Recreation Facility Management

SECOND EDITION

Brent A. Beggs, PhD
Illinois State University

Richard F. Mull, MS
Indiana University

Mick Renneisen, MS
Indiana University

Michael A. Mulvaney, PhD
Illinois State University

HUMAN KINETICS

Library of Congress Cataloging-in-Publication Data

Names: Beggs, Brent A., author. | Mull, Richard F., author. | Renneisen,
 Mick, author. | Mulvaney, Michael A., author.
Title: Recreation facility management / Brent A. Beggs, PhD, Illinois State
 University, Richard F. Mull, MS, Indiana University, Retired, Mick
 Renneisen, MS, Indiana University, Michael A. Mulvaney, PhD, Illinois
 State University.
Description: Second edition. | Champaign, IL : Human Kinetics, [2024] |
 Previous edition published 2009, with Richard F. Mull as principal
 author. | Includes bibliographical references and index.
Identifiers: LCCN 2023001930 (print) | LCCN 2023001931 (ebook) | ISBN
 9781492597629 (paperback : alk. paper) | ISBN 9781492597636 (epub) |
 ISBN 9781492597643 (pdf)
Subjects: LCSH: Recreation centers--United States--Management. | Sports
 facilities--United States--Management. | BISAC: BUSINESS & ECONOMICS /
 Facility Management | SPORTS & RECREATION / General
Classification: LCC GV429 .M85 2024 (print) | LCC GV429 (ebook) | DDC
 790.06/8--dc23/eng/20230322
LC record available at https://lccn.loc.gov/2023001930
LC ebook record available at https://lccn.loc.gov/2023001931

ISBN: 978-1-4925-9762-9 (print)

Senior Acquisitions Editor: Amy N. Tocco; **Managing Editor:** Chital Mehta; **Copyeditor:** Joanna Hatzopoulos Portman; **Proofreader:** Erin Cler; **Indexer:** Nancy Ball; **Permissions Manager:** Laurel Mitchell; **Senior Graphic Designer:** Nancy Rasmus; **Cover Designer:** Keri Evans; **Cover Design Specialist:** Susan Rothermel Allen; **Photographs (cover, from top to bottom):** vm / E+ / Getty Images, Cavan Images/Getty Images, Russell Monk / The Image Bank RF / Getty Images, and © Human Kinetics; **Photo Asset Manager:** Laura Fitch; **Photo Production Manager:** Jason Allen; **Senior Art Manager:** Kelly Hendren; **Illustrations:** © Human Kinetics, unless otherwise noted; **Printer:** Sheridan Books

Printed in the United States of America   10 9 8 7 6 5 4 3 2 1

The paper in this book is certified under a sustainable forestry program.

Human Kinetics

1607 N. Market Street	*United States and International*	*Canada*
Champaign, IL 61820	Website: **US.HumanKinetics.com**	Website: **Canada.HumanKinetics.com**
USA	Email: info@hkusa.com	Email: info@hkcanada.com
	Phone: 1-800-747-4457	

E8051

This book is dedicated to the memories of Linda S. Mull and J. Michael Dunn.

—To Linda, for her patience, understanding, tolerance, and cooperation during the early stages of thinking, writing, and rewriting the content

—To Mike, for his passion for facility design and commitment to the professional development of recreation professionals

CONTENTS

The recreation professional of today is responsible for a variety of recreation facilities that vary in type, scope, size, budget, and condition. These facilities may also have vastly different goals and expectations based on the type of management system and sector of the organization. Recreation facility management is an expansive and complicated subject that can vary greatly with the nature and objective of each facility.

The second edition of *Recreation Facility Management* continues to focus on recreation facilities and the products and services they provide. This edition includes key information related to facility trends in technology and sustainability. It also provides an understanding of universal and accessible design. These concepts are applied to a number of recreation facilities, such as parks and playgrounds, aquatic facilities, recreational sport facilities, schools, stadiums, fitness centers, sports complexes, recreation centers, golf courses, convention centers, tourism facilities, and theme parks.

Recreation administrators and those who use the facilities often don't appreciate the complexity of responsibilities associated with recreation facility management. The material in this text is based on a logical model incorporating information that prepares students to perform the responsibilities required of a recreation facility manager. Rather than take a theoretical approach to recreation facility management, this text analyzes and synthesizes the practical applications that recreation professionals should be aware of in facility management.

Recreation Facility Management is arranged into five parts. The content reflects a progression of concepts that aid in retention of infor-

mation for practical application. Part I covers foundations of the profession, including the definition of management and the description of duties of managing recreation facilities. Part II examines the development of recreation facilities, including needs assessment, planning, design, reading blueprints, funding, and construction. Part III includes information about managing resources such as equipment, money, and employees. Part IV analyzes strategies for utilizing recreation facilities in a safe and efficient manner. Part V examines, in detail, the operation of common types of recreation facilities.

Each chapter includes an Industry Profile feature and a case study with related questions. Also included in each chapter are objectives, summaries, and review questions. A glossary at the end of the book defines the key terms that are boldfaced throughout the chapters.

Students using *Recreation Facility Management, Second Edition,* also have access to HK*Propel*. Forms appearing in this book in thumbnail size are full sized in HK*Propel* as indicated by this icon:

These forms are from the files of actual facility managers. HK*Propel* also contains learning activities, discussion questions, and websites to help students further explore the ideas found in the book.

By using this text and the resources that come with it, students will develop a better understanding of the various types of facilities that exist in recreation and leisure services and the responsibilities associated with planning, designing, operating, and utilizing these spaces.

Instructor Resources on HK*Propel*

A variety of instructor resources are available online within the instructor pack in *HKPropel*:

- *Presentation package*—The presentation package includes more than 250 slides that cover the key points from the text. Instructors can easily add new slides to the presentation package to suit their needs.

- *Instructor guide*—The instructor guide contains several elements that enhance delivery of each chapter. The instructor guide includes activities that may be used in class or assigned as homework. These activities require that students conduct site visits to facilities on campus and in the community. In addition to these activities, the instructor guide provides discussion questions and answers related to the concepts in the text, as well as a list of websites that apply to the content of some of the chapters in the book. The instructor guide also includes answers to the end-of-chapter review questions and case study questions.

- *Test package*—The test package includes 30 questions per chapter in true-false, multiple-choice, essay, and fill-in-the-blank formats. These questions are available in multiple formats for a variety of instructor uses and can be used to create tests and quizzes to measure student understanding.

- *Chapter quizzes*—These LMS-compatible, ready-made quizzes can be used to measure student learning of the most important concepts for each chapter. Ten questions per chapter are included in true-false and multiple-choice formats.

Instructors also have access to all of the HK*Propel* student activities.

Instructor ancillaries are free to adopting instructors, including an ebook version of the text that allows instructors to add highlights, annotations, and bookmarks. Please contact your Sales Manager for details about how to access instructor resources in HK*Propel*.

ACCESSING THE HK*PROPEL* ONLINE CONTENT

Instructors

If you received this book or ebook as a desk copy, you should use the access instructions provided by your sales representative instead of the access code printed on this page.

All Other Users

Throughout *Recreation Facility Management*, you will notice references to HK*Propel* online content. This online content is available to you for free upon purchase of a new print book or an ebook.

HK*Propel* provides full-page forms that are applicable to many practical matters faced on the job. It also provides learning activities, discussion questions, and websites to help students further explore the ideas found in the book.

Follow these steps to access the HK*Propel* online content. If you need help at any point in the process, you can contact us via email at HKPropelCustSer@hkusa.com.

If it's your first time using HK*Propel*:

1. Visit HKPropel.HumanKinetics.com.
2. Click the "New user? Register here" link on the opening screen.
3. Follow the onscreen prompts to create your HK*Propel* account.
4. Enter the access code exactly as shown below, including hyphens. You will not need to re-enter this access code on subsequent visits.
5. After your first visit, simply log in to HKPropel.HumanKinetics.com to access your digital product.

If you already have an HK*Propel* account:

1. Visit HKPropel.HumanKinetics.com and log in with your username (email address) and password.
2. Once you are logged in, navigate to Account in the top right corner.
3. Under "Add Access Code" enter the access code exactly as shown below, including hyphens.
4. Once your code is redeemed, navigate to your Library on the Dashboard to access your digital content.

Access code: BEGGS2E-NZVY-CMLT-6RPW

Once you have signed in to HK*Propel* and redeemed the access code, navigate to your Library to access your digital content. Your license to this digital product will expire 2 years after the date you redeem the access code. You can check the expiration dates of all your HK*Propel* products at any time in My Account.

For technical support, contact us via email at HKPropelCustSer@hkusa.com. **Helpful tip:** You may reset your password from the log-in screen at any time if you forget it.

ACKNOWLEDGMENTS

We are grateful for the assistance and support of many people along the way in the development of this publication. In particular, we offer special thanks to the following people and organizations:

Donna Beyers, administrative assistant, who efficiently and tirelessly edited and assisted with the original publication and ensuing phases of this book

Kian Lam Toh, graduate assistant, for his resourcefulness and dialogue with the initial outlines

Mike Williams, graduate assistant, for his analysis of content and discussions providing valuable feedback

Chris Crume, aquatics assistant, for his original draft of the aquatics chapter with the advisory assistance from Bill Ramos, associate professor at Indiana University

City of Bloomington Parks and Recreation for charts and forms

Chris Nunes for his assistance with Industry Profile features

Support from the School of Kinesiology and Recreation at Illinois State University and the department of recreation, park, and tourism studies in the School of Public Health at Indiana University

PART I

FOUNDATIONS OF RECREATION FACILITY MANAGEMENT

All recreation services and core products are delivered in spaces known as *facilities*. To deliver core products, recreation facilities must be managed efficiently. Management of a recreation facility includes influencing agency resources such as employees, money, and equipment so that users have a positive experience. The management of a recreation facility varies based on the type of facility and the types of services being offered. Facilities can be natural or manufactured; they can also be indoor or outdoor spaces. Each facility is unique in how it provides core products, and numerous factors can influence the ability of a recreation facility manager to deliver products and services. Understanding these factors and how to manage resources is the foundation of facility management, and it requires extensive education and training.

CHAPTER 1

Understanding Recreation Facility Management

LEARNING OBJECTIVES

At the completion of this chapter, you should be able to do the following:

1. Define the term *management*.
2. Determine the administrative and operational functions of a recreation administrator.
3. Recognize the resources available to a recreation administrator for managing a facility.
4. Identify the importance of sustainable practices in facility management.
5. Review methods of marketing the leisure service product.
6. Recognize the types of goals to set for various types of recreation agencies.

If you are running a five-star resort or supervising a local senior center, you are managing a recreation facility. Whether you are supervising staff, operating a facility, maintaining equipment, or running a softball tournament, you are applying **recreation facility management** practices in one way or another. All leisure service organizations use some form of recre-ation facility management. The term **management** has several definitions and applications. However, all management functions share one common process: working with people and resources to achieve goals. This chapter introduces terminology and concepts to provide a practical understanding of management as it applies to facilities.

Managing the Product

In management, a person or a group wants to accomplish a specific directive. An organization usually has a stated vision and mission as well as a set of values, goals, and objectives to explain its intended direction. Organizational directives, such as a vision and mission, are communicated from the higher-level administrators of an organization; they are vital to establishing the role of the organization and putting policies in place. Lower-level directives, such as goals and objectives, are created within specific divisions of an organization; they are shaped by the vision or mission. As directives move from a higher level to a lower level, they become more specific. For example, the mission of an agency may be to provide outdoor facilities for its community. A specific goal related to the mission may be to design and operate a community skate-park. Objectives within that goal would establish a timeline for the development of the skate-park.

The organizational directive is considered a **product**; in overall management, it is the **core product**. The core product represents the primary focus for the organization, and it heavily influences management activities and initiatives. An organization's core product is created from the organization's core competencies. It exists for the customers, user groups, or participants. In park and recreation organizations, a core product often exists in the form of a service or experience that offers a benefit to the user. For example, a core product for a local park and recreation agency might be the

Hockey games are examples of core products, which are an organization's main interest.
Jamie Sabau/NHLI via Getty Images

provision of quality recreation facilities that offer diverse recreation opportunities for their community. In this example, the recreation facilities represent a product for the agency, and the core product for the community would be the diverse recreation opportunities associated with the facility.

Organizations often seek to accomplish something with the core product, such as success, profit, satisfaction, and participation.

Returning to the previous example, a local park and recreation agency may seek to increase the number of programs offered, improve user satisfaction levels, or increase membership revenue at their recreation center. Many park and recreation organizations will also track their efforts in these areas as a way to evaluate their progress in offering the core product to their targeted user groups.

CHECK IT OUT

Esports Programming as a Core Product for Universities and Colleges

Esports is estimated to be a US$1.5 billion market (Populous Events, 2018). Responding to this demand, college campuses in the United States have been quickly integrating esports programs into their core product line for students. In 2016, fewer than 10 colleges or universities had a varsity esports program; by 2021, that number grew to 175 (NCSA, 2021). As a core product for these institutions, esports represents yet another way for colleges and universities to recruit students and promote diverse interests on campus. Facilities to support these varsity and recreational esports programs have also increased, creating new products and opportunities for facility managers.

Often auxiliary directives exist that supplement the core product. These **core product extensions** usually support the core product and add to its success. Consider an example from a university that has an esports program. The core product for the university could be to offer high-quality varsity and recreational esports opportunities for students. Core product extensions might include offering coaching and lessons from expert gamers. Another core product extension could be a retail area where students could purchase esports gear, such as games, consoles, controllers, monitors, or seating. As a third example, the university may also wish to partner with academic programs in creating an esports research and development lab to support innovation and research opportunities for the campus community. Essentially, each of these examples supports the university's efforts to offer high-quality varsity and recreational esports opportunities (the core product) and has the potential to contribute to its overall success.

Defining Management

The basic premise of management can vary from field to field and from profession to profession. This section provides a meaning to the term *management* that is logical and reasonable and can withstand the diversity and extensiveness of the concept of management.

Management is often confused with concepts such as *administration* and *operation*, which are two components of management. Another component within management is leadership; however, the term *leadership* is not synonymous with management. Management represents a goal-oriented system in which leadership places emphasis on the people who are in the process of achieving organizational goals or on the people who participate in the core product.

Modern understanding of management is based on human interpretation and the capacities to share, coordinate, and cooperate. This understanding can be applied to recreation facility management by engaging people in the process of striving to achieve organizational goals. Considering both goals and people allows the establishment of a working description of management that is practical and applicable to all of its facets.

These various understandings of management can be best synthesized into a concise description that works for all systems where management is required: Management is influencing resources to obtain a goal.

This definition describes the human element in the functions and activities that are involved in striving to accomplish a goal.

Probably the most important term in describing management is *influence*. It incorporates the ideals of leadership, representing a modern interpretation of management instead of traditional interpretations involving terms such as *administer*, *direct*, and *control*. **Influence** means the power to affect an outcome. It is applicable to both personal and professional responsibilities.

It is important to understand the full meaning of influence as a key concept for management. If a product exists, management needs to find a way to make the product accessible and successful, bringing about satisfactory results for the organization as well as those who use the product. This goal is accomplished in two broad areas: **administrative functions** and **delivery operations**. These distinct systems of influence represent the various functions and operations in recreation facility management that bring about a desired result.

Administrative Functions

All professional and personal management starts with the responsible person or system having some type of authority. This administrative person or system represents the executive (upper-level) personnel in charge of producing a product. Most authoritative systems include these four administrative functions:

1. Planning
2. Organizing
3. Directing
4. Controlling

These four functions encompass a number of activities that help to influence everything that takes place in an organization. They can be

Is It Management or Leadership?

What's the difference between *management* and *leadership*? The two terms are often used interchangeably. While some overlap does exist between them, each one possesses unique qualities. Harvard Business School defines leadership as the development of positive, non-incremental change, including the creation of a vision to guide that change (Gavin, 2019). Leadership involves the empowerment of people to achieve that vision. In contrast, management involves the coordination of staff and resources to accomplish a common goal on a regular, recurring basis (Gavin, 2019). Leadership is more concerned with the creation of a vision for change or growth; management focuses on goal achievement and processes. Whereas a manager might administer, maintain, and focus on systems and structures, a leader would focus on people, innovate, and develop a vision for the future (Bennis, 2009). Managers set and enforce policies, and they coordinate tasks and activities to reach a goal or specific outcome. Leaders are less concerned with the organization of staff or other resources and are more focused on finding ways to align and influence them (Bennis, 2009).

described as the ultimate executive system that influences the organization's desired outcome.

Planning

Very little takes place without some degree of planning early in the effort. Most simply defined, **planning** is anticipating through thought and, when appropriate, documentation, all facets that should take an organization to an expected level of success. A plan is a predetermined and theoretical way to accomplish set goals and objectives. Planning can be short term (1-3 years) or long term (3 years and beyond). It may be simple, such as a conversation among a few people that establishes tasks and direction, or it can be a detailed, comprehensive process with several people, called **strategic planning**.

Planning is a critical aspect of recreation facility management. The importance of planning is evident in a number of areas in recreation facility management, including facility development, risk management, emergency and evacuation instructions, equipment purchasing and distribution, preventive maintenance, and budgeting. Evidence of planning can almost always be observed in successful recreation facility management, and lack of planning is just as evident in unsuccessful recreation facility management.

Organizing

Organizing involves recognizing and assigning specific tasks and responsibilities to employees and resources, as well as designing areas and time assignments that relate to the product. Much of this organizing is included in scheduling. In scheduling, certain steps are taken to efficiently allocate human and physical resources; therefore, it involves an appreciation for all facets of managing the core product. Resources can be categorized into the areas of information, equipment, human resources, and organizational resources so that management can coordinate the efficient delivery of a product and take appropriate steps for this process to occur in a methodical and timely fashion.

The organizing function incorporates more than the assignment of areas for specific activities. It also includes establishing a flowchart that reflects the authority structure of an organization (see figure 1.1), developing policies and procedures, and creating facility signage that designates areas and provides information. Organizing a facility uses all the elements of the facility to implement a meaningful process that influences the success of the product.

Directing

Directing is the process of guiding people or groups within an overall management

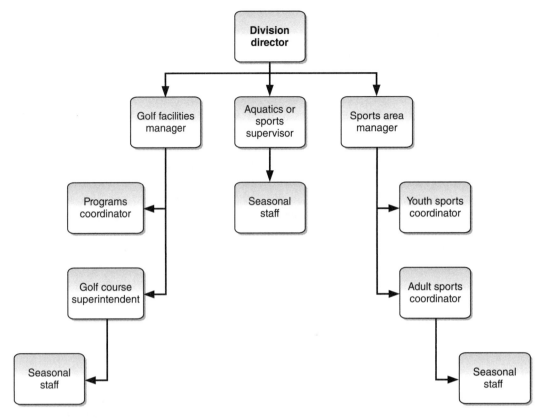

FIGURE 1.1   Sample organizational chart.

system. This managerial function ensures that employees understand the importance of their position and how they help the organization achieve its goals. Staffing, which includes recruiting, hiring, and training employees, is also important; however, successful directing requires creating an environment where those employees fulfill their role as intended.

Directing incorporates elements such as leadership style, training, delegation, communication techniques, coordination, and motivation. Having employees in place and fulfilling their obligations correctly is the foundation of ongoing success in recreation facility management. The directing function requires that employees be in place and fulfilling their obligations as outlined in their job description.

Controlling

Ideally, employees will perform every function in their job description in a timely and professional manner; however, this ideal does not always occur. Additionally, things often do not go as management planned. Therefore, employees, funds, facilities, equipment, and resources need to be monitored to ensure that they have a positive influence on the product and meet the expectations of management. This effort, called *controlling*, is similar to the process of directing, except it focuses more on monitoring resources. **Controlling** is the process of supervising, assessing, and correcting employee performance and resources to ensure successful product delivery.

Putting various controlling methods into practice can reduce or eliminate negative occurrences and can help deliver a product efficiently. Some examples of controlling methods include the following:

- Establishing expected performance standards
- Creating an evaluation system
- Implementing an award and recognition program
- Developing corrective procedures

- Formulating grievance procedures
- Using financial statements
- Recording inventory

Many factors are involved in the interpretation and performance of responsibility. In addition, management uses checks and balances to monitor efficient use of resources. However, even the best plans, organizational structure, direction, and control can't eliminate all problems, which is where delivery operations come into play.

Delivery Operations

Administrative functions initiate ideas and influence the product. In recreation facility management, presenting the product to the user is called *delivery operations*. **Delivery operations** integrate the resources and administrative functions that create interest leading to product participation or purchase, which results in a user experience that affects the success of the product. Delivery operations have four functions: production, support, auxiliaries, and maintenance.

Production

Arguably the most important area of delivery operations is the production function. **Production** is the basis of how the product is delivered. It includes communicating information to recreation facility users and allocating the human and physical resources and other elements that are critical to the delivery of the product. Production represents the detailed knowledge of employees and the responsibilities they perform to deliver a product.

In the recreation profession, production takes the form of programming, or providing various activities so that participants gain a sense of satisfaction from their experience. **Programming** is the designing and manipulating of leisure environments in an effort to promote the desired experiences of participants. Programming is not necessarily the responsibility of recreation facility managers; it is often the responsibility of other employees. In the tourism model, programming is often referred to as *event planning*. In the entertainment field, it

is the effort to show a movie, create an event, or produce a television show, play, or musical that spectators enjoy. In business, it could be the creation of a retail outlet or food and beverage outlet that brings the product to the customer for purchase. In the educational field, it is the delivery of information by the educator, including the methods for ensuring that students acquire knowledge.

Support

Support is another important delivery operation that affects the production effort. **Support** represents activities that take place behind the scenes by personnel who are typically not in contact with facility users. The support function is often not recognized as contributing to management efforts in relation to product delivery; in reality, support includes essential activities that are critical to the success of the product. These activities can be considered either internal or external support systems.

Internal Support Systems   **Internal support systems** take place within the organization. For instance, many organizations employ staff members to handle support duties such as the following:

- Clerical support (typing, record keeping, appointment scheduling)
- Payroll and benefit management
- Communications
- Bookkeeping
- Supply purchasing and distribution
- Mail service

These internal support employees play an important role in the operation of facilities.

External Support Systems   The support function can also take place externally. **External support systems** can involve outside contractual services such as the following:

- Legal work
- Medical assistance
- Accounting
- Information technology
- Consulting

These services are usually specialized and not within the basic activities of daily agency operations. Outside services are brought in to help with specific tasks where existing personnel lack expertise.

Auxiliaries

As mentioned earlier, certain product management needs can be considered auxiliary, or supplemental, to the primary product; they are called *core product extensions* or *ancillary spaces*. **Core product extensions** are areas in a facility that generate revenue through the provision of additional products or services. For example, a smoothie bar that provides healthy drinks to members of a fitness center is a core product extension. **Ancillary spaces**, on the other hand, are spaces in a facility that support the core product but are not designed to generate additional revenue. For example, the reception area and restrooms are ancillary spaces in a community recreation center. Essential to overall management, auxiliaries may represent only a small percent of product delivery. Auxiliaries may not be part of the primary product delivery, but in many instances, their elimination would have a negative effect on the success of the product. These auxiliary functions, although not usually as encompassing as the core product, could be significant enough to require their own production and delivery effort.

Maintenance

In the delivery operation of recreation facility management, **maintenance** (keeping facilities and equipment in proper and safe condition) can be considered a support function. However, maintenance is such a significant part of recreation management that it is considered a separate function. Maintenance functions can vary greatly. As organizations increase in size, maintenance responsibilities increase proportionately, making this effort more complicated. The day-to-day responsibilities can vary from simply cleaning areas to a full system of delivery incorporating repairs and preventive and cyclical maintenance.

Maintenance can incorporate specially trained staff who are either part of the agency

The reception area is an ancillary space in a recreation facility.
© Human Kinetics

Examples of maintenance functions associated with outdoor recreation facilities include mowing, caring of turf, and maintaining surfaces of ball fields.
© Human Kinetics

or an outside source contracted in a situation requiring certain expertise. Some of the tasks that relate to the maintenance function include facility and equipment repair, cleaning, mowing, watering, safety measures, inventory management, electrical controls, and equipment setup and takedown. Lack of attention to maintenance can have a negative short-term effect on the perception of a recreation facility as well as serious implications from a long-term perspective. Emphasis on maintenance is required in settings where appearance is important. It is essential especially in settings where health and safety of users and employees may be compromised if proper maintenance practices were not observed, such as at an amusement park or even a playground.

Managing Resources

Administrative functions and delivery operations rely heavily on **resources**. The most obvious management resources in the recreation environment are employees, money, equipment, and facilities. Each resource plays a

significant role within management. Being able to use resources effectively and efficiently is a recreation administrator's greatest challenge.

The capacity of management to influence resources as they pertain to the core product and core product extensions cannot be overemphasized. Management resources are of considerable importance to facilities; they are discussed in greater detail in later chapters. The following material summarizes how each can be interpreted as part of the recreation facility management process.

Employees

Human involvement and the management of that involvement are essential in the delivery of a product. A critical function of management is the capacity to influence **employees** to fulfill their obligations in the production or delivery of a product. This process is called *staffing*. **Staffing** includes the recruitment, hiring, and training of appropriate people to facilitate the requirements of a successful product.

A variety of formal and informal considerations are incorporated in the staffing function. A more formal staffing process is necessary as job complexity increases. Steps in providing proper staffing include the following:

- Classifying employees
- Establishing levels of authority
- Establishing a hiring timetable
- Creating a search-and-screen process
- Establishing selection criteria
- Announcing the position
- Interviewing potential employees
- Negotiating salaries
- Hiring staff

Each of these activities is significant in the appropriate placement of people within the management system. Allocating the appropriate responsibilities to the right people can be critical to meeting the product expectations of recreation facility users and management.

Money

As either a source of income or an expenditure, money is a critical component for any management system. The proper management of fiscal resources can have a significant effect on the viability of a recreation facility. Other terms relating to this resource include *funding*, *financing*, *fiscal*, *budgeting*, and *accounting*. The management of money, which is referred to as **budgeting**, must be planned in advance. The use of money must also include **accounting**, which is the documentation of income and expenditures associated with operating a facility. Money is a complicated resource that often requires specialized applications or processes.

Equipment

Equipment includes any item, mechanical or otherwise, that enhances the production and delivery processes. There are a number of ways to describe and classify equipment, which is addressed in later chapters. Equipment is an extensive resource that carries a great deal of responsibility, including purchasing, inven-

torying, receiving, storing, distributing, and maintaining. Equipment is often taken for granted; however, it represents a significant expense as well as a potentially labor-intensive problem when it does not work as expected. The ability of management to influence proper use and care of equipment can contribute to the efficiency and effectiveness of delivery operations.

Facilities

The **facility** is a resource that is critical to the production and delivery of the product. Recreation facilities, which can be indoor or outdoor structures, vary greatly. As a resource, facilities are initially the most expensive element in the provision of a recreation product. It is essential that management recognize the nature and scope of facilities in planning. The ability to understand the value of facilities to the product is the basis of this text.

Supporting Sustainable Practices

As noted in the previous section, effective and efficient use of an organization's resources is one of the recreation administrator's most important responsibilities. Engaging in sustainable practices while managing these resources is becoming increasingly important for organizations. While supporting sustainable activities is a factor in reducing the organization's carbon footprint, it can also lead to additional revenue. The 2015 Nielsen Global Sustainability Report (Nielsen, 2015) showed that almost three-fourths of millennial customers were willing to spend more money on products and services from organizations that supported sustainable practices.

Initiating sustainable practices within an organization typically involves the following methods: sustainability analysis, energy-efficiency updates, eco-friendly supplies, preventive maintenance, and recycling (Srivastava, 2018).

- *Sustainability analysis* requires that the organization review existing services and facili-

Recreation facilities can include anything from a fitness center to a community outdoor recreation center.
Kanok Sulaiman/Moment/Getty Images

ties to identify areas of wasteful energy use. The process typically involves a systematic review of existing practices to determine equipment efficiency, energy usage across seasons, and occupancy levels. Technological resources such as analytical and data tracking software are often used when completing a sustainability analysis.

• *Energy-efficiency updates* can be completed based on the results of the sustainability analysis. An organization's older physical resources were likely designed with little consideration for environmentally friendly features. Updating these areas within the organization will not only improve their sustainability but also improve efficiency and reduce costs. Examples of energy-efficiency updates include lighting upgrades; utilization of renewable energies such as solar, wind, and geothermal; installation of smart utility meters; heating, ventilating, and air-conditioning (HVAC) system updates; and integration of electric vehicles (EVs) into the vehicle fleet.

• *Eco-friendly supplies* to maintain the cleanliness of the organization's facilities can help in reducing the amount of toxic chemicals used and released into the environment. For instance, many public park and recreation organizations have implemented eco-friendly weed control methods, such as natural acids, soaps, salt-based herbicides, and weed torches, which no longer rely exclusively on glyphosate herbicides.

• *Preventive maintenance* performed on an organization's physical resources can help keep energy usage down and extend the life of these resources. Many organizations develop inventories and logs to monitor and schedule preventive maintenance activities for these resources.

• *Recycling* is often one of the first sustainability practices that organizations implement. An organization's efforts to conserve environmental and energy-based resources include recycling of various materials such as papers, plastics, metals, aluminum, mercury-based lighting, batteries, chemicals, and various pieces of equipment.

Understanding Marketing

No matter what the product is or how the resources are allocated, an organization needs a process in place to deliver the product to potential users. Whether a person makes a tangible purchase or enjoys the product as an experience, a system is needed to create interest in the product. The effort to reach an audience to deliver them a product is called **marketing**. This process involves assessing a targeted population and developing a strategy to create product awareness and availability, which is essential in meeting management goals for success.

Marketing is a complete field that involves several methods and techniques. The four Ps of marketing (product, promotion, price, and place) represent four different aspects of creating product awareness. They are defined as follows:

- **Product** is what the consumer receives from the business transaction. The product can be a tangible good or an intangible service.
- **Promotion** is the advancement of the status or value of a product or idea. Promotion includes strategies to deliver information, such as public relations, personal selling, sales promotions, publicity, and advertising.
- **Price** is the cost to the consumer to acquire a product. This expense goes beyond the sticker price and may also include time and opportunity costs, psychological costs, personal effort costs, and indirect financial costs.
- **Place** is where a product is distributed to target consumer markets.

Marketing also involves a process to evaluate the demographic characteristics of a population, thereby establishing a **target market** to help ensure the success of a product. Potential characteristics to evaluate in establishing the target market include age, gender, socioeconomic background, and geographic location. Lifestyle information, known as **psychographics**, can also be incorporated and assessed to reflect the influence of a product on the potential user. Marketing also uses **market segmentation**, which targets specific segments of users by recognizing their particular needs and interests and then attempting to meet them. Marketing has proven to be extremely important to product delivery and to ultimately accomplishing management goals for success.

Setting Goals

In describing the concepts involved in recreation facility management, this chapter has reviewed administrative functions and delivery operations, resources required to deliver the product, and marketing techniques for reaching potential users. No matter the product, management always wants to accomplish a predetermined goal. Ultimately, the desired outcome is reflected in the values, vision, and mission of an organization and will be evaluated using criteria that depend on the setting of the recreation facility. In broad terms, this desired outcome or goal can be service oriented or profit oriented. However, these categories are not exclusive.

Service-Oriented Goals

Management in the service category exists when an organization provides a meaningful experience for users without the incentive of profit. These types of services are often delivered in the **public sector**. Federal, state, and local taxes support the administration and delivery of services in the public sector; however, increasingly in the U.S. economy, service agencies are asked to become less reliant on tax dollars and generate more of their own revenue to support their operations.

Usually, public recreation agencies operate under the guidance of service-oriented goals. These outcomes are motivated by the idea that services should not be profit driven but should be based on the needs of society and made available to all. Many services in the public sector are recognized as necessary for the well-being of society. Examples of agencies that have service-oriented goals include schools, correction facilities, the military, and commu-

The exercise equipment room at a country club is an example of a facility in the private sector.
Getty Images/Blend Images/Space Images

nity agencies such as hospitals as well as fire, police, and park and recreation departments. The delivery of services in the public sector may involve charging fees to meet operational costs; however, the motivation is not to make a profit but to provide a public service and contribute to society.

Profit-Oriented Goals

Recreation facility management systems in the **private sector** provide products based on profit-oriented goals. Management with profit-oriented goals has traditionally operated very differently from management in service-oriented enterprises. In private management systems, all efforts are focused on the **bottom line**, an end result that management hopes will show a net profit. Products may be produced and delivered, but without **profit** (generating sufficient net income to exceed expenses), the recreation facility management system usually is unable to continue. All efforts within this type of management system are focused on the profit-oriented goal because it ultimately affects administration, delivery, resources, and the product itself. Positive user

experiences and good service are expected if a net profit is to be accomplished. Whether the production is the sale of an item or the use of a recreation environment for an experience, the ultimate goal is to generate income that exceeds expenses. Entities of this nature are privately operated. They include businesses, factories, corporations, and franchises that receive no tax support in delivering a recreation product.

Summary

Management is a complicated process that can be described as influencing resources such as employees, money, and equipment to obtain a goal. The goal for a recreation facility manager is to deliver the core product to users. The recreation facility manager must utilize internal and external support systems in delivering the core product and auxiliary spaces to users. Ultimately, the goals of management are established through understanding the values, vision, and mission of an organization. These goals are used to establish administrative functions, delivery operations, resource utilization, and marketing in the recreation facility.

REVIEW QUESTIONS

1. Develop an example of a core product and what a recreation-based organization may wish to accomplish with the provision of this core product.
2. What is the difference between management and leadership? Provide at least two distinct qualities for each.
3. What are the four resources available to a recreation administrator in managing a facility?
4. What are some ways an organization can support sustainable practices within their facilities?
5. Why is place important in the marketing of a recreation service?
6. Within which goal-oriented recreation management system is a private resort likely to operate?

CASE STUDY

Fitness Facility Expansion

You are a facility manager for the indoor sport complex with the Ellisville Parks and Recreation department, which serves a population of 70,000. The vision for the complex is *Deliver innovative programs and services that will be the standard for the city of Ellisville and exceed the community's expectations*. The mission of the complex is *Enhance the quality of life of Ellisville residents through positive recreation and sports programming and services*.

The 85,000-square foot (7,896 m²) complex includes an indoor track, basketball courts, an indoor soccer field, a snack shop, a climbing area, batting cages, and dance studios. Since opening 15 years ago, the complex has experienced growth in numbers of new members and users, and a majority of the complex's programming and services have been successful. Recently, the department's planning director informed you about the department's interest in offering health and wellness services to the community and possible plans for facility expansion. In particular, the department plans to construct a new fitness facility within the complex. Currently, no fitness facility or services are available within the complex or offered by the Ellisville Parks and Recreation department, so the department could acquire a new service area. The new fitness facility would include areas for free weights, weight machines, cardio equipment, and cross-training and space for fitness and dance classes. Your supervisor, the recreation director, has asked you for input on the impact of this expansion.

Case Study Questions

1. As the facility manager, what are some facility design recommendations you could share with your director to promote sustainability and eco-friendly processes within the newly developed space? Could this also be a good time to consider any eco-friendly upgrades to the existing facility? If so, what are some examples?
2. What impact would this new space have on existing resources (employees, money, and equipment)?
3. Review the department's mission and the vision of the complex. Can you identify a core product from these statements? How does this focus on health and wellness change (or not change) the department's mission or core product focus?

CHAPTER 2

Managing Recreation Facilities

LEARNING OBJECTIVES

At the completion of this chapter, you should be able to do the following:

1. Explain the fundamentals (definition, structures, and purpose) of recreation facilities.
2. Describe the steps in the facility development process.
3. Recognize the characteristics of indoor and outdoor recreation facilities.
4. Identify the key responsibilities of recreation facility management.
5. Explore career implications for recreation facility managers.

The delivery of the core product in leisure services can be done in a variety of ways depending on the service or product being provided. Regardless of what the core product is, it must be delivered in a space. The space where product delivery occurs is termed a *facility*. The facility is essential to the quality of the leisure experience. Despite the tremendous importance of facilities in providing leisure opportunities, the importance of managing recreation facilities is often underappreciated. The ability of recreation professionals to oversee a facility can have a significant impact on the success of product delivery. Recreation professionals can enhance their knowledge of recreation facility management with proper training and education.

Fundamentals of Recreation Facilities

Many activities that are part of everyday life take place in some type of facility. In this book, the term **facility** refers to an environment where leisure activities occur. Facilities can include naturally occurring resources, such as park areas and lakes, or they can be manufactured structures, such as museums and health clubs. A facility can be indoors or outdoors. It

In Decatur, Illinois, Nelson Park and Lake Decatur have together served as the recreational center-piece of the community for over a century; it began in 1912, when land was first acquired along the Sangamon River, and in 1921, when the river itself was dammed to create the lake (Decatur Park District, 2011). In 2011, the Decatur Park District completed a master plan for Nelson Park, and it established a clear vision and strategy for future improvements to the park. In developing this vision for Nelson Park, the district assessed the needs and interests of the community through several public meetings, community leader breakfasts, a website suggestion box, a survey, and a variety of group discussions.

One of the key findings from this assessment was the desire to develop destination attractions within the park. Residents of Decatur could enjoy these destination attractions, which would also attract regional visitors to the area. A permanent amphitheater overlooking the lake was identified as one of these destination attractions. Responding to this need, the Decatur Park District began planning, designing, and securing funding for an amphitheater. In 2018, construction began for the Devon G. Buffet Lakeshore Amphitheater. The construction of the multimillion-dollar facility was largely funded by the Howard G. Buffet Foundation; the venue was named in honor of Howard Buffet's wife, Devon.

Open since May of 2019, the Devon G. Buffet Lakeshore Amphitheater offers a wide variety of entertainment, such as musicians, comedians, big bands, movie nights, and family-themed entertainment. The amphitheater has a capacity of approximately 4,000 persons with lake views from almost every seat or viewing area. A variety of viewing areas were designed to support diverse spectator needs. For example, an open pit area is available in front of the stage for stand-ing-room spectators or for those who need to bring portable seating. Additional areas include reserved seating, a terrace level with artificial turf that allows spectators to bring their own chairs or blankets to sit on, a VIP party deck with a private bar, and a lawn area. Other amenities include USB charging stations as well as concessions areas for food and drinks.

can be as simple as a playground or as complex as an amusement park. In other words, facilities can take many forms, and they are of great importance to recreation professionals. To help you understand more about recreation facility management and its importance, this chapter first examines the fundamentals of facilities themselves, specifically the various types of structures and the purpose or function of a facility.

Structures

In simplest terms, **structure** refers to whether a facility is a natural environment or a manu-factured structure. In a natural environment, people have done little construction to create the main attraction; in a manufactured struc-ture, a management system has conceived, planned, designed, constructed, and occupied it to deliver a recreation product.

Natural Environment

Visitors to the Grand Canyon, Niagara Falls, or local wildlife areas experience a recreation facility in a **natural environment**. In this type of facility, little to no adjustment is made to the natural environment. A natural environment facility might include a lake, stream, cave, or other natural resource. The ski slopes at a ski resort are another example of a natural envi-ronment that is used in a recreational setting. Natural environments often have a manage-ment component that regulates use of the area in addition to providing auxiliary services to facility users, such as boat, canoe, kayak, or ski rentals. These types of facilities may be managed by a local, state, or federal agency or a private entity for general public use.

Manufactured Structures

A **manufactured structure** is a designated area that facilitates a process, operation, or course of

Natural recreation areas have little or no change from their natural evolutionary state. They can include settings such as waterways and caves.

RuslanDashinsky/Getty Images/Getty Images

activities; it is conceived, planned, and built by people to deliver a specific recreation product. Manufactured structures can be either indoors or outdoors. Outdoor manufactured facilities can range from local playgrounds or tennis courts to large water parks and sport stadiums. Indoor manufactured structures can take on many forms, such as bowling alleys, fitness centers, indoor arenas, or major resorts. Some structures may consist of both indoor and outdoor facilities, such as a swimming pool with a concession building and a locker room. Structures can be multifaceted with designated areas for many activities. A more detailed discussion of these multifaceted characteristics is offered later in the chapter.

Facility Purpose

No matter what the structure, essential to its existence is the production and delivery of the recreation product. All recreation facilities are built with the delivery of a specific product in mind; that delivery involves human creativity and initiative while managing resources efficiently. As the management process becomes more complicated and the facilities become more complex, they require more attention.

A track and field facility is a manufactured recreation facility, which can vary greatly in diversity and complexity.

Education Images/Universal Images Group via Getty Images

Manufactured Structures

Common Indoor Facilities

Sport arenas

Gymnasiums

Fitness and dance studios

Museums

Bowling alleys

Swimming pools

Resorts

Common Outdoor Facilities

Tennis or pickleball courts

Outdoor aquatic complexes

Golf courses

Parks and playgrounds

Sport fields

Beaches

Ski resorts

In order to manage a facility well, recreation professionals must understand the purpose or function of the facility.

A **single-purpose facility** typically has only one product that is developed and delivered. The administrative and delivery operations may be less complicated because of the single purpose of the product. **Multipurpose facilities** incorporate two or more products. Multi-purpose facilities may create more complicated management responsibilities because of the diverse applications and requirements of the products being offered.

Another way to look at the purpose of a recreation facility is to consider the size of the user base that it attracts. Bringing large numbers of people to a recreation facility creates many responsibilities that place various bur-

(a) A golf course is a single-purpose facility, and *(b)* a YMCA is a multipurpose facility.

Photo a nattrass/E+/Getty Images; photo b By Lauren A. Little/MediaNews Group/Reading Eagle via Getty Images

dens and technical requirements on recreation professionals. These responsibilities can result in additional staffing requirements, increased maintenance tasks, and greater attention to risk management, among other concerns.

Public or Private Recreation Facilities

Another way to determine the basic nature of a recreation facility is to examine how and why the facility came into existence. In other words, what is the primary goal of the facility? One basic premise is that local, state, or federal funds are used to support the construction and management of public recreation facilities. Many factors are involved in the creation of these facilities because of requirements associated with the use of tax dollars to fund them. The underlying philosophy of a public recreation facility is to create a service-oriented operation that meets the needs of the citizens who pay taxes for the operation and construction of the facility. Examples of public recreation facilities include sport complexes of park and recreation agencies, community centers, swimming pools, beaches, and tennis courts. Funding options to support these facilities vary based on the type of facility and the politics involved.

In general, private recreation facilities operate very differently from public facilities. Private facilities rely on the income generated from the product for facility construction and management expenses. Without adequate income, privately managed recreation facilities could not remain open. Some examples of private recreation facilities are golf courses, fitness centers, sport complexes, hotels, resorts, and marinas.

Facility Development Process

In order for a recreation facility to come into existence, a number of developmental stages must occur. Each stage has specific responsibilities and requires the completion of the previous stage before the next step can be undertaken. These steps form an evolutionary process of recreation facility development; they include assessment, planning, design, funding, construction, and management. Following is a brief description of these stages. They are discussed in greater detail in upcoming chapters.

Assessment

Whether a recreation facility already exists or needs to be created, an assessment should be conducted to determine the need for the facility. The assessment stage involves careful review of the space necessary to develop and deliver a product. It includes the recognition of weaknesses such as poor or inadequate lighting, inadequate space to produce the product, accessibility problems, or changing participation trends. These observations can result in recommendations to renovate an existing facility or design a new facility for better delivery of the core product.

Planning

Once it is determined that a recreation facility needs to be renovated or constructed, steps are taken to formally review how the facility can be modified or constructed. Planning often involves politics, prioritizing, and influencing various levels of administration and ownership

---

CHECK IT OUT

Prominence of Public Recreation Facilities in U.S. Communities

According to the National Recreation and Park Association's (NRPA) *Agency Performance Review Report*, nearly two-thirds of public recreation agencies in the United States have at least one recreation center in their community and operate from at least seven buildings (NRPA, 2022). The typical public recreation agency also has 13 playgrounds in its parks. At least half of these agencies have basketball courts, tennis courts, baseball or softball fields, multipurpose rectangular fields, dog parks, and outdoor swimming pools. Clearly, U.S. public park and recreation agencies oversee a wide variety of facilities.

to support the project. Plans can be short range or long range, and they relate to a corresponding master plan for the agency. Many components of a plan may be conceptual. This stage is where all needs, functions, and ideas are brought up for discussion.

Design and Funding

The design phase recognizes the need for a recreation facility and the acceptance of the proposed plan by the administrators of the agency. This phase also includes the formal process of designing the facility using architects and engineers, who provide guidance and detailed information regarding all aspects of the structure. Consultants often assist in this process to manage the technical details not commonly understood by management. The design phase is complicated, and it requires a great deal of attention to detail. It culminates in the completion of blueprints and specification books that are placed out for bid to obtain a price for the job from a qualified contractor before initiating construction.

Facility development cannot occur without adequate funding; therefore, funding efforts often occur in tandem with facility design activities. While the costs may vary depending on the size and scope of the project, funding is one of the most influential elements in the development of a facility. Funding methods and sources can vary based on the type of the project, overall costs of the project, and the type of agency responsible for the project. This phase requires the organization to thoroughly research the various funding options in order to maximize the cost efficiency for the project.

Construction

Planning for a construction project requires thorough review of information to justify the design of a recreation facility, and it involves the assistance of consultants to provide technical details. A recreation facility begins to take an identifiable form during the construction phase. As the construction phase evolves, it may require the professional assistance of construction management firms, contractors, and subcontractors to install building materials, finishes, and landscaping. It is a complicated stage that can be very rewarding when all facets of the project finally come together.

Management

Creating and maintaining a recreation facility as a functional space requires significant management effort. Various responsibilities and functions help make a product available. Of particular importance is the space where that product is produced or delivered. **Synthesizing** (bringing the recreation product and space together as a useful experience for the user) forms the basis of recreation facility management, a support process aimed at enhancing the success of the core product and its extensions. A more direct definition of recreation facility management is coordinating a physical workplace with the employees and goals of the agency while integrating the principles of management, architecture, and behavioral and engineering sciences. Facility management is just one component of the recreation environment; it functions in an indirect but crucial fashion by providing significant support to the delivery of the product.

The responsibilities of managing a recreation facility vary greatly because each facility has unique requirements. Recreation facilities serve a multitude of purposes, and they vary in size, volume, and square footage. As each of these factors grows, so does the responsibility in managing the facility. The **extensiveness** (number of products provided at a facility) indicates the complexity of managing it, which encompasses a wide range of responsibilities, including risk management and maintenance as well as unexpected disruption in product delivery (see figure 2.1). The responsibilities in facility management can be demanding, and extensiveness can be the greatest determinant of job intensity.

Each recreation facility is a unique result of the facility design and the product being delivered. Aquatic complexes present a good example of unique facility designs. Although nearly all aquatic complexes have a pool, water features, and locker or changing rooms, they

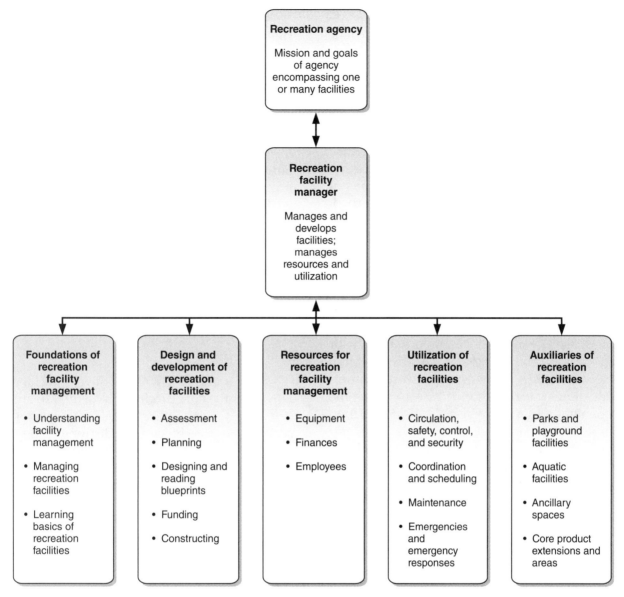

FIGURE 2.1   This facility management model provides a visual guide to the variables related to the extensiveness of a recreation facility.

each have a different design. The same can be said for health clubs, resorts, theaters, museums, and so on.

Administrative styles, management philosophy, staff composition, and leadership qualities all contribute to the **uniqueness** of a facility. In addition, the design often reflects the core product, architectural interests, environmental considerations, efficiency needs, and legal requirements. The unique structural design of a recreation facility can also reflect the marketing or visual promotion of the product. While the general functions of a facility manager may remain the same, the specific characteristics of each facility make them diverse.

Characteristics of Indoor Recreation Facilities

A fundamental requirement of recreation professionals is basic knowledge of the specific characteristics of recreation facilities; certain details about the structure should be understood. Following is an overview of basic characteristics of indoor facilities.

Site

All recreation facilities must be located in a specific location, or site. The site receives a great deal of attention as to how it will contribute to the successful delivery of the product. The makeup of the area can have a significant influence on the facility and its development. Typical site issues include natural barriers such as rock formations, drainage areas, weather conditions, and prevailing winds. Issues of site coordination also include the proximity of roads, utilities, and natural energy sources in addition to the proximity of other facilities and product competition. Additional site considerations are discussed in the following sections.

Topography

Topography is the natural condition of the land. Land conditions may be flat, hilly, or mountainous. Topography addresses area elevation, which incorporates water runoff and potential flooding. It also involves the orientation of the proposed facility (direction in relation to sunrise and sunset), layout, and potential access. A site with topographical problems could result in increased excavation costs or other management challenges.

Rock

Rock at or around facilities can provide aesthetic appeal; however, in most cases it creates tremendous disadvantages in construction. Rock may require excavation, blasting, and drilling to remove it from a location, possibly leading to unexpected construction costs. It can also create water runoff that can result in soil erosion.

Water

Unfortunately, recreation facilities are often not designed to protect against the potential impact of water sources. Architects and engineers must be aware of nearby rivers and streams because flooding may result from heavy rain or runoff. Sometimes recreation facilities are built in or near flood zones in order to save on land and construction costs. Other concerns involving water include leaking roofs or facility deterioration because of dampness. Sump pumps can be used to get rid of water seepage in a facility, especially from areas below ground level. Water in and around a recreation facility can have far-reaching implications if not managed properly as part of the site design.

Production Space

The most important factors relating to the basic nature of a recreation facility are the core product, the core product extensions, and the product delivery. Recreation facilities are developed with the product in mind, and specific areas are designed to enhance the production process. The production space and its characteristics are vital to the success of a recreation facility. This section addresses a number of these factors, which are essential for recreation professionals to understand.

Main Areas

The space that is necessary for developing and delivering the core product is essential to any recreation facility. Specific sizes, dimensions, and a variety of technical considerations should be considered when it comes to the design of primary product delivery areas. For example, sport fields or courts have dimension standards that must be followed to create an appropriate area for the delivery of the core product. The nature and efficiency of these areas play a critical role in the success of the product. In the design as well as in the delivery, all such areas should be planned in a detailed manner.

Surfaces

Generally, **surfaces** refers to three boundary areas in a recreation facility: floors, walls, and ceilings. Each surface has unique requirements to help an environment meet its intended purpose. Recreation professionals should be aware of the variety of surfaces that are available and how each surface may affect the production process.

- Floors have various characteristics depending on the type of activity that will take place in a space. Common floor surfaces are carpet, hardwood, synthetic, and tile. Each has different degrees of elasticity, resiliency, absorbency, and slide characteristics.

- A wall is a surface that acts as a sound barrier, reflects light, contains heat, and affects moisture and acoustics.
- Ceiling surfaces may hide conduits, electrical lines, steam lines, vents, duct work, communications wiring, and security devices. Ceilings often include a wide variety of lighting systems required for recreation facilities.

Indoor surfaces are discussed in more detail in chapter 6.

Illumination

Another factor that influences the production space is the illumination required for the area. The level of lighting can be generated by a variety of lights with different capacity and production requirements. The supply of energy required to brighten an area with light is measured using units called **foot-candles**. Energy supply and other considerations influence lighting choices, which can include indirect lighting (where light reflects off surfaces) or specialized lighting that is unique to the product. Popular features such as windows and skylights are sources of natural light, but they can create glare, shadows, and water leakage.

Types of light sources include incandescent, fluorescent, and density lighting. Each source has unique characteristics to meet a variety of product needs (discussed at greater length in chapter 6). Supplementary lighting includes emergency lighting, night-lights, and exterior lights for aesthetics. Motion-activated lights and flood lights contribute to the security of recreation facilities. The technical requirements associated with selecting the appropriate illumination for a recreation facility often call for engineering and consultant assistance.

Electrical Systems

Depending on the recreation product, a variety of electrical systems may be necessary. The wiring required to accommodate these systems can be diverse. Wiring can be the common type used in homes, or it may be more specialized types required for computers, laboratory equip-

ment, product equipment, lighting systems, scoreboards, and communication systems. All wiring must meet electrical codes as well as state and local fire regulations. Main service electrical panels should be located in restricted areas where users and employees have limited access. Sometimes secondary control panels are provided for staff members who open and close a facility. Electrical planning, design, and maintenance are complex tasks. Given the expensive and potentially hazardous effects of improper electrical system selection or installation, electrical systems are not areas to try to save money on during the construction phase. Often the services of electricians and engineers are needed to help with electrical system planning, maintenance, and repair.

Plumbing

Plumbing is a major factor in the design and operation of recreation facilities. Plumbing includes pipes that feed sinks, showers, toilets, water fountains, sprinkler systems, hot- and cold-water systems, and drains and garbage disposals. All of these areas contribute to the control of water flow. They require engineers and plumbers who can help with use, interpret code, and assist with maintenance.

Finishes

Finishes provide the final appearance of areas. Depending on the original design and ongoing maintenance, they can be attractive or unattractive to users of the facility. Finishes are usually applied in the final stages of a construction project. If not completed properly, they can create delays in the final stage of a project and public relations problems for management. Types of finishes include the following:

- Signs, which help in the circulation of facility users
- Wall coverings, such as paint, wallpaper, and tile
- Floor coverings, such as tile, wood, and carpet
- Keying access and exit control
- Doors and windows

Finishes require special attention because they are highly visible and regularly come into contact with users and employees. When implemented successfully, they can have a positive influence on the appearance of a facility; when implemented unsuccessfully, they can result in maintenance problems and have a negative influence on the facility.

Acoustics

Acoustics is the science of sound and its impact within an area. In some indoor recreation facilities, the quality of production space can often be judged by how well sound is projected, reflected, and received. Walls and ceilings can be designed to reflect and control sound based on the product and its delivery. Sometimes interior treatment of sound involves the elimination of unwanted noises that travel through ventilation ducts, pipes, walls, and floors.

Climate Control

Management should be concerned with the comfort level of people as they use or work in a recreation facility. User or employee comfort is mostly influenced by a climate control system, which can require specialists to ensure that environmental conditions are maintained at optimal levels.

Different regions can create unique climate control concerns in a facility. An indoor climate system can affect operating costs and user and employee comfort, so an efficient heating, ventilation, and air-conditioning (HVAC) system is important. Other considerations related to climate control include noise levels, insulation of hot and cold water pipes, exhaust, damp or dry air, air turnover per hour, and thermostat control.

Heating

Heating an indoor recreation facility to a comfortable temperature requires special mechanical systems. These heating units are unique to each recreation facility based on use and capacity. Generally, a larger and more complex facility requires a more complicated and expensive heating system. Air temperatures should generally be maintained between 64 and 72 degrees Fahrenheit (18-22 °C). Maintenance of heating equipment is a significant responsibility for facility management. When heating equipment breaks down, it can create a challenging or even emergency situation.

Ventilation

Ventilation circulates air within a facility, and it balances warm and cool indoor air with outside air. Ventilation ducts and motors, along with the heating and air-conditioning equipment, force air to move throughout a facility. The balancing of airflow is a technical responsibility that requires specialized design, daily attention, and maintenance.

Air-Conditioning

Air-conditioning, the process of cooling a facility, requires the same responsibility in controlling and maintaining equipment as heating equipment. In certain regions, air-conditioning can be essential to maintaining user and employee comfort levels. Air-conditioning affects not only the temperature but also the humidity of a facility.

Utilities

All indoor recreation facilities must have electricity, water, and a communication system in order to deliver a product. Certain facilities may also require natural gas. Utilities are essential to a functional recreation facility. Outside sources have the primary responsibility of providing utilities during the construction phase and throughout the life of the facility. Utility costs are usually paid monthly. The following is a brief overview of the various utilities and how they contribute to indoor facilities.

Electricity

Electricity is an energy source that feeds equipment, lighting, comfort systems, communication systems, and security systems. It is provided by an outside source or public utility that charges for the service. Often electrical systems are so important to the production process that facilities have backup generators in the event of an outage. Facilities with extensive lighting or other equipment that requires electricity have a significant energy bill, which can create additional monitoring responsibilities for recreation facility managers.

Sanitation

All structural recreation facilities must comply with laws that require the provision of restrooms. Wastewater or sanitation systems provide for the sanitary removal of contaminated water to the appropriate treatment facility in the community. Wastewater provisions should be planned in the design of any indoor recreation facility.

Water

Delivered to a facility by an outside source, water moves through the plumbing system that feeds water fountains, restrooms, fire hoses, sprinkler systems, showers, fountains, and pools. Water can also be used with hot water or steam heating systems to provide heat. Water temperature for these systems should not exceed 120 degrees Fahrenheit (49 °C). Water quality must be acceptable for human consumption, and it is monitored by local and state agencies. Facility managers are responsible for maintaining the water source so that it is safe and available at all times.

Communication

Indoor recreation facilities are served by local companies that provide communication systems, including telephone service, Internet access, security, and cable or satellite television. These systems are installed and maintained by outside agencies, but they are also monitored by management. Facility users and employees are particularly dependent on the conveniences that communication systems provide; when one malfunctions, it presents management challenges.

Exterior

Many options are available for the exterior of recreation facilities in terms of the materials used to create the desired appearance and structural soundness. This section describes some of those components and their potential applications.

Structure

One of the most notable aspects of any indoor recreation facility is its exterior or structural appearance. The structural appearance may be designed to help market the product, meet owner or administrative wishes, or create a level of attractiveness that makes a statement to potential users. The details that affect appearance are designed within the height, angles, material, size, windows, doors, rooflines, and siding of facilities. The comparison of different recreation facility structures demonstrates how diverse and extensive this aspect of indoor facilities can be, reinforcing the importance of design and construction as part of facility management.

Landscape

Almost all recreation facilities require landscaping, which may incorporate trees, lawn, plants, shrubbery, rocks, paths, medians, and walls. An attractively designed and maintained exterior can reflect the priority that management places on landscaping. Often, maintenance systems have to be in place with attention paid to growth patterns, temperature, and irrigation. Landscaping is a priority when appearance is a major concern. It can be a time-consuming responsibility for recreation facility managers.

Irrigation

Some recreation facilities develop landscape systems that require regular watering or irrigation. Irrigation systems can be aboveground or underground; they have the capacity to disperse water to help nourish trees, shrubs, grass, and other vegetation. Aboveground irrigation requires additional labor hours to apply water, which can have long-term cost consequences for a facility budget. Underground systems are often automated; they are programmed to turn on at designated times of the day or night. Automated systems cost more to install, but they require a lower labor cost in the long term.

Irrigation systems should be adequate for the vegetation present. The cost of irrigation can be significant, particularly in regions where water is a scarce resource. Facility managers are

Almost all recreation facilities require some type of landscaping. Plant material and walkways are effective ways to improve the appearance of a recreation facility.

responsible for the proper use of the system to adequately protect landscape environments and maintain appropriate appearance while conserving the use of a potentially expensive resource.

Vehicle Access

All recreation facilities need vehicle access. Roads should be considered not only in terms of user and employee access but also in terms of how they function in an emergency situation. Roads or access drives are also important for delivery of facility equipment and supplies. In addition, roads should have appropriate signage so that vehicles accessing the facility can do so easily without delay or misdirection.

Walkways

Walkways are essential for providing safe access to the recreation facility. These surfaces can include paths and sidewalks. They should be adequate in size, and they should be properly lighted. In the United States, they must be accessible (including the provision of ramps if necessary) according to the Americans with Disabilities Act (ADA) guidelines. They should be safe, without holes or raised areas where users could trip and fall. During inclement weather, sidewalks should be cleared of ice and snow in a timely fashion.

Parking

Adequate parking for users and employees is a consideration for all recreation facilities. The planning agency of each community may have specific requirements for the number of spaces at a particular recreation facility. Parking is usually designed to be close to a facility; however, in some cases it could be at a distance. When parking areas are more remote, management should consider transportation in the form of shuttles, monorails, or other options to conveniently move customers from parking areas to the facility. Parking areas should have proper security, including barriers, trees, and lighting. They should be designed with proper signage to clarify where people should park their vehicles, allowing for easy access to the facility while complying with ADA requirements. For a more detailed discussion on parking, see chapter 5.

Characteristics of Outdoor Recreation Facilities

Outdoor recreation areas can be simple or complex. Outdoor areas often incorporate landscaping, lighting, irrigation, and walkways. Although some information parallels that of indoor facilities, they have many distinct characteristics. Insight into these characteristics, especially as they relate to design, construction, utilization, and maintenance, is fundamental for outdoor facility management.

Site

Depending on the nature of the product, a number of factors affect the design and construction phases of outdoor recreation facilities. The site can have a significant impact on the daily operations of the facility. This section offers information that is relevant to the site of an outdoor facility.

Size

Before selecting a location for an outdoor recreation facility, the site must be assessed to ensure that it will be appropriate for the delivery of the product. Some products have specific dimensional requirements where length, width, and height are essential considerations. The size of the outdoor area must include adequate space for the primary product, support systems, safety zones, landscaping, access, and parking. In addition, management should consider that extra land may be desirable later; if the product is successful, expansion may occur, and land is rarely less expensive than when first purchased. Often the size of the area acquired for an outdoor facility is insufficient to meet the current or future production needs of the facility because the cost of the land limited the original purchase.

Topography

As mentioned in the discussion about indoor facilities, topography relates to the natural condition of the land. Topography includes elevation, slope, orientation, and any irregularities of the surface. The topography could have a tremendous influence on the construction process, including extensive excavation costs if a significant flat area is required to deliver a product. In most instances, topography plays an important part in the design of natural outdoor areas.

CHECK IT OUT
How Much Space Is Needed to Build a Playground?

Many elements in a playground, such as slides and swings, require additional space beyond the product's physical dimensions to ensure their safe use. In the United States, the American Society for Testing and Materials (ASTM) has developed minimum required standards for safety use zones for these products. Prior to building a playground, an organization should ensure the site is large enough to support both the product's physical dimensions and these safety use zones. One way to remain current with these standards and space requirements is through the Certified Playground Safety Inspector (CPSI) program. Offered by the NRPA, the CPSI certification program provides the most comprehensive and up-to-date training on playground safety issues, including hazard identification, space requirements, equipment specifications, surfacing requirements, and risk management methods (NRPA, 2021b).

Land

Ground surface composition can be altered by design and then construction. In this fashion, the organization can create a desired surface that contributes to the delivery of the product. Land concerns can affect maintenance, user safety, and landscaping costs. Some outdoor product areas require special surfaces that could include mixtures of topsoil, clay, and sand. Outdoor land areas could also include rocky and swampy parts; they could be designed as portions of the outdoor recreation facility or simply removed. Changes to land areas can drastically increase construction costs and maintenance expenses. The characteristics of the land chosen for an outdoor facility can have short- and long-range implications.

Surrounding Vegetation

Surrounding vegetation includes the trees, shrubs, and other plants that are already on-site or will be added to the site in the construction phase. Strategically placed vegetation can help reduce surface temperature, retain water, and minimize the effect of wind on the activities provided at the facility. It is wise to be aware of vegetation growth patterns and how they can affect the ecosystem of the area.

Water and Storm Water

Water located at or draining through a site can have an effect on the recreation facility. Natural water sources can aid the growth of vegetation, or they can cause erosion, flooding, and vegetation deterioration. Storm-water management

Generally a varied topography plays an important role in the design of an outdoor recreation facility, whereas a varied topography at the site of an indoor recreation facility could cause significant increases in construction costs because it may conflict with the desired design.

is the process of diverting surface water and draining subsurface water to drainage structures such as curbs, gutters, and detention or retention ponds. Storm-water management is an important factor in the design of any outdoor recreation facility. When not managed properly, it can have significant cost implications or require extensive rehabilitation to the area.

Climate

Climate refers to weather conditions such as temperature, rain, wind, humidity, and snow and how each can affect an outdoor recreation facility at various times of the year. Climatic conditions can have a major influence on the success of product delivery. Certain regions experience intense weather conditions such as heavy rainfall or lack of rain, excessive heat or humidity, or extreme wind that can affect the safety of participants and employees. The ability of recreation facility managers to evaluate these climatic conditions and schedule the use of the facility around potentially hazardous weather events is an essential contribution to the efficient use of a facility. Managers must evaluate climatic conditions in order to avoid dangerous situations. Managers must also be aware of the long-term effects of climatic conditions on ground surface, vegetation, and, ultimately, the product.

Production Space

Unlike indoor recreation facilities, outdoor areas require a management approach that accounts for the uncontrollable factors involved in outdoor spaces. This section discusses outdoor characteristics and their relation to production space.

Layout

Layout refers to how areas work together or relate to one another in the overall use pattern of the facility. Whatever the product, the areas of an outdoor recreation facility should be organized to maximize land use with the least amount of wasted space. Product dimensions, standards, and requirements dictate how much space is needed for the proper layout. For example, multipurpose fields with dimensions large enough to accommodate both American football and soccer fields are more efficient and provide more flexibility for management than facilities designed to accommodate only one of those sports.

Orientation

In the context of an outdoor recreation facility, *orientation* relates to the angle of the sun and prevailing wind direction and how they affect product delivery. To avoid improper orientation, this factor should be given the greatest attention during the design and construction phases. Some products could be seriously affected by orientation to the sun at certain times of the day or by prevailing wind direction. For example, if a baseball or softball field is situated with home plates in an eastern or western orientation, participants on the field will have the sun in their eyes at sunrise and sunset. In golf courses, holes are often designed to incorporate prevailing wind direction. For example, longer holes are designed to be downwind, whereas shorter holes can play into the wind to increase their difficulty.

Drainage

Unexpected or excessive rain can affect the delivery of products at an outdoor recreation facility. Drainage is the removal of unwanted water from a facility in an effective and timely fashion. Some sites have natural drainage, creating few problems. Lack of drainage can seriously affect product delivery by creating delays, inconveniences, and significant maintenance expenses, which can result in dissatisfied users and potential loss of user interest and facility income. Excessive water that does not drain properly can also damage surfaces and vegetation, making areas unattractive and less functional.

Barriers and Fences

In the outdoor production process, barriers and fences can play an important role in segmenting areas as well as controlling use. These elements can help create secure and isolated use, thereby limiting potential liability. Some facilities require controlled access with specific

Proper orientation of an outdoor tennis facility keeps the sun out of the eyes of participants.
Digital Vision/Photodisc/Getty Images

entrances and exits. Barriers and fences can provide the necessary control methods to limit access. They limit user access to one area and direct users to the entrance for the purposes of tracking attendance and collecting any fees associated with use of the product. They can also help control unwanted noise, sun, and wind.

Landscape

One of the intrinsic benefits of an outdoor recreation facility is users' appreciation of being outdoors. An attractively designed outdoor area that blends into the terrain can create a high level of satisfaction for users. The proper selection and placement of flowers, mounds, trees, shrubs, and walkways that tie together the landscape of an outdoor environment can enhance users' experiences. Proper use of landscape techniques can contribute to the appear-

ance of the facility and assist with drainage, layout, and orientation.

Surfaces

One of the most significant considerations in the delivery of products at an outdoor recreation site is the land surface used for the production process. Outdoor surfaces can influence safety, maintenance, and user satisfaction. Surface qualities to consider include function, appearance, resiliency, longevity, and maintenance costs. Several outdoor surface options are available; they are discussed in chapter 6.

Support Systems

Support systems that contribute to product delivery are fundamental to most outdoor recreation facilities. These systems are usually not noticeable to users, and they can be very

A fence is helpful to control user access and provide security for a facility.

Robin Alam/Icon Sportswire via Getty Images

specialized depending on the nature of the facility. Following are some examples of support systems found at outdoor facilities.

Access

Every outdoor recreation facility needs to have easy access for users. Many facilities are located away from populated areas, with external and internal roads, internal sidewalks and paths, and parking areas created to support access. The design should facilitate access without hindering users' ability to get to where they desire. Easily visible signs and directional indicators should be strategically placed throughout the facility. Pedestrian and vehicle traffic flow should eliminate hazards and congestion, incorporating barriers and fences to help control movement, crowds, emergency vehicles, program registrations, and other activities.

Utilities

Utilities play a significant role in safety, product quality, and maintenance. Operations at most outdoor recreation facilities would be hampered without the availability of water, electricity, and communication capacity. Some outdoor recreation facilities can function without utilities; however, complex outdoor facilities have a greater need for utilities. Water is required for irrigation, drinking, and delivery of food and beverages. Electricity is required for equipment, lighting, security, public-address systems, scoreboards, and food and beverage services. Communication systems may not be necessary for all outdoor facilities, but they can be extremely important for more diverse operations. Communication systems include telephones, security systems, computers, and televisions.

Lighting

Many outdoor recreation facilities depend on lighting to deliver their product beyond daytime hours. Illumination systems for outdoor recreation facilities can be elaborate, and they may require certain levels of lighting for television broadcasting. Various types of lighting exist for specific facility needs such as safety, specialized product activity, parking areas, and security. The importance of lighting at some facilities may necessitate specific maintenance arrangements to ensure uninterrupted service.

Irrigation

An irrigation system is critical for outdoor recreation facilities that emphasize appearance and protection of surfaces and vegetation. Product delivery can cause damage to turf surfaces. Heavy use combined with heat and humidity can destroy turf unless it is maintained properly. An irrigation system can be beneficial to the maintenance and protection of these areas. Irrigation systems can be as simple as handheld hoses and as complicated as computer-controlled networks. Along with chemical applications, irrigation is key for maintaining usable, safe, and attractive outdoor surfaces.

Conveniences

It is common for users to stay at a recreation facility from 1 to 3 hours. During this time, users may require conveniences such as restrooms, food and beverage services, public telephones, and water fountains. These areas can vary from facility to facility, with the more complex facilities requiring more sophisticated spaces to deliver the conveniences. These areas are usually identified with appropriate signage so that they can be located easily.

Seating

Spectator viewing areas are a significant element of delivering a product at many outdoor recreation facilities. Depending on the activity, the seating required can vary greatly. Seating areas can range from open space for chairs to permanent stadium seating. Seating options may require the use of ushers, ticket takers, ticket sales, and other considerations. The management of seating areas takes on greater responsibilities as the facility becomes more complex and diverse.

Trends in Recreation Facility Management

Today's recreation facility manager is concerned with utilizing a facility to its capacity while maximizing revenue and minimizing expenses. The better a facility is utilized, the more it is perceived as beneficial to the mission of an organization. Professionals should understand current trends in recreation facility management in order to maximize a facility's potential. Prominent trends include sustainability, demand for functional space, technological advances, legal code interpretation, risk management, liability protection, and cost reduction.

Examples of Sustainability Efforts in Facility Management

- *Disposal methods:* Waste prevention, recycling programs, and composting efforts
- *Energy-efficient supplies:* Implementation of a tracking or accounting system to monitor energy-efficient strategies; staff training on energy-efficient operation of equipment and supplies; utilization of equipment automatic control features
- *Green initiatives:* Development of supportive, green-thinking workplace culture; identification of areas for improvement and action plan implementation; evaluation of expected versus actual energy usage
- *Leadership in Energy and Environmental Design (LEED) certification:* Development of water savings, energy efficiency, materials selection, and indoor environmental quality of a facility to obtain LEED certification (silver, gold, or platinum)

Some facilities require just enough lighting to be able to play a game at night, whereas other facilities require lighting at television broadcasting standards for a night game to be shown on television.

Marc Atkins/Getty Images

Sustainability refers to operating a facility while minimizing its long-term effect on the environment. For facility managers, sustainability is a process of implementing and maintaining economic, social, and environmental conditions that support both current and future facility users. From initial assessment activities to the management of the completed facility, sustainability efforts should occur within every phase of the facility development process.

Being green is another term referring to ways that a facility can be more efficient and lessen its negative influence on the environment. Because many leisure service organizations serve as stewards for the environment, recreation facilities are being designed and operated using technological advancements in materials and efficiency systems that minimize their effect on the environment.

Demand for Functional Space

Today, recreation professionals are placing more importance on analyzing and assigning space to maximize its use. Functionality of space is critical to administrative plans and expectations because few facilities can afford to have space that is not being used or is creating expenses without producing revenue. In an effort to maximize resources, recreation professionals are constantly analyzing the product and seeking to make all facility areas a functional part of the production process.

Energy Star

The Energy Star label is found on a variety of products, including heating and cooling, appliances, water heaters, lighting, building products, office equipment, and electronics. In the United States, Energy Star is the government-backed symbol for energy efficiency. Energy Star provides both consumers and organizations with energy efficiency information on products that help save them money and protect the environment. Partnering with the U.S. Environmental Protection Agency (EPA), products are reviewed and, when appropriate, certified as an energy-efficient and cost-saving product. Since 1992, Energy Star and its partners have helped U.S. families and organizations save 5 trillion kilowatt-hours of electricity, save more than US$450 billion in energy costs, and achieve 4 billion metric tons of greenhouse gas reductions (Energy Star, 2021).

Advanced Technology

Technology has created a more complicated work environment for management where operating equipment, efficiency systems, registration applications, and maintenance functions all affect the production and delivery processes. Properly functioning and successful facilities require highly automated systems along with technological applications that are integrated with human capacities. They can include anything from computer-oriented efficiency systems to technologically complicated equipment that must remain operational to meet demands. Recreation professionals face constantly changing technology that emphasizes obtaining and assessing information to enhance the efficiency of human resources and any equipment that delivers a product.

Legal Code Interpretation

State and federal governments have written codes that protect the welfare of all users and employees. Interpreting and applying these regulations requires professional attention to protect a recreation agency and its users.

Recreation professionals have the responsibility of ensuring that all codes are observed in the design and operation of facilities. The Americans with Disabilities Act (ADA) and the Equal Employment Opportunity Act are just two examples of legislation that influences recreation professionals. In addition, risk management policies must be considered in facility design and operations. Negligence in this responsibility can have serious consequences, resulting in formal reprimands, lawsuits, termination of employment, or even the demise of an organization.

Risk Management

Recreation professionals have always been concerned with safety within their facilities. Efforts to assess and minimize risk is at the forefront of every recreation organization's mission and operations. The COVID-19 pandemic is a recent example of the importance of risk management for the recreation professional. As federal, state, and local COVID-19 guidelines changed almost daily, recreation professionals were required to work closely with local health departments in their decision-making and planning efforts. Regular communication and collaboration across the local agencies became increasingly important, leading to the development of new safety protocols such as masking, social distancing, and the cleaning of high-traffic and heavy-use areas. These dynamic conditions required recreation professionals to balance newly established protocols while continuing to provide essential recreation services to their user groups.

Protection Against Liability

Currently in the United States, it is common for people to take legal action against someone or something that negatively affects their lives. Lawsuits can be expensive and time consuming, and some can eventually destroy an organization. Recreation administrators have responded to this challenge by attempting to prevent such actions. They emphasize the need to have a safe working environment for employees to protect their health, and the same consideration is extended to the people who use the recreation product. Recreation professionals must take every precaution to protect users of their product. They must establish risk management strategies, providing facilities and equipment that are free of both mental and physical dangers. Sound recreation facility management practices play a major role in protecting the administration from legal consequences while delivering a product.

Cost Savings

Maximizing revenue while minimizing expenses has become a demanding requirement in all areas of the recreation profession. All costs related to operating recreation facilities, including utilities, maintenance, labor, and facility financing, have come under scrutiny of facility managers. Close analysis of these expenses has resulted in far-reaching implications in terms of maintaining environments and equipment. Sustainability (discussed earlier) also has cost implications. By finding ways to use resources more efficiently, facility managers can lower operational costs.

Key Responsibilities of Recreation Facility Management

Recreation facility management is a complex blend of the facility's purpose and functions, the employees, and the users. A direct link between the recreation facility and the organization's mission, goals, and objectives must also be present. Furthermore, facilities must be managed to support the core product and the core product extensions. This rule applies to small facilities with part-time facility employees as well as large facilities that require not only a professional administrator but various types of staff to support the overall operation. This section describes the roles and responsibilities of recreational facility managers in greater detail in relation to product delivery and human resources.

Ensure Delivery

Ensuring delivering of the core product and core product extensions involves coordinating facility areas and space. Recreation professionals are responsible for properly coordinating all spaces, including scheduling the areas for appropriate use and assigning the appropriate equipment and staff resources to those areas. Employees must recognize their role as part of a team in bringing together all activity and functions with the smallest amount of resistance and disruption in the production and delivery of the product. Employees should report any activity that can negatively affect the delivery of the product; then they should take the necessary steps to ensure proper delivery.

Operate Efficiently

Facilities and equipment play a key role in the production process. Recreation professionals have to be aware of whether the facility and equipment are functioning efficiently. They are responsible for making sure that space, equipment, and weather do not negatively affect delivery. Employees keep a comfortable environment with proper ventilation, maintain clean and attractive spaces for users, and apply preventive measures to areas and equipment in order to efficiently deliver the product. Other areas that require attention to operate efficiently include mechanical systems, vehicles, and electrical and plumbing components.

Be Flexible

Flexibility is crucial in managing a recreation facility. The delivery of a product can require so much attention that recreation facility managers sometimes unintentionally neglect facility-related concerns. Even though facility management responsibilities are important, they often do not receive the same kind of enthusiasm and attention as the efforts associated with product delivery. The ability of recreation professionals to be flexible and remain aware of the need for adjustment can play a significant role in the success of the agency. Activities that can challenge recreation facility managers' flexibility include administrative-imposed priorities, production difficulties, conflicting interests, last-minute changes, communication problems, politics among employees, and challenging personalities. Sometimes not all demands can be addressed. It is the responsibility of facility managers to address all variables to help the administration recognize how these demands can influence facility operations.

Be Cost Efficient

A critical responsibility of recreation professionals is attending to the finances of the resources assigned to them and accounting for spending. Recreation facility managers find themselves assessing space in order to make it as efficient as possible in terms of revenue and expenses. Typical areas of **cost containment** include controlling utility costs by evaluating use patterns, reviewing labor costs and employee scheduling practices, and monitoring the purchase and use of supplies and equipment. Energy costs in particular have skyrocketed in recent years. Facilities are expensive to operate; recreation facility managers need the capacity to interpret facility functions from a cost perspective and make appropriate decisions to control costs without affecting the delivery of services.

Maintain Effective Human Resources and Relations

Staffing a recreation facility requires a diverse range of employees to perform the necessary roles associated with product delivery. One of the most important functions of recreation facility managers is managing personnel and working effectively with people, or **employee relations**. Recreation professionals must be able to communicate appropriately with employees. They should be sensitive, and they should motivate, coach, mentor, and discipline

employees. Interacting well with staff requires more attention than any other aspect of the recreation profession because it is also one of the most critical aspects of a successful facility.

Closely related to employee relations is **user relations** (or **customer relations**). By responding to user needs, maintaining open communications, and enforcing agency policy while maintaining high levels of customer service, recreation professionals can establish a positive relationship with users. The task of addressing human relations, whether with employees or users, can be challenging and time consuming. Recreation professionals must have the ability to stay composed, thoughtful, organized, and tactful when it comes to human relations.

Career Implications for Recreation Facility Managers

The wide variety of responsibilities associated with the recreation profession, as well as the diversity of facilities that exist, indicate a significant demand for qualified people who can fulfill such numerous obligations. Expectations for qualified recreation facility managers vary based on the diversity, complexity, and extensiveness of the agency. Consider the variety of facilities that currently exist, including convention centers, professional sport arenas, theme parks, fitness centers, community centers, resorts, cruise ships, aquatic centers, sport complexes, community parks, theaters, museums, galleries, playgrounds, and golf courses. All of these public and private facilities need trained recreation professionals.

It is certain that the role of recreation professionals is necessary and is continually receiving more attention. Career opportunities in the recreation profession have expanded dramatically in the last 20 years because of the proliferation of new facilities in the marketplace. In addition, administrators have come to understand the value of employing personnel with academic training in the recreation profession. This section discusses the professional activity of the field and the numerous responsibilities of recreation facility management.

Employment

Considering all the recreation and tourism-related agencies that exist (the United States alone has more than 4,000 recreation organizations), the opportunity for employment in the recreation profession is virtually endless. Organizations with the responsibility for large populations (e.g., military bases, community systems, colleges and universities, correctional settings, schools, hotels and resorts, stadiums and arenas, recreation centers, and hospitals) provide even more opportunities for employment. As an organization increases in size, the need for greater and more formal recreation professional knowledge increases.

Overseeing resources will continue to be a tremendous responsibility. As organizations grow and more are created to meet the increasing demand for recreation services, employment of recreation professionals will increase. In addition, owners and administrators now understand the need for professional management of agency resources. Both the public and private sectors will continue to hire qualified people as well as contract with professionals for recreation-related services, which will create enormous growth in the profession.

Associations

Most professions have at least one formal membership-based organization consisting of professionals who meet regularly to address issues relevant to their field. People in leadership roles have created a number of associations that work to enhance the management of recreation agencies. A widely recognized association is the National Recreation and Park Association (NRPA), with a membership of 22,000 recreation professionals. Since its formation in 1965, it has been meeting members' needs by conducting research, providing educational opportunities, assisting in the development of strategies for recreation management, promoting advanced technology, addressing structural and equipment needs, and providing other valuable assistance. The NRPA also includes a variety of branches and sections to meet the needs of recreation professionals in areas such as aquatics, armed forces, commercial recreation and tourism, education, and therapeutic recreation.

Many other national associations incorporate the importance of resource management within their mission. These associations address facilities and equipment that are specific to their particular field. Their recognition of subjects related to the recreation profession can be observed at their national and regional meetings and within their publications. They address content that reflects trends, research, safety and legal matters, professionalism, and systems of efficiency and effectiveness in facility management. Here are some associations that are invested in the importance of recreation agencies:

- National Education Association (NEA)
- International Association of Convention and Visitor Bureaus (IACVB)
- Resort and Commercial Recreation Association (RCRA)
- American Alliance for Health, Physical Education, Recreation and Dance (AAHPERD)
- American Therapeutic Recreation Association (ATRA)
- North American Society for Sport Management (NASSM)
- Association for Experiential Education (AEE)
- International Festivals and Events Association (IFEA)
- National Collegiate Athletic Association (NCAA)
- National Intramural-Recreational Sports Association (NIRSA)

A complete listing of recreation professional associations and organizations is lengthy, and it continues to grow as the need for information increases.

Formal Training

A variety of jobs and levels of employment require training in the delivery of products at recreation agencies. Expectations can range from no training to on-the-job training to formal academic learning requirements. Some roles require specific training and certifications; examples include electricians, plumbers, landscape architects, golf-course superintendents, lifeguards, youth sport administrators, and personal fitness trainers.

Many agencies seek the services of recreation professionals to meet agency goals and expectations. These professionals usually come from four-year college or university degree programs. Most graduates from these programs have been exposed to a body of knowledge that helps guide them to competency in all areas of the recreation profession. Usually, such degrees are broad in nature and are not limited to classroom experience; they also include internships, volunteer experience, and practical skills.

Summary

Recreation facilities are instrumental in the delivery of the core product in that they are the spaces where core products are available to users. Recreation facilities can take many natural and manufactured forms, and they can be extensive in the variety of products and services they provide. The recreation facility manager must be aware of the positive and negative influences of users and employees on a facility. In order to minimize negative employee influences, recreation facility managers need to properly train employees and have their own opportunities for professional development. Facility managers need to continue to understand trends in sustainability, technology, risk management, fiscal responsibility, operational efficiency, and human relations with both employees and facility users.

REVIEW QUESTIONS

1. What are the two broad types of structures for recreation facilities? Provide at least one example of a recreation facility for each type.
2. Describe the differences between a public recreation facility and a private recreation facility.
3. What are the steps in the facility development process? Provide a brief description of each step.
4. Identify at least one way in which the characteristics of an indoor recreation facility are similar to the characteristics of an outdoor recreation facility. Next, identify at least one way the two facilities differ.
5. Describe two ways a recreation professional could promote sustainability practices within a recreation facility.
6. Why are professional associations important for the recreation facility manager's career development?

CASE STUDY

The Growth of Esports

You are a facilities director for a campus recreation department at a public university. Located in the northwestern United States, this town has 55,000 residents, and the university has an enrollment of 10,000 undergraduate and graduate students. You have been with the campus recreation department for seven years; you currently oversee the operations at the student recreation and fitness center and outdoor adventure facility.

Two years ago, the university added varsity and recreational esports programming to their list of student services. Campus recreation provides the oversight and coordination of these programs. Both the varsity and recreational esports programs are housed in a wing of an existing building on campus. The space was originally two computer labs, and it was repurposed to support this new programming. As the facilities director for campus recreation, you have been involved in the development of these spaces. While this repurposed space is adequate for your department's esports programming, you think a new space could lead to new opportunities and significant growth for these programs.

The university's position on this relatively new programming has been as follows: *If, after five years, the esports program is deemed a success, long-range plans could involve the development of a new, state-of-the art space for these programs.*

Case Study Questions

1. As someone who is new to the esports field, where could you go to obtain resources and support for esports programming?

2. How will success be determined for the esports program? What criteria could be used to measure the program's success over the five-year period?

3. You want to be prepared in the event the esports program is deemed successful and the university decides to pursue the development of a new, state-of-the art esports facility. What are some tasks you could work on now to help prepare for this potential facility development project? (Hint: Consider the steps in the facility development process.)

PART II

DESIGN AND DEVELOPMENT OF RECREATION FACILITIES

When creating a new recreation facility, moving forward with the design project requires justifying its funding. An organization can employ assessment strategies to establish this justification. Information learned through assessment is important also in the planning of a new facility. A planning committee examines facility needs and communicates them to a design team, which makes decisions about the function, structure, and aesthetics of the new facility. The design team works with an architect; together they follow building codes and ordinances to develop building blueprints and other construction documents. Finally, the construction manager and contractors use these documents to aid in building the project.

CHAPTER 3

Assessment

LEARNING OBJECTIVES

At the completion of this chapter, you should be able to do the following:

1. Understand the influencing factors to consider when reviewing facility needs.
2. Recognize and apply the various methods of formal and informal needs assessment.

Assessment is an important component in the successful delivery of leisure experiences. Because recreation agencies strive to provide a product that users desire, understanding user needs is essential. Identifying what users want guides recreation agencies in determining what to provide. However, assessment isn't only about understanding user needs; it is also about determining whether providing the product is feasible for the agency and within the scope of its mission. Assessment is an important part of determining what programs a recreation agency will offer. It is also important in facility design and development.

Assessment serves as the foundation of a recreation facility development project. The assessment determines the need for a facility, and it greatly influences the approach to con-

struction. Assessment methods range from very formal to very informal. Formal assessments include the following:

- A **needs assessment** helps an agency understand additional services and facilities that users would like to have.
- A **feasibility study** is used to determine if a facility design project is financially viable for an agency.
- A **prospectus** is a formal summary of a business venture or facility project that may be used to justify funding or attract investors.

These formal tools are objective in nature, and they involve considerable research. In contrast, informal methods used in assessing facility needs are more subjective. They may include gathering facts that reflect facility needs through having casual conversations with facility users and observing their behaviors.

In the case of constructing a new recreation facility, the assessment process begins with the recreation service provider or a stakeholder (someone who has a vested interest in an agency or facility) recognizing a need for it. Once this need has been identified, the next step is to assess its importance to the recreation agency and to users. Often, consultants are commissioned to help assess the need for a new facility or the renovation of an existing one. The organization may enlist the help of consultants to justify the expense of a recreation facility project. Assessing the need for a facility project can involve many considerations. This chapter discusses factors that influence facility assessment, and it describes assessment techniques. In addition, it offers a suggested initial proposal process that communicates the message of facility needs to administrators and decision makers.

Influencing Factors in Facility Assessment

In facility assessment, influencing factors are the issues that need to be reviewed and documented when observing concerns at an existing facility or when recognizing a void that a new facility could fill. The more serious and potentially expansive the project, the greater attention these factors will require in order to influence desired results. The following factors may also be applied to facility equipment limitations: safety, satisfaction, participation, efficiency, comparison, and modernization.

Safety

A fundamental requirement of any recreation facility manager is to provide a safe environment for all users and employees. To create a safe environment, risk of harm must be minimized as much as possible. When assessing facility safety, the organization should determine if the design or use of the facility creates potential for injury. Examples of safety concerns include the following:

- A hardwood basketball court surface may have warped boards or worn areas that create a tripping or slipping hazard.
- An outdoor tennis or basketball court may form cracks that could lead to users getting injured.
- An outdoor baseball or softball facility has potential for foul or overthrown balls to hit people who are playing or watching.

Pools present liability concerns for management because of the risk of drowning.
© Human Kinetics

- A beach or swimming pool facility includes the risk of drowning and therefore presents potential liability.
- A parking lot at any type of facility will have moving vehicles and pedestrians in the same area, potentially leading to collisions.
- The design of a golf hole may be problematic when drives regularly hit off the tee and land in areas of another hole, putting other golfers at risk of injury.
- The outfield fences of two baseball or softball fields that are too close together create a potential problem when home runs from one field fly into the other field.

Recreation facilities follow national standards recommended by the governing body of a particular sport. Some tourism facilities follow the requirements established by a franchise hotel chain. Architects may also provide recommendations for facility design that will minimize risk factors. When building a new facility or updating an existing one, it is necessary to be aware of minimum safety requirements and to consult experts to minimize risk. Unsafe facilities become a liability, so they may require changes to prevent legal problems. These changes may require some type of facility project that could result in repairs, renovation, or new construction. Safety concerns can play a big role in the need for facility improvements or development.

Satisfaction

Satisfaction is the degree to which the expectations of facility users have been met. The degree of satisfaction among users is a determinant in the success of the core product. Facilities only have one chance to make a first impression on users. A perceived lack of quality or a bad experience while using a facility can negatively

In addition to potential liability to the organization, cracks or worn areas on court surfaces may cause user dissatisfaction.
miromiro/iStock/Getty Images

influence users' satisfaction. Recreation facility managers should attempt to ascertain how users perceive the facility and what additional services they might enjoy. Facility managers can conduct participant satisfaction surveys, establish suggestion boxes, or simply interact with customers to determine their level of satisfaction.

User satisfaction can be affected in a negative way if the facility is perceived to be of substandard quality. For example, golfers may become dissatisfied with the conditions of a golf course if regular maintenance (e.g., fertilizing, overseeding, controlling weeds) isn't performed. Negative experiences from poor customer service can also contribute to unsatisfied users. Determining who the users are and their requirements for satisfaction can help recreation facility managers be aware of problems that need to be corrected or facility needs that are unmet.

Participation

In recreation facility management, the term *participation* refers to the number of people using a facility. Facilities are designed to accommodate a specific number of users, or participants. Even the best architects and consultants have difficulty predicting the usage patterns and capacity of the facilities they design. Some recreation facilities become so popular that they attract more users than they were designed to accommodate. Facility managers should recognize when usage creates a sense of overcrowding, which can have a negative impact on user experience. For example, an increase in the use of fitness equipment at an indoor facility can lead to participants waiting in line for a particular piece of equipment. Eventually, this condition may cause users to become dissatisfied with management for not providing additional equipment or adding space to accommodate the increased interest in personal fitness equipment. This dissatisfaction may lead to users seeking another recreation facility that has sufficient space and equipment.

Efficiency

Efficiency relates to how well management uses a facility and other resources in maximizing revenue opportunities while minimizing expenses. It also involves allocating space to allow for maximum use without decreasing customer satisfaction. Often the design of a facility can cause problems with the efficient provision of the core product or core product extensions. For instance, if in order to access a basketball court a user must first walk across a running track, the design is not efficient because crossing the track could be problematic for both court and track users. However, recreation facility managers can influence the delivery of a product with their management practices. By

regularly evaluating staff, equipment, and facilities, managers can determine whether goals and objectives are being achieved in an efficient way. They should conduct regular assessments to determine whether a better facility improves the efficiency of the product delivery. If so, efficiency concerns can help demonstrate the need for facility improvements or a new facility.

For example, the design of an older golf-course clubhouse may have separate spaces for the pro shop and concession areas. A renovation that combines them into one area not only improves the efficiency of the space for users by allowing one-stop shopping for registration and purchasing golf supplies and concession products; in addition, it improves efficiency for management by eliminating the need to staff two separate operations.

Imagine that a recreation facility manager is responsible for an aging ice arena that has outdated and poorly performing compressor (ice-making) equipment. This equipment

This gift shop situated in a recreation facility is an example of how user needs can be managed efficiently.
Jeffrey Greenberg/Education Images/Universal Images Group via Getty Images

consistently fails, causing regular closures of the facility. As a result, customers are frustrated that they can't access the facility as intended. Over time, they begin to find other facilities to pursue their recreational interests. This change causes a loss of revenue for the ice arena and creates a poor image of the facility management. Clearly, this inefficiency indicates a need for a facility improvement or renovation.

Comparison

Whether they work in the private or public sector, all recreation facility managers are involved in comparing their products with those of their competitors. Termed *benchmarking*, this comparison is initiated so that management can ascertain what products their competitors are providing and how well they are providing them. Facility operations have many aspects to compare, but the most important is determining how a facility measures up in space functionality and appearance. Most recreation facility managers want to be in a leading position or at least equal with their competition. Benchmarking with comparative information from other facilities can be a valuable tool in influencing administrators to recognize the need to renovate or construct a facility.

Consider an example of the development of resorts in Las Vegas. Before designing a new resort, it is common to examine other resort and casino developments in the area. These facilities have gone through considerable change from their early years (1940-1970) when they simply consisted of hotels with casinos. In the 1980s, there was a shift toward creating a family experience. But the greatest change in resort and casino developments occurred in the 1990s when a greater emphasis was placed on luxury and entertainment for adults. Now resorts and casinos include entertainment venues, shopping malls, restaurants, amusement parks, water parks, and nightclubs. These developments are a result of benchmarking.

Modernization

Many facilities are constructed with state-of-the-art materials and furnished with the most up-to-date equipment. Over time, however, they become outdated as new technology creates improved options in a variety of facility applications. Recreation facility managers should be attentive to these new options and plan and budget for necessary improvements.

New trends developed by industry manufacturers and interests expressed by users can create an opportunity to upgrade an existing facility or construct a new one. When new technology becomes available and managers do not make related improvements to facilities, those facilities can quickly become out of date. Facilities can also be less productive if they don't take advantage of new options. In short, a facility is either *up*dated or *out*dated. An outdated facility can lose customers to new competitors or facilities that have been continually updated. Technology advancements in materials and equipment could prevent injury, create new experiences, improve user satisfaction, and even improve the appearance of the facility. Managers of fitness-related facilities frequently see the introduction of new exercise equipment, products, and services. Those managers who don't replace old equipment with the latest updates find themselves at a competitive disadvantage with other facilities in their market. This result also applies to tourism-based facilities, including hotels and resorts. Upgrading rooms, replacing old furniture, and adding new televisions, video games, and Internet access can enhance the appeal of such facilities.

Influencing Techniques in Facility Assessment

Sometimes the previously mentioned influencing factors may not be enough to accurately determine facility needs. Recreation facility managers can use additional techniques to gauge support for the renovation or construction of a facility. These techniques can help inform administrators, board members, financial officers, and politicians to recognize the circumstances that warrant attention and response. They include site visits, surveys, focus groups, comments and opinions, petitions, history, and asset management.

Site Visits

One of the best ways to bring about support for facility projects is to take a representative group of users and administrators to visit existing facilities with problems or other facilities that may become a model for a new facility. These site visits are usually done in the early stages of development or renovation. They are particularly effective because personal experience and a visual assessment of facility problems (or of a state-of-the-art facility) is a great way to create insight for what needs to be accomplished. This personalized experience and visual evidence can help obtain support among administrators, politicians, and financial backers.

Technological advances have expanded site visit capabilities for many recreation agencies. Many agencies have created virtual tours of their facilities as a way to attract new users and showcase facility amenities. An indirect benefit of these virtual tours is the ability for other agencies to initially view these facilities without having to travel to the site. The use of drones with video and image capturing has also afforded recreation agencies a low-cost opportunity to obtain aerial images of the facility and the community in order to assess existing or potential sites. Other advances in technology, including geographic information system (GIS) mapping and satellite imaging websites, have also made virtual site visits more accessible.

Surveys

Surveys have traditionally been the most common method for obtaining information. Several types of surveys solicit input. An internal survey can be used to obtain user or employee feedback regarding the facility. An external survey can be used to obtain comparative (benchmark) information from facilities with similar products. A benchmark survey shows facility managers how their facility compares with a competitor's facility. External surveys can also assist in discovering user or employee habits, interests, attitudes, and opinions. Obtaining objective facts about comparable facilities resulting from a formal benchmark survey can be instrumental in persuading administrators of the need for a facility project. Benchmark surveys should be in written form with appropriate questions that can be completed within a reasonable time frame. Surveys that compare one facility with another or written survey information from users and employees can be useful for convincing administrators that a facility has deficiencies.

Online surveys first emerged in the 1980s, and they have grown into one of the more

CHECK IT OUT

What Is GIS, and How Can It Help With Facility Assessment?

According to the United States Geological Survey (USGS), a geographic information system (GIS) is a computer system that analyzes and displays geographically referenced information (USGS, 2022). GIS analysis and mapping are widely used when assessing the location and type of recreation facilities and amenities within a community. By mapping the geographic locations of a community's recreation facilities (e.g., playgrounds, trails, recreation centers), the recreation agency can better identify and assess areas that are possibly underserved while also better locating desirable locations for new facilities.

popular survey formats. Largely attributed to their low cost and fast turnaround times for data collection, online survey formats have exploded in popularity, and recreation agencies have enthusiastically embraced them. Several vendors of online surveys allow agencies the ability to create their own surveys with instant access to the results. The two most common approaches to recruiting participants for online surveys are river and panel sampling techniques (Lehdonvirta et al., 2020).

- *River sampling* is the most common online survey sampling technique. Participants are invited with a link to the survey, which is often included in an email, posted on a web page, or shared on a social media site. The term *river* refers to the idea that the agency is dipping into the traffic flow of a website, mass email, social media site, and the like, and hopes to catch some of the participants who are floating by.

- *Panel sampling* involves working with an online survey panel provider that has recruited a so-called panel of participants through advertisements on websites or social media. These providers invite participants to join an online panel based on the participants' interests and background. The recreation agency works with the panel provider to distribute online survey invitations to participants who are associated with specific panels. Online panels typically yield higher response rates and allow the recreation agency to target specific groups that may not typically complete surveys using the river sampling technique.

Focus Groups

A **focus group** consists of people who represent various segments of users and stakeholders. Group members are simply asked to share their thoughts on subjects related to facility development; a facilitator guides them through questions regarding facility needs. Focus groups generally range in size from 5 to 12 participants. Managers may choose to use multiple groups to better understand the diverse needs of participants. For example,

focus groups could be divided by gender or another factor. These groups could be broken into smaller segments based on marital status, age, income level, and other characteristics. The value of having different groups is that each group possesses different opinions and values. Understanding the needs of various segments of the population can play an important role in facility design.

Comments and Opinions

The comments and opinions of facility users and employees are important to consider when assessing user satisfaction. These pieces of information, both positive and negative, can provide valuable feedback for management. Both users and employees offer distinct perspectives of a facility that management does not have. User and employee opinions should be solicited in several ways. Comment cards and suggestion or complaint forms should be available for users and employees to express their concerns, and online options should also be provided as an alternative to written forms. User and employee dissatisfaction should be carefully reviewed, and concerns should be addressed in a timely and professional manner. Concerns should be documented in a system that maintains a record of such information. At some point, these records could be a helpful resource to convince administrators of the need for a facility project.

Opinions can also be solicited through opinion polls. Opinion polls are designed to obtain user opinions regarding satisfaction with the condition of a facility or the perceived need for a new facility. Such polls are usually conducted through online apps or web-based services. They tend to have fewer than 10 questions, and they can be completed in a few minutes. For example, users may be asked if they are in favor of the development of a community theater or if they would be interested in attending events put on at a community theater. This technique is effective for getting an initial impression about a project that is under consideration, especially if public support is vital to the feasibility of the project.

Petitions

A **petition** is a document stating that people agree on a certain issue. The petition usually has a formal statement that helps demonstrate interest in a project. Petitioning is a common form of creating awareness of the need for a project, especially if the user has an interest or a stake in the facility. The petition should include petitioners' identification information, such as name, address, and telephone number, along with a signature. Sometimes petitions have certain legal requirements. These requirements often pertain to funding sources being considered for a facility project and may vary by location. More information about petitions can be found through government agencies. Recreation facility managers should research these requirements if petitions are being considered.

History and Asset Management

Recreation facility managers should know the history of the facilities for which they are responsible. The age and condition of the structural systems and construction materials are crucial information that affects the need for timely replacement or renovation of infrastructure. Many facility materials have predictable life spans. For example, roofing materials typically need to be replaced on a 20- to 30-year cycle. Paving materials in parking lots typically have a 15- to 20-year life cycle.

Facility managers should document when materials and equipment are installed and then budget accordingly for when they need to be replaced. Documenting facility renovations and updating records on the age and condition of materials and equipment are critical to facility maintenance. The concept of documenting the age and predicted life span of facility components is called **asset management**. The history of a facility can track outdated building materials, design and layout, mechanical systems, and structural equipment including doors, windows, and railings. It is also important to document whether the core product has changed but the facility has not. For example, consider a facility that was originally designed

for physical activity, such as an aerobics room or dance studio, but is now being used for office space or for educational purposes. Visual documentation through video recordings or digital images is an excellent way to represent changes in physical condition. Simply showing how outdated a facility is can create the necessary support for an improvement or construction project.

Initial Proposal

An initial proposal is a formal way of communicating the need for a facility improvement or for the construction of a new facility. Generally, the party creating a case for the improvement or development project (most likely a facility manager) creates this document, then delivers it to administrators, owners, investors, governing bodies, or other agencies that control funding. The initial proposal is not a formal plan; it is merely the communication of the need for a facility project. Nevertheless, this written statement of need should include as much detail as possible to ensure clear communication of concerns and prevent those reading it from making assumptions that hinder progress.

The initial written proposal should describe the need or title, limitations, problems, and opportunities involved in the project; an outline for the proposal is described here:

- *Need or title*: Assign a specific name or brief description of the project that identifies what is wanted or needed.

- *Recommendation*: Make a formal, short statement of the proposed action or outcome. The statement should be concise and complete.

- *Introduction*: Express the need by creating awareness of the forthcoming proposal. Provide an overview of what the document will contain and what it is to accomplish.

- *Rationale*: Create a case with logical points of information. Emotional points can also support the proposal. Establish the fundamental reasons for the need.

- *Justification*: Provide real data, background information, and other facts to support the need.

- *Funding*: Summarize the fiscal requirements and opportunities of the facility projects. Share the income and expenditure information. Identify estimates or real construction or renovation costs involved. Show how the proposal fits the funding circumstances.
- *Impact*: Share the potential benefits of the project.
- *Conclusion*: Summarize by restating the recommended need.

This written proposal is a reasonable and professional way of communicating a facility project need to the entities that must approve such a project, and it can prove to be helpful in gaining initial interest and support for the project. In some cases, adding a verbal presentation may be required as well. The verbal presentation can be used to complement a written proposal when communicating to board members, potential investors, and stakeholders.

Summary

In most instances, the need for a facility project must be justified. Managers can provide this justification by addressing shortcomings of current facilities and by showing user demand for facilities. Various formal and informal methods exist for assessing influencing factors in a recreation facility. To understand user needs, a recreation facility manager may use techniques such as surveys, focus groups, comment cards, and petitions. These assessment strategies are essential knowledge for recreation facility managers; they are used in making the case for facility improvement and development projects and in preparation of initial proposals for those projects.

REVIEW QUESTIONS

1. Why is it important to regularly complete facility safety assessments?
2. Provide an example of how a facility manager could assess user satisfaction and user participation rates within their facility.
3. How can comparison (benchmarking) data be useful when assessing facility needs?
4. Define river sampling and panel sampling for online surveys.
5. Describe the primary elements to include when drafting an initial proposal for a renovated or new facility project.

CASE STUDY

Community Considers Closing a Soccer Facility

"The grim realities of the community's indoor soccer climate could lead Dyersville YMCA leaders to contemplate closing one of their indoor soccer facilities," the Young Men's Christian Association (YMCA) executive director, Betty Slagle, said Tuesday. The discussion came as part of the YMCA's annual indoor soccer focus group meeting. Indoor soccer enthusiasts filled the room to hear a presentation of the status of the indoor soccer program and provide their input about its future. The YMCA owns two complexes: the Indoor Soccer Center (ISC) and the YMCA Indoor Soccer Planet (YISP).

"What's indoor soccer going to look like in the future? Are we going to be able to sustain indoor soccer the way it looks today?" Slagle said, after the meeting. "If you look at the national trends and look at the trends in Dyersville, it will tell you probably not." YMCA Board President Warren Chrisman said no decision had been made, despite ongoing rumors about a potential closure. "I think we're going to talk about financing in the future," he said. "Whether that entails closing a facility or not, I don't know. I think we've got budget questions coming up, and we'll see." Overall, financial data presented a bleak picture. Despite cuts to staff and other expenses and continued efforts to diversify offerings, the two indoor soccer complexes continue to lose money. "Indoor soccer's decline in the city reflects national trends, with dwindling youth numbers for the ninth consecutive year," Slagle said. In addition, the game generally isn't drawing as many young adults as it did 15 years ago.

During the focus group meeting, one indoor soccer participant asked directly about the possibility of closing YISP and what could be done with the banquet facility within that facility. "I don't think any decisions have been made, but it will be a topic of discussion going forward, how we're going to create a sustainable future," Slagle answered. "The reality is that we're going to have to talk about that. We have to talk about sustaining an entire YMCA system." Speaking after the meeting, Slagle said the YISP would be the most logical option if YMCA leaders did decide to close a facility. "Given the participation numbers, given all the indicators that you would use in making a decision, I think that would be probably the first place you would have to look," he said. "I think we'll have to talk all the way through that and determine what the future would be."

According to the YMCA's presentation, the two indoor soccer complexes together will see an expected 1,750 participants this fiscal year. That number represents a dramatic decrease from 7,833 participants in the year 2000. Indoor soccer is one of the YMCA's many offerings, some of which attract more participants. Several indoor soccer participants suggested some type of discount, such as cheaper team fees for weekend evening games or lower tournament fees to encourage more participation. This past year, YMCA officials did reduce fees at the YISP by 20 percent in an effort to draw more players. While the number of participants at the YISP increased, participation at the ISC decreased. Overall, the numbers were not high enough at the YISP to make up the discount. "You have to consider that when you reduce prices, you have to increase volume," Slagle said. "Right now, in our environment, we're really not increasing volume." John Davis, a former candidate for the YMCA board, suggested that the YMCA pursue more competitive tournaments and add video gambling. The latter comment drew some chuckles from the crowd. "OK, we laugh, but gambling machines are very popular, and they bring in a lot of revenue," Davis said. Wes Hillen, assistant women's soccer coach for the local community college and one of the event's younger attendees, said he didn't think gambling or small price adjustments were the answer. Instead, he said the YMCA must find ways to attract youth and their families as well as young adults, who could eventually raise their children with the sport. "When it comes down to it, it really is the younger kids," he said.

Case Study Questions

1. If you were the executive director, how would you respond to this situation?
2. If you were charged with collecting additional input from the community, who would you want to engage with to obtain useful information about the indoor soccer needs and interests within the community?
3. What techniques would you recommend for obtaining input from the groups you identified in question 2?
4. In addition to obtaining stakeholder information and input, what secondary sources would you pursue?

CHAPTER 4

Planning

LEARNING OBJECTIVES

At the completion of this chapter, you should be able to do the following:

1. Define the concept of project planning, and explain the two approaches in project planning.
2. Explain the concepts of a comprehensive, master, and strategic plan, and understand how each is related to facility planning.
3. Recognize the typical steps in planning.
4. Explain the various development options and when each would be appropriate.
5. Understand the purpose of the project statement and the components of it.

Planning is the foundation for successful recreation facility development and operations. This critical stage is where ideas are transformed into details that result in solving problems that recreation facility managers face. It is especially important to plan ahead and forecast future facility needs as much as is possible. The planning stage is distinct from the earlier assessment process in that it incorporates all information gathered in the assessment phase and transforms that information into the details that result in the construction or renovation of a recreation facility. This chapter outlines and describes the planning process, which includes planning options, common plans in recreation, typical steps in planning, planning and development considerations, development options, and program or project statements.

Planning Options

In recreation facility management, **project planning** is the systematic anticipation of information through careful thought and documentation to develop a facility project. The

Industry Profile

Partnering with the City of Pittsburgh and founded in 1996, the Pittsburgh Parks Conservancy is a 501(c)(3) nonprofit agency focused on improving the city's park system and facility amenities. The strategic initiatives of the Pittsburgh Parks Conservancy include advocacy, equity, and sustainability as well as a *green first* focus. The organization has raised over US$130 million for City of Pittsburgh parks, and it has completed over 20 major improvement projects. One of its recent projects, the Frick Environmental Center, is a certified Living Building that supports hands-on, experiential environmental education for learners of all ages. The Frick Environmental Center also achieved a platinum level in Leadership in Energy and Environmental Design (LEED).

In 2018, the Pittsburg Parks Conservancy launched a community assessment and outreach initiative titled the Parks Listening Tour (PLT), which was completed in two phases. Phase I (2018-2019) of the PLT consisted of community meetings and events throughout Pittsburgh. The Pittsburgh Parks Conservancy partnered with the City of Pittsburgh to collect feedback from more than 10,000 residents across more than 70 neighborhoods to better understand what they enjoyed about their parks as well as identify potential improvement needs within the city's parks. The Parks Conservancy agency sought to obtain input from as many residents as possible; it worked with neighborhood associations, schools, businesses, and other community groups to ensure diverse and equitable representation.

Launched in 2019, phase II of the PLT involved the City of Pittsburgh and Parks Conservancy leaders revisiting the various locations throughout the city and sharing the results of the data obtained during phase I. Based on the community input collected during phase I, an equitable Parks Plan was presented to residents. The agency also shared facts, figures, and investment maps for the equitable distribution of resources across the city's parks system.

A component of the Parks Plan that the organization said was developed *by the community, for the community*, included strategies for addressing the city's US$400 million shortfall of deferred capital repairs and a $13 million annual maintenance deficit (Pittsburgh Parks Conservancy, 2020). Driven by the community input garnered during the PLT, a ballot initiative to establish a Parks Trust Fund was proposed; the fund would raise funds to address the budgetary shortfalls. The residents of Pittsburgh approved the ballot item, resulting in a guaranteed $10 million per year to Pittsburgh's parks, in perpetuity, funded by a US$0.5 million levy on property taxes (Pittsburgh Parks Conservancy, 2020).

project is planned to meet user and employee needs and to remedy the shortcomings observed during the assessment of an existing facility.

Generally, managers can accomplish the planning of a recreation facility in two ways: an administrative approach or a participatory approach. The chosen planning option is usually determined by the nature of the agency, whether it is in the public or private sector, and the management philosophy of the agency. In addition, the political environment of the agency may influence decisions. For instance, in an agency where employees do not work well together or have a difficult time making group decisions, an administrative approach

may be best. In the situation where an administrator is trying to get employee support for an idea or create a stronger bond between employees, a participative approach may be more appropriate. Understanding both of these options should assist recreation administrators in determining which option is best suited for a particular project.

Administrative Approach

The administrative approach to planning a recreation facility is used in the private sector or at agencies where few or no tax dollars are supporting the project. In this approach, although a number of people may be involved in the process, all technical information, responsibilities, and priorities are decided by the administration (executive level). If users, facility staff, consultants, and other specialists are involved, it is only because an administrator sought their input in order to make informed decisions regarding the project. Progress revolves around the administrator or a small team of recreation professionals who are responsible for all planning aspects of the project. The administrative approach often does not appreciate the value of involving others in the planning of a facility project.

Participative Approach

The participative approach is typically used in public agencies where tax dollars are the primary funding source for facility projects; input from those who pay taxes is encouraged and sometimes required. The participative process involves a variety of people who have an interest in the project. Input is solicited from users, employees, consultants, and other specialists, and their role in bringing about the project is emphasized. This process assumes that administrators may not possess all the knowledge necessary to determine recreation facility needs. It is a good way to obtain additional information, encourage involvement, and gain support. The level of participants' involvement varies during different phases of the planning process based on the need for their contribution. The participative process can be a time-consuming approach, but if carefully managed, it can create a positive team atmosphere and generate support for the project.

Common Plans in Recreation

Planning is a critical element in nearly every aspect of a recreation agency's operations. Many of these planning activities culminate in the development of a formalized planning document that guides the agency's future initiatives and activities. Three types of plans are regularly linked to the operation, renovation, and development of recreation facilities: comprehensive, master, and strategic plans. While these three plans have some similarities, which can lead agencies and facility managers to refer to them interchangeably, they in fact have distinct differences.

Comprehensive Plans

Comprehensive plans are designed with the entire agency in mind; they typically focus on all known physical, financial, and human resources within the agency. The interrelationships among these resources as well as current and anticipated external trends within the agency's service market (e.g., demographic shifts, societal trends, geopolitical trends) are considered. Comprehensive plans typically provide a long-range (10- to 20-year) outlook for the agency. Because of their longer-term outlook, these plans provide a more generalized overview of the agency's operational activities and are more concentrated on capital projects such as extensive facility renovations, land acquisition, and new facility development.

Master Plans

In contrast to the agencywide focus of comprehensive plans, master plans are typically developed for specific physical resources such as a group of facilities, an individual facility, a cluster of parks, or an individual park site. Focused more on onsite-specific aspects of the agency, a **master plan** is a formal, comprehensive document that identifies the needs of the facility and prioritizes which construction or renovation will occur. A master plan is usually maintained at the administrative level of an agency. It creates a road map for facility needs in the future. Often, a master plan contains an inventory of existing agency facilities, including their current condition and any need for renovation. It considers the desires and needs of users and employees, and it projects those needs in a long-range time frame of 5 to 15 years, providing the big picture for the future. In addition, the master plan includes action plans for implementing those goals.

Strategic Plans

Strategic plans emphasize the development of a vision for the agency's desired future condition. A **strategic plan** involves developing strategic goals and initiatives that will be used to achieve the agency's desired vision. While comprehensive and master plans generally embody longer-term outlooks, strategic plans have a shorter-term (3- to 5-year) focus for the agency.

Each of these plans must result from considerable research, evaluation, and anticipation of future needs. This attention to detail is essential to a progressive mindset with concern for an agency's ongoing success. The size of the agency, the human and financial resources available, and the planning skills of the people involved in the process greatly affect the complexities associated with each type of plan. In many instances, agencies hire consulting firms to facilitate the planning process.

Typical Planning Steps

In addition to the two approaches to planning, the steps and specific ordering of the steps for planning vary. Planning can range from a process of 10 or more phases with additional tangents based on the results of a particular step in the planning process to models that outline the cyclical nature of planning. Despite this variation, most planning activities in recreation involve these steps:

- Planning organization
- Engagement
- Analysis
- Plan development
- Implementation

Planning Organization

The organization of the overall plan and corresponding activities should be initiated very early in the process. While the specific details associated with the organization phase can vary depending on the specific plan and agency, at a minimum, three tasks should be addressed: establishing a planning team, developing a planning process and schedule, and determining a stakeholder engagement strategy.

Establishing a committee (team) should kick off the overall planning process. For an administrative planning approach, the team is primarily composed of employees holding executive-level positions. In contrast, agencies implementing a participative approach are likely to seek input from a variety of internal and external sources, including the following:

- *Facility users.* People who experience the core product are those who use the facility on a daily basis. Facility users are key members of planning committees because their hands-on experience with an existing recreation facility provides a unique perspective.

- *Staff.* Staff are responsible for all the details involved in bringing the core product and core product extensions to the users of the facility. Staff are knowledgeable about the shortcomings of existing facilities and can provide unique observations because they live the consequences of facility limitations that affect their ability to deliver a product. Their insight can be invaluable in the planning process; in most instances, multiple staff members across multiple departments are involved. For instance, a representative from the maintenance department would be able to speak for those involved in the facility's support functions, including equipment setup and takedown, landscaping, storage, equipment repair, waste removal, delivery of equipment and supplies, and daily operations.

- *Facility administrators.* Facility administrators or owners bring a unique perspective to the project because they oversee the master plan for the facility. They have the responsibility for determining priorities and making project budget decisions. Their support and commitment in a facility project must be secured before progress can be made.

- *Consultants.* Consultants are usually specialists in the design, architectural, or engineering fields who bring detailed information, trends, and insight to a project. Consultants assist the committee or administration in developing concepts, ideas, and alternatives while establishing priorities in the building project.

Their expertise can guide a project, taking into consideration agency strengths and limitations, construction and equipment needs, cost assessment assistance, comparative data, and other factors that may be involved. Consultants usually have access to comparative information regarding recently constructed recreation facilities similar to the one being planned.

• *Architects.* Almost any level of facility project, whether a minor renovation or new construction, requires the services of an architect. Architects bring expertise and technical knowledge that is invaluable, and the selection of an architect should receive special attention. A request for proposal (RFP) is used to solicit the services of qualified architects for a recreation facility project. This document usually defines the scope of the project and asks respondents to list similar experiences or qualifications that make them suitable for this particular project. Selecting the appropriate architect for the project is a crucial step in the planning process. Architects bring together concepts, needs, technical information, related facts, and interests, creating the documents that guide others to construct the recreation facility. (These documents are discussed later in this chapter.) Typical fees for an architect range from 8 to 12 percent of the total construction cost.

Once a planning team has been established, they should complete a process and schedule for developing the plan. As noted earlier, the specific planning steps can vary depending on the agency, the facility, and its needs. Before they begin, the planning team should discuss the desired steps, the ordering of these steps, and a schedule. For example, the team may determine that the collection of internal input will occur during the first four weeks of the planning process, and external data will be obtained during weeks 5 through 12.

Engagement

Arguably the most important step in the planning process is the engagement of internal and external stakeholders. Only through their input can a plan truly be successful. The development of a stakeholder engagement strategy should also be completed during the organization phase of the planning process. Stakeholders are all parties who will be affected by or will affect the facility's strategy. Stakeholders can be internal or external to the agency; a successful plan should include the engagement of both internal and external stakeholders.

Internal Stakeholders
- Employees
- Management
- Boards
- Volunteers

External Stakeholders
- Facility users
- Community leaders
- Facility or agency partners
- Civic organizations

A variety of data collection methods can be utilized to engage with stakeholders; examples include questionnaires, interviews, focus group sessions, and observations (see chapter 3 for an overview of assessment techniques). In addition to stakeholders, the planning team should review secondary sources that are relevant to the facility or agency. Common secondary sources include agency inventories, resource assessments, population information, existing plans, benchmarking data, and external standards.

CHECK IT OUT
Avoid the Usual Suspects

When establishing a planning team, agencies should avoid creating a team of only the agency's inner circle. Rather, consider a cross-sectional representation of staff and departments. It can even be helpful to include one or two contrarians because they can help provide rigor and credibility to the team and processes.

Tips for Establishing a Planning Team

- *Select a chairperson (or co-chairs)*: Consider someone with experience in conducting major problem-solving meetings; if necessary, the chair could also be a nonvoting member of the team.
- *Determine a communication plan:* Identify one or more team members to record notes from the meetings, document team decisions, help prepare meeting materials, and disseminate outcomes.
- *Agree on ground rules:* Before beginning, members of the planning team should agree on the processes for discussion and activities. For example, members may criticize ideas, but they may not criticize each other personally.
- *Outline roles:* Flush out the expected roles for each member of the team prior to starting the process.

Analysis

At its core, the analysis phase is about identifying needs and issues from the stakeholder engagement and review of secondary sources. A list of facility needs and concerns should be extracted from this data. From the data reviewed, the team may identify a list of the highest-priority items. While the number of items can vary, a list of 10 to 20 items is typical. Some of these items may be relatively quick fixes (e.g., minor facility renovations or updates), while other items may be more difficult to address (e.g., new facility requiring funding that is not yet in place). At this stage in the process, each of the highest-priority items should be included on the list regardless of their feasibility.

Plan Development

Guided by the priority items identified during the data analysis phase, the next step is plan development. The number of items and their scope are often fleshed out based on the specific plan (comprehensive, master, strategic, etc.). For instance, during this phase, a team working on a strategic plan may determine a vision for the types of services and facilities their stakeholders will have in the next five years. Regardless of the type of plan, the goals and objectives to support the vision are often developed during this phase. Goals are based on the highest-priority needs and concerns, and they are written as broad statements of lon-

ger-range aspirations that set overall direction for the facility and its stakeholders. Objectives should be measurable, specific, and directly tied to a specific goal, and they should include timelines.

Implementation

The plan's goals and objectives provide the facility manager with a road map for future activities and initiatives. Despite having this clear outline for the facility's future, implementing the plan is not without challenges. The facility manager must carefully prevent a scenario in which the plan quickly becomes ignored and is rarely considered when making facility-related decisions. Taking the following steps can increase the likelihood of successful implementation:

- *Develop a resolution.* Once completed, the agency or facility should present the plan to a governing council or administrative leadership team for formal adoption.
- *Implement the plan quickly.* Implementing the plan as soon as possible helps the team to capitalize on the momentum from the planning team's efforts and stakeholder engagement processes.
- *Update the plan.* The facility manager should be cognizant of change, making a commitment to review the plan on a regular basis and revise it as needed.
- *Develop a planning task force.* To keep stakeholders engaged in the process, the

facility manager can develop a planning task force to regularly monitor the plan and the facility's progress with it.

- *Strike a balance.* Finding the sweet spot between being too ambitious and doing too little supports successful implementation of the plan.
- *Take ownership.* It is important to establish an individual or single entity for the completion of each priority or initiative. This process can increase accountability and support successful completion of each priority or initiative.
- *Use appropriate resources.* The plan requires the use of adequate and properly designated resources in order to be successful.
- *Provide annual updates.* Regular updates on the plan and the agency or facility's progress on the plan's goals can help maintain momentum.

Facility Planning and Development Considerations

New facility projects represent a common outcome (goal) of many planning documents. No matter what planning option is being applied, these facility development projects require certain preliminary considerations. Some of these points of information will be integrated into the planning steps outlined in the previous section. Regardless of the timing, it is important to consider site analysis, structure, cost projections, and area impact during the initial stages of facility planning and development.

Site Analysis

Planning for a new facility includes a discussion about the potential location for the project. This phase of planning is called the **site analysis**,

The location of this waterway might influence the development of certain facilities at this site.
Arnokx/iStock/Getty Images

which evaluates a variety of factors related to the specific location desired for a facility. These factors include environmental aspects of the site such as terrain, water, topography, climate, and vegetation. They also include zoning or governmental restrictions as well as potential historical significance of the site. Community planning agencies may have ordinances that limit how much land can be developed in certain areas. Along with storm-water storage, tree and other green-space preservation often limits the development of certain sites. It is also important to understand the accessibility of utilities to the site (e.g., electrical, sewage, telephone, cable) because it could affect development costs. Often projects are delayed or canceled because of site problems. When preparing a site analysis, a site visit is essential for identifying these concerns.

Structure

Ultimately, some type of facility will be identified during the planning process. That end product must be depicted in a way that can be shared with others involved in the process, including those who will provide the funding. Although the final design may not be ready after the site has been analyzed, the potential structure should be conceptually represented. The detail and technical aspects of the facility are not necessary in this step; however, an architect will likely need to create these details at a later stage. The potential structure can be represented in a sketch, rendering, or schematic design that reflects the information obtained in the assessment. The architect is typically responsible for preparing this representation.

Cost Projections

After a structure has been conceptualized, cost projections are necessary to solicit financial support and to make progress. These projections involve two types of costs: capital and operational.

- **Capital costs** are required in order to construct the facility. Architects can provide an estimate of capital costs based on their knowledge of construction costs in the area where the facility is to be constructed. Managers of other facilities in the area can also provide insight into the anticipated construction costs. No matter how the informal cost projection is determined, it helps the team think about the reality of paying for the project and is therefore a critical component in the planning process.

- **Operational costs** are the day-to-day operation of the facility. In addition to the construction costs, careful consideration of the resources required to support operational costs is necessary. Comparing a new facility with a similar facility already in existence can help provide a general estimate of operational costs.

Area Impact

Area impact is about the impact of the area on a facility and vice versa. In determining how an area may affect a facility, information such as demographics of the service area is important. The term **service area** refers to the people within a certain distance of a facility who will be users of—and therefore served by—the facility. Distance can be measured in actual geographic distance from a facility, or it

CHECK IT OUT

Satellite Imagery Resources

There are several free or inexpensive satellite imagery resources that can provide agencies with a quick, close-up satellite view of Earth. Many of these programs allow the user to overlay various geopolitical landmarks, provide weather and heat maps, and project measurements onto a site. These programs can help provide agencies with a preliminary assessment of a potential site and its relationship to other facilities and spaces within the area.

can be measured in the amount of time it takes to get to a facility. For instance, many users of a campus recreation facility may be within walking distance. In this case, the walking distance from dormitories, classroom buildings, or off-campus student living areas is a primary focus. When a facility location requires users to drive, drive times and access routes play a more important role. For a community center where people may walk and drive, the service area should be understood in terms of both walk and drive times. In the instance of a resort or other tourist destination, accessibility of major highways and airports is an important consideration. For a resort to be successful, it must be accessible to users. This accessibility has been a key to success for tourist attractions such as Walt Disney World and the Las Vegas Strip; they are accessible from airports throughout the United States.

Area impact also includes how a facility project will affect the area around the facility. Types of area impact include economic impact, environmental impact, and social impact.

- **Economic impact** refers to money that users and employees will spend directly at the facility or indirectly at other businesses in the community. For instance, other businesses in the area may benefit from the addition of a new facility, and the new facility may benefit by being located near other businesses. Having multiple businesses in the same area creates a **gravity effect**; in other words, people are drawn to the area by a specific business but end up spending additional money at nearby establishments.

- **Environmental impact** is typically negative and relates to the damage that the facility may have on the environment, such as pollution or overuse of natural resources. As discussed in chapter 2, this is an opportunity for facility planners to think in terms of sustainability as they strive to minimize environmental impact.

- **Social impact** explains how the facility will affect people living nearby or using the facility. It includes understanding the demographics of users and of nearby residents.

Development Options

When planning to enhance a facility or correct existing problems, the team must consider various development options. The solution could range from a simple repair to a completely new facility. Most facility development projects involve one of the following: repair, renovation, retrofitting, or new construction (including facility expansion). All four options require construction work where specialists or contractors may be necessary to complete the project. Each option has its own application to solving facility limitations.

Repair

Probably the simplest and most common improvement option is the repair of an existing facility. Repair is desirable when a facility simply wears out from overuse or age and needs to be rebuilt or made to function as it was intended. Repairs usually address minor problems where the goal is to revitalize the area to its intended state. Repairing a facility and restoring it to a sound condition helps in the production and delivery process. A major concern in repairing a facility is the cost. If the cost to repair a facility is high, it may be more reasonable to build a new facility. Generally, if the cost to repair a facility is more than half the cost to build a new one, then building a new facility is a better option.

Renovation

Renovation requires greater planning and supervision than repair. **Renovation** is the rehabilitation of an existing facility with steps taken to rearrange the space within an existing structure. This option usually includes changes that create a more efficient operation or a more attractive facility, make the facility safer, or meet legal requirements. Some structural changes are usually made, but using the original structure is a crucial planning component. Renovation is less expensive than new construction, and it usually extends the life of

Unlike with repairs, while a new facility is under construction, the old facility can still remain in use so that no revenue is lost during construction.
shock/iStock/Getty Images

the existing facility. The downside is that the facility is often unusable during the renovation, leading to revenue loss. In addition, the old structure may experience other problems in the future. The same guidelines regarding costs for repairs apply to renovation: If the cost to renovate a facility is more than half the cost to build a new facility, then building a new facility is a better option.

Retrofitting

The concept of retrofitting involves updating a facility. More specifically, **retrofitting** is the addition of new technology systems to an existing facility. Retrofitting is used when the space in a facility still has a high degree of functionality but needs to be modernized. New systems can include security systems,

computer systems, video, cable, identification-card equipment, and ticketing. Usually, the function of the facility sees few changes to activities during retrofitting.

New Construction

New construction of facilities is the most significant and demanding of the development options. New construction involves planning a facility from the establishment of a need for development through the final stages of moving everything in. An advantage of new construction is that it is an opportunity to develop the ideal facility and still maintain the function of the old facility without losing revenue. This option also includes expanding an existing facility. A tremendous number of details are involved in the planning process for a new facility. Recreation professionals must understand the complexity of constructing a new facility. The remaining chapters in part II of this book address the details involved with planning such an undertaking, including design and blueprints, funding, and construction.

Project Statement

Throughout the planning process, it is important to document information and use it in the formal facility design stage (discussed in chapter 6). This documentation is called the *project statement*, or program statement, and it will assist in the architect's design of the facility. The information comes from the early assessment and planning efforts; when approved by administrators, it represents the first formal commitment in the planning process. A **project statement** is a written report on a variety of subjects providing direction for the architect. It serves as a transitional document between planning and design. This information specifically relates to the facility and its purpose. Often facility managers lack the expertise in accurately bringing this information together. Consultants or architects can play a valuable role and provide the necessary assistance during this stage. The more detail and clarity the statement has, the easier it will be for the project designer to translate it into a building or facility design. The project statement should include the following components: objective, basic assumptions, trends, comparisons, primary space, auxiliary space, service needs, space relationships, environmental impact, sustainability, and equipment and furniture list.

Objective

The objective describes the specific delivery of the product and how the facility will serve its potential users. It should state the ultimate objectives or anticipated outcomes of the facility, including the primary core product delivery areas of the facility. For example, in designing an aquatic park, a primary objective is to provide a facility that will increase the number of aquatic activities for users.

Basic Assumption

The basic assumption cites how the facility will solve the facility's current problems. This section often identifies current programs and facility offerings. In addition, it identifies desired activities and programs that the agency would like to offer. This statement makes it easy to identify problems in the current facility. In addition, it highlights how the renovated or new facility will address the problems by describing new activities and programs that can be offered.

Trends

Trends reflect how society is changing and how those changes affect demand for the product. Trends may play a major role in driving the project. They could include technological advancement, legal requirements, population growth in the area, and public interest in the core product.

Comparison

The comparison section compares existing facilities or competition and how they affect the core product and core product extensions of the proposed facility. It also reflects comparisons with recreation facilities in other communities that may be perceived as desirable. This comparison can create political support for a facility. It demonstrates how existence or nonexistence of a potential facility will affect the market in the community and how a new facility might compare with others.

Primary Space

The **primary space** section describes the spaces needed to provide the core products of a facility. The description should include a list of the spaces that are being planned within the facility, along with the size and function of each area.

Auxiliary Space

The **auxiliary space** section lists the names and sizes of the core product extension areas. This

A running track at a track and field facility is an example of a primary space.
© Human Kinetics

list should include the requirements of each area and any specialized equipment to be used. This space includes food and beverage outlets as well as equipment rental or checkout, office, parking, and reception or lobby areas.

Service Needs

The section on **service needs** describes the maintenance functions that the facility will require. This part of the program statement is often poorly addressed (and sometimes even omitted) by the planning team. An indoor facility could incorporate areas for custodial service, trash removal, storage, plumbing, mechanical rooms, custodial supplies, and equipment repair. An outdoor facility could incorporate equipment storage for mowers and other equipment, space for lighting systems,

and irrigation controls. This category would also include the use of maintenance at the existing facility and how it will contribute to the future success of the facility.

Space Relationships

The section on **space relationships** describes how all the areas of a facility will relate to one another, including flow of users and employees throughout the facility. In other words, it addresses how users and employees use the facility and what spaces should be located in proximity to each other. This section summarizes the overall operation of the areas, bringing them together effectively and efficiently. It could include diagrams depicting the functional relationships of all production and delivery areas.

Environmental Impact

This section provides a detailed description of the surrounding environment and how the facility may affect it. Typical environmental concerns include water runoff, vegetation impact such as tree loss or other loss of natural vegetation, facility appearance, and effects on habitat. The architect should appreciate community concerns about how the facility will influence the environment and consider opportunities for sustainable development.

Sustainability

The project statement should include a description of the facility's planned sustainable practices. Typical information within this section includes energy-efficiency plans, use of eco-friendly supplies, preventive maintenance activities, and recycling practices. In addition, the team should develop a description of how and where (within the facility) these efforts will occur.

Equipment and Furniture List

The equipment and furniture list is an extensive identification of all moveable and fixed facility items. It includes all the items (mechanical and others) that will be needed for the production and delivery operations of the core product and core product extensions.

Summary

Planning is a key element in the development of a facility. By establishing a diverse planning committee and considering many sources of information in the planning process, agencies can communicate their facility requirements to an architect, and a facility can be designed that meets the needs of the agency and its stakeholders.

REVIEW QUESTIONS

1. Describe the two approaches to planning.
2. What are the typical timelines for a comprehensive plan, a master plan, and a strategic plan?
3. What are the typical steps in the planning process?
4. Why is it important to visit the future facility site during the preliminary stages of facility planning and development?
5. Describe the importance of a project statement in the facility planning process.
6. What are some differences between primary and auxiliary spaces within a facility?

CASE STUDY

The Graying of the Blue Wave Aquatic Facility

You are an aquatics coordinator for the Blue Wave Aquatic Facility, which is located in the town of Valley Falls. The Blue Wave Aquatic Facility is a public facility that includes a 25-yard (about 25 m) outdoor pool with two diving board areas, locker rooms, an outdoor seating area, an equipment storage room, and a concession area. The facility has been a mainstay in the Valley Falls community since it was originally developed nearly 40 years ago. Since that time, numerous renovations and repairs have been completed to ensure the complex meets local safety codes and national aquatic standards.

The Blue Wave Aquatic Facility is, once again, in need of renovations and updates. The director of the Blue Wave Aquatic Facility has asked for you to assemble a planning committee to determine the appropriate course of action for the facility. The director wants you to chair the planning committee and appears to be embracing a participative approach to planning. Possible options range from renovating the existing facility to constructing a completely new aquatic complex. The planning committee's charge is to help the director determine the plans for the site.

Case Study Questions

1. One of your first tasks would be to organize a planning committee. Who are some individuals you could invite to serve on the planning committee?

2. What are some things you would want the committee to consider related to the planning and development or renovation of the Blue Wave Aquatic Facility?

3. Would you encourage the committee to seek input from others to help inform the plan? If so, whom might you engage with?

CHAPTER 5

Designing Ancillary Spaces and Core Product Extensions

LEARNING OBJECTIVES

At the completion of this chapter, you should be able to do the following:

1. Define the terms *ancillary space* and *core product extension*.
2. Identify the various elements in parking lot design.
3. Examine the functions and amenities of a facility's locker room space and reception area.
4. Recognize the various types of food-service operations used in facilities.
5. Understand factors associated with child care operations and equipment rentals or checkouts.

A recreation facility manager's primary focus is to provide the core product to users. However, users often seek additional services when using a facility. These additional services may simply enable a user to use a facility or enhance their use of a facility. Facilities are supported by ancillary spaces (areas that support the core product). In most facilities, the core product could not be made available to users were it not for the supporting ancillary areas. Recreation facility managers need to understand ancillary areas, such as parking and locker rooms, and how they affect recreation facility management. While ancillary areas do not exist as sources of revenue, facilities often have spaces that support the core product and generate revenue. Revenue-generating products and services that complement the core product are called core product extensions. These extensions play an important role in meeting user needs. Core product extensions are similar to ancillary spaces in that they support the core product of the facility. However, they have one notable difference: Core product extensions are designed to generate revenue. They can take the form of commodity outlets, food service, child care, and equipment checkout or rental.

Ancillary spaces represent those spaces within a recreation facility that support the core product. The most common ancillary spaces in recreation facilities include parking areas, reception areas, and locker rooms. Each of these spaces serves a vital role in supporting the core product and services within the facility. They are discussed in the following sections.

Parking

Recreation facilities can use two kinds of parking areas. The most common type is **surface parking**, an area consisting of a single, level surface. The second type of parking area is a parking structure or garage. These structures contain multiple levels of parking, creating more parking area while using less land. Parking structures are useful in cities and other areas with space restrictions. However, they are much more expensive to construct than surface parking.

Parking Options

Three types of parking options are typically offered at recreation facilities: self-parking,

gated parking, and valet parking. Each type has unique considerations. The nature of the core product typically determines which parking option will be used and to what extent.

Self-Parking

Self-parking (when drivers park their own vehicles) is the most common parking option. This option is typically used when a recreation facility has access to public streets or a parking lot in close proximity. It may be free of charge for facility users, or a fee may be charged based on length or time of use, which typically is regulated by parking meters. In some instances, such as at a campus recreation facility or health club, users may be required to purchase parking permits.

Gated Parking

Gated parking can be designed to combine self-parking and a system that controls vehicle access and security. Gated parking is often controlled by one-way access and an exit with an attendant to check vehicles in and out as well as to collect fees. This option often incorporates a gate that is controlled using access cards. In this instance, the user swipes a card through a magnetic card-reading device, or a device is attached to the vehicle that trips an electrical signal. These systems activate the gate to open or close. They often have a variable fee structure and membership options. Higher fees offer

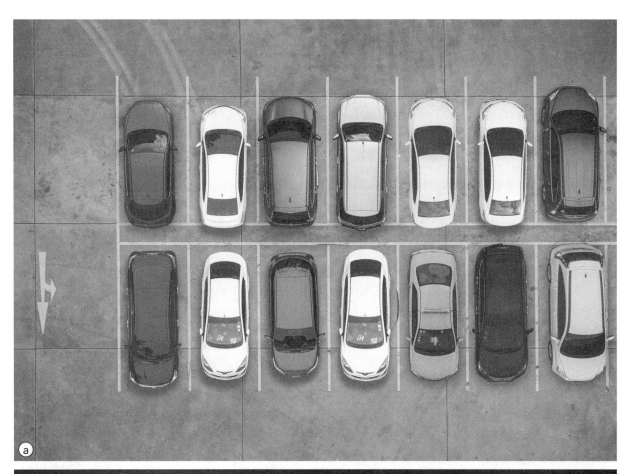

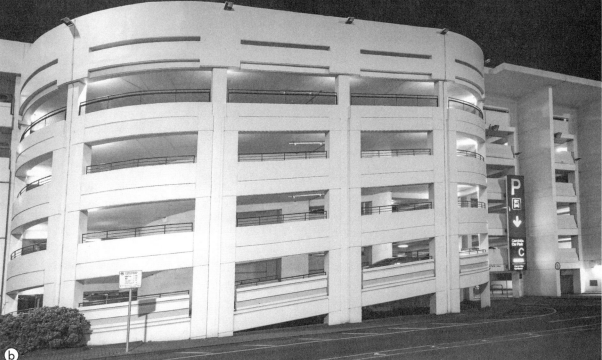

The two basic kinds of parking areas are (a) surface parking and (b) parking structures.
Photo a nonnie192/iStock/Getty Images; photo b mikroman6/Moment/Getty Images

benefits that may include specified parking spaces; spaces that are closer to the facility have a higher fee than more remote spaces.

Valet Parking

Valet parking provides maximum customer convenience. A valet service provides staff members who greet customers at the entrance of the facility and take the vehicle to a different location or parking area. It is a convenient form of parking, requiring little effort on the part of the vehicle owner. A numbered ticket is given to the owner, who gives the ticket to the valet upon leaving. The valet matches the number and returns the vehicle. Generally, valet parking costs more than other types of parking. Management must have access to nearby parking areas and provide vehicle security. Management must also have insurance coverage for this type of service. Valet parking is most common in urban areas, country clubs, hotels, and resorts.

Parking Operations

It is generally understood that recreation facilities should provide some form of parking as part of the facility or at least nearby. Usually, community-planning agencies require facilities to provide on-site parking to prevent congestion and overflow on local streets. The efficiency of a parking area projects a message about the management of the facility. It can be reflected in parking access, signage, maintenance, and security.

Access

An important consideration is how accessing and exiting a parking facility occurs. If a large parking area connects to a main street in the community, it may cause considerable delays for customers exiting the parking area. A system of control and communication should exist in the event that a special event creates heavy use or when the parking area is full. The facility may need parking attendants to direct vehicles to appropriate parking areas or security personnel to facilitate safe entry and exit of a parking facility that connects to a busy street.

Parking area signage should be easy to read. If applicable, it may provide information on time limits, parking rates, and where to pay.
Tobias Titz/fStop/Getty Images

Signage

Signage provides critical information for drivers using a parking facility. Recreation facility managers should provide readily identifiable directional indicators so that drivers know how to find and enter the designated parking areas. Signs to consider include directional, handicapped, visitor, compact car, and space or lane restriction signage. Signs are also useful for advertising; indicating rates; and communicating rules, regulations, policies, and how to pay. Some community ordinances place restrictions on the size, location, and amount of signage that may be allowed. Signage in a parking area should be consistent in size, color, and location throughout the parking area to provide easily identifiable information.

Maintenance

When it comes to the maintenance of a parking area, consider these three things:

1. *Attend to structural needs of the parking facility as required.* Management has to respond to harsh conditions, extreme weather, vehicle weight, and general wear and tear on the parking area.

2. *Keep up with the daily maintenance functions required to keep a parking facility in working order.* These tasks include ensuring that the surface is in good shape,

parking lines and signage are visible, and meters and gates are operational.

3. *Attend to the appearance of the parking area by keeping the area clean and attractive.* This responsibility can include attending to landscaped areas and providing adequate water to support vegetation in addition to providing trash receptacles and removing waste.

Security

Parking operators need to be concerned for the safety of users and prevention of vehicle theft and damage. Special attention is required to provide complete protection of vehicles and personal property. If adequate security is not provided, courts could hold an agency liable for damage and criminal acts. A key factor in parking security is the provision of proper lighting. Overhead lighting with adequate brightness can limit security concerns. Where feasible, security guards can supervise parking areas. In the event of an incident, some form of emergency communication device, such as an alarm, intercom, telephone, or security camera, should be available.

Parking Design

Recreational facility managers often dedicate little time to parking once a facility has been designed and is operating. However, it is vital that time and effort be devoted to the design of the parking area during the planning phase of parking operations. Parking design requires many considerations, including shape, angles, codes and ordinances, space size and number of spaces, sidewalks, landscaping, and drainage.

Shape

The shape of a parking area can be greatly influenced by topography and architectural requirements. A rectangular parking area is the most efficient and most common. Irregularly shaped lots are often the product of site constraints and usually result in an inefficient design.

Angles

Parking spaces are usually at 90-, 75-, 60-, or 45-degree angles. In some cases, local ordi-

nances require spaces to be at designated angles. However, the angle of a parking space is most frequently dictated by the amount of space available for parking and the desired number of parking spaces. Spaces at 90-degree angles allow for the most parking spaces in two-way traffic flow; however, in one-way traffic flow, angled spaces (usually 45 or 60 degrees) require less row width and may use space more efficiently.

Codes and Ordinances

Codes and ordinances can affect parking areas. They usually apply to areas with more than six parking spaces. Codes and ordinances depend on the interpretation of community planning agencies; each community has its own requirements. Codes may require a ratio of parking spaces per facility user tied to the capacity of the facility. For example, a code could require one parking spot for every six potential users and employees. Other factors that could be affected by codes include the appearance, overall design, entrance and exit locations, and location of the parking area in relation to the facility. Management should inquire about codes and ordinances in order to be in complete compliance. Accessibility for users with disabilities is governed by the Americans with Disabilities Act (ADA) Standards for Accessible Design.

Space Size and Number of Spaces

A parking space needs a minimum of 20 inches (51 cm) of door clearance; 24 inches (61 cm) is preferable. The general width for most parking spaces is 8 feet (2.5 m). The ADA establishes guidelines for accessible parking spaces. In addition to being located at the shortest walking point to building access points, accessible parking spaces should be at least 8 feet (2.5 m) wide. Parking access aisles should be 5 feet (1.5 m) wide for standard cars and 8 feet (2.5 m) wide for vans, and they should be part of an accessible route to the facility entrance. Two accessible parking spaces may share a common access aisle. Parking spaces and access aisles must be level, and at least one space must be van accessible.

The number of parking spaces required for a facility is also often dictated by local ordinances; however, some general guidelines follow:

- *Universities*: One parking space for each employee and one parking space for every four to six students
- *Community or recreation centers*: One parking space for every 200 to 250 square feet (18.5-23 m²) in the facility
- *Stadiums*: One parking space for every three or four seats
- *Parks*: One parking space for every 4,000 to 5,000 square feet (371.5-464.5 m²)

The ADA also includes guidelines for the number of accessible spaces, which is based on the total number of spaces at the facility (see table 5.1).

Generally, parking areas should be located in close proximity to the facility. Typically, users do not want to walk far to access a facility. However, in instances where space is inadequate or for an event where a large number of vehicles need to park, management should provide perimeter parking options, which require a longer walk or even a shuttle service to and from the facility.

Sidewalks

Sidewalks are essential for safety, especially with large parking lots. Sidewalks should be distinguished from the roadway and parking areas and should be raised 3 to 6 inches (8-15 cm). In situations where sidewalks are not raised, they should be properly painted, placing adequate emphasis on them for easy visibility, especially in crosswalks.

Landscaping: Shading, Screening, and Buffer Zones

Landscaping greatly contributes to the appearance of a parking area and can even increase property value. Landscape design can also help control traffic and increase safety in a parking area. In addition, the planting of berms, trees, and other types of vegetation can assist in shading a parking area. It not only is helpful in keeping vehicles cool but also helps maintain asphalt by limiting direct sunlight. Vegetation is also useful in screening neighboring areas and creating buffer zones from the parking area, which is required by many local ordinances. Screening or buffer zones can also be created with walls, fencing, or other types of dividers.

Drainage

Parking areas should have proper drainage to prevent pooling and flooding from rainwater. The parking area should have a flat surface with a slight slope (1%-4%) to allow for water runoff. The slope should be minimal, and it should not create a hazard for users. In most

TABLE 5.1 MINIMUM ACCESSIBLE PARKING REQUIREMENTS

Total number of parking spaces	Required minimum number of accessible parking spaces
1-25	1
26-50	2
51-75	3
76-100	4
101-150	5
151-200	6
201-300	7
301-400	8
401-500	9
501-1,000	2% of total spaces in lot
1,001 and above	20, plus 1 for each 100 over 1,000

Reprinted from the United States Access Board (www.access-board.gov).

cases, the slope is not noticeable to the naked eye.

Reception Area

A reception area is an ancillary area that can be vital to recreation facility usage and product success. The reception area represents an extension of the administration and delivery operations, creating initial contact with customers and providing a first impression of the facility. A reception area should establish a comfortable, uncongested, and unconfusing atmosphere that helps users gain access to the product.

A reception area serves as a transitional area from the outside boundaries of the facility to its inner operations. How well the reception area functions can make a lasting impression on users. This section includes some critical points for placing emphasis on a reception area.

Initial Appearance

An aesthetically pleasing reception area creates a favorable first impression by being well maintained and well organized. A disorganized and unattractive reception area can cause users to draw negative conclusions about the facility and its management. Conversely, a positive image projected by the reception area can recruit new users and help maintain repeat use from current users.

Efficiency

The efficiency of a reception area may be more important than its appearance. *Efficiency* refers to how well the staff communicates with users. A knowledgeable staff that is properly trained and understands organization procedures is vital in order to maintain consistency at the front desk and share correct information with users.

A reception area has many functions for a recreation facility. An aesthetically pleasing and comfortable reception area can create a favorable first impression of the facility.

ProfessionalStudioImages/E+/Getty Images

Attitude

Information and aesthetics go a long way in creating a positive impression in the reception area, but attitude is equally as important. Guests should interact with staff members who are friendly and helpful. Reception staff members are often asked the same questions over and over. Nevertheless, they should make users feel as though they are pleased to answer their questions and enjoy the interaction. A smile and a warm greeting go a long way in making users feel welcome.

Functions of Reception

The reception area may serve a variety of functions depending on the facility. In a health club, the reception area may simply provide a point to sign in or get information. In a hotel or resort, the reception area will also include a check-in area. Regardless of the facility, they all have certain common functions, including access control, fee collection, communication, and schedules, among others.

Access Control

The reception area controls user access. Nearly all indoor and many outdoor recreation facilities require some way of limiting user access. Not all areas of a facility are appropriate for users to enter. Outdoor recreation facilities may have sensitive environmental areas where user access should be limited in order to protect the area. Indoor facilities may have mechanical or other equipment areas that users should not enter for their safety and to prohibit tampering with important equipment.

If the facility has a requirement for controlled access, much thought should be put into the design of the reception area and any lobby or atrium that complements the reception area. The reception area can play a major role in the security of the facility because many reception areas are responsible for opening and closing functions. Most importantly, a reception area

Many recreation facilities have an attendant or receptionist check photo identification cards to control access into the facility.

Getty Images/andresr

is often designed to limit user access by the use of gates, barriers, or controlled doors.

Facilities may use a variety of access-control systems. Spectator sport facilities such as college and professional arenas or stadiums may require tickets, passes, or names on a pass list to gain entry. Community centers, YMCAs, and public and private fitness centers may also limit access by requiring some type of identification card or pass.

The facility access area can fulfill this obligation through several techniques. Typical access-control devices include gates, turnstiles, counter areas, card-reading equipment, and metal detection or X-ray devices. Typical personnel involved in the process of facility access include attendants, receptionists, customer service representatives, security personnel, ushers, and ticket takers.

Fee Collection

Some recreation facilities collect a fee before permitting access. Reception areas can fulfill this obligation with an attendant using a cash register, credit card machine, or computer to assist with fee collection. They can collect other types of fees, including membership fees, late fees, registration fees, rental fees, or fees from the sale of merchandise. Recreation facilities may collect fees each time a user accesses a facility (admission, participation fees) or in one lump sum (memberships, season passes) to allow access and use of the core product or core product extensions.

Information and Communication

Facility reception and access areas are commonly where facility information is shared with users. Facility hours, policies, procedures, rules, regulations, fees, registration deadlines, and any facility control policies are often communicated from this location. Information on the core product, the core product extensions, and all relevant details are also communicated when a user inquires. Information exchange can occur face-to-face, through verbal contact on the phone, through the facility's social media sites, or through a website. Additional communication techniques include signs posted in the reception area.

Schedules

Recreation facilities require use of coordination and scheduling practices that can be quite involved. These arrangements or reservations for use result in a schedule that can be maintained and communicated at the reception area. Types of schedules include employee schedules, area and space schedules, and access and use schedules. A reception area can also facilitate schedules for simple or major maintenance tasks that need to be done on a particular day at a certain time. Reception area staff could be responsible for producing the actual schedule, or they could simply post schedules for users and employees to view.

Other Functions

Typically the reception area is the first area to open and the last area to close, so it is common for a reception area to be responsible for the opening and closing of the whole facility. These responsibilities may include unlocking and locking the facility, turning on and off lights and other equipment, setting alarm systems, compiling and printing facility usage or other required reports, and depositing receipts from daily use. Many facilities have a variety of activities that may require registration or other forms to be completed. These forms are often maintained and filled out at the reception area.

Response to a facility emergency could also originate in this area. Reception staff could be responsible for emergency response actions such as first aid, cardiopulmonary resuscitation (CPR), crowd control, or contacting other facility or external staff about the situation.

Reception areas may present an opportunity to assist with facility control by using a public-address system to communicate announcements and use considerations. Reception areas may also be the location where lost and found items are turned in, stored, and claimed.

Contributing Areas

Reception areas vary in function, size, and location from facility to facility. Several areas contribute to the reception area. These areas may include the lobby, administration offices, and other contributing areas.

Lobby

The most common space in a reception area is the lobby. All recreation facilities have some type of entrance that introduces the product to its users. For example, a facility could have an atrium that includes a small or large lobby with furnishings that match the reception area. Lobbies can function as welcoming areas that may include special decorations, displays of awards and achievements, play areas for children, and reading materials for those who are waiting for other users or employees. A lobby should be designed to help the user feel comfortable and to create a positive impression of the facility.

Administration Offices

Another ancillary space usually located near the reception area is administration space. Some facilities have a combined reception and office area. These areas are combined to maximize available space or for more efficient facility operation. In addition, combining them allows administration personnel to assist customer service staff and respond quickly to customer questions. In many respects, a reception area is an extension of administration offices.

Other Contributing Areas

Facility directories, digital display boards, video monitors, and bulletin boards are often located in the reception area, and reception staff maintain them. The area may also include some type of showcase displaying facility information, such as its history, successes, promotions, or awards.

Reception Area Design

Recreation facility managers should be aware of the importance of a reception area and how its design enhances the functionality of the facility. Most important in the design of the reception area is its location, especially if the area is intended to perform numerous functions. It should be in the center of activity so that users can easily identify it.

The reception area should also be located in such a way that it guides users through the facility. A reception area by nature has the potential to cause lines to form. In certain recreation facilities, such as amusement parks, users may have to wait a significant length of time to access the product. The design of any recreation facility should incorporate adequate space to accommodate customer waiting. Recreation facilities that attract large numbers of users and have long lines with considerable waiting time should receive special consideration.

The ability of a recreation facility to effectively receive its users can have a tremendous impact on user satisfaction. Recreation facility managers and those involved in the design or renovation of a facility should pay attention to the number and types of doors, ADA requirements, and how users can make their way through the reception area without difficulty or unnecessary delays. The desk or counter needs to be designed in such a way that the space, size, height, and working area are conducive to users' reception and employees' ability to do their job. For example, ADA requirements necessitate a counter height of 30 inches (76 cm) to accommodate users with disabilities. Receiving all users properly and creating a sense of comfort in the receiving process is an important consideration in the design of the area.

Locker and Shower Areas

In some recreation facilities, such as health clubs, aquatic parks, or campus recreation centers, facility managers could be responsible for operating a locker and shower area. Whatever the setting, this area can present unusual management challenges. As an ancillary space, it could be a support service that is a key to the success of the core product. Locker and shower areas are usually a service provided to users and employees. They require specialized knowledge and attention to detail that should not be taken for granted.

Functions of Locker and Shower Areas

Certain locker and shower functions are compared with other areas of a recreation facility.

This space should be secure, private, and, where necessary, supervised to protect the users. Fundamental functions to the provision of locker and shower areas include hygiene, grooming, lockers, showers, restroom areas, therapy, and information and communication. Many of them vary between facilities.

Hygiene

A basic function of any locker and shower area is to provide an area for users to perform personal hygiene functions after using the facility. A locker and shower area becomes a necessary service where physical exertion creates a need to shower, clean up, or perform other personal hygiene functions. All areas and surfaces must be kept clean and sanitized at all times. If not attended properly, this function can create an unsafe environment and have a negative impact on the success of the core product.

Grooming

Grooming (performing tasks associated with maintaining personal appearance) requires space in a locker and shower area. This activity usually requires a sink, mirror, electrical outlets, shelving, hair dryer, and other personal items such as shaving cream, hair spray, hand cream, brushes, and combs. Most facilities require users to bring personal grooming items to the facility. However, some upscale country clubs or private fitness facilities may offer these products as a benefit for members.

Lockers

Lockers are important when the core product requires users or employees to store their belongings in a secure space. Typically, users are responsible for providing their own lock, or they can rent or check out a lock at the facility. Lockers vary in size; they are typically smaller at outdoor facilities where users may be storing only valuables, such as at a water park or amusement park. Lockers should be larger at facilities where users may be changing clothes and showering. A facility should include enough lockers to serve all users during peak hours of operation. This number should be planned before the locker room is designed because adding lockers at a later time can be expensive.

Ample space should be provided in and around lockers to allow for users' comfort as they dress before or after using a facility. The space around the lockers should be adequate and include seating such as benches or chairs. Enhancing user comfort also includes paying attention to the color of the locker area, lighting, music or television, and type of floor covering. The flooring chosen for a locker area should provide comfort for users and be a safe, nonslip surface. Users will often be coming from the shower area and may still have wet feet, which can lead to injuries related to slipping on a surface that does not absorb or displace water.

Showers

An adequate number of showers should be available for the number of potential users at any given time. Shower systems can be provided in several ways. To maximize space, sometimes showers are placed in a group in an open area. In circumstances where providing privacy is of greater importance, individual showers are separated with partitions. Appropriate hardware for dispensing the water should be available with adjustable showerheads. Water temperature and velocity should be adequately regulated so that users do not have to feel the discomfort of irregular water pressure or temperature. Soap dispensers or bars can be provided. The showering area should be separate from but close to the locker area.

Restroom Areas

All locker and shower areas should provide appropriate restroom facilities, including toilets, urinals, and sinks, as appropriate. In general, these facilities should include partitions to provide privacy. Other considerations include whether to use automated or manual mechanisms for toilets and sinks, type and number of paper towel dispensers to provide, and the provision of scent-enhancing devices to keep areas fresh. Restroom areas must be kept clean and sanitary at all times, with disposable covers for toilet seats where necessary or required. The

ADA requires that restroom areas comply with specific dimensions to accommodate users with disabilities. Recreation facility managers and administrators must consult ADA regulations before designing or renovating any restroom area. A link to this information is available in HK*Propel*.

Therapy

In more elaborate locker and shower facilities, therapeutic functions may be provided for users. Therapeutic services could include access to massages, a hot tub, a steam room, or a sauna. A training area may also be provided where users can receive prescriptions for health concerns, weight and blood pressure checks, and treatment for injuries. Some private health spas and centers design their services around these needs. Indoor recreation facilities that feature therapeutic services, including heart rehabilitation services and customized exercise and nutrition programs, are becoming more common. Provision of therapeutic functions greatly depends on the nature of the facility, and it should be managed appropriately.

Information and Communication

The final consideration for the locker and shower area is using the space to communicate information to facility users. A locker and shower area is an excellent place to convey a message because it is a location where people congregate. Signage or digital display boards can be placed in highly visible locations in a locker and shower area to disseminate information about upcoming activities, services, deadlines, and so on. Public-address announcements could also be incorporated along with other creative methods for conveying information.

Locker and Shower Area Design

Each subsection of a locker and shower area has unique needs in terms of its function. These factors should be addressed in the design phase of a facility project. Proper circulation of the areas and user safety should be a primary consideration in the overall design. Spacing of a locker and shower area should be considered in terms of user circulation or flow; users' ability to move from one area to another should be facilitated and easily monitored. Additionally, adequate space should exist in each functional space—lockers, showers, grooming areas, and restroom facilities—so that personal comfort zones can be respected. User movement should be safe and free of objects, barriers, and slippery surfaces. Entrance and exit traffic should be anticipated to control unwanted intrusion and congestion.

Locker and shower areas are generally contained units with minimal or no windows. The activities of a locker and shower area, by their nature, create odors, humidity, and other by-products, so ventilation is also critical. Ventilation systems must accommodate adequate air circulation, especially during times when many showers are in use. Without proper ventilation, humidity can build up and temperatures can increase, which can have a negative impact on the structure and fixtures in the area, not to mention the comfort of users. Appropriate ventilation should be maintained at all times, with regulated temperature and humidity checks to prevent odor and moisture containment.

The surfaces in a locker and shower area are also important for maintenance and safety. Showers can create wet surfaces that are hazardous for walking. Where wet conditions exist, slip-resistant surfaces should be incorporated. Management must be particularly sensitive to floor surfaces in this area because they can be a liability if not designed and maintained properly.

Environmental and sustainability considerations are also important elements in design of locker rooms and showers. For instance, the provision of green hand sanitizers can help improve hygiene without requiring customers to use water or paper towels, and green shower products can reduce the amount of harsh chemicals that are rinsed down the drain and into the water supply (Cipolla, 2013). Installation of low-water-use plumbing fixtures and light-emitting diode (LED) lighting can reduce energy consumption and lower operational costs. The use of recycled materials for lockers, benches, and flooring can reduce the amount of raw materials required for the development of the facility.

Finally, security needs should be a top priority in locker and shower areas because users will be storing personal belongings, showering, and changing. Valuable belongings are often stored in lockers, so security measures should be implemented to minimize theft. Locker areas should be designed to have open sight lines and provide easy angles for observation from facility staff to help minimize inappropriate activities. Surveillance cameras may be used to assist with security; however, they are limited to the entrance of locker areas, and they can be expensive to install and monitor. Theft in locker areas is more common when users leave personal items out in the open or do not use locks. Ultimately, users are responsible for ensuring that they keep their belongings in a secured locker.

Core Product Extensions

Core product extensions are the revenue-producing products and services that support the facility's core product. While the core product extensions can vary from one facility to the next, more common ones include commodity outlets, food service, child care, and equipment rental or checkout. Each of these core product extensions are discussed in the following sections.

Commodity Outlets

A core product extension that can enhance revenue generation for a recreation facility is a **commodity outlet**, which sells gifts, supplies, apparel, equipment, and specialty items. These outlets can provide purchasing opportunities to regular users as well as visitors. Common terms used to describe these operations include *retail*

Including a commodity outlet in a recreation facility provides the facility with another means of revenue generation.
MANDEL NGAN/AFP via Getty Images

outlet, store, pro shop, specialty shop, and *gift shop.* They can be found in a variety of recreation settings with a variety of systems and layouts.

Before opening a commodity outlet, creating a written business plan is a must. This plan should document a mission statement, goals, objectives, and a timetable or action plan. The business plan should include details such as items to be sold, item quantities to be purchased, prices of items, expected expenses by category, and anticipated revenue. Recreation facility managers should try to anticipate and analyze every aspect of the commodity outlet before opening for business. The plan should reflect situations such as when to offer discounted sales, staff hiring and training, item layout adjustments, merchandise return policy, purchase and delivery timing, type of inventory system, security measures, and advertising and promotions. Detailed planning can help avoid problems before they occur as well as provide the necessary background to make good decisions.

Commodity Outlet Operations

The delivery responsibilities for a commodity outlet are to prepare and enhance the sale of items to users. Recreation facility managers should be aware of the following principles: merchandising, vendors, pricing, staffing, sales, displays, and enhancing success.

Merchandising   The core product plays a key role in determining the commodities that can be merchandised to facility users. There should be a complete understanding of the items being sold and customers' needs and interests, as well as some expectation of how the product will be received. For example, selling ice skates, sticks, athletic tape, and other hockey supplies makes sense at an ice arena, whereas selling athletic shoes and apparel may not be well received in the same facility.

Merchandising requires a sincere commitment and enthusiasm from facility managers and employees in bringing the product to customers. Those responsible for purchasing merchandise for resale should remove emotion and personal preferences from their decisions to buy products. Some items do not sell, and an emotional buyer could make a bad decision.

Purchasers must also remember that they may not be able to accommodate all customer interests. Accepting that accommodating a small niche is better than trying to offer too many items will lead to fewer unsold items and greater profit for the agency.

Purchasers should take special interest in understanding product lines and how they might appeal to a particular customer base. They should also recognize that men and women have differing purchasing habits regarding styles, types, quality, and price points. As an example, a fitness center may be tempted to purchase and resell a wide variety of nutritional supplements to try to meet the needs of all members. However, this approach could lead to some products selling and others rarely selling. It's better to tell customers that the facility doesn't carry their preferred item than to have too much inventory of items that don't sell enough to make a profit.

Vendors   Vendors provide a wholesale service to commodity outlets. Maintaining a good working relationship with vendors is a key component to the success of commodity outlets. When considering which vendors to use, recreation facility managers should carefully assess vendor pricing, delivery, financing terms, consignment terms, product availability, and overall service. Ask questions such as the following: Do they provide a display for the product line? Do they advertise locally, regionally, or nationally? The size of a commodity outlet will determine how many vendors are necessary to supply the appropriate merchandise. It may be wise to keep the number of vendors to a minimum to simplify operations.

Pricing   Pricing is critical to the success of a commodity outlet. It simply comes down to whether the user will purchase what is being sold for the designated price and whether the outlet can afford to sell the items for that price and make a profit. Management can do some things to allow some flexibility in pricing merchandise. As appropriate, the manager of the commodity outlet may offer quantity purchases (large numbers) and special sales (buy one, get one free). These tactics are often used to move items that have not sold well or are outdated.

Commodity outlet operators can also look at the standard in the industry for the sale of comparable items and maintain similar pricing. Different regions, settings, and facilities are able to set prices based on their unique environments. For example, a golf course at a resort in Hawaii could charge more for the same piece of logo apparel than a municipal golf facility could charge. Operators should continually evaluate competitors' prices.

Assessing product popularity and customers' willingness to pay will have a significant impact on setting a price for a product. Prices should meet the cost of the operation, which includes the cost of goods to be sold, labor, and any overhead such as utilities, insurance, and equipment, as well as build in a margin of profit. A common pricing strategy is to use a keystone markup, which is to double the cost of the goods to be sold. Applying the keystone strategy for a golf shirt that costs US$20 from the vendor would result in a retail price of US$40.

Staffing   All staff should show sincere interest in customers by greeting them in a friendly fashion. They should also be capable of attending to customers in a competent manner and answering questions about the products. Sometimes when a commodity outlet has been operating for a while, staff enthusiasm wanes, personnel become complacent, and even management loses sight of this aspect of their responsibilities. Facility managers may consider scheduling regular training sessions that include techniques for motivating staff to maintain a positive and professional approach to their responsibilities. Staffing is critical to the success of any commodity outlet. Emphasizing training and supervising and evaluating employees is vital because staff members play such an important role in the purchase transaction, satisfaction of the customer, and ultimate success of the commodity outlet.

Sales   The goal of all commodity outlets is to sell or move a product. A variety of methods can be used to accomplish this goal. Even unpopular items (known as *dogs*) need to be moved. Managers can create sales as opportunities to move those items. Items could be sold at a discount, or they can offer a lower price for quantity purchases. For example, a sleeve of golf balls, with three balls per sleeve, may sell for US$10. However, a quantity discount scenario would offer four sleeves of golf balls for $35. This strategy encourages customers to purchase a larger quantity and helps reduce the inventory of a commodity outlet.

Another option for moving difficult products is to offer special payment plans. An example of this option is to offer a monthly payment plan of $50 per month toward the purchase of a set of golf clubs priced at $600. The $600 price may be too much for potential buyers to pay at once, but $50 each month may allow the buyers to purchase the desired product and create a vested interest in completing the purchase. All customers like to believe they're getting a good deal when they purchase an item. Being creative with sales and promotions can greatly enhance the success of a commodity outlet while at the same time creating customer satisfaction.

Displays   Most commodity outlets arrange, present, and display their products for two purposes:

1. Displays present opportunities to store items.
2. Displays attract potential customers.

Displays can be set up to create a flow of traffic that contributes to sales. They can also be set up with items that complement the main product of the outlet so that the buyer recognizes the extra item and may choose to make a purchase. Displaying impulse items at a cash register or entrance is another application of this technique. Examples of impulse items include athletic socks, sweatbands, and water bottles at a fitness center; golf balls, gloves, and tees at a golf facility; or key chains, magnets, and pens at a resort or gift shop. These displays should always be attractive and go with the decor of the facility. Displays should be modified, adjusted, and moved to various places in the outlet to keep the environment from becoming stagnant. Moving displays also generates interest in products that were previously out of the main flow of traffic.

Digital Signage

Digital signage in facilities has increased dramatically as the costs associated with these services and equipment have decreased. Digital signage includes video monitors, projections and display walls, and digital images. Popular ways that facilities have utilized digital signage include the following (DGI Communications, 2020):

- Promotions for products, services, events, and sales
- Listings of general service offerings
- Inspirational quotes, mission statements, and vision statements
- Interactive forms and games for facility users
- Social media streams and news
- Facility or agency memos for recognition
- Calendars and event schedules
- Interactive maps and directories
- Emergency messages

Enhancing Success   Not all items sell as readily as others. Additional options can help inform customers of what is available and encourage them to make a purchase. All staff associated with a commodity outlet should be knowledgeable about products and able to share information about their benefits. Related responsibilities may include providing demonstrations of the product or offering to help in any way possible. Some options to attract customer purchases include gift wrapping, free or discounted shipping, extended warranties, quantity discounts, open houses to feature certain items, liberal return policies, special deliveries, trial uses, and reminders (newsletters or emails) of sales or activities associated with the commodity outlet.

Managers should analyze what techniques have previously produced successful results; they should repeat what has been effective in the past, anticipate trends that could affect the product, and adjust techniques and products as necessary. For example, tight-fitting athletic shorts for men were replaced with loose-fitting, long shorts, and moisture-wicking fabrics became more popular than standard cotton blends. Knowing what trends are popular is critical to making appropriate purchase decisions and thus enhancing the success of a commodity outlet.

Commodity Outlet Design

A number of design elements are associated with a successful commodity outlet. An architect or consultant who may be part of the design process of a commodity outlet can provide this information. Often, commodity outlets are added to a facility during a renovation project. On these occasions, recreation facility managers may be responsible for making recommendations for the design of the commodity outlet. It is imperative that facility managers be cognizant of design elements in order to enhance the success of this core product extension.

Location   A commodity outlet needs to be located where users of the facility see it and can take advantage of it. This location should be in an area with significant user traffic flow. Successful locations are typically close to reception areas where fees, tickets, or other admission-based payments are collected, such as at entrances to facilities or near spectator areas in stadiums. Making a commodity outlet visible and easily accessible to customers improves the likelihood of success.

Appearance   The appearance of the commodity outlet parallels location in terms of importance. All elements of aesthetics dealing with decorations, wall and floor coverings, paint colors, windows, and lighting should receive attention to enhance customer comfort and contribute to product sales. The image of the product and the appearance of the commodity area should be designed carefully with the knowledge that appearance can affect customer moods.

Signage   Commodity outlets can use a variety of internal and external signs to influence sales. Internal signs can communicate a message or help feature a sale. External signs help potential customers become aware of the location of a commodity outlet as well as communicate sale opportunities. External signage should be considered during the design phase. Local codes can affect what sizes and types of signs are allowed. Both internal and external signage should be attractive, laid out well, and presented in a fashion that draws customers' attention, creating a positive impression.

Security   Unfortunately, most commodity outlets have to deal with theft. Theft can occur both internally (by staff) and externally (by customers). In the design stage of a facility, security should be planned for the commodity outlet in order to observe customers and staff and to help prevent theft while the facility is open or closed. Some security options include mirrors, security doors, motion lights or sensors, monitoring cameras, and alarm systems. Additional options include affixing special sensors to items that must be removed by a staff member or they will set off an alarm located at the exit. Simply limiting employee access to keys to certain parts of a facility can minimize internal theft. In addition, conducting strict and frequent inventory of products can limit employee theft. Although it is not easy to think about this responsibility, it is a reality that should be addressed during and after the design phase of a commodity outlet.

Changing Area   Most commodity outlets include the option of purchasing some type of apparel. An area that is set up for customers to try on apparel should have adequate space, hangers, benches, and mirrors, even if it is incorporated into a restroom. When offering changing areas, commodity outlets should also implement security measures. Changing areas present the opportunity for customers' personal items to be stolen and for customers to steal merchandise. Additional staff may be required to monitor changing areas, particularly in larger retail operations.

Other Design Considerations   Other considerations for commodity outlets include area lighting to enhance certain products. Enhancing customer comfort by controlling the temperature of the commodity outlet encourages customers to stay longer. Providing appropriate seating encourages longer visits by giving nonshopping family members the option to wait. Commodity outlets require a higher number and different types of electrical outlets to accommodate displays, special lighting, counters, and other equipment. A commodity outlet is a specialized facility that can become very expensive if not designed and managed properly. It can also be very profitable if the right items are sold at the right price in an environment that encourages customers to make the purchase.

Food Service

Food service is a common core product extension. Food service can be a demanding responsibility for recreation facility managers. At the same time, it can be a vital part of the overall product delivery and increase user satisfaction by meeting a need.

Food and beverage operations could range from simply selling candy, ice cream, and sodas to a complete restaurant with hosts, servers, cooks, a full menu, and a comfortable environment. No matter what type of food service is offered, the operation should be customer service oriented and be sensitive to health concerns and requirements related to this type of service. All food and beverage environments are regulated by local and state laws.

Types of Food Service

Food and beverage outlets can vary in size, length of season, menu, and even mobility, moving from place to place or facility to facility. The most common food and beverage outlets are snack bars, vending machines, cafeterias, full-menu restaurants, and catering.

Snack Bars A common type of food-service outlet is a snack bar, which usually features a limited menu, provides fast service, requires a small staff, and is relatively easy to operate. Often called *concession stands*, these operations exist at golf courses, stadiums, theaters, resorts, hotels, arenas, public pools, and community recreation centers. They may include a grill or a small cooking area for short-order items such as hamburgers, hot dogs, or sandwiches. Usually, items are served that require less food handling, such as candy, cold beverages, popcorn, and ice cream. In some applications, snack bars also sell alcohol, placing greater responsibility on management. Although alcohol sales

can produce significant profit margins, they require additional staffing and supervisory measures in addition to creating greater risk for the agency. Agency policies and goals should be carefully considered before offering alcohol at a food-service outlet, and a liquor license will be required.

Vending Machines Many facilities may not have enough customer demand, sales volume, or space for a snack bar that would require staff. In this case, vending machines may best serve the needs of the facility. Vending machines allow for certain food, beverage, and specialty items to be offered with no staffing or extended management responsibility. Vending machines can contain a variety of food and drinks. They require little maintenance, create

Snack bars or concession stands are common in many recreation facility settings.
© Human Kinetics

few health concerns, and require minimal security or management attention. Some vending machines can offer nontraditional items such as sandwiches, milk, fruit, and juices that may require additional attention. These types of machines are usually maintained and stocked by an external vendor who owns the machine. Vendors typically have a schedule for stocking machines based on purchasing habits at the facility. However, should there be an unforeseen increase in vending machine use, a recreation facility manager can notify the vendor to restock machines prior to the normal schedule. Usually, the gross earnings from the vending machine go to the vendor, and a negotiated percentage of the sales is paid back to the recreation agency. Managers can select products that will appeal to the user base. For example, a fitness center may choose to stock vending machines with nutrition or energy bars, sport drinks, and bottled water.

Cafeterias A cafeteria is slightly less involved than a restaurant. This food-service option allows customers to select food and beverages by serving themselves or being served by staff as they go through a line. Such operations generally require the same food preparation as a restaurant. Benefits of cafeterias include no wait staff, a less diverse menu, and patrons serve themselves and clean off their own tables. Cafeterias are often offered in golf facilities, on cruise ships, in fitness centers, and in community centers.

Full-Menu Restaurant Some facilities offer a full-menu restaurant as part of their conveniences. Restaurant operations are typically found at hotels, resorts, stadiums, arenas, and country clubs. They require a much greater level of responsibility compared with snack bars and vending machines. Restaurants also require a greater commitment from management in terms of food preparation, quality, and service. Restaurants can be thought of as a separate management unit, particularly at extensive facilities. Careful analysis of the customer base along with specialized knowledge and training should precede any attempt to provide a restaurant operation.

Catering Many agencies have to arrange for food to be delivered to the facility and served because of the product, lack of food preparation area, or users they attract. This situation may necessitate the use of a caterer. Arrangements of this nature require advance planning. Hiring a catering service delegates all food responsibility to an independent operation that is contracted to provide food service for the facility. For example, a caterer might be used for a golf tournament or outing at a golf facility. This type of event usually creates demand beyond the ability of a typical food-service outlet at a golf course given the high number of participants and the need to provide food service within a limited window of time. All details should be discussed in advance, leading to a written agreement or contract. The planning stages include making many decisions, such as the users' food and beverage interests, the time of the event, the location of the food-service area, and the number of people to be served. The menu and food quality for such occasions can be diverse. Catering costs can be extremely high; therefore, the written agreement should stipulate guarantees for food quality, quantity, timing, and service. Sometimes additional accessories and equipment may be necessary to ensure that all expectations of the catering service are met.

A fundamental consideration when offering food and beverage service at a facility is whether the service can or should be provided in-house or outsourced. Each option has benefits and drawbacks. Generally, the benefits of in-house operation include control of the food and beverage products offered and a higher income potential. Drawbacks include additional staffing and training requirements and more risk associated with preparing and serving food. The benefits of outsourcing include reduced risks, a more experienced and knowledgeable staff, and a guaranteed revenue stream. Drawbacks include lack of control of operational concerns, such as hours of operation, menu, price, and staff selection and training, and, in general, less income from the operation.

External Influences

Food-service outlets are regulated by predetermined codes, standards, and laws, or external influences. Any facility that offers food and beverage service accepts a responsibility that can affect people's health. This serious responsibility has far-reaching implications involving people's well-being. Negligence can result in lawsuits that can be extensive and damaging to a management system and its reputation. In the United States, these standards and codes are provided by the Occupational Safety and Health Administration (OSHA), public health agencies, state liquor agencies, and local ordinances.

Occupational Safety and Health Administration (OSHA)   In the United States, OSHA checks various elements in the food-service industry. It enforces laws that ensure safety of employees, conducting inspections to assure compliance with these laws. It regulates how workers function in preparation and service as well as the condition of the environment where food is prepared. It also observes functions such as storage, cooking procedures, food handling, and employee protection. OSHA can require the facility to make specific adjustments. If a facility is not in compliance, they can levy fines or even close the facility.

Public Health Agencies   A public health agency is an extension of the federal, state, or local government that stipulates requirements, provides assistance, and performs inspections for food-service operations. These agencies influence many aspects of food service, including food preparation, food supplies, storage, food temperature, personnel, equipment, sanitation, water, waste removal, restrooms, personal hygiene practices, and insect and pest control. Each U.S. state has a publication that outlines this information and any local requirements. Public health agencies also conduct inspections to check the quality of food as it relates to health problems that can result from food consumption.

State Liquor Agencies   In the United States, state liquor agencies are involved in the licensing required for serving alcohol at a facility. They place limits on the distribution of alcohol at a food-service outlet. State liquor agencies control the minimum age of customers, consumption levels, and server rules and regulations. Significant legal implications can result when a food-service outlet does not follow state liquor agency requirements. Management should carefully consider the pros and cons of offering alcohol products before including this option in a food and beverage operation.

Local Ordinances   Most communities have governing bodies that observe food-service outlets. In the event that food and beverage requirements are neglected and immediate action is required, local ordinances supersede all other laws and agencies. Situations and conditions can vary considerably between communities. Facility managers are encouraged to

---

CHECK IT OUT

Compliance With OSHA Regulations

OSHA inspectors can visit restaurants to determine compliance and identify any violations. Violations to OSHA standards can result in a fine and a deadline for correcting the violation. Failure to make this correction by the specified deadline can result in the closure of the restaurant. General strategies to maintaining OSHA compliance include (Quan, 2018) the following:

- Maintaining clean and dry flooring surfaces
- Engaging in proper food-handling practices
- Maintaining fire safety
- Providing optimal working conditions
- Observing age limitations

know about local ordinances before opening a food-service operation.

Child Care

Child care is a core product extension created to provide the service of caring for children while adults use or work at a recreation facility. As a planned extension of the facility, it provides a supplemental service and, when possible, additional revenue. It is crucial that parents feel confident that their children will receive proper care. Child care operations often do more than watch children; they also provide activities that are designed to enhance the children's development and experience.

The child care industry is extensive. For some, it is a professional career that can be managed within an existing facility, or it can be independently delivered as a separate operation.

Child Care Age Levels

Overseeing the child's safety and well-being is a primary responsibility that requires constant attention. Recreation facilities that have this option may be more attractive to parents with young children. Recreation facility managers must realize to what extent a facility may need to provide such a service. Child care options can be grouped into three age levels: infant, preschool, and school age.

Infant   The infant level includes children from birth to age 3. Many factors make this age group challenging for child care staff. First, they are

Child care at recreation facilities is a supplemental service for both users and employees that could provide additional revenue.
nilimage/iStockphoto/Getty Images

tasked with easing the anxiety of parents who are concerned about leaving infants in the care of others. In addition, the ratio of staff members to children may be regulated by local ordinances. Management must be meticulous in fulfilling the various child care requirements and responsibilities. Each infant's schedule and care should be designed on an individual basis, and care of this nature is usually provided for a large portion of the day. Caring for infants requires strict regulations and caution for the child's health and safety at all times; in short, it can be demanding work.

Preschool   A preschool operation provides care for children from 3 to 5 years old. Preschool care exists in both public and private organizations that need to extend services to employees and users of the facility. This type of care usually parallels the daily schedule and annual calendar of the local schools. Similar to infant care, the organization must comply with many rules and regulations, which are available from the individual U.S. state's regulatory agency, such as a Department (or Division) of Children and Family Services (DCFS). If the preschool operation is not run properly and according to guidelines, it will affect the facility's public image.

School Age   School-age care centers typically provide after-school care for children and early adolescents from 6 to 14 years old. Children in this age group have more flexibility and opportunity to participate in programs offered, so staff-to-child ratios decrease. Therefore, supervision becomes more challenging for staff. For this age level, managers should focus on providing recreational and educational activities that are designed to stimulate the children's physical, mental, social, and emotional growth. This focus should include providing quality supervision, nutrition, and programs in a safe environment. Managers should consider arrangements for parents' drop-off and pickup areas and children's activity areas. School-age child care should be directly related to local grade school schedules. State rules and regulations are in place for licensed school-age child care as well.

Child Care Functions

Although the types of child care operations may differ, some common operations apply to all situations. These operations may vary within the technique and methods depending on the ages of the children. When possible, parents should have the opportunity to be informed of operational practices through observation and conferences.

Health   The most important aspect of child care operations is ensuring the children's health and well-being. No matter what the age or activity level, a child's physical and emotional health is the top priority. Operational policy should direct staff to frequently wash their hands and the surfaces in their environment. This policy is even more critical if changing diapers is involved. Every effort should be made to prevent the risk of infection that could result from activities or environmental conditions. Staff should disinfect toilets or potty chairs after each use to avoid spreading germs. Where snacks or meals are provided, cleanliness of the preparation, storage, serving, and eating areas must be a priority. Depending on their age, some children should have naps. Quiet times, including listening to stories, can be included during rest breaks to provide a settling time for active children. Management must be fully aware of local and state health requirements, and they should be prepared for an inspection from health agencies.

Safety   No matter what kind of child care is being delivered, management should be concerned for children's safety, taking every precaution to avoid injuries. All space, equipment, access areas, and activity areas should be constantly monitored to ensure that hazardous situations do not develop. Staff should know the location of all children at all times. If an injury does occur, first aid supplies should be available along with emergency telephone numbers and parental contact information. All electrical sockets should be checked for appropriate covers so that children cannot insert fingers, pencils, pens, paper clips, and other objects. Safety cannot be overstated; it is the child care provider's greatest responsibility.

Education   Another key function of child care is providing educational programs to help children develop their intellectual capacities. Fundamental to learning is creating meaningful connection to information and a sense of comfort. Staff can facilitate this process by showing care, patience, and understanding for each child's individual differences. For example, depending on the ages of the children, staff members can read stories to help them learn to read in addition to influencing their appreciation of the importance of reading.

Playing games can help children learn to think spontaneously and creatively. Children can learn motor skills, discipline, and other skills through low-level sport or creative play. Child care centers can also provide a setting that allows children freedom to explore their surroundings and interact in informal social situations. Even watching educational tele-

vision programs (if properly monitored) can expand the minds of children by exposing them to unique places, concepts, and experiences. Parents place a high priority on their children's ability to learn new things. Child care operations that provide this opportunity can create and maintain parental support.

Recreation   Although recreation activities are offered for fun and entertainment, they also emphasize the learning component of child care. Children like to be active, and they should have the freedom to express themselves through recreational activities. These activities may include noncompetitive sports, cultural activities such as music and dance, or simply playing in an open area where they explore and interact with one another. Quiet play, such as reading books, exploring arts and crafts, and playing with toys, can also be

Recreation activities allow children to be active, express themselves, and learn how to get along with other children.
FatCamera/E+/Getty Images

important recreational activities. Recreation and education programs can help to keep children meaningfully engaged in physically and intellectually stimulating activities.

Coordination   All of the previously mentioned functions of child care should be coordinated in an efficient and effective fashion. Coordination influences the quality of experience of children and their parents' perceptions. Haphazard scheduling not only creates control problems but also can be counterproductive to the growth and development of children. Functions should be coordinated into a meaningful schedule to provide the best experience possible for children and to reflect positively on the facility.

Security   When parents leave their child in a child care environment, they expect every precaution to be taken for their child's security and well-being. In outdoor activity areas, appropriate fences should be in place so that children are not able to leave the premises. Although the technology is expensive, some child care centers may have surveillance cameras connected to a monitoring system so that parents or staff members are able to observe the children either from home or at the site. Depending on the location of the center, access control could be a concern. Unauthorized people should not be allowed access to the premises. Implementing a strict sign-in and sign-out policy helps to monitor who is allowed to enter a facility and who is allowed to take children out of the facility. Emergency lighting should be in place in the event of an electrical outage, along with appropriate fire prevention equipment, alarms, and properly functioning exits. Emergency exit and severe weather plans should be in place and practiced regularly.

Child Care Operations

Delivering a child care operation requires understanding and appreciating certain functions relating to general management. Parents want to know that the child care service is suitable and that their child is in attentive hands at all times. Recreation facility managers should be concerned with the child care delivery functions of staffing, training, and policies.

Staffing   The child care industry refers to people child care providers as *caregivers*. They are considered a substitute for and representative of parents. Management should make sure that staff are educated and have the skills and knowledge required. Depending on the children and the center, caregivers can vary in age. Management must be aware of caregivers' ages and experiences and assign responsibilities to staff accordingly. Training is a crucial component for all staff at a child care operation. Supervising staff should know basic concepts about child development and information about age-level needs. An appropriate number of caregivers, as dictated by state departments of children and family services, should be on duty to observe and control activities at all times. Staff should have an aptitude for working with children, knowing that children will not always be obedient and will often challenge their patience. Staff should be certified in CPR and first aid because a quick and appropriate response to emergencies is crucial. All staff should be personable and have the ability to communicate well with children and their parents.

Training   Recreation facility managers should pay attention to the training of both child care administrators and caregivers. The employee selection process should focus on applicants' experience, credentials, interest, and commitment to the concept of child care. In addition, before an employee is hired, reference and background checks should be conducted. Training should include developmentally appropriate activities for children, activity limitations, rest requirements, special arrangements related to mental or physical health, nutrition, facilities and equipment, hygiene, maintenance, and food service. All caregivers should have job descriptions that outline their specific responsibilities. Where necessary, training should be completed to verify that the staff is prepared to handle unique problems that might occur.

Policies   Statements that direct staff and the operations of a child care service are called *policies*. Policies help staff properly run the center and let parents know appropriate information.

Recreation facility administrators should establish policies that incorporate the following:

- *Fees.* How much will the center cost to operate? How much will be charged per participant? Do special fees apply for certain services? What can parents expect for their fee?
- *Food.* Will food be served? What kind of food? What procedures will be followed in food service?
- *Hours.* What hours will the center be open? Are those hours flexible? Is early and late pickup available? Is the facility open during holidays? Can parents make vacation and holiday arrangements?
- *Emergency.* Who should be contacted in case of an emergency? What are the emergency procedures?
- *Infant supplies.* Will the caregiver or the parents provide infant supplies and other necessities required for an infant? Do certain children require special supplies for their stay?
- *Nap.* Will the child have the opportunity to take a nap during the day? What conditions will be available for napping? Will parents need to provide a blanket and pillow for napping, or will these items be provided?
- *Discipline.* How will the child be disciplined? How will parents be notified in the case of a behavioral problem?
- *Spare clothing.* Will parents need to leave spare clothing in the event that additional clothing is necessary?
- *Medical concerns.* Does the child have medical conditions, such as allergies or illnesses, that staff should be aware of? What permission do staff members have regarding medical treatment? What doctor should be called in the event of a problem? What is the protocol for dispensing medication?

Regulations   Regulations for child care operations vary from state to state. These regulations can include the following:

- One staff person must be present for every five children.
- Only a certain number of children are allowed per room.
- No more than two children under 30 months of age are allowed per caregiver.

Group size in child care centers can be regulated because the smaller the group, the better the care and control. Some safety codes that affect child care operations include fire emergency procedures, food presentation and consumption, lighting levels, equipment, and use of chemicals. Some regulations also affect the size of certain areas, including restrooms, play areas, and fence heights and types. Management should understand and enforce these regulations, and they should include them in any training of administrative staff.

Insurance   Recreation facility managers should be aware of the liability associated with child care. Although facilities usually do not operate under the premise that they are going to be sued, unfortunately that potential exists, especially when taking care of children. Parents can sue child care providers if they think caregivers were negligent or failed to exercise reasonable care and an accident, injury, or even death resulted. An essential preparation for running a child care operation is finding an insurance company to help the facility maintain appropriate liability, accident, and property insurance.

Maintenance   Maintaining a child care operation requires greater emphasis than maintaining a facility where only adults are involved. While all facilities should be kept clean and functioning properly, child care facilities (especially those with services for infants) need even more attention to maintenance. All toys, equipment, and surfaces should be kept as hygienic as possible. Top priorities include establishing a regular cleaning schedule, using disinfectant, and taking care of all repairs that would pose safety concerns as soon as possible. Equipment, locks, sprinkler systems, exits, and security equipment should be inspected routinely. Debris, water, and snow should be removed as soon as possible to prevent children and parents from slipping, tripping, and falling.

Cost   The cost of providing a child care operation varies by facility. Some recreation facilities may subsidize the cost of the operation, which may entice users. Where possible, child care should be inexpensive, especially in communities where income may present challenges to affording child care at a recreation facility. Parents are more often likely to pay for a child care service that is monitored by state regulations; however, unregulated or private individual operations can cost less. The cost of a child care operation is often proportional to the cost of other facility programs. A more extensive recreation facility will likely have a more involved and expensive child care service.

Child care should receive special review in determining fees for the services provided. Parents' ability to pay should be a consideration; if available, a facility can offer scholarships or payment arrangements to accommodate special circumstances.

Child Care Design

Similar to other core product extensions, child care centers have unique design requirements. Attention should be directed toward design, appearance, functionality, and maintenance needs that are important to daily operations.

The location of a child care center should always provide access for parents with appropriate control of all entrances and exits. The location should be visible and provide easy

Indoor play areas should be designed to stimulate children's creativity, encourage creative play, and provide social opportunities.
FatCamera/E+/Getty Images

access for parents to pick up and drop off their children. It should have minimum pedestrian traffic so that children are safe from potential interactions with outsiders. Sensitivity to such problems should be heightened depending on the crime rate and other factors related to the location.

The dimensions of a child care facility must be planned for in a recreation facility. The general guideline is 35 square feet (3.25 m²) of activity space for each child. In some situations, size and space can determine whether a child care operation can attain licensing from a state regulatory agency such as DCFS. Therefore, it can affect the existence and success of a child care center. The design should accommodate the number of children in the facility at any one time. It should also include extra space for isolating children with behavior or health concerns. Large areas can be a nuisance, create noise problems, and be difficult to staff when trying to meet a proper ratio of children to staff. When space is too large, it can lead to reduced attention span on the part of children and increased supervisory personnel. Areas that are too small with a high density of children can be associated with aggression and a decrease in satisfactory solitary time for children. The size of the production space is a key component of a child care operation. Ideally, size parameters are considered in the design stage of a facility.

Because of the nature of a child care operation, administrative space sometimes is limited and can be integrated into the general production space of the facility. Wherever possible, an administrative area should be separated with easy access to the child care area and adequate space for work and conferences with parents. Ideally, this space should include space for an assistant, office equipment, and a lobby and reception area. Sometimes recreation facility administrators are directly involved in the delivery of programs or activities. Administrative space should have appropriate viewing capacity and access to child care operational space.

Indoor Play Area   Many auxiliary child care areas are primarily indoor play areas. It is often the case if they are associated with recreation centers, resorts, or private fitness facilities. Indoor play areas should be designed to help children remain occupied and to encourage creative play and social opportunities. Recreation facility managers should determine the number of children that may be in this area at any one time, leading to an appropriate amount of space. The area should be large enough that children can run and play without congestion, avoiding interfering with children doing other activities or trying to rest. The indoor play area should also receive design attention for children who need to be alone, especially if they are experiencing stress, discomfort, or behavior problems. This area should be configured in such a way that it can be supervised with as little intrusion as possible. All equipment and furniture in the indoor play area should be arranged so as to avoid injuries or accidents.

Outdoor Play Area   Most states require that children play outdoors for a certain number of hours per week. An outdoor play area should have a fence surrounding it so that outsiders' access is limited and children cannot leave the area on their own. The layout should allow staff to observe the entire play area from a central location.

Depending on the ages of the children, the outdoor area should be large enough that they can participate in different activities. The surface should be object free and act as a cushion for falls. The three most common playground surfaces are sand, bark mulch, and poured-in-place rubber. Because of weather elements and possible deterioration, equipment should be monitored for any developments that could cause injury. The outdoor play area should be located away from driveways, roads, and any other hazardous conditions. For more information on how to develop and design a playground area as well as the surfaces required for outdoor playground areas, see chapter 16.

Kitchen   The design of a kitchen area in a child care center will depend on the type of facility it is in as well as the length of stay for the children. The kitchen should be centralized for easy access and distribution of food. It could include the potential for on-site food preparation as well as food delivery. It should have adequate tables and chairs for dining. Ideally, kitchen areas include the following: a receiving area, food storage, a cooking area, a cleanup area, equipment storage, refrigeration, and a separate waste storage and removal area. The kitchen area must adhere to health codes, laws, and standards discussed in the previous section on food-service regulations.

Restrooms   Child care centers need two separate restrooms: one for adults and one for children. The children's restroom should have lower fixtures and include a changing area for infants. Lights should always be on during operational hours, and light switches should be out of the reach of children. Restroom areas should be frequently inspected for cleanliness, restocking of supplies, and the general safety of children.

Storage   Storage is needed for administrative purposes, play equipment, and other objects. Unfortunately, most child care centers are designed with inadequate storage space. Equipment that is improperly stored can create a hazard. Adequate storage allows for items to be put away out of the reach of children. Additional storage is needed for children's backpacks and personal belongings. Often, specially designed cubicles are installed to create storage space for these and other items.

Equipment Checkout or Rental

Many recreation facilities offer equipment rental or equipment checkout as a core product extension. Equipment checkout or rental systems must ensure that the equipment is distributed and returned properly. Equipment distribution operations can be costly if they are poorly managed with no systems in place to monitor distribution.

One option for equipment distribution is a simple checkout system for facility users with a requirement to return the equipment after use. The other is a more involved approach; equipment is rented with certain rules and regulations that state what is expected. Both systems require managers to apply fundamental policies and procedures.

Equipment checkout and rental areas should be located in a highly visible area of a facility where users have easy access to their equipment needs.

Photosampler/iStock/Getty Images

Equipment Checkout or Rental Operations

Whether a facility maintains a checkout or rental system for distributing equipment, a thorough system that controls the equipment exchange is essential. The nature of the facility and the equipment to be distributed usually dictates the system. Some facilities exist solely for the purpose of distributing equipment. For example, the primary purpose of a dive shop may be renting scuba gear to potential customers. Other facilities, such as golf courses, have rental clubs, range balls, and golf carts that are directly related to the core product. Some basic points that could be incorporated in an equipment checkout or rental operation include exchange, policies and procedures, waivers, insurance, and tracking.

Exchange   Any equipment checkout or rental area creates an exchange between the equipment owner (the facility) and the customer. This exchange requires an understanding of the expectations between the owner and the customer. Often, a form is completed that provides pertinent information such as name, address, telephone number, signature to verify understanding of return policy, deposit, and equipment condition. The form could include a statement of understanding that explains the consequences of equipment damage, breakage, use, or theft. Often the customer must provide proof of identification, such as a facility identification card, picture identification card, driver's license, or credit card.

Equipment rental and checkout procedures have typically been a direct sales experience between staff and the customer, but technology advancements in the form of online exchanges have revolutionized the process. Through the use of online rental forms, facilities are able to interact with customers 24 hours a day. Many of these online rental platforms allow customers to review available equipment and schedule a specific date and time to rent the equipment.

Policies and Procedures   Sometimes equipment operations need formal policies and procedures to help manage equipment distribution. Where rental fees are involved, the prices for using equipment need to be established, printed, and posted. It may be necessary to establish time stipulations regarding the following:

- Duration between when a request is received and responded to by the agency
- Duration equipment can be out
- Deadlines for returning the equipment
- User requirements or any experience required before use

Written policies often include a statement of consequences for equipment that is lost, stolen, or damaged. A policy statement should also stipulate any penalties for late returns of equipment. In addition, a policy statement may be required to establish a priority system when equipment is in high demand. A common priority system provides access to equipment on a first come, first served basis. Other priority systems may restrict equipment use to certain classifications such as adults only or facility members only.

Some equipment may require previous user experience. A policy could require proof of experience through certification, license, letters of reference, or similar documentation. This requirement is common in the car rental business. In the recreational setting, climbing equipment rental often includes the requirement of previous licensing or experience. Sometimes the distribution of equipment could require identification before the exchange, such as showing a membership card, verifying age, or providing other pertinent information. Fundamental to any distribution system is posting all policies and procedures for potential users to read before an exchange. Often these policies and procedures are outlined in a signed waiver.

Waivers   Some equipment inherently holds the potential for injury. In such a case, an identifiable means of communicating that risk may be necessary. Immature or inexperienced users should be advised of the hazards that could be associated with the use of the equipment. A written statement (liability waiver) expresses the dangers involved. Users must read and sign a waiver to indicate that they recognize the risk they are accepting. Although waivers do not relinquish the responsibility of the facility, they do reflect the intent to care for user safety while also informing users of potential risk. Risk levels can vary depending on the type of equipment that is being distributed. Generally, potential for injury is minimal, and any harm is usually a result of improper equipment usage.

Insurance   Some equipment exchanges could require users to provide proof of insurance that covers potential injury and damage to the equipment. This situation usually exists with expensive equipment that requires certain control and demonstrated ability. Sometimes insurance is included in the usage, rental, or deposit fee that is charged for the equipment. All equipment presents some risks of injury that could have negative implications for management. Insurance needs should be evaluated, and appropriate coverage should be obtained based on the specific risks posed by whatever equipment is exchanged.

Tracking   An inventory system should identify available equipment for distribution as well as the status of equipment that has been rented or checked out. An inventory system should identify what equipment is available, what has been checked out, when it was checked out, what condition it was in when it was checked out, and when it will be returned. User information, including name, address, and phone numbers, should also be recorded and maintained. Computer software can be helpful with both inventorying and monitoring equipment. It is important to have a system that accounts for all equipment in order to minimize lost, missing, or stolen equipment.

Equipment Checkout and Rental Design

A major consideration with an equipment area is its location in the overall recreation facility. Users should automatically be aware of and have easy access to the equipment area. An equipment area should be located where the flow or circulation of facility users through a facility creates traffic to the area.

In addition to location, the size of the equipment checkout and rental area is important. This area should always have ample space to fulfill its functions as well as provide for the comfort of employees assigned to the area. Far too often, equipment areas are too small to meet equipment distribution needs. However, a more common problem is providing adequate space for the storage of equipment.

A variety of methods can be used to assist with equipment storage, including cabinets, shelving, bins, racks, and hanging devices. Some equipment may require humidity and temperature control to protect it from deterioration. A well-planned and accessible storage area facilitates efficient distribution of equipment. Providing easy access to equipment can contribute greatly to getting the equipment to users in a timely fashion.

Some facilities may need to consider laundry of items such as towels or uniforms in relation to equipment checkout and rentals. Laundry can be a service and a convenience to users, eliminating the need to bring towels. Facilities may even provide cleaning services for personal clothing. This function requires advance planning, and it will be contingent on available

CHECK IT OUT

Tagging Your Equipment

A recognized method to promote a safe and reliable inventorying of the equipment within a facility's equipment rental or checkout is a labeling, or tagging, program. An effective tagging program should clearly identify each piece of equipment and be linked to the facility's equipment inventory system. Relevant information (e.g., its age, condition, and usage rates) can also be recorded for each piece of equipment. A recommended approach is to use noun names or alphanumeric codes on the labels that can provide a concise and meaningful description of the equipment being identified. The labels should also be placed in a consistent location of each piece of equipment for uniformity and ease of access. The use of bar or quick response (QR) codes on the labels can be a helpful way to quickly access and process the equipment.

Adequate equipment storage areas are critical for securing, protecting, and accessing equipment to be rented or checked out to the users.
© Human Kinetics

funds as well as the type of facility services expected by customers.

Summary

Ancillary services and core product extensions play a key role in supporting the core prod-uct. These functions are essential for efficient facility operations and providing users with services that are typically expected in a recre-ation facility. Each of these spaces has unique design requirements as well as functions and operations that must be considered in planning the design of a recreation facility.

REVIEW QUESTIONS

1. Describe the similarities and differences between ancillary services and core prod-uct extensions.
2. What are the three primary considerations associated with the maintenance of a parking area?
3. Why is the location of the reception area the most important factor to consider when designing this space?
4. Identify the primary functions of a locker room and shower area.
5. What is OSHA, and why is it important in a facility's food-service operations?
6. Why is an inventory system important for a facility's equipment rental or checkout procedures?

CASE STUDY

Updates Needed for 30 Year-Old Facility

You are a facility manager of the Bluestem Community Recreation Center (BCRC). The BCRC is an 84,000-square-foot (7,803 m²), 33 year-old facility. The facility includes four multipurpose courts; a four-lane, one-eighth-mile (0.2 km) track; a racquetball court; a climbing wall; a dance and aerobics studio; a fitness area; locker rooms; a child care area; and a snack shop. Overall, the BCRC is a popular facility within the community, as is evident by the stable membership and participation rates during the past three decades. Despite the facility's popularity, a few areas, such as the racquetball court and the snack shop, have experienced waning interest.

As the facility ages, it needs some renovations and updates. Needs assessment data from the community and feedback from BCRC members also suggest upgrades to the locker rooms and snack shop as well as the general signage in the facility are warranted. Your supervisor has asked you to investigate the development of additional revenue-producing services and products to support your facility's core operations. Possible options are renovating the services provided at the snack shop to include equipment rental options, or repurposing the racquetball court to a space for merchandise sales.

Case Study Questions

1. Given the BCRC is over 30 years old, what are some specific upgrades to the locker room area that would support eco-friendly and sustainable practices?

2. From an operational perspective, what are some things you would want to consider if you were to pursue the development of an equipment rental or checkout service within the BCRC?

3. You approve the purchasing of 10 digital monitors to improve the BCRC's signage. What types of facility information could you include on these monitors?

CHAPTER 6

Designing Recreation Facilities and Reading Blueprints

LEARNING OBJECTIVES

At the completion of this chapter, you should be able to do the following:

1. Identify the various roles of individuals on a design team.
2. Recognize the design considerations to be reviewed by the design team.
3. Identify the types of surfacing and appropriate applications of each.
4. Identify the types of lighting and appropriate applications of each.
5. Recognize the construction documents used in the design process.

The **design stage** of a facility development project brings together all relevant details of assessment and planning, integrating them into documents that describe what will be constructed. At this stage, the facility starts to take shape. All of the ideas generated during the earlier stages must fit together as a puzzle. The design team usually develops multiple variations of a design that are discussed and reworked to come up with a final design. The final design is a commitment that represents the formal start of a project. At this stage, design documents and blueprints are prepared.

Design Team

The **design team**, which usually evolves from the assessment and planning stages, consists of a team leader or an architect, an administrator, and the construction manager. This group works in a cooperative and professional fashion to bring the project to reality.

Team Leader or Architect

Usually the architect serves as the team leader. The selection process for an architect has to be thorough, ensuring that the architect has adequate experience in planning and designing facilities. These tasks are part of the selection process:

- Check the architect's references and previous work for quality of work.
- Determine if they have done similar jobs.
- Talk to contractors who have worked with the architect to get their feedback on the architect's work.
- Contact the Better Business Bureau (BBB) to see if they have had any reports filed against them.
- Check with the local building and code office to see if they have worked with the architect.

Architectural services can be expensive; fees usually range from 8 to 12 percent of the total construction budget. In other words, for a US$100,000 project, that could be US$8,000 to US$12,000. Nevertheless, because of their expertise, architects are an absolute necessity for design teams. The architect is typically responsible for all design documents and drawings associated with the project and for understanding legal and technical requirements. In addition, the architect is expected to be knowledgeable about trends in design and materials.

Design documents will ultimately reflect an architect's training, experience, and ability. When additional consultants cannot be afforded, an architect can provide predesign services such as project statement assistance, funding ideas, and site selection. Available funds or projected costs often dictate which architectural firm will be chosen. It is important to hire the best firm based on a balance of qualifications in combination with the fee proposed for services provided. Allowing politics and personalities to affect the selection process can result in unsatisfactory results.

Administrator

Along with the architect, the administrator is an important part of the design team. The administrator will make many—if not all—final decisions. Depending on the project, this role could be demanding not only during the design stage but also throughout the project. The agency administrator is typically the leader of the organization and in a private setting, may be the owner of the organization or facility. Often the facility manager has significant decision-making responsibilities too; at the very least they assist the administrator.

In developing a design, the design team is involved in many long meetings. It is often the administrator's role, along with the architect, to organize and plan these meetings. The meetings require special leadership skills in addition to an understanding of the content involved in developing a recreation facility design. The administrator also plays a key role in keeping the project on schedule. Although the design team as a whole works to put together the schedule for construction, the administrator is responsible for seeing that the project stays on schedule. Project timetables are determined by the following:

- Desired groundbreaking date
- Seasonality
- Desired opening date
- Changes to the design
- Inclement weather
- Construction material availability
- Subcontractor availability
- Financial concerns

Aside from the recreation facility manager, no one has more invested in the project than the administrator. This person is the only member of the design team involved in operation of the facility once it has been completed. The administrator is also the member of the design team most affected by the politics surrounding the project. It is critical that the administrator commit to the project timetable and keep others focused on the desired completion schedule. The administrator's role is to monitor everything from the perspective of the agency, avoiding undue expense and keeping everything on schedule and reflective of the final design. This role can be an enormous responsibility, especially with the many project stages and people involved in the process.

An administrator must be able to recognize, analyze, and discuss the details associated with delivery of the core product. Most likely the administrator is the only person who has specific knowledge about the core product and will be able to guide a successful design process. The administrator also needs to be able to interpret costs for all the product areas and equipment that will be in the new facility as well as to represent all facets of product and delivery operations. During design, some desired options may need to be eliminated because they are too expensive, do not work in the project plan, or are not as high a priority. It is the administrator's role to keep costs within the project budget by making these difficult decisions, all while ensuring quality control. The administrator functions as a watchdog to make sure that all plans and design information are followed according to design specifications. Sometimes architects have their own agenda, bias, or interest in a project. It is the administrator's job to make sure the architect adheres to the design goals and represents the interests of the agency.

Construction Manager

During the construction phase, it is desirable to hire a construction management firm to observe the stages of construction. A **construction manager** from the construction management firm ensures that contractors are performing the work as described in the blueprints and specifications for a project. If this option can be afforded, it usually costs 5 to 10 percent of the cost of construction. This service can be well worth it to ensure that contractors adhere to the design specifications and the agency gets what it paid for.

CHECK IT OUT

Safety Matters!

Location? Size? Budget? Timeline? Amenities? These factors are important for the design team and architect to consider, so much so that another factor can often be overlooked: safety. Make safety a top priority for the design team. Consider drafting a safety statement for the facility, its daily operations, and management. Establish safety as part of the culture in the design team recruitment and selection process. Outline safety goals for the project. Hold everyone accountable for these goals. Monitor progress toward these goals, and update them as needed (Boyd, 2019).

Design Considerations

Before an architect can complete actual design work, the design team needs to discuss certain topics. Some of these discussion topics include the site, structure, materials, lighting, mechanical systems, aesthetics, and schematics. Team members should provide insight into and direction on these design considerations because they will help guide the architect.

Site

Facility location is a major design decision. The product will revolve around where it is produced and delivered. A recreation facility can have significant impact on the surrounding area; many facilities are substantial in size and have requirements that can affect the surrounding community. Some sites will not have all the requirements needed to comply with product delivery. After conducting a comprehensive site analysis during the planning stages (discussed in chapter 4), the design team will have the information necessary to discuss site issues.

Structure

The structure needs to be conceptualized in the design discussions for what it is intended to provide or produce. Much of this information comes from the project statement (discussed in chapter 5). Considerations include the following:

- Structure size
- Structure shape
- Area impact
- Square footage

The design team must review these factors thoroughly. As mentioned, all of the structural details are derived from the information in the project statement. These discussions help to create a mental image of the facility that is important to the architectural work.

Materials

Structural material refers to the materials that are used to construct the facility, including wood, cement, steel, concrete block, fiber cement board, stucco, or a combination of them. A variety of factors determine what materials to use. The most important factor is related to the purpose or function of the facility. For example, a facility that will be hosting events such as concerts will want to select materials that will allow for heavy speakers and lighting to be suspended from the roof of the facility. Closely related to function are the design needs established by the architect. The design needs of the architect reflect facility function and aesthetic needs identified by the architect and design team. The environment is also an important factor to consider; some materials may be better to use in certain types of environmental conditions. In addition, local government may have requirements on the types of materials that are allowed. A more recent trend related to selecting structural materials is selecting materials that are sustainable. Sustainable (green) structural materials means that the material is a renewable resource and environmentally friendly. Numerous green structural materials are available, such as sustainably harvested wood, baked earth, calcium carbonate, sandstone, and clay. Regardless of the factors that influence structural material selection, materials are a significant part of the project because they influence all other areas of design in addition to representing a major cost in the total budget for a project.

An important consideration when discussing materials is the type of surfacing that will be incorporated in the facility. **Surfacing** in facilities refers to floors, walls, and ceilings. Walls and ceilings primarily serve as space dividers, but they can be important in program delivery because they have acoustical characteristics and moisture absorbency qualities. Typical materials used in interior walls and ceilings include wood, ceramic tile, plaster, and concrete blocks. Ceramic tiles and concrete blocks are the best materials to have in spaces with a lot of moisture, such as in a locker room or aquatic space. In office spaces and classrooms, plaster and wood are more common because of acoustical characteristics. Walls and ceilings are important to the structure of a facility, but floor surfacing has a greater effect on the types of

It is becoming increasingly common for construction teams to use sustainable materials in the building or renovation of a recreation facility.
iStockphoto/Justin Horrocks

activities that can take place in a facility. Types of flooring in a facility should be considered based on the purpose of specific areas in the facility. For example, a room that is used for a dance class will need a different surface than a locker room or lobby. Surfacing also varies for outdoor structures such as a playground. Surfaces beneath areas where children climb will be different from surfaces on other parts of a playground. For a more detailed discussion on outdoor surfaces, see chapter 16.

Floor Surfaces

The surface used in an indoor area should be selected based on the **area function** (the activities that will take place in the area) and the cost of the surface. Some activities may require a surface that has some **elasticity** (give) such as basketball or aerobics. Other activities, such as volleyball or dance, may require **slide characteristics** (how much the surface allows

people to slide when participating in activities). In addition, whether an area will be exposed to water (e.g., a pool area) may also affect the surface that is selected.

When considering costs, it is necessary to calculate initial cost, installation costs, maintenance costs, and life expectancy of the surface. This information can help determine the cost of the surface over its lifetime.

Six types of flooring are commonly used in indoor facilities:

Carpet. Carpet is typically used in lobby areas, office space, and spaces where no physical activities take place. Carpeting is the least expensive of the surfaces, but it only lasts 7 to 11 years before it needs to be replaced. It is relatively easy to maintain, but it offers no elasticity and limited slide characteristics. Carpet should not be used in areas that may get wet because it easily stains and hosts mold growth.

Options for eco-friendly carpets are becoming increasingly important for facilities. These products are made with low volatile organic compounds (VOCs), nontoxic dyes, and easily separated backing for more efficient recycling. The use of carpet tiles can also support sustainable practices because single tiles can be replaced when stained instead of removing and replacing the entire carpeted space.

Vinyl. Vinyl surfaces usually involve tiles used in locker rooms or spaces that have limited physical activity, such as office space or classrooms. They are easy to maintain, and they can last up to 15 years. The slide characteristics vary depending on the type of finish; vinyl surfaces typically have good slide characteristics. They are not commonly used in areas of physical activity because they have no elasticity.

BioBased Tile. BioBased Tile (BBT) is another surface option that holds many of the same advantages as vinyl but represents an eco-friendlier alternative. BBT is made from 40 percent recycled materials and VOCs. Most BBT products are also free of plasticizers, derived from rapidly renewable plant-based materials, and can last up to 15 years.

Cork. Another renewable flooring surface option is cork. Cork can be glued down or applied as a floating surface. Cork flooring costs US$10 to US$15 per square foot (.09 m^2) with a life expectancy of approximately 15 years. Cork surfaces are most commonly used in multipurpose rooms, fitness areas, and offices.

Synthetic. Synthetic surfaces, which are also called *poured* or *rolled surfaces,* can have considerable elasticity but typically have limited slide. These surfaces are common to multipurpose rooms and weight rooms, and they are occasionally found in gymnasiums. The life expectancy of a synthetic surface is approximately 20 years, and maintenance is inexpensive.

Hardwood. Hardwood surfaces are the most expensive type of surface, and they also have higher maintenance costs than the other surfaces. In certain spaces, the use of reclaimed hardwood may be feasible, which can help in cost reduction and serve as an environmentally friendly alternative. In general, a hardwood floor can last up to 50 years.

Hardwood surfaces also provide elasticity and slide characteristics. This type of surface is often used in aerobic areas, dance areas, and gymnasiums.

Outdoor Surfaces

Outdoor areas also require various surfaces, including natural stage (existing soil and dirt), turf (sod and grass), masonry, concrete, asphalt, and aggregates (gravel, graded stone, and cinders). Most outdoor spaces take advantage of the natural surface, such as grass or dirt. These types of spaces can include parks, trails, open spaces, or playing fields. The surfaces are typically in areas that are meant to be in a natural state and where **fall protection** (or a safe play experience) is not an issue. Specialized areas such as those designed for playgrounds require surfaces designed for a safe play experience. In other words, usually these spaces have no elevated areas where someone can fall. In addition, asphalt and concrete can also be considered outdoor surfaces. They are used in parking lots, basketball courts, and skate parks. Such surfaces are typically selected because of functionality, and they are used in spaces where vehicles may travel or where activities require a hard or smooth surface.

When discussing outdoor surfaces, the major concern is usually the type of surface used in areas where children play and where elevated equipment exists. Therefore, the most important consideration in these areas is fall protection, which is similar to elasticity in indoor surfaces. Some surfaces provide better fall protection than others. Four important considerations in fall protection include the following (see chapter 16 for more details):

- Accessibility to play areas is governed by the ADA. Playgrounds and play structures should be accessible to everyone. Detailed guidelines regarding elevated play structures and the number of play structures that should be accessible are available through the ADA (www.ada.gov).

- Adequate use zones are the areas beneath a structure that should have a surface that provides fall protection. Standard use zones include the space beneath a piece of equipment plus at least 6 feet (2 m) around. Slides and swing structures have larger use zones;

in the United States, they are governed by the Consumer Product Safety Commission (CPSC). Any new structure should include manufacturer guidelines for use zones.

• Structure height obviously affects falls; the greater the height of the structure, the greater the fall protection surfaces should provide. Depth of material is closely related to the height of the structure. However, some materials provide greater fall protection and do not need as much depth to maintain safe fall protection. Detailed information regarding how deep certain materials should be in relation to the height of equipment is available from the CPSC at www.cpsc.gov.

• Outdoor surfaces for playgrounds are considered either loose-fill surfaces or unitary surfaces, and the depths of these materials are major considerations in fall protection. **Loose-fill surfaces** are the most common; they include sand, pea gravel, wood chips, and mulch. These loose-fill surfaces are common, but they are not considered accessible. Accessible loose-fill surfaces include synthetic wood fiber and shredded rubber. These surfaces also provide better fall protection and do not need to be as deep as the other loose-fill surfaces. Loose-fill surfaces need to be added to on a regular basis in order to maintain adequate depth. This maintenance is not an issue with unitary surfaces, which have some of the same characteristics of indoor synthetic surfaces. However, unitary surfaces can be expensive and need to be professionally installed. **Unitary surfaces** are surfaces that can include a rubber mat or rubberlike materials bound together to give it a consistent depth and shock absorbency qualities.

Lighting

Similar to surfacing, a variety of spaces within a facility require lighting. The most important consideration for lighting is the number of foot-candles given off by a light. Larger areas

Loose-fill surfaces are very commonly used in playgrounds, but not all loose-fill surfaces are accessible. However, unitary surfaces can be very expensive and also need to be professionally installed.

© Human Kinetics

CHECK IT OUT

Foot-Candles and Lumens

Lumens measure the total amount of light emitted from a source, whereas foot-candles represent the amount of light falling on a specific point or object. Typical foot-candle levels vary by type of recreation facility area (see table 6.1). These terms are connected, but they describe lighting from different perspectives. The lumen focuses on the light source, and the foot-candle describes how intense light is in a space. Foot-candles are commonly used by architects in calculating appropriate lighting levels in spaces. When purchasing lighting, lumen level information should be provided in product descriptions and labeling.

or areas where physical activities take place typically require more **illumination** than other spaces. Four types of lighting are used in facilities: incandescent, fluorescent, LED, and high density.

Incandescent Lighting

Many people have incandescent lights in their homes. They are easy to install, and they turn on with no delay. Although they are inexpensive to purchase, they are the least cost efficient of the three types of lighting because they give off the lowest amount of illumination and require regular replacement. Incandescent lighting is usually found in office and administrative areas.

Fluorescent Lighting

Fluorescent lighting has a longer life expectancy than incandescent lighting. It is much more cost efficient because it is only slightly more expensive but provides up to four times the illumination. These lights turn on after a slight delay, and they make a dull sound. Fluorescent lighting is used in offices, small classrooms, storage spaces, and other administrative spaces.

LED Lighting

Light-emitting diode (LED) lighting has existed for more than 50 years, but it didn't become a viable lighting option for many facilities until the early 2000s. The higher brightness, increased energy efficiency, and longer life span of today's LEDs are largely responsible for that recent growth (Myrick, 2019). LED lighting provides brighter illumination and has almost twice the life of fluorescent lighting. While LED lighting is still more expensive than fluorescent lighting, the cost has decreased significantly. It is also much more energy efficient than the other lighting options. LED lighting is used in nearly every indoor and outdoor facility area, including parking lots, athletic fields, gymnasiums, offices, small classrooms, storage spaces, and other administrative spaces.

TABLE 6.1 TYPICAL FOOT-CANDLE LEVELS BY RECREATION FACILITY AREA

Recreation facility area	Typical foot-candle level
Trails, sidewalks, parking areas	2-10
Meeting rooms, banquet areas, auto maintenance areas	10-25
Operations/maintenance work areas, gymnasiums, indoor tracks, football fields, soccer fields	25-40
Fitness areas, studios, multipurpose areas, gymnastics areas, baseball or softball fields, tennis courts	40-55
Food prep areas/kitchen, offices, competitive-level athletic fields or courts	60+

Adapted from Peterson (2022).

High-Density Lighting

High-density lighting provides high levels of illumination and lasts much longer than incandescent and fluorescent lighting. Although some facilities still use high-density lighting, LED lighting is quickly replacing most of it, despite being more expensive in initial costs. Most high-density lights turn on after a slight delay, and they cannot be turned off and back on quickly. Three common types of high-density lights are as follows:

1. *Mercury vapor lighting* is the least expensive and least efficient of the three.
2. *Metal halide lighting* is the most common high-density lighting used in recreation facilities.
3. *High-pressure sodium* provides the greatest illumination and is the most cost effective of the three.

High-density lighting is used in gymnasiums, large activity spaces, aquatic areas, and outdoor fields.

Mechanical Systems

All facilities have mechanical systems that contribute to facility utilization. These systems are categorized as indoor or outdoor support systems. Indoor support systems include communication systems, HVAC systems, and plumbing installations. These systems require additional space in a facility, which is especially relevant to indoor facilities. Some outdoor support systems, such as irrigation and lighting systems, also require specific spaces. Usually, architects and engineers provide all necessary details for these areas; however, the design team needs knowledge of the mechanical support systems required for the project.

Aesthetics

The appearance (aesthetic) of the facility is also a discussion topic for the design team. The aesthetic of a structure depends on how the design team envisions the style and feel. For example, will the facility appear institutional and purely focus on function, or will it look more interesting in order to attract users? Team feedback provides information for the architect to accomplish the appropriate aesthetic. In addition to the nature of the product, project funding plays a big part in determining the overall aesthetic design and appeal.

Schematics

To communicate a design option, an architect can work with the program statement, site, and related information to create a preliminary mock-up (schematic) of the project. A *schematic* is a graphic or model form that represents the details planned for the project. During the design stage, an architect may produce either a schematic drawing or a three-dimensional model. Both can be helpful for the design team and anyone else interested in the project. They both allow interested parties to see a visual representation of the facility (see figure 6.1).

Drawing

Most projects of any significance have a schematic drawing that represents the general design of the facility. This representation shows the core product and core product extensions; it may include diagrams of walls, rooms, stairwells, corridors, outside topography, landscaping, and access roads. Drawings represent only a few details of the project; they are simply used to create a feel for the facility. They also provide a footprint, which shows how the facility is laid out as part of the overall site.

Model

Often with large projects, a schematic model is developed so that the team can visualize the actual exterior of the structure or facility. A *model* is a tabletop rendition of the facility that may include landscape, elevations and roads, and a fairly accurate depiction of how the facility will look. This model can prove to be valuable when trying to influence project funding. Models can also be created digitally using computer-generated graphics.

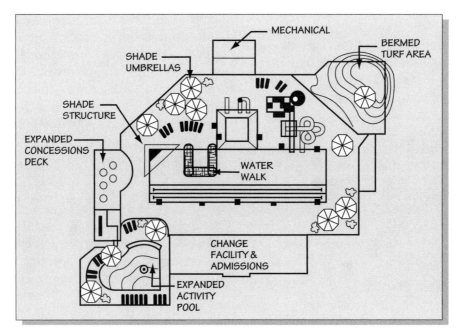

FIGURE 6.1   A schematic drawing depicting what a renovated or new facility will look like when completed.
Adapted by permission of Water Technology, Inc. (www.wtiworld.com).

Blueprints and Design Documents

As with all facility projects, the architect-created design documents represent a great deal of general and specific information that is communicated to the contractor. At various times during design, the administrator and the rest of the design team review these design documents to make sure everything is going as planned. These documents are called *blueprints*. They can be a drawing of a particular part of the project, or they can be integrated, overlapping with other sections of the blueprints. Blueprints become more individualized as the size of the project increases. Larger projects also require more pages and detailed sections that depict all the elements of the facility. Design documents cover all areas of a project, including the demolition or preparation, site, structural, mechanical, electrical, landscape, and other design documents.

Demolition or Preparation Blueprints

Most projects require some degree of land preparation for construction. The demolition

or preparation blueprint represents the design that will lead to removal of existing material and vegetation from the site. In addition, the preparation component may include changing the elevation of the site by removing or adding dirt to level some areas and raise others. This phase may also include moving utilities as well as the demolition of existing structures, roads, sidewalks, and trees. Some planned facilities may be in a flood zone or may require leveling, which could necessitate filling in the area with extra dirt or other material to support the structure. Some sites may have too much elevation that requires removal of dirt or other materials. The demolition or preparation documents show exactly what is expected in order to prepare the site for construction.

Site Blueprints

The site blueprints show how the facility is situated in relation to the entire area where it will be built. Site blueprints include information about utilities, environmental concerns, zoning ordinances, and land requirements. They also identify where all aspects of the facility will be placed on the site, including existing structures, access roads, sidewalks, landscaping, utility lines, and drainage.

Demolition is not just removal of an existing building; it may also include removal of existing vegetation, roads, sidewalks, trees, dirt, or other materials from a site.
RapidEye/E+/Getty Images

Structural Blueprints

The first blueprints to be prepared are the structural prints. They are usually extensive drawings that diagram all rooms, corridors, stairwells, entries, exits, floors, and ceilings, as well as other details. The structural section of blueprints may require many pages to capture the necessary information. It shows the areas that will house the core product and its extensions with appropriate details that indicate exactly what needs to be developed structurally. Structural blueprints not only reflect the overall facility layout but also the foundation plans. The foundation is what supports the structure. In an outdoor facility, structural blueprints represent the different areas and their layout; they include separate blueprints of any buildings that may be required.

Mechanical Blueprints

Mechanical blueprints have separate design information but are almost always integrated with the structural blueprints. Anything that is mechanical in the facility (e.g., plumbing, heating, air-conditioning, ventilation, lighting, drainage) is drawn in detail. Mechanical drawings require special knowledge that administrators and architects usually do not have, so engineers often help the architect with the detailed interpretation and application of the technical requirements.

Electrical Blueprints

Electrical blueprints are also integrated with the structural blueprints. No utility requires greater knowledge and adherence to technical standards to ensure safety than electricity. This section of blueprints is often too complicated for the design team, so the project engineer provides the technical expertise required. Everything that requires electricity in order to operate and support the administrative and delivery operations is represented in these blueprints. All detailed wiring is shown with diagrams identifying exactly where and how everything is located, sized, and connected. The project engineer must define the degree and level of all systems such as communication, lighting, and security, as well as HVAC systems. The actual locations for all electrical outlets are shown (including hookups) for cash registers, public-address systems, junction boxes, computers, alarms, security cameras, lights, and other electrical devices.

Landscape Blueprints

Landscape blueprints diagram the details of exterior aspects, such as trees, shrubs, mounding, fences, grass, flowers, and irrigation systems. Details include the type and number of plants, grasses, trees, and other vegetation in addition to how to plant and where to locate these materials. Other information includes maintenance of plant materials. The landscape blueprint is a significant element of outdoor facilities that include many types of vegetation, such as parks.

Other Design Documents

Some design documents may be vital to the design of the facility but are not in the form of a blueprint. These documents include information regarding the structural equipment; the finish plan; specifications; and laws, codes, ordinances, and standards.

Structural Equipment

Often the structure of a facility requires certain equipment to be attached to the facility. This equipment, such as a sound system or scoreboard, is necessary for the production of the product and is usually integrated into the structural blueprints showing designed locations, hookups, and installation requirements.

Structural equipment is considered part of the facility; in some cases, the facility could not be what it is designed to be without it. Other equipment and furnishings are purchased later with the input of the administrator and architect. Additional equipment needs do not require as much detail as other components in the blueprints.

Finish Plan

Although not an actual blueprint, the finish plan (or finish schedule) is a design document that cites information for the finishes for all facility areas, including paint colors, types of doors and hardware, floor coverings, ceiling types, light fixtures, sinks, toilets, partitions, and windows. During the design phase, the administrator provides input about finish details. It can be difficult for the design team to understand and interpret all of the options associated with a finish plan. An architect can provide assistance in interpreting the information. The layout and organizational scheme is a condensed way to present information to the contractor, subcontractors, and vendors.

Specifications

The **specification book** (also called the *spec book*) describes the blueprints in a narrative, descriptive format. Although not always used, these documents provide detailed directions on each item to be used in the project. Spec books contain a greater number of pages and details as the scope of a project increases. They provide information for contractors, subcontractors, and vendors, and they are written so that every page is coded in reference to the appropriate blueprint. This cross-referencing assists users in interpreting what they are to do so that no mistakes can be made in relation to the intended design.

Laws, Codes, Ordinances, and Standards

All architects must follow laws, codes, ordinances, and standards in the design stage of any project. This information must be incorporated in both blueprints and spec books.

Failure to adhere to laws, codes, and local ordinances can cause delays with the timeline; if discovered after construction is complete, it can even result in substantial monetary losses for the agency. In the United States, common requirements governing facility design and accessibility are included in the ADA guidelines (www.ada.gov) for all types of building construction. In designing a playground, architects need to consider requirements and guidelines established by the Consumer Product Safety Commission (CPSC) and state agencies for children and family services (e.g., DCFS). Other examples of requirements include municipal building codes, fire and life safety codes, National Register of Historic Places (NRHP) requirements, and environmental ordinances. The details regarding electrical, security, plumbing, access and exit areas, and building capacities all have to conform to local or state codes and laws.

This information should always be drawn in the blueprints and stated clearly in the spec book. Contractors or subcontractors may miss or ignore requirements if no one monitors their work. Architects and engineers are fully aware of these requirements and are obligated to meet them by law or be penalized by their professional associations. These requirements do not end with the design phase; they are also prevalent throughout the construction stage of a project and use of the facility. Primarily for that reason, an architect should remain on contract with a project through the implementation of the design and the conclusion of the construction. For a small construction or renovation project where the services of an architect may not be necessary, the builder or contractor may be responsible for adherence to requirements. Recreation agencies can hire construction managers or rely on local inspectors to monitor this kind of work.

Reading Blueprints

Whether they involve rehabilitating a building or designing a park, all design projects require blueprints. A critical role in designing a recreation facility is reading and interpreting blueprints. Recreation professionals need to be able to visualize what has been drawn, no matter how complex it may appear at first. Blueprints are a road map that offers formal information about all aspects of the project, diagramming how everything should be developed.

The architect is responsible for the majority of the blueprint content. The engineer is also involved in preparing the blueprints. An administrator or designated representative (often the facility manager) may be required to interpret the blueprints in order to assist with the project. This responsibility can require technical knowledge and an understanding of terminology used in design and construction documents. With study and practice, reading and interpreting blueprints will become second nature.

To gain a clearer perspective, recreation professionals must imagine themselves in the area that is detailed in the blueprint, orient themselves to the view and direction of the drawing, and visualize the finished project. Most importantly, evaluating the blueprints is the last chance to represent, correct, or change what will ultimately be developed for the core product and core product extensions. Mistakes in the design that are not caught and corrected will cost more to fix later in the process. If mistakes are not corrected before construction or renovation begins, facility managers will be forced to work with the facility as it is designed in the final, approved blueprints.

To better understand how to read blueprints, consider an outdoor skate park as an example (figure 6.2). The components of the skate-park blueprints included in this chapter are not difficult to read. The blueprints are integrated, and they include overlapping aspects of the construction project because it is a single-purpose project that is not large or complex. The skate-park blueprints consist of two sections of drawings. All blueprints include specific sections of important information to assist in understanding the document. These sections include the title block, direction indicator, drawing index, scale, drawing title, drawing area, notes, legend, schedules, symbols, keys, and cross section.

Title Block

The title block contains standardized information about the drawing. It is usually in the lower-right corner of each page of the blueprints. The title block contains significant information about the overall project as well as specific identification for the drawing being viewed (see figure 6.2). Some of the details include the administrative seal, project number, drawing title, architectural company, project sponsor, date of drawing, engineer's name, drawing identification number, and client's or company's name. This area also has space for the architect's authorization of approval, allowing for a signature and date for each page of the blueprints.

Direction Indicator

The direction indicator shows the facility in relation to north with an arrow pointing in that direction as it would if a compass were part of the blueprint (see figure 6.3). When reading blueprints, it is important to be aware of the direction being viewed. A direction indicator simply helps the reader realize north, south, east, and west, and it provides an orientation to identify the particular area being viewed.

Drawing Index

The drawing index is a coded list of the drawings. Similar to the table of contents of a book, it lists the various blueprints that are involved with the project (see figure 6.4). These corresponding letters and numbers are located in the title block on each page, telling readers what blueprint page or section they are reading or searching for.

Scale

The scale of a blueprint is a ratio of the drawing measurements (for this example, in inches) to the actual size of the facility (for this example, in feet). It represents the size of the structure, which makes the blueprint an accurate representation of the facility. In blueprints, the following symbols or abbreviations are used to indicate inches and feet: inches = ",

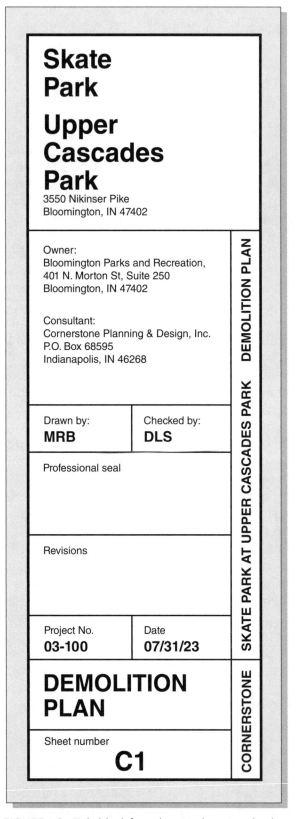

FIGURE 6.2 Title block for a skate-park project that lists the name of the project, architectural firm, and other pertinent project information.

Adapted by permission of Lawrence R. Moss and Associates (www.lrmassoc.com).

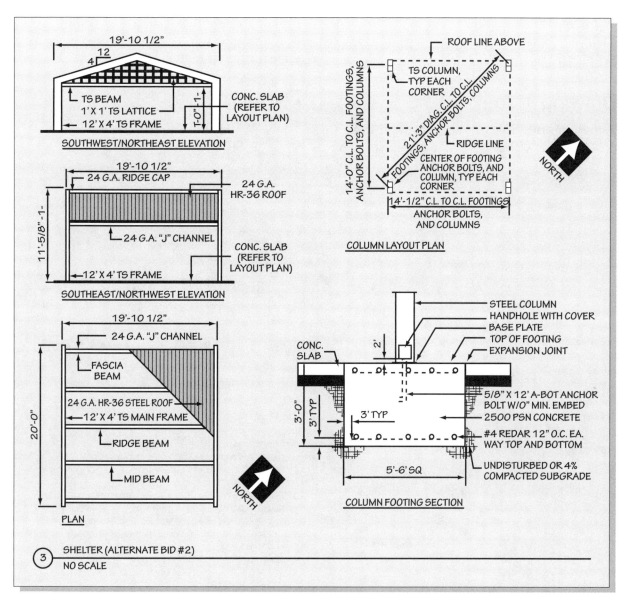

FIGURE 6.3 This drawing area for shelter buildings includes a direction indicator depicting where the shelter is in relation to north.

Adapted by permission of Lawrence R. Moss and Associates (www.lrmassoc.com).

FIGURE 6.4 Similar to a table of contents in a book, a drawing index is a coded list of drawings.

Adapted by permission of Lawrence R. Moss and Associates (www.lrmassoc.com).

INDEX TO DRAWINGS	
DRAWING NUMBER	DRAWING TITLE
C1	DEMOLITION PLAN
C2	LAYOUT PLAN
C3	GRADING AND DRAINAGE PLAN
C4	EROSION CONTROL PLAN
C5	UTILITY PLAN
C6.1	CONSTRUCTION DETAILS
C6.2	CONSTRUCTION DETAILS
L1.01	SKATE PARK GRADING PLAN
L2.01	SKATE PARK LAYOUT PLAN
L3.01	SKATE PARK CONSTRUCTION PLAN
L4.01	SKATE PARK CONSTRUCTION DETAILS
L4.02	SKATE PARK CONSTRUCTION DETAILS
L4.03	SKATE PARK CONSTRUCTION DETAILS
L4.04	SKATE PARK CONSTRUCTION DETAILS
L4.05	SKATE PARK CONSTRUCTION DETAILS

and feet = ′ (see figure 6.5). In the skate-park example, 1 inch (2.5 cm) equals 10 feet (3 m), or 1″ = 10′.

Drawing Title

Sometimes multiple drawings provide details of a section within the same blueprint. The drawing title indicates the area being viewed (see figure 6.6). In this case, it also includes a scale for the drawing.

Drawing Area

The drawing title includes detail that reflects more specific information about the drawing;

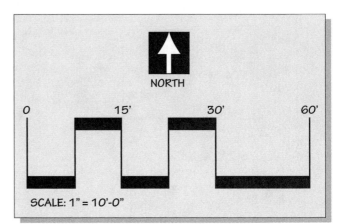

FIGURE 6.5 Scale for measuring various elements of a particular page of the blueprint, where 1″ = 10′.
Adapted by permission of Lawrence R. Moss and Associates (www.lrmassoc.com).

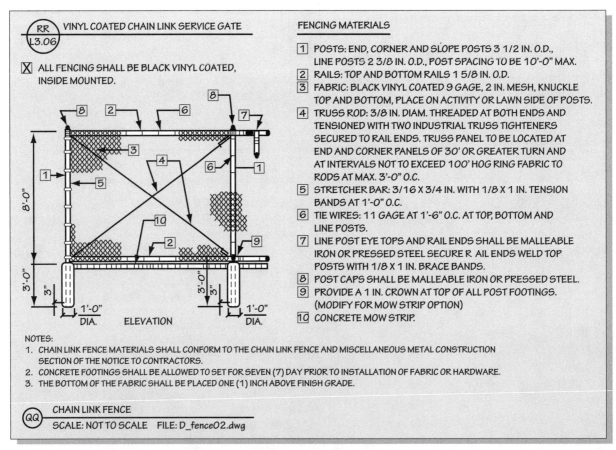

FIGURE 6.6 Drawing area for a chain-link fence section of the skate park.
Adapted by permission of Lawrence R. Moss and Associates (www.lrmassoc.com).

the subtitle reflects a particular drawing area. In this case, it is part of the total area or view, providing a specific descriptive title that names the area (see figure 6.6). In general, the drawing area gives the reader a closer look at a certain area, showing details from a top view. It can include electrical outlets, fixtures, cabinet work, walls, dimensions, telephone jacks, and doors. In the skate-park example in figure 6.6, the drawing area represents a wall section with the drawing title Vinyl Coated Chain-Link Service Gate and details on how to construct this particular area.

Notes

Some blueprints can include notes that provide special information for the contractors or subcontractors. This area is labeled *Notes*, as seen in figure 6.6.

Legend

The legend indicates how each surface is labeled on the drawing and what to do with the surface. By looking at the legend in figure 6.7 and looking for the similar pattern on the corresponding blueprints, readers can find out what areas are to be removed from the site and what surfaces will remain.

Schedule

Blueprints can include a number of construction schedules. They are usually charts that coincide with the blueprints and provide detailed information for the contractor. The schedule depicted for the skate-park project in figure 6.8 shows the electrical components that are part of the project, and it includes details on the parking-lot lighting, sump pump,

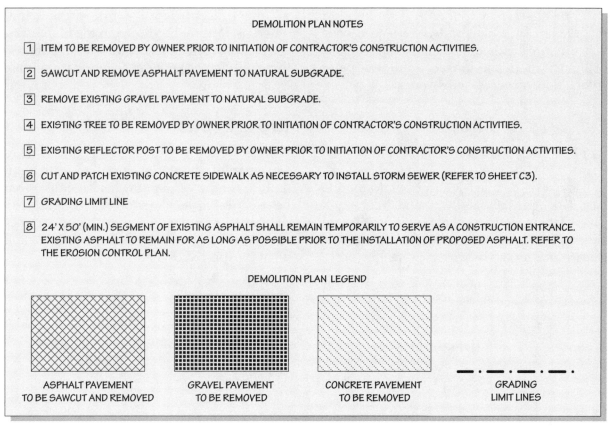

FIGURE 6.7 Notes provide the contractor with additional details about a particular element of a blueprint.
Adapted by permission of Lawrence R. Moss and Associates (www.lrmassoc.com).

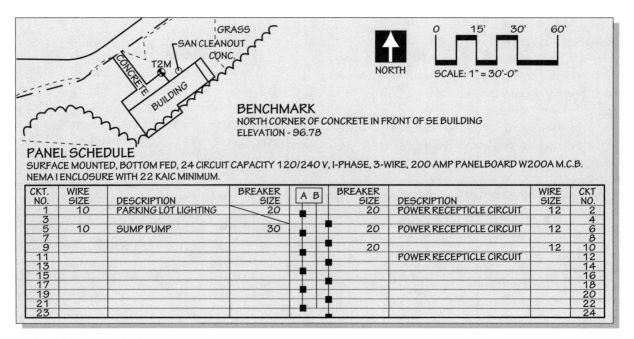

FIGURE 6.8 This schedule shows electrical components that are part of the skate-park project.
Adapted by permission of Lawrence R. Moss and Associates (www.lrmassoc.com).

and power receptacle circuits. Although not included in these blueprints, often included is a facility finish schedule that maps the details of lights, doors and hinges, windows, paint colors, floor surfaces, and so on.

Symbols and Keys

Symbols are pictures that represent certain items in the blueprints that need to show location as well as detailed descriptive information (see Fencing Materials section in figure 6.6). They diagram and describe specific design considerations such as name, size, type, and model number for lights, switches, and telephones.

Keys present detailed information that otherwise cannot be shown in the blueprints. A key describes elements in a certain area so that contractors know exactly what they are expected to do.

Cross Section

A cross section is a dissected or side view of some part of a blueprint (usually a wall, foundation, roof, tree planting, or signpost) that helps show the details involved (see figure 6.9). A cross section demonstrates the importance of details in helping contractors to understand what is expected of them.

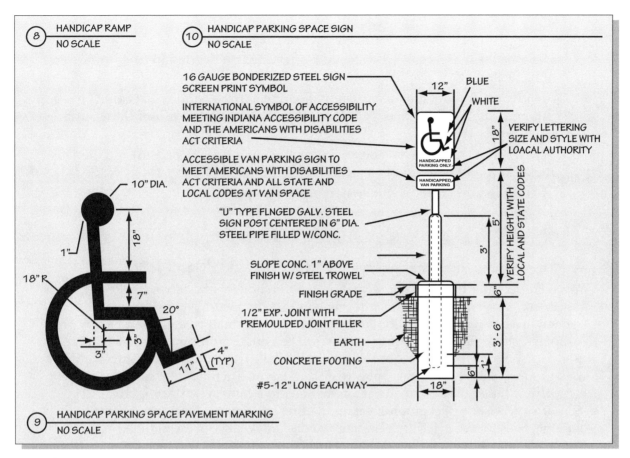

FIGURE 6.9   A cross-section view of the details for a handicap parking sign.
Adapted by permission of Lawrence R. Moss and Associates (www.lrmassoc.com).

Summary

The design team must consider many types of information in the development phase of a project. In addition, they are required to make many decisions about the structure, its function, and how it will look. All of these decisions must be made considering the guidelines and laws, codes, ordinances, and standards of various agencies. The design team must ultimately come up with a completed design that can be used to develop the final blueprints to be followed in construction. The architect provides the blueprints and other design documents, which include a great deal of information for the contractor. The design team should regularly review these documents to make sure the project is proceeding as planned.

REVIEW QUESTIONS

1. Describe the individuals who should be included on the design team for a recreation facility.
2. Identify two environmentally friendly flooring surface options that could be used in a recreation facility. Specify an area in a facility where each of these surfaces could be installed.
3. What type of lighting would best support an indoor basketball court and the activities that would occur in this space?
4. Identify and describe two different types of blueprints.

CASE STUDY

Surface, Lighting, and Sustainability Needs for the Resort's New Facility

You were recently hired as the recreation coordinator for the Bluestem Resort. Your supervisor, the general manager, informs you that the resort is considering the development of a small indoor facility that would include a small reception and lobby area, restrooms, storage area, two administrative offices, and a multipurpose area that can be used for tennis, basketball, volleyball, and pickleball. The multipurpose area would be used to support recreation-based play (e.g., leagues, instructional clinics, free play) with competitive-based play occurring at another facility on the resort's property.

Your supervisor's background is in marketing and finance, and they have a limited amount of experience in facility planning and design. Because of their limited experience, they ask you to join the facility design team. The design team will include an architect, a construction manager from a local firm, your supervisor, and you. Your supervisor is looking to you for input on the facility's design and its relationship to the intended uses and activities within the facility.

Case Study Questions

1. Your supervisor would like to carpet the reception and lobby area floor. They are concerned about its longevity, and they want to find the least-expensive option. Based on your expertise, how would you respond?
2. Your supervisor is also unsure of flooring options for the multipurpose area. Based on your knowledge of facility design and the intended uses for this space, what flooring options would you recommend?
3. The architect is discussing lighting needs with your supervisor. The architect refers to *foot-candles* and *lumens*. Your supervisor is confused by these terms. To help your supervisor, how would you explain the difference between *foot-candle* and *lumen* to your supervisor?
4. What type of lighting (incandescent, fluorescent, LED, high density) would you recommend for the reception and lobby area? What would you recommend for the multipurpose area?
5. Your supervisor is also interested in creating a green building (building that reduces the impact on human health and the natural environment). Identify two things or initiatives the resort could consider to support a sustainable building.

CHAPTER 7

Funding and the Bid Process

LEARNING OBJECTIVES

At the completion of this chapter, you should be able to do the following:

1. Examine the various hard and soft costs associated with a design project.
2. Identify the construction options for completing a facility project.
3. Explain the bidding processes used for public and private agencies.
4. Articulate the various funding options in facility design.

A facility development project will have a price tag attached to it. Whether it is a smaller project (e.g., retrofitting an aerobics room) or a large project (e.g., building a water park), it cannot be done without adequate funding. Funding is perhaps the most important part of starting a design project. Numerous funding methods are available for recreation facility projects; they are based on the type of project, the cost of the project, and the type of agency responsible for the project. Regardless of these variables, a design project is more likely to be funded if the design team researches the funding options available. This chapter addresses details associated with locating funding for a recreation facility project by examining project costs, construction options, the bid process, contract arrangements, and funding options.

Before examining costs and funding, it is important to establish the need for the project during the assessment stage. It is also necessary for the design team to have administrative support for the project. The ultimate success of a facility development project will depend on the support given and interest generated for funding the project.

Truist Park is a 41,000-seat stadium that is home to Major League Baseball's (MLB) Atlanta Braves team. Located 10 miles (16 km) northwest of downtown Atlanta in Cobb County, Georgia, Truist Park hosted its first baseball (exhibition) game on March 31, 2017, and its first regular-season game on April 14 of the same year. Construction for the stadium began in September of 2014. The total construction budget was approximately US$670 million, which included the ballpark, parking, and other related infrastructure (Cobb County Government, 2022).

Funding for the construction of Truist Park involved a public–private partnership between the Atlanta Braves organization, Cobb County, and the Cumberland Community Improvement District. More specifically, that Braves organization invested about US$372 million (55%), and local contributions were about US$300 million (45%). The public involvement in the shared funding of the stadium was predicated on the view that the new stadium would create a significant impact on the local community in the form of job growth, increased tourism and spending, and increased property values in the surrounding area. According to an annual report from Cobb County, property values in the area known as The Battery rose from US$5 million in 2014 to US$552 million in 2019. Hotel or motel and rental car tax revenues also reached all-time highs in 2019.

As part of the public–private agreement, a portion of the Cobb County tax revenue that is directly linked to activities associated with Truist Park is reinvested into the county government and state and county boards of education. Revenues drawn from business licenses, drink (liquor) tax, sales tax, and property taxes from Truist Park and its operations are given to these public agencies. For example, in 2019, these public entities received nearly US$23 million from the revenues previously mentioned.

Project Costs

Funding for a design project is closely associated with the cost of the project. Once recreation administrators understand how much a project will cost, they can examine funding options. Early in the development of a project, projections are made to help estimate cost in order to give planners an idea of what they are creating and at what cost. The eventual construction costs result from the design, bid process, negotiations, and signing of a final contract for construction. Throughout the design stage, costs are assessed by calculating the detailed budget aspects associated with the design and construction process for facilities, which are called hard and soft costs.

Hard Costs

Hard costs are the elements of a project that are fixed; in other words, they are a permanent part of the facility, and they include all that directly relates to the construction process. Hard costs stay with the project barring any unforeseen circumstances or change orders. They can change early in the planning or predesign dis-

cussions if a decision is made to use different construction materials. Hard costs that affect the construction of the facility include these categories:

- Construction
- Construction management
- Furniture
- Equipment
- Signage

Construction

Considering all of the steps required to complete a project, estimating the cost of a construction project can be challenging. Typical construction elements include the demolition, site-work, structural, electrical, mechanical, and landscaping stages. Here is a basic formula to establish the construction cost of a facility:

Quantity of material × cost of material + labor = construction cost

Construction costs are variable. The predominant factors that influence this variability include location, building type, materials, finishes, and labor.

Equipment, such as a lawn mower, is part of the owner-purchased equipment for a facility; it factors into the hard costs for a facility.

© Human Kinetics

- *Location* influences construction costs; some areas of the country are simply more expensive than others. Location-specific factors, such as access to materials, labor costs, desirability of the area, climate, and precedents set by other constructed buildings in the area, influence overall construction costs.
- *Building type* (number of levels) also influences the overall construction costs.

The structural needs and the property size required to support the facility will influence the costs associated with building it.

- *Materials* (e.g., the structure of the building, windows, doors, and customizable amenities) and availability of desired facility features vary, and they influence construction costs.
- *Finishing touches* to the facility, such as floor-to-ceiling windows, exterior siding choices, and flooring surface selections, will have a significant effect on costs.
- *Labor* costs can vary by area and need, which will influence overall costs.

Another way of looking at the cost is a monetary amount per square foot of the facility. A square foot is 1 foot by 1 foot (30 cm × 30 cm). Square-foot costs vary by the type of facility, region, and climate. The monetary amount per square foot generically applies to all areas of a facility. However, it also allows for variations in cost for the different areas planned for the facility. The design team and contractors assess what it will cost to develop the facility using gross square footage, assignable square footage, nonassignable square footage, and structural square footage.

Gross square footage (GSF) is the total number of square feet of space in a facility. GSF is established by measuring the perimeter of a facility and multiplying the result by the number of levels. Multiplying the length by the width by the number of levels will provide the total number of square feet, establishing the total area of a structure (table 7.1). GSF is made up of assignable square footage (ASF),

CHECK IT OUT

Location, Location, Location!

While location is a key factor in selling real estate, it also matters in construction costs. According to Cumming's U.S. Construction Per Square Foot Data (Scalisi, 2022), the average costs (in US$/ft²) to construct a community center or school in four U.S. regions are as follows:

- Eastern United States: $317 to $381 per square foot
- Western United States: $341 to $417 per square foot
- Midwest United States: $242 to $290 per square foot
- Southern United States: $217 to $260 per square foot

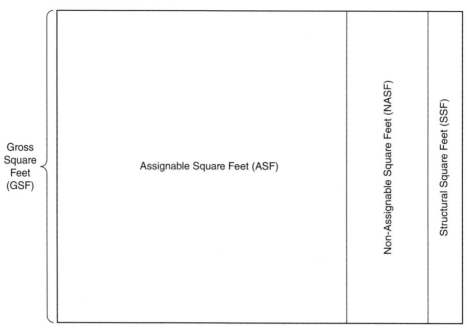

FIGURE 7.1   Types of square footage.

TABLE 7.1   SQUARE FOOTAGE TERMS AND CALCULATIONS

Square footage type	Description	Formula	Example
Square footage (SF)	General measure of space in a facility; 1 SF = 1' × 1'	length × width	30' × 45' = 1,350 SF
Gross square footage (GSF)	Full building area, including all space	Sum of total SF of a facility; ASF + NASF + SSF	A facility with 2 levels; each level is 22,000 SF. 22,000 + 22,000 = 44,000 GSF
Assignable square footage (ASF)	Usable SF where activities will take place and core product extensions and services are provided; may include some ancillary spaces (meeting rooms, offices, lobby, locker rooms, child care, concessions)	Sum of total SF where activities will take place and core product extensions and services are provided	A facility with the following areas: • Multipurpose area (10,000 SF) • Concessions area (1,000 SF) • Offices (200 SF) • Hallways (400 SF) • Storage closet (300 SF) • 10,000 + 1,000 + 200 = 11,200 ASF
Nonassignable square footage (NASF)	Spaces where activities do not take place, consisting primarily of nonactive ancillary spaces and circulation areas (hallways, stairways, mechanical, storage)	Sum of total SF where activities do not take place	A facility with the following areas: • Multipurpose area (10,000 SF) • Concessions area (1,000 SF) • Offices (200 SF) • Hallways (900 SF) • Storage closet (500 SF) • 900 + 500 = 1,400 NASF
Structural square footage (SSF)	Construction materials that make up the walls and permanent facility structures	Sum of total SF of the construction materials that make up the walls and permanent facility structures; width of walls × total length of all walls	A facility has 1,500 linear feet of walls. Construction materials (metal framing material or studs, gypsum board, exterior siding, etc.) in the walls are 1' thick. 1,500 × 1' = 1,500 SSF

nonassignable square footage (NASF), and structural square footage (SSF), as illustrated in figure 7.1.

All facility designs consider the number of square feet needed to deliver the core product and its extensions. **Assignable square footage (ASF)** is the total number of square feet that can be assigned for actual use or that are required for product delivery. When considering the ASF, it is important to include appropriate use zones for the specific activity designated for that particular space. Some spaces in which a sport or activity can take place outside the dimensions of the space require use zones. **Use zones** are the safety buffers around spaces such as basketball courts, volleyball courts, and tennis courts that support the safe engagement of the activity. Activity spaces have different use zone recommendations based on the types of activities taking place in those areas (table 7.2). Often facilities have activity spaces with multiple courts arranged side by side. In these instances, the courts can share a use zone. For example, basketball courts should have a 10-foot use zone around all four sides of each court. Two basketball courts that are side by side could share a use zone, so they would need only 10 feet between them. Figure 7.2 depicts four basketball courts with a track around the perimeter. To calculate ASF for this space, follow these guidelines:

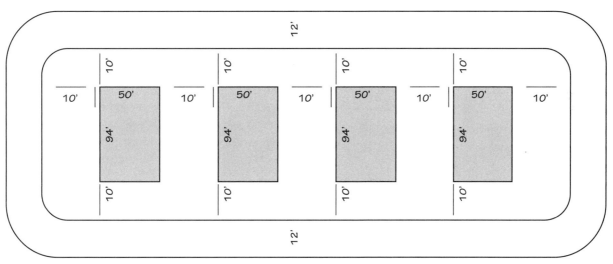

FIGURE 7.2   Activity spaces and use zones in a space with four basketball courts and a three-lane track.

TABLE 7.2   RECOMMENDED USE ZONES FOR INDOOR ACTIVITY SPACES

Activity space	Activity space dimensions	Use zones
Basketball court	94' × 50' (Courts for high school and under can be 84' × 50')	10' (all sides)
Hockey rink	200' × 85'	None
Track	Varied, with lanes typically at 1.33 yd (1.22 m) each	None
Racquetball	20' (width) × 40' (length) × 20' (height)	None
Swimming pool (Olympic size)	25 m × 50 m (~82' × 164')	Vary Minimum = 4' (all sides) Recommended = 15' (all sides)
Tennis court	36' × 78'	Back = 22' Wall side = 15' Court side = 12'
Volleyball (Indoor)	59' × 29.5'	10' (all sides)

Calculating ASF for Figure 7.2

- Calculate the width of the basketball courts. Each court is 50 feet wide with 10-foot use zones.

$$50' + 50' + 50' + 50' + 10' + 10' + 10' + 10' + 10' = 250'$$

- Calculate the length of the basketball courts. Each court is 94 feet long with 10-foot use zones on each end.

$$94' + 10' + 10' = 114'$$

- Overall dimensions of four basketball courts (with use zones): 250' × 114'

- Determine the inside track dimensions: Based on the dimensions of the four basketball courts (with use zones), the inside dimensions of the track would be 250' × 114'.

  - A three lane track (each lane is 1.22 m or 1.33 yd):

$$1.22 \text{ m} \times 3 = 3.66 \text{ m (4 yd, which is also 12')}$$

  - Total width of (outside) track:

$$250' + 12' + 12' = 274'$$

  - Total length of (outside) track:

$$114' + 12' + 12' = 138'$$

  - Total area (rectangle) outermost edge of track:

$$274' \times 138'$$

  - Total area (rectangle), which includes the track and four basketball courts with use zones:

$$274' \times 138' = 37,812 \text{ ASF}$$

In contrast, **nonassignable square footage (NASF)** is the total number of square feet for those places where activities do not take place; it consists primarily of nonactive ancillary spaces and circulation areas. Typical NASF spaces include hallways, mechanical areas, and storage closets.

Structural square footage (SSF) represents the square footage made up by the construction materials used for walls and permanent facility structures.

Another important consideration when reviewing construction costs is **building efficiency**, a measure of the percentage of the facility that is used to deliver the core product and core product extensions. It is determined by calculating the percentage of the building that is ASF in relation to the GSF of the building. The general formula for calculating a building's efficiency is

$$\text{ASF/GSF = Building efficiency}$$

For example, consider a facility that is 50,000 GSF and has 40,000 ASF. The building efficiency would be calculated as follows:

$$40,000/50,000 = .80$$

In this example, the facility has a building efficiency of .80, or 80 percent. On average, the building efficiency for recreation facilities ranges between .70 and .80.

Construction Management

When administrators cannot or do not want to oversee the construction phase of a project, they can hire a construction management firm. These firms are usually hired for large projects or when the facility owner or administrator does not have the experience to oversee the project. A construction management company has the expertise to make sure the contracted work is done safely, properly, and according to the plans for the project. The specification books and blueprints guide construction managers through completion of a project. Construction management firms charge a fee for their service that is generally a percentage of the total construction cost. This fee is in addition to the contractor's construction costs, and it is included in the hard costs for a facility.

Furniture

All facility projects require furniture. Typically, the administrator has a cost allowance to select furnishings up to the amount allocated in the budget. Furniture includes all the items to be placed in the facility, such as desks, chairs, sofas, lamps, conference tables, filing cabinets, and bookcases. Often, the amount allocated for furniture is less than sufficient to furnish a facility. Any furniture not funded by the budget may require that the owner provide additional funds to meet this expense.

Recreation facility managers could take a sustainable approach to furniture by recycling old furniture from a former facility (if possible) rather than buying all new furniture. This approach keeps costs down and reduces waste.

Equipment

The **equipment** for a facility generally includes structural equipment and owner-purchased equipment. Both are included in the hard costs of a facility. **Structural equipment** is permanent, and it is critical to the core product and extensions. Common examples of structural equipment include HVAC systems and scoreboards. Owner-purchased equipment includes anything that is not permanent but is critical to product delivery. Examples of owner-purchased equipment may include lawn mowers, golf carts, and ice groomers. Often the owner includes an allowance for equipment as part of the hard costs. Equipment can be expensive; as with furniture, the budget may not allow enough funds to fully equip a facility.

Signage

Signage encompasses all the attached signs throughout a facility. All facilities have a directional system that helps users get to where they want to go. Typical facility signs include directories, wall signs, posted areas, regulatory signs, and informational signs. Signage also includes signs required by the ADA. Depending on the size and complexity of a facility, a significant number of signs may be necessary. The recreation facility manager is responsible for identifying what kind and how many signs should be located at a facility. They should view the need for signage from the perspective of a user who has never visited the facility.

Soft Costs

Soft costs are expenses that are necessary to get a project started and to meet extended or unexpected costs. These costs include architectural fees, engineering fees, consultant fees, permit fees, reimbursable costs, and contingencies. Soft costs can be one-time expenses as well as ongoing expenses throughout the project.

They do not relate directly to the construction process.

Architectural Fees

In most facility projects, an architect is hired to design and oversee the development process. Architects have great influence on the entire project. Their fee is generally a percentage of the total estimated construction cost of a project; it ranges from 8 to 12 percent of the project budget. Sometimes a flat fee is negotiated with an architectural firm. However architectural costs are determined, they are included in the soft costs of a facility project.

Engineering Fees

Most facilities require help with the design of certain areas and equipment. Engineers with technical backgrounds and expert capacities in specialized areas such as heating and cooling, aquatics, and structural design are hired to review the design detail to make sure no problems exist. Their services are an invaluable complement to the architectural effort. Often an engineering firm partners with an architectural firm on a facility project. It is common for the engineer's fees to be included in the 8 to 12 percent associated with the architect's fees.

Consultant Fees

Consultants have extensive experience in a field, and they can bring unique knowledge to the project. They are usually part of the planning and design team, providing advice on everything from product design and feasibility studies to mechanical and equipment needs. Their role is most common in the early phases of a facility project, and they often assist recreation agencies in establishing a need and support for the project.

Permit Fees

All construction projects are required by law to obtain certain permits. Each locality has regulations regarding permits. Typically, grading, building, and environmental permits are required. Often, it is the administrator's role to determine what permits are needed, apply for them, and obtain permission to proceed. Others associated with the project, including architects, engineers, contractors, and construction management firms, can also perform this responsibility. Permits should be obtained once a design has been agreed upon but before construction begins. A fine may result for working without a permit. A building permit could stipulate requirements that must be met before a construction project is approved, such as the development of roads, sidewalks, access, and parking. These requirements are designed and presented as part of the project; they are depicted in the blueprints and specification books.

Reimbursable Costs

Reimbursable costs repay the architects, consultants, and engineers for any costs outside the direct project cost. This line allows for expenses beyond contract costs, such as travel, lodging, meals, supplies, or phone services, that are not accounted for in the design or construction management fees.

Contingencies

A **contingency** is money set aside in the overall project cost to take care of unexpected developments that arise during construction. Contingency funds allow for correction of design flaws or mistakes, or substitution of different construction materials or equipment. The amount usually allowed for a contingency fund is 10 to 20 percent of the construction cost. Omission of a contingency fund in the project budget can prove to be unfortunate. Inevitably, unanticipated situations occur that can negatively affect the funding plan if a contingency fund is not in place.

Other Costs

It is important to be aware of the construction cost, but in some respects it is even more important to be aware of the potential cost of operating the completed facility. An awareness of **operational costs** can affect the design and construction process. Architects and engineers can incorporate certain elements in the design that can reduce operational costs. For example, a sustainable approach to operating a facility may result in building materials that are more energy efficient, which in turn will reduce utility costs. Consideration of operational expenses in the design phase is wise in order to avoid building or renovating a facility that cannot be properly maintained or kept operational because of unexpected, avoidable expenses.

Construction Options

Part of the funding analysis is determining which of the available construction options is most appropriate for the project. These options are greatly influenced by the cost of the project, the setting (public or private), and what the owner is willing to pay. In selecting a construction option, it is important to consider available funding and the time frame for completion of a project. The construction options include conventional, design-build, fast track, and turnkey. They provide recreation professionals with options to save money, time, or both during the construction process. Each option will vary based on the setting and expertise of the company bidding the project. When companies bid a project, they are essentially informing the recreation agency what it will cost to complete the project.

Conventional Option

The most common construction method is the conventional method. This process takes the completed design for the project and formally bids out the project to interested contractors. Bids are generally submitted in a lump sum or fixed amount for the entire project. The recreation agency reviews them, and the lowest and most responsive bidder is usually awarded the contract. The contractor then develops the facility according to the blueprints and specifications completed by the architect and engineers during the design process. The conventional method is most often used for recreation projects in the public sector.

Public-sector recreation facilities are often funded using the conventional method.

Jeffrey Greenberg/Universal Images Group via Getty Images

Design-Build Option

Under the design-build option, one company is responsible for both the design and the construction of the facility. This option results in design cost savings because a price for both the design and construction of the project is established early in the design process. This construction option may also accelerate completion of the project. As the plans for each segment are completed, that stage can begin construction rather than wait for the total project design and bid process to be completed. Additional expenses can be added to a project if administrators are not sure of what they want as a finished product. This option is often used in the private sector. In many areas, this option is not available to the public sector based on laws regulating the bid process.

Fast-Track Option

The fast-track process compresses the time between the start of design and the completion of construction. To save time, construction begins on selected parts of the project before the completion of the total design effort. The fast-track process requires careful cost allocation to ensure sufficient funds for the entire project. This time-saving process also restricts the designer's ability to incorporate desired changes into the project after the initial construction contracts are awarded. This option is often used in the private sector. It may not be available for public-sector projects based on laws regulating the bid process.

Private-sector facilities often choose the fast-track process in facility construction.
Jacob Ammentorp Lund/iStockphoto/Getty Images

Pick Two?

An old principle in construction is represented as a triangle of *good*, *fast*, and *cheap* (figure 7.3). The principle asserts that an agency can select only two of the three elements when building a facility. For example, an agency may select *good* quality and lower cost (*cheap*), which means the facility will not be completed quickly (*fast*). Alternatively, the agency may opt for lower cost (*cheap*) and completed quickly (*fast*), which means quality won't be *good*. What do you think? Is this construction triangle still relevant today?

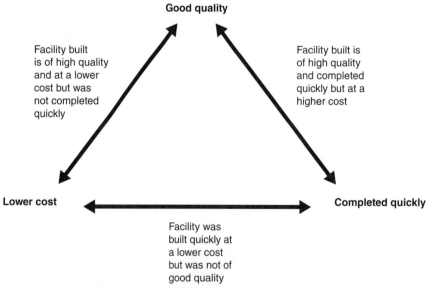

FIGURE 7.3   Principle of *good*, *fast*, and *cheap* construction.

Turnkey Option

In a turnkey project, the contractor bids a lump sum for all aspects of the project; obtains all necessary design work, financing, and permits; and then develops the facility. Once the project is complete, the contractor exchanges the title of the facility for the full payment or an agreement for future payments. The turnkey approach saves money because the contractor controls many details, negotiations, and communications. The turnkey process can be used in either the private or the public sector.

Bidding the Project

Part of funding a facility project is making the transition from planning and design to obtaining financial quotes or bids from potential contractors who will commit to build the facility. In the facility construction, administrators, architects, and contractors come together as a team to build the facility. Before that collaboration can happen, contractors need the opportunity to bid on the project. The owner and architect agree on what is to be developed (through the design); then potential contractors submit a price or bid based on their estimated costs to construct the facility and their margin for profit. This process usually takes three to five weeks. It requires that all pricing information submitted by contractors be kept confidential, allowing contractors to work independently of one another. Most of the time, the bidding process can be competitive, with pricing (total package) as the only variable under consideration. However, the bidding process does have some variations between public and private projects.

Public- Versus Private-Sector Projects

Not all facility projects must go out for bid. Private agencies can do whatever they want in finding a contractor to complete construction work for a project. If an owner feels comfortable with a contractor who has a good reputation, it is not uncommon for that contractor to be awarded the contract without going through a bid process, which can be long and costly. Some private agencies use the bid process to save money because many contractors will lower their quote when they are put in a competitive situation. The bid process can be applied to private projects if judged necessary or advantageous.

On the other hand, public-sector projects must go out for bid to find the lowest price and the best contractor. Public projects go out for bid because they use taxpayer money and are required by law to create fair competition for all interested contractors. In this situation, all contractors and vendors should have an equal and objective opportunity to bid on the project. Because the bidding process for public agencies is more involved and can be more complicated, bid information must be made available to all interested firms.

Quotations

Whether used in the public or private sector, the bid process results in a quotation submitted by a potential contractor to the agency bidding out the work. A quotation indicates the contractor's cost for a facility project. It represents the contractor's cost analysis and calculation that incorporates all aspects of the project. In the bidding process, contractors and administrators can choose one of two quotation options. One option is the **lump-sum bid**, also called a **fixed-priced bid**. With this option, all designs and specifications for the project are awarded to one general contractor to complete all the work. A lump sum results in a single sum of money paid for all work to be accomplished. The general contractor is responsible for making all arrangements and paying all subcontractors.

Another quotation method is **separate-bid pricing**, where quotes are solicited from different general contractors for separate elements of the construction process. These separate elements include excavation, plumbing, landscaping, electrical work, structural work, and mechanical work. The separate-bid process may save money by eliminating the general contractor's markup for overhead or profit. However, it places greater responsibility on the recreation agency to make sure that subcontractors get things done in a timely fashion, requiring the administrator to work closely with the various contractors.

Alternates

Often agencies bidding a project are not sure whether the amount they have budgeted for the project will cover all components. To ensure that they don't have to throw out all bids and start over, agencies often include alternates in the bid documents. Alternates are parts of the project that are bid on outside of the original bid package. They may be identified as extra or not as necessary to the project because they may be expensive or beyond the anticipated budget. However, alternates may be important project components. They do not affect the original bid price, but if the original bid comes in under the budgeted amount, it may be possible to include the alternate components of the bid in the construction project. Often, alternates are left for later inclusion when funds are available or when decisions are made to put an alternate into the project. Using an alternate-bid process helps keep costs manageable. It is the discretion of the agency owner or administrator and the architect to decide if the alternates should be included; the decision is dictated by the funds available.

Bonds

Along with the bid, contractors submit a **bond**, usually a large percentage of the project cost, which guarantees their quote as a commitment to complete the project. The bond is returned to all other contractors that do not get the business or contract; it stays with the winning bidder, and it is applied to the project or returned at the completion of the project.

Bid Process

Although quotation options and alternates are mentioned, the bid process can take on varying degrees of formality, and requirements are often determined by the recreation agency as well as the government. Sensitivity to this

process is important, especially when working in the public sector.

The bid process begins with making the design documents (blueprints and specification books) available to all interested parties after a public announcement is made that the bid is available to all who are interested. A formal timetable is established with deadlines for when the bids are due to allow all potential contractors a fair and impartial chance to submit their bid. The bid requires that every monetary cost be accounted for as related to every detail in the blueprints and specification books.

At the end of the timetable, all contractors are invited to a public opening of the bids to see how their bid compared with those of competing contractors. At this formal bid opening, each bid is opened and read aloud for the benefit of all in attendance. The agency may then take the information received before a public or private board before awarding a contract, taking the bids under advisement until the project design team can examine all the details. Generally, after bids have been reviewed for accuracy, the most responsive contractor with the lowest bid is awarded the contract. Bidders may withdraw their bid for any reason before the contract is awarded. Once a contractor is awarded the project, contract arrangements can be finalized.

Contract Arrangements

At the end of the bidding process, the owner or administrator, architect, and contractor meet to begin their team collaboration on the project. Although the contract commits the contractor to many obligations, the team has formal conversations to make sure everything about this complex process is clearly understood. During the contract arrangements, the administrator and contractor move toward a written document that ties everything together in the form of a detailed understanding. They must establish agreements and guarantees to protect themselves from any misunderstanding. As they move toward a formal agreement, they consider the following:

Value Engineering and Assessment

With the lowest bid received and the contract being awarded, the contractor and the owner or administrator work together on the bid details to make sure everything is designed and interpreted properly. A number of elements in the project could require detailed assessment and interpretation. At this stage, the two parties may seek assistance from architects, engineers, and specialists to make sure the bid prices accurately reflect the details in the specifications. This process of looking at prices and specifications is referred to as **value engineering**. The team of specialists looks at the blueprints and reviews the pricing to make sure that the owner does not pay too much money and that the contractor receives fair compensation for work performed. The team works toward solving problems that the administrator or contractor may not have been aware of during the planning, design, and bidding processes. No one wants to learn during construction—when it will cost much more to correct—that a mistake was made. Value engineering benefits both parties; it can catch details that were missed during earlier phases, and it can lead to negotiations to ensure that both parties agree and that all details are understood and correct.

Insurance Coverage

In the final stages of contract arrangements, contractors have to demonstrate that they have appropriate insurance covering all aspects of the project during the construction stage. The insurance package should protect against any situation that could occur at the construction site, including workers' compensation and property and casualty loss. The contractor's insurance coverage is important because the owner should not be responsible for anything that goes on at the construction site. The contractor is at great risk because construction sites can be dangerous. The contractor should take every precaution to protect against claims of injury, with insurance established in case something does occur.

Contractors must show facility administrators that they have insurance to cover any accidents that may occur at a construction site.

© Human Kinetics

Financing Plans

Just as contractors are held responsible for their work with a bonding and insurance plan, recreation agencies are responsible for providing an adequate amount of money to pay for the project and a system for distributing payment as the project progresses. Every project should have a financial plan and an established system for the contractor to request payment for work completed. It is appropriate for the contractor be aware of the financial system that the administrator has arranged to pay for the facility.

In making these financial arrangements, the recreation agency will have to justify the cost of the facility to the mortgaging or loaning entity. Sometimes financial arrangements can influence the viability of a project. Without adequate financial planning, the agency might not receive the necessary funding and therefore may have to decide whether to continue the project. Recreation administrators must justify the cost of a facility as well as assess the highest potential for reward and the lowest financial risk. The construction cost of a facility is usually the greatest financial consideration for administrators. Lenders expect the existence of a way to ensure repayment of the loan. Recreation administrators can perform calculations to determine the net amount of investment required for the project, the return expected for the investment, and what rate of interest will be charged. When the amount of the loan is determined, the agency can seek financial assistance from a financial institution or private lender.

When recreation agencies are looking for loans to finance projects, they must carefully look at the terms of the loan. Loan terms include interest that will be charged on the loan, the length of the loan, the closing costs, the penalty fee or charge for a late payment, and any financial consultant fees required to complete financing details. Although most of these concerns are administrative, contractors should be aware of this information because they are entering into a contract with the agency.

Controlling Costs

A contract arrangement is designed to protect the facility owner and the contractor from unexpected construction costs. No matter what plans are made to move the project along, facility administrators should be aware of unexpected costs that could occur during construction. The contract can establish a maximum price for completion of the facility. Administrators can offer financial incentives for contractors if they can reduce the construction cost. Administrators can also pay the actual cost of all materials and labor, plus a fixed percentage or fee to the contractor, to help keep the final cost of the project from rising. These two contract concepts can contribute to the overall effort in getting a facility developed and keeping costs under control.

Signing the Contract

After all the discussions, meetings, engineering assessment, and other arrangements have been determined, and after the administrator and the contractor have finalized and authorized the formal blueprint and specification books, a contract can be completed. Recognizing and accepting all responsibilities as documented in the blueprints and specification books, both parties sign the formal contract at an established time and place. Once the contractor and the administrator sign the finalized contract, the price cannot be changed unless both sides agree with an appropriate cost-adjustment agreement. The formal contract binds the price and establishes the work to be completed.

Funding Options

Many possible sources exist for funding a recreation facility project. Some facilities can receive funding from a single source, whereas others can receive funding from a combination of sources. Some sources may apply to certain facility projects only. This section provides a sampling of funding options.

Mandatory Fees

An agency can establish a fee requiring payment from users of the product. This mandatory fee can be designated to pay for new construction, renovation, or repair. Mandatory fees are most often associated with public agencies; they are usually established by a governing body, trustees, or a representative administrative system. A mandatory fee can be designated to pay for an expensive project over an extended duration, usually from 5 to 30 years. Mandatory fees can be attached to other ongoing user fees or payment obligations, such as memberships, monthly dues, payments, or school tuition. Often, mandatory fees are designed to meet operational expenses as well as construction or renovation costs.

An **assessment fee** is another type of mandatory fee that can help fund less expensive projects. Assessment fees are usually collected for a short duration; generally, they do not exceed a year. Usually members, customers, or patrons make monthly payments for an improvement to a facility. For example, private golf courses often use assessment fees to pay for facility improvements. However, mandatory fees or assessments can be unpopular with those who must pay. Attention should be given to opposition to make sure everyone understands and appreciates the need for the facility project.

Tax Levy

A **tax levy** occurs in the public sector and earmarks a portion of local taxes for a recreation facility project. Usually, this type of funding requires a great deal of community support, and it can take years to evolve. A number of public boards, commissions, and elected officials may have to authorize this type of funding. A tax levy is limited to a certain amount based on the conditions imposed by governing bodies. It is often used for community projects such as schools, fire stations, and recreation centers, as well as state facilities such as universities and government buildings.

User Fees

User fees come from people who pay to use the core product of a facility. The amounts charged for services usually equate to the type of use, the user's ability to afford the services, and what others in the market are charging. User

User fees come directly from people who pay to use the facility's core product.
kali9/E+/Getty Images

fees often come in the form of memberships, monthly dues, payments, or school tuition. They differ from mandatory fees in that mandatory fees are additional fees related to facility construction and operation whereas user fees are not related to facility development. The agency provides a competitively priced product that users will benefit from in the hope that it leads to repeated use and satisfaction. Income and expense analysis should be conducted to make sure the fee is fair and that users will not be discouraged by the amount. Accurate projections of income from user fees are critical in the planning stage. User fees can be a primary source of revenue for private agencies that depend on this type of income to meet facility expenses. Public facilities can also institute user fees to help offset expenses. In the public setting, user fees are usually lower and may be less critical to the support of the facility because of funding generated through taxes.

Bond Issue

A **bond issue** is a method of raising funds for public facilities. It is often the primary source of funds for local or state facility construction projects. The process offers tax-exempt bonds for the general public to buy with a return of the principal amount, plus interest, after a certain amount of time. The state bonding authority controls the process, and it has the authority to allow or deny such an option. Prior to final approval by the state bonding authority, local boards and elected officials will be required to authorize the sale of the bonds. Citizens in a community can object in writing to a bond issue if they do not want their taxes to be used for a particular project. Requirements for the approval of bond issues vary from community to community. Generally, financial consultants are hired to assist with projects funded by bond issues. Bonds of this nature are sound investments because they are supported by tax income, which is safe and regular income that can be counted on to pay off the loan on a facility mortgage.

Revenue Bond

A revenue bond is for a public project. It relies on projected revenue that will be generated by the facility for repayment of a loan. A revenue bond is backed up or supported by property taxes in the event that the revenue collected is less than projected. This type of funding is used only when a facility project is able to generate substantial revenue from its core product. Examples of public facilities funded by revenue bonds include water parks and golf courses.

Donations and Contributions

Additional sources of funding for facility projects include gifts, donations, and contributions from interested individuals and groups. These sources come from supportive people or businesses that usually have a vested interest, possibly from past involvement with the receiving agency. Contributors may have the financial ability and benefit from making donations of this nature for tax purposes. Sometimes agencies campaign to raise funds of this nature. Such campaigns often use fundraisers who have expertise in raising money for causes. Some contributors can have requirements that the agency must meet, such as using the contributor's name in recognition of a particular area of the facility or in naming the facility.

In-Kind Gifts

Another source of outside assistance in funding a project is **in-kind gifts**. They represent a unique approach that can get some aspects of a facility project completed that otherwise may not be possible. With an in-kind gift, a contractor or other interested party provides labor or materials to a facility at no cost in exchange for a tax deduction for the amount that is donated. The recreation environment provides opportunities to solicit a potential contractor or vendor for an in-kind gift by targeting people or businesses that use the facility. Often, the emotional tie to a program offered

Depending on the size of the donation, some contributors may require a facility to use their name when naming a facility area or the entire facility.

Wesley Hitt/Getty Images

at a recreation facility creates the appeal for a business or individual to donate an in-kind gift. In-kind gifts are a good way to get minor repairs, renovations, and small parts of a new project completed at a lower cost.

Grants

Agencies can approach many granting institutions about helping with the funding for a facility project. Grants are an excellent option for public projects, especially if the requesting agency has a similar mission, interest, or purpose as the granting agency. Grant funds can be provided by the government, private institutions, or public or private foundations. These sources usually require a formal grant proposal before the grant is awarded. Gen-

erally, the directions for writing a grant are straightforward. However, a recreation professional seeking grant dollars may want to participate in grant-writing workshops provided by professional recreation organizations and grant-writing agencies. Granting sources may have certain conditions that must be met in order to award the grant. In some cases, sources may place no restrictions on how the grant funds can be used. The grant process can be very involved and competitive. Larger recreation agencies often have a full-time staff member designated to research and apply for grants. Funds from grants can vary from several thousand to several million dollars. Grants can provide a significant funding source for a project if the criteria for the grant match the mission of the agency applying for the grant.

Sponsorships

The construction of a new facility often provides an opportunity for outside entities to provide funds so that their business receives recognition of some type at the facility. This relationship is usually established through a contractual arrangement before construction, with detailed understanding regarding the level of funding support to the project in return for recognition at the facility. It is common to see professional sport facilities named after a business in exchange for a significant amount of money. These arrangements may become more prevalent in the recreation environment as agencies attempt to raise funds for projects. In such cases, matching facilities with businesses that may benefit from exposing their name to the users may be a winning combination. Common examples of sponsorship opportunities include exposure of sponsor names on scoreboards, fences around sport fields, and hole signs on golf courses. Sponsorship opportunities are available for both public and private recreation facilities.

Combination Funding

Usually private entities do not have access to the same sources of funding as public agencies.

Private facilities generally rely on mandatory fees, user fees, and private investors as their primary sources of facility funds. The public sector has greater latitude in seeking funds for a project, often resulting in a combination of the funding sources mentioned. In addition to fees and charges, public-sector agencies are funded through tax dollars and are often eligible for grant dollars. Public-sector agencies also occasionally benefit from individual and corporate donations. Recreation professionals should be aware of all funding options and be creative in considering the mix that may work best in accomplishing the project.

Campaign Funding

Often facility development projects require significant persuasion of administrators, investors, the general public, and politicians in order to create the necessary progress to fund a project. This approach especially applies with a large project that requires extensive financial support. The effort to create awareness among the parties mentioned could be viewed as a campaign that helps people to realize the need for a facility project. The ability for facility advocates to influence people and create an interest in funding support is instrumental to the success of a project. The two primary

Some businesses may decide to sponsor part of or an entire facility in exchange for having their name prominently displayed at the facility.

Kevin Abele/Icon Sportswire via Getty Images

methods used to influence attitudes toward funding a project are individual selling and specialty firms.

Individual Selling

Often, the person responsible for initiating the support for funding a facility and taking on the task of individual selling is the recreation agency administrator or facility manager. Raising support for a facility project means spending extra hours on the job outside the daily routine. Typical duties include speaking on behalf of the project by attending functions where knowledge and enthusiasm for the project can be shared. In the individual selling effort, the aim is to disseminate accurate information about the project to all interested and influential parties through methods such as direct conversations, telephone calls, petitions, special presentations, fliers, press releases, and press conferences that focus on the benefits of the facility. The ability to network or interact with others who can sell the vision and assist in obtaining the necessary funding for a project can play a huge role in gaining financial support.

Specialty Firms

Firms with fundraising expertise can be hired to help lead a funding campaign for a facility project. Hiring a specialty firm as a consultant to assist with a project comes at a cost that varies depending on the size of the project.

These firms retain professionals who know how to reach target audiences that recreation agencies may not usually consider. They also possess the knowledge and skills to present the appropriate message or pitch that leads to a successful fundraising campaign. Such firms are typically hired when a project is expansive and affects a large number of people, when it has conflicting interests or complicated funding requirements, or when recreation administrators or facility managers recognize that their help is needed. Specialty firms may be brought in on a project when an independent perspective of the need for a project may help to assuage public and political dissension. Often, these firms specialize in damage control. When a project is very large, they may devise methods to soothe public and political concerns and ultimately influence the funding process.

Summary

Funding a facility development project is a serious consideration in the evolution of any facility. Funding could be described as the process for acquiring money to support a project and allow it to become a reality. Without funding, a facility simply remains a plan with a design. The funding of a facility project can be complicated. It involves considering funding options, project costs, construction options, the bid process, and contract arrangements.

REVIEW QUESTIONS

1. Describe the differences between assignable and nonassignable square footage.
2. Provide an example of (a) a hard cost and (b) a soft cost.
3. In a construction project, describe a turnkey option and the conventional method.
4. List the typical funding options for a recreation facility project. Which options would a public recreation agency be more likely to pursue?

CASE STUDY

Developing a Much-Needed Indoor Space for a Midwestern Community

You are the recreation director for the town of Green Prairie. Green Prairie is a smaller, Midwestern community (population: 7,500) located 20 minutes outside of the major city of Lawerencetown. Two years ago, you completed a needs assessment for your residents with the assistance of a group of graduate students from the local university. The results of the needs assessment indicated a strong interest in an indoor recreation center to support indoor sports programming during the winter months. In particular, residents identified the following programs as their household's first, second, third, or fourth most desired programs:

- *First choice*: Senior walking opportunities (77% of residents were supportive of this programming)
- *Second choice*: Adult basketball leagues (55% of residents were supportive of this programming)
- *Third choice*: Adult fitness classes (52% of residents were supportive of this programming)
- *Fourth choice*: Youth and adult volleyball leagues (50% of residents were supportive of indoor space to support this pursuit)

Currently, your community does not have any indoor facilities for winter programming. Five years ago, your agency received a land donation from a community member. This parcel of land is located in the middle of town, and it is approximately 2.5 acres (1 ha) in size. This donated parcel of land sits right next to a city-owned parking lot. The parking lot can accommodate 50 cars and currently has one ADA accessible parking space.

Your agency also just received a large financial donation from a local business that wishes to fund the development of a recreation center in your community. While the local business will not fund the purchase of a site for the facility, it is willing to pay for 100 percent of the facility construction. Of course, the local business also requests naming rights to the recreation center.

You are hoping to use the 2.5-acre site for this facility project. You also want to include as many facility spaces as you can to support the residents' top four programming interests. You are currently thinking about a recreation center that includes the following:

- Reception area (700 ft²)
- Fitness room (40' × 40')
- Two locker rooms that can each accommodate about 15 people at a time
- Hallways and stairwells (1,000 ft²)
- Space to store equipment and supplies (2,500 ft²)
- The main area of the center (5 basketball courts and a 6-lane track surrounding the courts)
- An outdoor area that includes a pavilion and small playground (21,780 ft²)

Case Study Questions

1. Calculate the square footage for each of the following areas:
   a. Fitness room
   b. Two locker rooms (assume 15 ft² per person is needed)
   c. Main area of the new recreation center (5 courts and 6-lane track)
2. Not including the outdoor area, what is the anticipated total assignable square footage (ASF) of the proposed recreation center facility?
3. The residents' fourth programming choice was volleyball, but the current recreation center plans do not mention these spaces in its current design. Why? More specifically, where could these spaces be integrated into the existing plan without increasing the facility's square footage?

CHAPTER 8

Constructing Recreation Facilities

LEARNING OBJECTIVES

At the completion of this chapter, you should be able to do the following:

1. Recognize the various issues and elements involved in the construction phase.
2. Identify the factors that influence a construction schedule.
3. Understand the role of the construction manager.

The construction stage of a facility development project is an exciting time; all the work to this point starts to take shape into an actual structure. It is often a time of celebration and ceremony, especially with larger projects. Design project construction frequently begins with a groundbreaking ceremony and concludes with an opening ceremony.

Before the construction begins, a ceremony is often held to recognize the official start of the project. This step, called a **groundbreaking**, recognizes the project as having gained the necessary support to become a reality, and it initiates the construction process. To get to this stage takes a tremendous effort, and it often involves many people. The groundbreaking is a time to recognize the people and groups that helped bring the project to this stage. The ceremony can range from an informal gathering to an elaborate program involving speakers and a literal groundbreaking (or shoveling) activity. A newspaper article, photos, and media coverage can also be part of the groundbreaking ceremony, communicating the event to a greater audience.

Construction Documents

After design documents or blueprints have been reviewed during the value assessment

On August 6, 2019, residents in Sedalia, Missouri, voted on two ballot issues: an additional one-eighth of a cent sales tax and the removal of the sunset (provision of the tax code that expires at a certain date) for the capital improvement tax. Both of these issues had direct implications for the potential development of the Heckart Community Center; passing them would mean more public funds would be available for the project. Both ballot issues passed on June 11, 2020, and a groundbreaking ceremony was held to kick off the construction of the facility. On March 18, 2022, the Heckart Community Center held its grand opening ceremony (KMMO, 2022).

The Heckart Community Center is a 92,000-square-foot (8,547 m²) facility located in the central part of Sedalia. The center's location was carefully selected for multiple reasons. First, being centrally located supports equitable access by all members of the community. Next, the location provides great visibility for those traveling in and out of Sedalia. The center serves as an eye-catching jewel in the town; its high visibility to both residents and out-of-town travelers creates a welcoming and vibrant environment for the community. Finally, the community center's location is the former Jennie Jaynes Stadium property. The Jennie Jaynes Foundation was established in the Sedalia area with a goal of bringing quality recreational opportunities to the community. Locating the Heckart Community Center on the former Jennie Jaynes Stadium site aligns with the Foundation's original goal to support community recreational opportunities in Sedalia.

The Heckart Community Center embodies a true community recreation feel, as is evident by its diverse amenities, including the following: an aquatic center with a zero-depth entry pool, water slide, lazy river, lap lanes, diving boards, and an eight-lane competition pool; a multipurpose gymnasium; a child watch area; a party and meeting room; a kitchen; a senior center; community rooms; administration offices; an elevated track; and a fitness area with cardio studios. Motivated by her parents' dream of a community center in the city of Sedalia (population of about 21,000), Sue Heckart provided a donation of paying the interest on the bonds used by the city to construct the center. The Sedalia Parks Department manages the Heckart Community Center, and it plans to cover the operational costs through user fees and facility-based services.

and engineering steps, the architect creates final drawings reflecting adjustments decided on by the administrator, architect, contractor, and construction manager. These revised documents are called *construction documents*. As mentioned in chapter 6, as the size of the project increases, so does the number of blueprint pages. Each design area within the facility (structural, mechanical, electrical, landscaping) has its own layers of blueprints with specific details. With smaller projects, these design areas could be incorporated into fewer pages with some of the blueprint areas overlapping each other. The following documents are generally understood to be the construction documents that are provided to the contractor. They represent the project in detail, and they are the formal communication among the members of the design team (the administrator, architect, construction manager, and contractor).

Final Blueprints

The **final blueprints** are the design documents that communicate the details of what is to be constructed. The final blueprints indicate how the contractor is to complete each component of the project. These documents are also copied and given to subcontractors and craftspeople to serve as their guide for how to construct their part of the project. They are carried to the construction site, where they will be referred to frequently throughout the project. The contractor is financially responsible for all errors, so every detail must be followed as drawn. Mistakes can be costly, are time consuming to correct, and compromise the safety of the facility. It is crucial that the final blueprints be accurate to ensure accurate construction of the facility.

A groundbreaking symbolizes the beginning of the construction phase for a project, and it recognizes having garnered the necessary support to see the project come to this stage.

Rachel Luna/Getty Images

Specification Book

The **specification book** (also called the *spec book*) is an important part of communicating the specifications of a project to the contractors. It provides written detailed references to the blueprints. When problems and misunderstandings arise, the spec book can clear up the differences. As the project increases in size, so does the amount of detail in the spec book. Small projects may not even require a spec book if the blueprints provide enough detail. Spec books are an extension of the contract and final blueprints. They include design information as well as requirements for the design, including codes, laws, and standards that need to be conveyed accurately to the contractor and subcontractors.

Shop Drawings

Another step in the construction process that assists contractors with design expectations involves creating **shop drawings**, which support blueprints and spec books. Shop drawings are the contractor's (or subcontractor's) interpretations of the blueprints that are approved by the architect. The architect or the contractor can create the shop drawings; they can be simple and informal, or complex and formal. Whatever is included in the shop drawing is subject to final approval by the administrator. Shop drawings help ensure that details in blueprints are understood and accurate as they relate to specific items, customized areas, or unique design elements. This component of facility projects can be time consuming. With the extent of details that many projects require, shop drawings help clarify the design expectations and avoid problems in the long run.

Change Orders

No construction project proceeds exactly as planned. Contractors, architects, and administrators may discover problems during the process. Change orders occur for the following reasons: errors or omissions in the design, a change in the method or construction material, or contractors recognizing a problem from their experience with the project. When these situations occur, the construction manager initiates a change order to communicate what needs to be corrected and to authorize the change. The **change order** is a written amendment to the contract that authorizes the contractor to make the proposed changes in the work at the construction site. These changes can have serious cost implications that all parties want to avoid. However, it is usually understood that making a change during construction will be less expensive than correcting it later. Change orders should be approved by administrators, architects, and contractors.

Project Schedule

One of the most interesting and comprehensive construction documents is the **project schedule**, a conceptual plan that reflects all phases of the project. The project schedule can be presented in the form of a book, or it can be a poster displayed on a wall. The layout represents all aspects of the project, including site preparation, demolition, architectural developments, electrical work, mechanical installation, and landscaping. It also communicates deadlines for each stage of the project, including the day, month, and year. This schedule is usually set up with all construction functions, tasks, and responsibilities listed down the left side and proposed dates for completion across the top. Bars or lines depict when each stage is estimated to be completed. At first glance, a project schedule appears difficult to comprehend. Once studied, it clearly presents the entire picture of a project from beginning to end.

Construction Management

More often than not, administrators do not have the capacity to supervise a construction project, especially if it is large and complicated. As noted in chapter 6, companies exist that can bring expertise to overseeing all aspects of a construction project. These firms provide construction management expertise, and they can contractually assume the role of the administrators, working with the architect to ensure that all project requirements are accomplished in a timely and suitable fashion. Construction managers are responsible for all phases of a construction project. They have the knowledge, insight, and ability to supervise all phases of the project. This arrangement should be formalized in writing between the facility administrator and the construction management company. The following are functions that are usually fulfilled by the construction management team, whether this team includes a construction management company or not.

CHECK IT OUT

What's the Deal With Change Orders?

Change orders can be additive (adding something to the facility), or they can be deductive (requiring a reduction or decrease of something in the facility's development). Regardless of the type of change order, common change order requests include the following (Farley, 2018):

- Moving the location of a wall (to accommodate another design element)
- Changing the flooring surface
- Adding a window to an area that did not have one in the original plans

Weather is one type of delay that can occur and lead to greater problems, which are discussed at construction progress meetings.

Erkan Davulcu/EyeEm/Getty Images

Conducting Progress Meetings

The construction management team schedules and conducts regular **progress meetings** with key people involved in the project. Attendees include the administrator, user representative, architect, vendors, contractors, subcontractors, and (when necessary) engineers and consultants. At these meetings, all aspects of the project are discussed in detail. Any existing or potential problems should be resolved to avoid project delays that can lead to greater problems. Some problems that can affect construction include weather, worker productivity, material imperfections, materials delivery, timetables, accidents, changes, conflict, quality concerns, and coordination challenges. At each meeting, the construction management team leader

makes verbal and written progress reports detailing everything that happened since the previous meeting. Progress expectations and timetable details are also addressed and confirmed in progress reports.

Coordinating the Project

The many facets associated with the construction of a recreation facility require attention in order to avoid conflict and ensure that work is progressing as planned. Coordinating the various aspects of a project can be challenging because of the number of workers, subcontractors, vendors, timetable requirements, unexpected problems, inspections, and weather delays that often occur. Coordination of a project is a critical role for the construction manager because delays can cost money, create tension, and negatively affect the completion schedule of a project.

Establishing and Managing the Project Schedule

During a construction project, many phases transpire between groundbreaking and occupancy. Along with the administrator and architect, the construction manager is responsible for establishing this detailed schedule for each phase of the project. The schedule identifies work functions for each part of the construction team. It includes timetables for each function, which the construction management firm monitors. The construction manager is responsible for keeping construction progressing according to the project schedule.

Performing Quality Checks

One of the most important functions of a construction manager is to review the work of contractors and subcontractors. Occasionally, contractors do not have the same commitment to a project as the architect or administrator. Contractors may try to find cost savings through workmanship and material substitutions in order to enhance their profit margin. In addition, some contractors may attempt to hide worker mistakes and oversights to avoid additional costs. The construction manager is responsible for monitoring contractors' work, which includes identifying problems and taking the necessary steps to rectify situations as needed. A construction manager is the agency representative; they must ensure that the agency receives what is outlined in the blueprints and specification book.

Interpreting Legal Requirements

Administrators often do not initially realize how many local and state codes are involved in the construction of a recreation facility. Construction managers serve a valuable role in interpreting these codes, which must be observed during construction. Specific codes are available through local government agencies and state governments, and they are usually available on the Internet. Construction managers make sure everything is done accurately and meets specific design requirements. The watchdog role of the construction manager comes into play with electrical, mechanical, plumbing, and structural details, as well as the legal codes that must be applied to each phase of the project. Failure to follow certain requirements can result in lawsuits that affect all those involved with the project.

While local codes may vary, construction managers in the United States should be aware of the federal standards associated with facility construction. One of the most recognizable federal codes surrounding facility construction is the Americans with Disabilities Act (ADA). Part of the Civil Rights Act of 1991, the ADA prohibits discrimination against people with disabilities in multiple areas, including employment, public accommodations, communications, transportation, and access to public programs and services. The ADA provides the legal support to ensure reasonable accommodations in public places, prohibits discrimination based on disabling conditions, and provides a definition of disabilities (Sourby, 2022).

A supporting philosophy called *universal design* builds on the tenets of the ADA with an emphasis on a wider spectrum of abilities, and it aims to exceed minimum standards to meet the needs of the greatest number of people. Seven principles embody the philosophy of universal design. They are listed here, followed by their applications to recreational settings (Sourby, 2022):

1. *Equitable*: Designs that address a wide range of needs
2. *Flexibility in use*: Hands-free operation of equipment and facility amenities
3. *Simple and intuitive use*: Comfortable equipment that is easy to use (e.g., high-contrast, large on–off controls).
4. *Perceptible information*: Large buttons on remotes, phones, and touch screens
5. *Tolerance for error*: Nonslip surfaces, glare reduction surfaces

6. *Low physical effort*: Amenities that support a wide range of abilities

7. *Appropriate size and space for approach and use*: Wide doorways, roll-in showers, and bathroom stalls for wheelchairs and walkers

Scheduling and Overseeing Inspections

Construction managers are also involved in scheduling and overseeing inspections that are conducted by local governing agencies. Inspections are a required part of a construction project. An inspector's role is to act in the best interest of the future employees and users of the facility by ensuring that the construction process does not create inconveniences or dangerous situations.

Inspectors can examine any number of elements at a construction site. Throughout construction, outside agencies inspect specific situations, items, or areas to assess the workmanship and ensure that contractors are in compliance with all codes. The construction manager is responsible for working with inspectors to help them do their job. In addition, the construction manager should always be prepared for inspectors, knowing that they could show up unannounced. Items that inspectors scrutinize include electrical work, plumbing, accessibility, and structural requirements.

Managing Changes

No construction or renovation project progresses to completion without changes. Changes are expensive; therefore, the construction manager needs to make sure each change is necessary and that it is best for the project. Construction managers must coordinate any changes with contractors, architects, and administrators.

Once the administrator and the construction manager informally discuss a change, the construction manager initiates the change order

One part of a construction manager's job is to schedule inspections during the construction process to ensure that the construction does not create hazards, inconveniences, or dangerous situations.
Andreswd/E+/Getty Images

and forwards to the architect; the architect then reviews and forwards the change order to the administrator for documented approval. After the administrator authorizes the change, it is then returned to the contractors for correction. Construction managers keep track of all change orders and coordinate when the work is to be completed.

Ensuring Site Safety and Security

Every construction site is a potentially hazardous area. Contractors cannot have people visiting the site without authorization because they could be seriously injured. Contractors are liable for keeping people out of a construction site. Typically, barricades or fences are put up to control access. Construction managers play a key role with this responsibility, using techniques that include monitoring access, posting signs, installing tape warning barriers,

and hiring guards and watchdogs to monitor the site. Efforts to secure a site at night may require additional security measures, such as hiring security guards or using surveillance equipment, to keep people away. Given the potential danger for and cost of any accidents that might occur, construction managers should take these security measures seriously.

Controlling Visitation

Those invested in a facility construction project enjoy experiencing the progress of a project. Construction managers have the responsibility to control this interest through a process called *visitation*. Traffic at the construction site is controlled with strict rules for all visitors, including the facility administrator and the architect. A well-planned visitation system can help significantly with public relations while at the same time ensuring the safety of the visitors. Every precaution is taken to avoid dangerous areas

When a visitation from people with a vested interest in the construction project occurs, ensuring the safety of the visitors is a top priority of the construction manager.
Ilkercelik/iStock/Getty Images

during visits. All visitors are required to wear hard hats. They are usually required to sign in, be supervised by the construction manager throughout the tour, then sign out at the end of the visit.

Final Stages

Late in any construction project, after all the structural, mechanical, and electrical work is done, steps are taken to complete the facility. This fine-tuning brings to the facility those things that make the core product and core product extensions function as they were intended. As with the other phases of the project, the construction manager plays a key role in directing all aspects of the final stages by seeing that everything is done in a timely and proper fashion. Following are the final-stage activities that occur before the facility is occupied.

Operator Training

Toward the end of a project, certain aspects of a facility, including the use of equipment, needs to be explained and its proper use needs to be demonstrated. Usually, training is provided for operators of technical equipment that requires

special knowledge to operate or maintain. It may also be important for facility managers to participate in training in order to train future staff and assist in operation and maintenance of equipment and systems. Examples of this vendor transfer of information include the following:

- HVAC systems
- Security equipment
- Lighting
- Public-address systems
- All core product and core product extension areas
- Equipment

The construction manager organizes and schedules these training sessions, making sure the appropriate people are in attendance. These sessions may be the only times the administration or its representatives will learn what is necessary to know about specialized equipment or systems.

Maintenance Manuals

Many facility areas and equipment require specific maintenance attention. Maintenance manuals provide instructions for taking care of

CHECK IT OUT

Pursuing LEED Certification

Leadership in Energy and Environmental Design (LEED) is a worldwide green building certification rating system. LEED-certified facilities are recognized for saving money, demonstrating efficiency, and having low carbon emissions. A facility can earn one of four levels of LEED certification:

1. Certified
2. Silver
3. Gold
4. Platinum

LEED certification involves a four-step process:

1. The administrator completes the necessary paperwork and submits payment to register the facility.
2. The administrator applies for LEED certification.
3. The Green Business Certification Inc. (GBCI) reviews the application.
4. The GBCI grants a certification decision.

these areas and systems. Maintenance details about the care of product equipment, utilities, mechanical systems, electrical systems, and landscape areas must be conveyed to the administrator. The construction manager organizes the transfer of maintenance information, which is an important responsibility. If maintenance requirements are not fulfilled properly, areas and equipment will not meet expectations; if equipment fails at some point, a vendor, contractor, or administrator will be responsible.

Finishing Stage

One of the most significant aspects of construction is the **finishing stage**. The finishing stage includes work the contractors do, such as painting walls, installing light fixtures, hanging doors, and installing windows and floor coverings. The finishing stage is the fine-tuning of aesthetics, acoustical considerations, and other appearance details, and it also includes moving in equipment and furniture. Usually, a finish schedule or design chart or system guides the contractor through every aspect of this phase.

Key System

All facilities will eventually need to be secured from inappropriate access. The extensiveness of a project will dictate just how complicated a key system will need to be. From the beginning, key access should be planned, designed, and controlled with a number or coding system to identify the specific key with an area or piece of equipment. Key systems can be divided into the following categories:

- Masters (open all doors)
- Submasters (open interior locks)
- Individual keys (for each area)

Types of key systems available for recreation facilities include the following:

- Combination locks
- Magnetic-strip cards
- Bar-code cards
- Smart locks

Common key systems include (a) a card reading system, (b) a keypad system, and (c) a magnetic strip card system.

Photo a krisanapong detraphiphat/Moment/Getty Images; photo b undefined undefined/iStock/Getty Images; photo c Galina Zhigalova/iStock/Getty Images

Each facility has its own key requirements. The construction manager's role is to help administrators interpret the details and responsibilities involved that will result in the appropriate key system for their facility.

Signage

Directional signs are necessary to inform users of facility locations. A common mistake made by facility administrators is not providing adequate signage to direct users to appropriate areas. Planning and designing signage requires the capacity to visualize the total use of a facility. The perspective of a first-time user should be considered when designing signage that links all areas into a logical flow that gets people to where they want to be. Signs communicate directional information that includes entrances and exits, area identification, directories, and information about facility policies and procedures. The same type, style, size, and color schemes should be followed throughout the facility so that signage is uniform and visible and also matches the aesthetics of the facility.

Punch List

Near the conclusion of a facility construction project, a system of assessing and recording everything that is to be finalized is compiled into a **punch list**. During a final walk-through of the completed facility, usually a handful of items or areas do not meet design expectations, are incomplete, or are completed below acceptable standards. The construction manager plays a critical role in influencing the contractor to recognize these conditions and ensuring that the necessary adjustments are completed. It is generally accepted that all identified items on the punch list will be fixed, completed, or installed by the contractor before the administrator will accept the facility. As items are corrected to meet design expectations, they are removed from the punch list. The admin-istrator should not provide final payment to the contractor until the entire punch list has been completed.

Furniture and Equipment

Planning, designing, purchasing, and coordinating the installation of furniture and equipment can be one of the most demanding aspects of a facility project. Many detailed decisions on furniture size, quantity, and layout will have to be addressed. Depending on the facility, the same equipment decisions regarding functionality, quality, and quantity must also be discussed. The selection and placement of furniture and equipment requires a great deal of planning and leads to a purchasing process. The administrator ultimately makes many decisions regarding what the contractor will be responsible for as part of the project and what the administrator will provide with separate funds.

During this stage, the construction manager coordinates all items that the facility administrator and project vendors have brought to the facility in the most cooperative and effective way possible. Vendor responsibilities can include shipping, delivery, receiving, and installation. They can be difficult to schedule without complications and communication problems. Sometimes items are delivered outside planned times, requiring patience and cooperation between the contractors (who are still on the site) and the facility employees (who are anxious to occupy their new facility). Planning ahead and budgeting extra time for this stage are essential efforts to avoid inconveniences and the extra labor costs associated with the move-in process.

CHECK IT OUT
Think Universal Design!

Planning and purchasing the furniture and equipment for the facility can be an exciting task. During this time, it is important to consider accessibility in the selection of these important facility amenities. Consider the seven principles of universal design (discussed in Interpreting Legal Requirements). Networking with similar agencies who have successfully employed these principles in their facilities can also be helpful.

Acceptance and Occupancy

As noted in the previous two sections, the final stage of a facility project involves moving in the furniture and equipment in addition to finalizing all items on the punch list. The construction manager coordinates the final stage, which concludes with administrator acceptance and occupancy. Often, facility employees need to take over or move in while a few minor aspects of the construction process are still being completed. This timing may be necessary for facility employees to prepare for the delivery of the core product or product extensions. The construction manager should consult with contractors to allow for this transition unless serious problems need to be resolved. Facility management employees may not move in without contractor approval. Sometimes items on the punch list are allowed to linger, but it is agreed that they will be completed by a certain date after occupancy.

With the acceptance of the project, the administrator formally acknowledges that the facility is complete. Final steps including key and maintenance-manual exchanges, employee training, and final payment to contractors culminate with employees being allowed to occupy the facility. Once acceptance of the project has occurred and the administrator has occupancy, the opening ceremony occurs.

The opening ceremony is a culminating event or celebration that may be similar to the groundbreaking ceremony. This ceremony creates an opportunity to publicly thank everyone involved with the project as well as promote the official opening of the facility. It can incorporate a ceremony including speakers and a ribbon cutting, as well as photographs, tours,

Opening ceremonies, which often include a ribbon cutting, present an opportunity to recognize that a facility project goal has been achieved as well as to thank those associated with the project.
© Human Kinetics

and commemorative gifts to those who played a significant role in the project.

The ceremonial activities involved in the construction phase are just a small part of actual construction. The construction stage of the design process is

- when plans have come together;
- design documents have been put out for bid, reviewed, and accepted;
- value assessment has been finalized; and
- all contractual arrangements have been made and signed.

Depending on the size or type of project, the construction process can involve many details, and recreation facility managers should be aware of these variables. The responsibilities associated with any construction project can involve diverse interpretations and applications, and much of this information is included in the construction documents.

Summary

The construction phase is where all of the planning and hard work start to take shape. It is important that construction documents have been properly prepared so the construction manager can facilitate the construction process and oversee the many responsibilities included in that position. Once construction is finished and the administrator is satisfied that all work has been completed to specifications, the project is deemed complete. At this point, the agency is prepared to start using the facility.

REVIEW QUESTIONS

1. Describe the difference between a final blueprint and shop drawings.
2. Why is a project schedule so important during the construction of recreation facilities?
3. Identify the seven universal design principles. How do these principles differ from ADA mandates?
4. What is the purpose of an opening ceremony for a facility, and why is it important to do?

CASE STUDY

Construction Challenges at the Aquatic Complex

You were recently hired to serve as the facility coordinator for the Swim Happy Aquatic Park & Entertainment Center (SHAPEC). The SHAPEC is currently in the construction phase, and it is scheduled to open in 12 months. The SHAPEC includes a lazy river; zero-depth entry leisure pool with a wet deck, interactive play structures, and vortex; a 10-lane lap pool with a rock climbing wall and zip line, two diving areas, and three body slides. A full-service concession area will also be available at the SHAPEC.

While regular meetings have not been scheduled, you have met with the SHAPEC construction management team and toured the construction site. It appeared contractors and construction crews were busy working on various parts of the SHAPEC during your site visit and everyone appeared friendly and eager to meet you. This large-scale project definitely has a lot of moving parts!

After about a month on the job, you are quickly noticing some issues with the construction phase of the SHAPEC project. In particular, you have already been involved with three change order requests and received multiple complaints from various contractors regarding delays in their crew's work as a result of needing to wait on other contractors to complete the needed prep work required at the site. You are already worried about the delays in opening the facility due to weather-related setbacks, and these issues are only compounding your concerns. Furthermore, you are receiving several calls, emails, and social media posts from community members and media outlets asking about the status of the project and its schedule. A project schedule has not been made available to the community or media, and the last update they received was during the ground-breaking ceremony last year.

Case Study Questions

1. What are some strategies you could employ to address the lack of organization and communication occurring at the construction site and among the various contractors?

2. How should you respond to the community and media requests for information regarding the status of the SHAPEC project? What can you do to foster an improved information-sharing process for those groups?

3. As you reflect on the SHAPEC project, what are two or three ways you could encourage environmentally friendly and sustainable practices during the current construction phase of this project? How about once the facility has opened?

4. What are some ways you can ensure specific legal requirements (local, state, federal building codes) and ADA Design Standards are supported during the construction of the SHAPEC?

PART III

RESOURCES FOR RECREATION FACILITY MANAGEMENT

Recreation facility managers must manage resources in order to deliver the core product. Most recreation facilities have three basic resources: equipment, financial resources, and people. Equipment includes many objects that must be purchased, distributed, used, and maintained so that users can enjoy them while at a facility. Although the consumer does not directly use them, financial resources are vital to the operation of a facility. Practicing fiscal responsibility and understanding financial practices are parts of everyday life for a recreation facility manager. People (the employees at a recreation facility) are also a vital resource for a recreation facility manager. Managers must take great care in hiring, training, and developing employees.

CHAPTER 9

Managing Equipment

LEARNING OBJECTIVES

At the completion of this chapter, you should be able to do the following:

1. Recognize the diverse types of recreation equipment and their purpose.
2. Examine the processes and procedures used in purchasing equipment.

Recreation facility equipment could be described as items that enhance, make functional, and complete the administrative and delivery operations of a recreation product. Anything in a facility that contributes to the administrative and delivery operations can be considered equipment. Managing and understanding equipment initially seems simple, but it can be logistically and technologically demanding. Specialized knowledge and procedures may be involved in purchasing and maintaining equipment. It would be virtually impossible to describe in one chapter all the unique equipment that exists in recreation facilities. This chapter provides an overview of the basics of facility equipment and general information on types of equipment.

It also includes practical information on purchasing equipment, receiving and distributing equipment, renting and leasing equipment, and using equipment in the recreational setting.

Overview of Recreation Facility Equipment

Any recreation professional with management responsibilities should have a basic understanding of equipment in order to realize its potential. This section outlines the key concepts of equipment diversity, complexity, use, and status to illustrate the scope of equipment in facilities.

Equipment Diversity

Every recreation facility has equipment that contributes to its core product and core product extensions. Each piece of equipment has a unique role within the delivery of the product. Equipment may serve a maintenance, protective, decorative, or administrative function. **Equipment diversity** simply means that equipment designed to help deliver a specific product can serve a variety of purposes. Recreation facility managers should seek out information about potential equipment and be knowledgeable of the many equipment options that exist.

Equipment Complexity

Some recreation facility equipment is easy to use and requires little instruction or preparation before use. However, some equipment can be complex and create greater responsibility for management. Complexity factors include the following:

- Special instructions
- Warranty concerns

- Start, operation, and shutdown procedures
- Maintenance requirements
- Storage
- Employee training
- Safety

Laws and standards could also influence equipment management. For example, an ice arena that uses an ammonia system requires a piece of equipment called a *compressor*. A compressor is so critical to the function of an ice arena that if it fails to operate, the facility will not be usable. Laws and codes related to the safe operation of an ammonia-based compressor system may require detection and alarm devices to warn customers and employees of unsafe conditions that may result from the compressor.

In addition, equipment delivery, distribution, installation, inventory, and maintenance all have to be monitored properly. When more complex equipment is used in a recreation facility, it requires recreation facility managers to be educated about potential problems or costs associated with use of that equipment.

Equipment Use

Each piece of equipment has a unique application toward enhancing product success. Use of certain recreation equipment could require training that ranges from basic to extensive. Some equipment even requires certification before use. For example, chemical-application equipment for outdoor facilities may require an employee to obtain a certification to apply the chemicals. Management must be sensitive to all facets of these requirements. Any equipment use can have potentially hazardous consequences for users and employees. Examples of equipment that can have harmful consequences for employees include mowing equipment, chain saws, and bucket trucks used to repair lights or other items off the ground. Organizations should take every precaution to warn users and employees of the potential dangers of and detailed instructions for using equipment. Some pieces of equipment have user manuals that provide instructions, descriptions, precautions, and safety measures. More technical equipment requires greater awareness of use and protection. Management must be aware of the use requirements of all facility equipment, making sure that proper training takes place and appropriate supervision is available at all times.

Equipment Status

Equipment status refers to the condition and availability of equipment for users. In determining the status of equipment, recreation facility managers must consider the following:

- Product warranties
- Preventive maintenance
- Projected life span
- Replacement schedules
- Repair factors

A compressor used at an ice arena is a complex piece of facility equipment that is regulated by laws and codes so that people are warned if unsafe conditions exist.
FatCamera/iStock/Getty Images

Equipment that is not functioning affects the ability to properly provide services to recreation facility users. Malfunctioning equipment could create inconveniences and unnecessary expenses. Management should have a system in place that provides information regarding the status and condition of equipment. Appropriate equipment management and maintenance practices (discussed in more detail in chapter 14) include the following:

- Assessing the status of equipment
- Scheduling equipment for and providing funding for preventive maintenance
- Scheduling appropriate repair or replacement

The concept of performing and documenting these practices is part of asset management (see chapter 3).

Types of Equipment

Equipment is anything in a facility that contributes to administrative and delivery operations. When considering details such as how much it costs and how it is used, recreation equipment can be categorized as permanent, expendable, and fixed (table 9.1).

- **Permanent equipment** is not affixed to the facility, but it is necessary in order for the facility to fulfill its intended purpose. It usually costs more than US$5,000, and it has a life expectancy at least 2 years. This type of equipment usually receives special maintenance con-

sideration, and it is managed carefully because of its initial cost to purchase and ongoing operational expenses. Permanent equipment includes specialty mowers, vehicles, golf carts, and scoreboards.

- **Expendable equipment** generally costs less than US$5,000, and it has a life expectancy of less than 2 years. Expendable equipment mostly relates to the delivery process, and it is used with the expectation that it may get lost, broken, or worn out. By some definitions, this equipment might also be called **supplies**. It includes items such as basketballs, softballs, and netting for sports, or furnishings such as beds, desks, tables, and chairs at tourism facilities.

- **Fixed equipment** is firmly attached as part of the facility structure, and it is usually installed during construction. Removal has a negative effect on the appearance and functionality of the facility. Fixed equipment includes efficiency systems (e.g., HVAC), fencing, athletic goals or posts (e.g., football, soccer, basketball), playground apparatuses, and restroom fixtures.

Equipment can also be classified in a more specialized manner. It can be categorized as part of efficiency systems, structural equipment, administrative equipment, delivery equipment, or maintenance equipment (table 9.2). These descriptions define equipment as it relates to its function within each type of equipment and recreation operations.

TABLE 9.1   TYPES OF EQUIPMENT IN RECREATION FACILITIES

Equipment type	Description	Examples
Permanent equipment	Not affixed to the facility but is necessary in order for the facility to fulfill its intended purpose; has a useful life of at least 2 years and usually costs more than US$5,000	Specialty mowers, certain fitness equipment (treadmills, weight machines), vehicles, scoreboards
Expendable equipment	Relates to the delivery process and is used with the expectation that it may get lost, broken, or worn out; has a useful life of less than 2 years and usually costs less than US$5,000	Athletic equipment (balls, bats, netting, etc.), chairs, desks, tables, uniforms
Fixed equipment	Attached as part of the facility structure and is usually installed during construction	Fencing, athletic goals or posts, playground apparatuses, restroom fixtures

TABLE 9.2   SPECIALIZED CLASSIFICATIONS OF EQUIPMENT IN RECREATION FACILITIES

Specialized classification	Description	Type of equipment	Examples
Efficiency systems equipment	Electrical, technological, and mechanical systems of equipment that support the overall use of the facility	Primarily permanent and fixed	HVAC systems, irrigation, servers, routers, Wi-Fi support, lighting
Structural equipment	Permanent, attached part of the facility structure; usually installed during the construction phase	Primarily fixed	Doors, windows, railings, permanent seating
Administrative equipment	Supports the administrative and executive operation of the facility	Primarily permanent and expendable	File cabinets, phones, cash registers, copy machine, computers
Product delivery equipment	Relates to the delivery of the product or service for which the facility was designed	Primarily permanent and expendable	Fitness facility's exercise equipment; esports facility's computer equipment

Efficiency systems are the electrical, technological, and mechanical systems of equipment that support the overall use of the facility. Efficiency equipment includes HVAC systems, irrigation, servers, routers, Wi-Fi support, and lighting systems. It maintains comfort, efficiency, and security for users and employees. It is installed during construction, and it requires technical ability to operate and maintain.

Structural equipment is a permanent, attached part of the facility structure. It is usually installed during construction, and it is included in the construction cost. It is not movable; if it were eliminated, it would negatively affect facility design and functionality. This category of equipment includes doors, windows, railings, permanent barriers, and permanent seating.

Every recreation facility has space and **administrative equipment** that supports the administrative and executive operation of the facility. Recreation facility users typically do not use administrative equipment unless they interact with the administration. Often this equipment takes on a sense of ownership among employees even though it belongs to the facility. It includes all computers, scanners, and printers; telephones; file cabinets; cash registers; and copy machines.

Each recreation facility has **product delivery equipment** that relates specifically to the delivery of the product for which the facility was designed. Employees use this equipment when providing services to customers, and users may operate it when using the recreation facility. Examples of product delivery equipment include the following:

- A fitness facility may provide weight-lifting or cardiorespiratory equipment for users.

- A golf course may provide golf carts, pull carts, rental clubs, or range balls for users.

- A white-water rafting company often provides rafts or canoes for participants.

A variety of maintenance equipment helps keep both recreation facilities and their equipment in proper working condition. Many types of maintenance equipment require qualified, capable personnel to operate them safely and properly. For such equipment, the necessary training may be provided in-house. Maintenance equipment includes lawn mowers, vehicles, chemical sprayers, fertilizer spreaders, floor cleaning equipment, and custodial equipment.

Rafts are product delivery equipment for a white-water rafting company.
tdub303/E+/Getty Images

A few other equipment items should be incorporated into the management process because they assist with the delivery of the core product and core product extensions. They include all forms of equipment that are planned, designed, and purchased to be used in the management of a recreation facility, such as the following:

- Supplies
- Keys
- Furniture
- Security equipment
- Fire protection equipment
- Decorative equipment
- Signage

Supplies are expendable items that are consumed during the production process. Examples include office supplies (e.g., paper, pencils, staples, paperclips, pens), cleaning products (e.g., toilet paper, paper towels, soap, trash bags), and similar items. They are generally used in administrative and delivery responsibilities to help present or support the delivery of a product, but they are not as costly as other forms of administrative equipment. Supplies require processes that are similar to other equipment when it comes to storage, inventory, stocking, and replacement.

Although keys and locking systems are not often thought of as equipment, they involve similar responsibilities as part of recreation facility management. All recreation facilities need to be secured or locked outside of business hours. It is also important that recreation facilities have key and locking systems in place during business hours to keep unwanted people out. The process or system for securing a facility can be very involved. (Options in key styles, systems, and sizes are discussed in detail in chapter 12.) Technology-supported equipment for securing recreation facilities include bar-coded cards and even fingerprint or other technical access options. Keys or cards require a system of control for distribution and inventory. They are distributed in a process that is similar to that for other equipment, including recording the person the key is assigned to, the date assigned, and the date returned (see figure 9.1). Keys should be subjected to regular inventory checks. Locking systems can also vary from those built into doors and gates to padlocks that are externally attached.

Furniture is another recreation facility item that generally involves the same planning and purchasing process as equipment. Furniture is permanent. It is purchased, inventoried, and distributed in a similar manner as all other equipment. It includes office desks and chairs, credenzas, conference tables and chairs, lounge chairs, sofas, coffee tables, end tables, and television equipment. Furniture often requires repair because of abuse, overuse, or parts that no longer work as intended.

Facility security requires **security equipment** that is in place to protect the employees and users as well as the facility and its equipment. Some examples include turnstiles, barriers, identification readers, video cameras and monitors, alarms, specialized exit doors, and metal-detection devices. Security equipment can be permanent or expendable.

Fire is the most common form of serious emergency or disruption in recreation facilities, and legal codes are in place specifically for fire protection. All recreation facilities must be designed, constructed, and maintained in such a way that they adhere to fire codes. To protect users and employees in the event of a fire, they must be prepared with fire protection equipment. Fire protection equipment includes smoke sensors, exit signs, sprinkler systems, fire hoses, fire extinguishers, and fire alarms. This protective equipment is assessed regularly and repaired or replaced as needed.

Decorative items make the recreation facility more aesthetically pleasing, adding to the appearance and pleasantness to help users and employees feel comfortable. These items can include window coverings, pictures, sculptures, displays, plants, and floral arrangements. Recreation facility managers should make these items a priority and maintain them as they do other expensive equipment.

Signage is another type of item not commonly recognized as equipment in a recreation facility. Items of this nature are planned, designed, purchased, and usually installed at the time of construction. Some examples of signage include facility directories, interactive touch screens, directional signs, arrows, floor and wall guides, individual area signs, and emergency signs. The signage style and content can be changed or replaced as facility areas take on new functions.

Purchasing Equipment

Appropriate equipment has to be purchased and placed in the recreation facility in order for the facility to fulfill its purpose. The timeline for purchasing equipment varies based on the type of equipment being purchased and the timeline for construction. Recreation facility managers should refer to the construction schedule, research how long it takes to get a piece of equipment delivered, and determine an appropriate timeline for purchasing the equipment. The process of purchasing equipment for a facility includes these steps:

1. Research
2. Purchase requisition
3. Bid process
4. Purchase order

Staff Key Checkout and Return Agreement

Checkout

Date_____

Staff checking out key _____   _____
                        Print   Signature

Staff receiving key_____   _____
                    Print   Signature

Check-in

Date_____

Staff checking in key _____   _____
                      Print   Signature

Staff returning key _____   _____
                     Print   Signature

From B. Beggs, R. Mull, M. Renneisen, and M. Mulvaney, 2024, Recreation Facility Management, 2nd ed. (Champaign, IL: Human Kinetics).

FIGURE 9.1   Key check-in and checkout form.

5. Shipping
6. Invoicing and payment
7. Warranty purchasing

This section provides a detailed description of each step.

Research

Equipment purchasing usually begins with a recreation facility manager providing a written description of need and interest that is based on sound rationale, or research. Research is a prepurchase action, and it is necessary for identifying the most appropriate equipment for the desired function and the best price. This process involves reviewing available options in terms of quality, durability, price, and payment. It also involves understanding the amount of time required for obtaining a piece of equipment.

Purchase Requisition

Once a piece of equipment has been identified through the research process, recreation facility managers must make a request to purchase the equipment. The preliminary request for obtaining equipment is called the **purchase requisition**, which is a written request to administration indicating a need for a particular piece of equipment. Employees usually complete a standard form that allows space for justification for the purchase (see figure 9.2). The form also

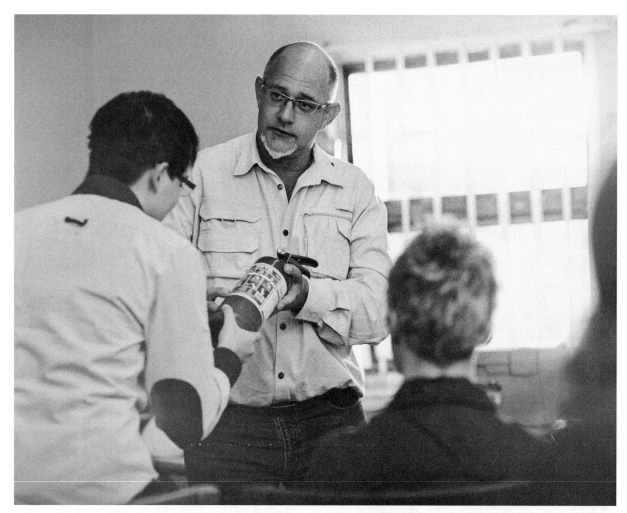

Training all staff how to use a fire extinguisher is crucial because fire is the most common form of serious emergency or disruption in recreation facilities.

Purchase Requisition

Location, facility, and program _____

Requested by _____ Date requested _____

Purchase justification _____

Vendor _____ Address _____

City, state _____ Zip code _____

Phone _____ Fax _____

Quantity	Unit	Description (type, size, model)	Unit price	Amount
			$	$
			$	$
			$	$
			$	$
			$	$
			$	$
			$	$
			Shipping/freight	$
			Total	$

Delivery to _____
_____
_____
_____

Approved by _____ Date _____

Other _____

From B. Beggs, R. Mull, M. Renneisen, and M. Mulvaney, 2024, Recreation Facility Management, 2nd ed. (Champaign, IL: Human Kinetics).

FIGURE 9.2 Purchase requisition form.

allows for specifications that include the type, size, model, cost, quality, and delivery timetable. They may list a recommended vendor who has provided assistance with the details of the purchase or has already submitted the most competitive price.

Bid Process

In some instances, a bid process is involved before a purchase can be made. The bid process allows vendors an equal opportunity to obtain the business of a recreation facility. The bid process entails the solicitation of price quotes, either formally or informally, from two or more vendors. A bid process is not required in all recreation facilities; some recreation facility managers can purchase items directly without having to solicit prices from vendors. A formal bidding process is usually required by public agencies, especially as the cost of equipment increases. Different agencies have different guidelines for when the formal bidding process must take place. On some occasions, private businesses use this process in order to obtain the best price. It's best for recreation facility managers to follow agency guidelines for the bid process.

Once all the details (specifications) are established, the request for bids is made available to prospective bidders and then the bid process begins. All information submitted by vendors remains confidential until the deadline for submittal. This process ensures fairness, eliminates favoritism, and stimulates competition to reduce pricing. A deadline is set, and a bid opening is announced so that all vendors may attend the bid opening to hear the outcome. The equipment order usually is awarded to the lowest and most responsive bidder. (See chapter 7 for more details on the bid process for contractors.)

Purchase Order

Once a vendor is selected, a formal written request is initiated to order the equipment and arrange for delivery. This form is called a **purchase order**, which can include quantity, size,

Playground Equipment Costs

How many children will use the playground equipment at one time? The answer to this question can help in determining an estimated budget for a playground. Playground budgets are typically around US$1,000 per child. A playground with 30 children (using the playground at the same time) would equate to about US$30,000. Approximately 50 to 60 percent of this cost will be for the equipment; about 30 percent will be associated with the installation costs, and 10 to 20 percent will be for site preparation and equipment shipping costs (GameTime, 2020). Clearly, the playground equipment itself represents a significant cost for the overall project!

color, model number, warranty information, delivery information and timetable, price, and method of shipping. It is a contract with the vendor that states the intent and understanding of the purchase. The vendor who receives this purchase order is expected to meet the specifications as presented and deliver the equipment in a timely fashion. A purchase order is used when purchasing equipment on an account or through a billing process. The equipment should be ordered well in advance, allowing ample time for shipping and receiving.

Shipping

Shipping and delivery should be included in the bid process. Time and place of delivery are important considerations. Equipment arriving at the wrong location can create additional work for delivery personnel. It may delay access to the equipment or even delay the opening of a new facility. Equipment could require additional arrangements for handling and installation; in particular, large or costly equipment, such as playground equipment or picnic tables, may need special attention.

Invoicing and Payment

Shortly after delivery, the vendor usually sends an invoice requesting payment. After the equipment is assessed to determine whether it has arrived undamaged and performs as intended, the payment process follows. This process can be as simple as writing a check or paying in cash or a more elaborate process that may take several weeks before a vendor receives full payment. Sometimes a percentage of the payment is withheld until the equipment is known to fulfill its intended use and performance requirements are met. Holding a percentage of payment under these terms is called *retainage*. Each recreation facility has its own process for completing a purchase transaction based on the accounting controls established by the administration.

Warranty Purchase

Another way to ensure that the equipment performs as it should is to purchase equipment that comes with a warranty. A warranty includes a period after the purchase where the vendor is responsible for replacing or repairing the equipment should it not function properly. In such instances, the manufacturer or a third party must repair or replace the equipment. Warranty arrangements are usually built into the purchasing arrangement, especially with expensive equipment. Other factors to consider when purchasing a dealer's or manufacturer's warranty include whether installation and training are provided, access to any parts that may be needed, and service or maintenance expectations until the expiration of the warranty.

Receiving and Distributing Equipment

Whereas shipping and delivery are the vendor's responsibility, receiving and distributing equipment is the responsibility of management. When the equipment is delivered, the facility manager accepts it while understanding that from the point of delivery forward, it will be difficult to return; this process is called *receiving*. Before officially receiving equipment, facility managers must be sure they got what they ordered both in quality and in quantity. Vendors can make mistakes in the shipping process, and the order should meet expectations as stated in the purchase order. Equipment orders also should be inspected for damage that may have occurred during shipping and handling. Equipment can be rejected and returned to the vendor at no cost if it was damaged during delivery or shipping. Management should not accept equipment that cannot be used or does not meet expectations.

Once the manager has received a piece of equipment, they must document the transaction and temporarily store the equipment before distributing it. Inventory is the process of recording the receipt and ownership of equipment. Through an inventory system, equipment arrival, condition, and status can be recorded and maintained. An inventory system should also include the following equipment information:

- Date received
- Cost
- Condition
- Quantity
- Identification number

A computerized equipment inventory system can help with the organization process. Many software- and application-based inventory management programs are designed for specific industries. Regardless of the specific program utilized, the equipment inventory and tracking system should, at a minimum, support the use of barcode labels and asset tags to track equipment. Many of these programs also include an inventory for tools and spare parts to provide the facility manager with quick access to parts replacement orders, which helps to avoid extended equipment downtimes.

Once it has been inventoried, the equipment will either be immediately distributed or temporarily stored. Sometimes equipment, particularly a specialty item such as a fitness monitor, requires arrangements for storing and protecting it until it is needed for use. When storing equipment, security measures to consider include proper lighting, locks, and inventory controls. Also, the storage environment could affect the equipment, so temperature and humidity are key considerations. In addition, size and shape of equipment could affect where items may be stored. Finally, prioritizing accessibility ensures that equipment can be easily distributed.

Space for equipment storage is critical. However, when designing a recreation facility or when additional space is needed for another purpose, equipment storage areas are usually the first to be eliminated. Before making decisions that affect allocation of space, facility managers should recognize the importance of adequate storage space for equipment.

It is especially important to make advance arrangements for delivery and installation of larger equipment, such as this playground equipment.
Jane Tyska/Digital First Media/East Bay Times via Getty Images

According to Krysiak (2022), the most popular equipment inventory and tracking software systems include the following:

- Aptien
- Asset Essentials
- Asset Panda
- AssetCloud
- AssetTiger
- Cheqroom
- EZOfficeInventory

Distribution of equipment to the appropriate employee or area should be linked to the inventory records and tracked annually or semiannually. Usually, some type of arrangement is made so that the user or employee accepts responsibility for proper use and care of the equipment. Management also may require training, experience, or certification before certain equipment is made available for use, such as in the instance of climbing equipment, certain aerobic and strength equipment, and equipment used for specialized maintenance.

Renting and Leasing Equipment

Sometimes facilities require equipment that the agency does not own or desire to purchase. In other situations, certain equipment may only be necessary for a short duration or to meet a specific need. The purchase of extremely specialized equipment may not be justifiable because of the expense involved. In this case, two options to consider are renting or leasing. For small recreation facilities, renting equipment is common because it requires few arrangements and usually minimal expense. Renting generally requires some paperwork, valid identification, a deposit (which is returned when the item is returned undamaged), and a rental fee.

Leasing equipment is an option to consider when equipment may be needed that is not available for rent or when the cost of the equipment is too great to consider purchasing in one payment. Usually, an equipment lease is for a designated period with a signed contract that stipulates the leasing agreement between parties. An advantage to leasing equipment is that it can be less expensive than a new purchase. In addition, most leases cover maintenance and insurance costs. Commonly leased or rented equipment includes the following:

- Tables and chairs
- Sound systems
- Specialty cleaning and maintenance equipment
- Temporary or portable playground equipment
- Concession equipment

Using Equipment

The purpose of having equipment is to make it available to employees to assist in delivering the product or to make it available to users. Most equipment is available for open use, such as fitness equipment or play structures. Facility employees are responsible for ensuring that equipment is in good operating condition and that it is used properly. Recreation facility managers should have systems in place for employees to monitor the condition of equipment and supervise its use.

When a fee is charged for using the equipment for a certain period, the transaction is considered a rental. Equipment rental systems should record the condition of the equipment at the time of checkout and when it is returned. Depending on the original cost of the equipment, the facility may require a deposit, which is returned when the equipment is returned undamaged. Checkout systems can have many rules, including advance reservations, user experience or training, damage responsibility, and proof of age or insurance. Facility staff can keep a master file as a record for equipment that has been checked out; this file includes the user's address, phone number, and email. Depending on the complexity of the checkout system, tracking software could be useful. The facility is responsible for providing equipment that functions as intended, and the user is responsible for using it properly. Both parties are responsible for meeting expectations established at distribution.

Summary

Equipment plays an important role in delivering the product in a recreation facility. Equipment includes many objects, and equipment needs are unique to each recreation facility. Therefore, recreation facility managers must prioritize learning about equipment. They should carefully consider the types of equipment needed for a facility and proper ways to purchase, distribute, use, and maintain that equipment to support the goal of creating optimal experiences for staff and users.

REVIEW QUESTIONS

1. Describe the characteristics of permanent equipment, and provide two examples.
2. Describe the characteristics of expendable equipment, and provide two examples.
3. List the steps associated with purchasing equipment for a recreation facility.
4. What is a purchase order, and when is it used?
5. Provide an example of when a recreation facility might choose to rent equipment rather than purchase it.

CASE STUDY

Missing Inventory at the State Park

A couple of months ago, you were hired as the park superintendent for Walnut Grove State Park. You actually began your career as an intern for Walnut Grove State Park nearly 10 years ago. Upon completing your internship, you remained in the state park system and accepted a position as an assistant site superintendent at Douglas Lake State Park. After working at Douglas Lake State Park for 5 years, the park superintendent position opened up at Walnut Grove. You applied, and were hired, for the position. You are excited to be back at Walnut Grove State Park. You look forward to working with the staff, and you have several ideas for making improvements to the park.

In addition to expanding the Walnut Grove State Park's trail system, replacing the furniture in the nature center, constructing a playground near the Pin Oak campsite, and establishing a wildlife restoration program, you also believe some of the park's policies and procedures need to be reviewed and, possibly, updated. Before pursuing these initiatives, you think it is important to meet with staff to get their input on the issues and opportunities within the park.

During a few of these staff meetings, a theme begins to emerge. In particular, you have heard from both the office and maintenance staff that during the past 5 years, a larger percentage of capital inventory (primarily permanent equipment) has been missing each year. The park's current definition of a capital inventory item (developed in 2020) is that "it is an item that costs in excess of US$500, is tangible, has a useful life exceeding 1 year, and is not materially reduced in value immediately by use." The park currently uses a paper-and-pencil and file folder inventory system that tracks the following:

1. Each piece of equipment
2. The date it was received and how many were purchased
3. The cost of the equipment

Closer inspection of the inventory system indicates the park is currently missing nearly 40 percent of the inventory.

Case Study Questions

1. What are your initial thoughts about the missing inventory? What are some possible factors that could have contributed to the missing inventory?
2. What are some strategies you could employ to improve the so-called missing inventory from happening in the future?
3. Would the utilization of an inventory and equipment tracking software system help Walnut Grove State Park? Why or why not?
4. Outline the steps you would take to purchase new furniture for the nature center.
5. Needs assessment data and park participation rates suggest the new Pin Oak Playground would be used by approximately 20 to 25 children at one time. What would you estimate the budget would be to construct a playground to support the anticipated participation and usage at Pin Oak?

Managing Finances

Chapter 7 discussed fiscal responsibility in terms of funding and the bid process for construction; this chapter addresses fiscal responsibility related to managing a facility. Although the basic principles that influence funding for private and public recreation facilities are different (as discussed in chapter 7), many of the concepts are similar. Since the turn of the century, increased expenses, including inflation, wages, and utilities, in addition to higher expectations from users, have made fiscal responsibilities more involved for recreation facility managers in the United States. Also, recreation facility managers need to be able to minimize the expenses associated with the deterioration of recreation facilities and equipment. Recreation administrators play a role in preparation, implementation, review, and control of all related funding sources as part of managing finances.

Expenses associated with recreation facilities fall into two categories: construction expenses and management expenses. Construction expenses for a recreation facility can be extensive, and they vary greatly. The planning, design, and construction expenses are overhead expenses that will exist for management as long as the facility exists. Planning and design costs are considered a part of the construction costs of a facility; although they are categorized as soft costs, they are typically included on part of the long-term financing package of a facility.

Management-related expenses are ongoing costs to operate, maintain, program, supervise, promote, and renovate a facility; they include salaries, supplies, equipment, marketing costs, and more.

It is not uncommon for users (and, to some extent, employees) to have little appreciation for the expenses associated with recreation facility construction, maintenance, and management. The expenses associated with product delivery in a recreation facility are much more involved than most people realize.

Expenses

Numerous expenses have an effect on recreation facility management. These expenses can be extensive, and they are greatly influenced by the success of the product in generating the income necessary to support management responsibilities. A high percentage of total recreation agency expenses revolves around facilities and their employees, maintenance, utilities, repair, and renovation expenses. Typ-ical recreation facility expenses can be broken down into two broad categories: structural expenses and support expenses.

Structural Expenses

The presence of a recreation facility as a structure creates **structural expenses**. These expenses are associated with maintaining or improving the physical structure of the facility, which can include repair, renovation, and retrofitting. They can also include loan or mortgage, depreciation, tax, reserve, and insurance expenses.

Repairing, Renovating, and Retrofitting

Over time, facilities and equipment deteriorate, no longer fulfilling their original purpose. When they have reached this point, expenses are incurred to keep them functional. Typical repairs to recreation facilities include repairing broken doors, windows, locks, and other equipment or spaces. Sometimes facilities undergo a complete renovation that modifies the original layout and design purpose. Some renovation projects include expanding existing facilities, creating greater recreation production space, and expanding administrative areas or other in-demand spaces. Retrofitting also modifies a structure by adding new or more modern systems to a facility. For example, a facility might add new plumbing or retrofit the facility with a new security system. All of these situations require proper planning and budgeting (as discussed in chapter 4).

Developing a schedule of capital outlays associated with the facility can be helpful in organizing expenditures as well as supporting both the short- and longer-term financial planning efforts. A schedule of capital outlays (see table 10.1) provides the facility manager with a list of each major piece of equipment and capital purchase within the facility. The schedule of capital outlays for each item the facility owns should be considered as part of a long-term—at least 5 years—financial plan to forecast spending. A multiyear budget plan provides a picture of what the facility's financial status is likely to be. With a preview of where possible shortfalls or surpluses may occur, plans can be changed well enough in advance to avoid crises. Planning is especially important for capital improvements such as facility renovations, major maintenance to facilities (e.g., pools, community centers), repairs to vehicles and other equipment, or facility expansion efforts. Planning ahead allows a facility manager to identify future needs, provide long-term financing for those projects, and better coordinate any future growth.

Loan or Mortgage

One of the greatest ongoing expenses for recreation facilities is the monthly or quarterly loan or mortgage payment for construction or purchase of a facility. This arrangement can be in the form of a bank loan or bond payment; it commits management to repay the debt for the purchase or construction of a recreation facility over a predetermined period. The payment includes the cost of purchase or construction plus interest, which varies according to market conditions. The predetermined period for satisfying the obligations of the loan is usually between 10 and 30 years. One of a facility manager's responsibilities is generating enough income to meet this expense.

Bonds

Arguably the most popular way public agencies finance the construction of a new facility is through the issuance of debt. The issuance of debt is typically in the form of bond financing. In general, bond financing is a form of long-term financing in which the public agency pledges its full faith and credit (taxing power) to repay the debt over a specified period. A general obligation bond, repaid over a 20- to 30-year period is the most common type of bond utilized by public agencies.

Reviewing and understanding the facility's schedule of outstanding bonded debt can be important in assessing financial obligations and future expenses. A schedule of outstanding bonded debt typically includes a description of all debt issued by the agency, the purposes for which the debt was issued, the issue and

TABLE 10.1   SAMPLE SCHEDULE OF CAPITAL OUTLAYS

Item	Estimated cost (in US$)	Less trade-in of existing equipment (in US$)	Net cost
Turf lawn mower	$18,000	−$3,000	$15,000
Oak Park sidewalk improvements	$8,000	−$0	$8,000
Computer and registration software	$10,000	−$0	$10,000
Pool pump and filtration system	$15,000	−$3,000	$12,000
Storage shed construction in West Park	$32,000	−$0	$32,000
Placement/establishment of 15 interactive digital monitors in community center	$54,000	−$0	$54,000

Facility renovations can be extensive and are considered a structural expense.
Stanislaw Tokarski - Fotolia

maturity dates, the amounts outstanding at the end of the current fiscal year (the same amount that will be outstanding at the beginning of the first day of the upcoming fiscal year), and the amounts of principal and interest payments that must be made during the upcoming fiscal year (see table 10.2).

TABLE 10.2   SAMPLE SCHEDULE OF OUTSTANDING BONDED DEBT

Issue	Purpose	Amount issued (in US$)	Issue date	Maturity date	Amount outstanding
Limited-tax general obligation bond	Construction of concessions building	$150,000	08/01/02	08/01/32	$45,000
Limited-tax general obligation bond	Acquisition of land for splash pad and park development	$550,000	11/01/11	11/01/31	$277,345
Limited-tax general obligation bond	Acquisition and construction of parks and recreation facilities: Outdoor sports complex	$450,000	02/15/19	12/01/39	$420,000
Limited-tax general obligation bond	Construction of disc golf course	$150,000	08/15/00	07/01/25	$135,000

The schedule of outstanding debt can also help the facility manager outline the amount of principal and interest that will be required for the next year as well as for subsequent fiscal years (until the bonds are retired).

Depreciation

As soon as a recreation facility or piece of equipment is purchased, it begins to lose value. The decrease in value of recreation facilities and equipment by a certain percentage each year is called **depreciation**. The amount depreciated can be recorded as an expense for tax purposes.

Taxes

A major difference between public and private agencies is that public recreation facilities may receive tax support for construction or operation. Another significant difference is that public recreation facilities may be exempt from paying certain taxes on income generated from a product or from paying property taxes. A private facility can be at a serious disadvantage when in direct competition with a public recreation facility that benefits from tax-supported income in addition to not paying taxes because of its public status. In the private sector, the responsibility of paying taxes must be factored into operational expenses. Recreation professionals, particularly in the private sector, are encouraged to seek advice from accountants or financial planners in order to maximize tax deductions and correctly prepare facility tax returns.

Reserve Fund

In order to protect against spending from the daily operational cash flow, a reserve is created as an expense management category. A reserve fund is a sound fiscal practice of setting aside money for potential facility problems. Unexpected situations include vandalism, weather damage, fire, and equipment breakdowns. These situations vary greatly from facility to facility; they are often unpredictable and sometimes unavoidable.

Insurance

Competent recreation administrators or facility managers budget for adequate insurance coverage. Insurance should cover potential losses for management with a policy that defines the conditions for coverage. Several categories of insurance may be necessary at any given rec-

reation facility; in fact, a typical facility may need all these forms:

- Liability insurance
- Accident insurance
- Workers' compensation
- Property damage or theft insurance coverage

Not all problems can be anticipated. Insurance is key to covering costs related to unexpected problems, such as user or employee injuries or fatalities, equipment damage, or destruction of facilities. Management should purchase adequate insurance to cover these and other potential problems.

Support Expenses

Another category of expenses relates to supporting the operation of the facility. These support expenses include costs associated with employees, maintenance, equipment, utilities, and contractual services.

Employees

In a recreation facility, one of the highest expenses is labor costs. People who keep facilities and equipment functional require expenses such as the following:

- Salary
- Hourly wages
- Payroll taxes
- Benefits
- Training
- Professional development

Employee compensation is important to understand and manage because it can easily account for 50 to 80 percent of the budget. (Employees are discussed in more detail in chapter 11.)

Maintenance

Allocating adequate funds to support maintenance is paramount. Some recreation agencies consider facility maintenance to be one of the most important aspects of presenting their product. Proper maintenance of recreation facilities and equipment is not only a serious consideration for the comfort and efficiency of product delivery; it also contributes to facility and equipment longevity by preventing unnecessary wear and tear. Maintenance expenditures should be analyzed, including routine, nonroutine, and preventive maintenance. (These categories are discussed in more detail in chapter 14.) Maintenance costs include both building and ground maintenance tasks, such as performing custodial services, lubricating machines, painting, fixing broken equipment, repairing fencing, repairing lighting, maintaining turf, and removing snow and leaves.

Equipment

A primary responsibility of recreation administrators is budgeting funds for the purchase and care of all equipment. An extensive array of items, objects, and equipment within a recreation facility can vary greatly in cost. Equipment expenses include not only the initial purchase of the equipment but also ongoing costs to keep it functioning as intended. Some equipment can be extremely expensive. An ice resurfacing machine (commonly known as a Zamboni) may cost US$80,000 to US$99,000. Certain types of mowing equipment for golf courses may cost between US$35,000 and US$50,000. Annual maintenance-related costs associated with the type of equipment can be 5 to 10 percent of the original purchase price. If equipment is not functioning, it can cause frustration for facility users and employees. As with maintenance costs, recreation administrators and facility managers must allocate adequate funds to keep equipment functioning properly.

Developing an equipment replacement plan can aid the facility manager in determining (a) the equipment that needs to be replaced and (b) the amount of money to set aside to support these replacements. Creating an equipment replacement plan requires the following steps:

Snow removal is one of the numerous potential maintenance costs involved in managing a recreation facility.
Kevin Sabitus/Getty Images

1. *Determine a budget.* Review previous capital and operating budgets as well as equipment purchase records to determine the average costs associated with equipment repairs and replacements.

2. *Review the manufacturer's life span.* Use the manufacturer's projected life span for the equipment as a reference for determining a replacement timeline.

3. *Prepare financial reports on the equipment.* The costs associated with repairs and other expenses should be itemized for each piece of equipment.

4. *Gauge the need for replacement.* Develop a need scorecard for each piece of equipment (indicating critical, moderate, low need), and rank them to create a prioritized list of all equipment within the facility.

5. *Determine replacement costs.* Collect quotes for those pieces of equipment that received higher rankings (see itemized financial reports). Categorize the costs into levels (low, moderate, high).

6. *Score equipment priorities.* Review the need and cost data obtained in steps 3 and 4. Move equipment that received high need and low cost to the highest priority, and move those with low need and high cost to the low end of the priority list.

7. *Develop a plan.* Spend time writing and implementing an equipment plan. Share the plan with staff and stakeholders to generate awareness and excitement for the plan.

8. *Perform an ongoing evaluation.* Regularly monitor the replacement plan, and update it as needed (Trotter, 2019).

Utilities

Virtually no recreation facility can function without access to water and electricity, and sometimes other utilities. Each utility represents an expense category that usually has to be paid for on a monthly basis. Recreation facility managers must maximize the use of a facility and scrutinize the utilities to minimize their cost where possible. Recreation facility managers can compare past usage information to help monitor costs and identify savings through more efficient use. Computer software can assist in minimizing the costs associated with utilities by analyzing usage and determining the most efficient way to operate.

Additional utility expenses include provisions for communication devices commonly used at recreation facilities. This equipment can come in many forms, including telephones (both land lines and cellular phones), two-way radios, computers, and cable or satellite television. Monitoring expenses so that employees do not abuse these services and create unnecessary expenses presents an additional challenge for managers.

Contractual Services

Another facility expense category is outside contractual services that assist with facets of the facility that cannot be managed internally. Typical contractual services include repairs to HVAC systems, janitorial services, garbage removal, landscaping, design assistance, consultant assistance, and snow removal. Usually, these arrangements are made with interested vendors; they bid for the job, and the contract goes to the lowest and most responsive bidder. Outside contractual services (also called **outsourcing**) can be an important means of meeting recreation facility needs. Contractual

CHECK IT OUT
How Much to Set Aside?

How much money should be set aside each year for equipment replacement? According to industry benchmark data (see Trotter, 2019), facilities should allocate about 3 percent of the annual operating budget for equipment replacement.

service expenses should be planned, negotiated, and agreed upon with careful attention to the need for outside assistance and the costs of providing the service.

Income

For a facility to be viable, it must generate income. Income generation is critical to the success of recreation facility managers in delivering the core product to the user. Many decisions regarding the delivery of a recreation product focus on pricing the core product and core product extensions and the ability for those products to generate income. This income is categorized, classified, applied, and analyzed carefully to meet monthly, quarterly, and annual expenses.

Income generated is categorized as gross income or net income. **Gross income** is the total amount of money generated over a specified time; **net income** is the remaining funds after all expenses (including taxes) have been paid. Net income is also termed *profit*, which is the primary source of revenue for private recreation entities.

Income sources for recreation facilities can be complex and diverse. A number of income sources exist for facilities, depending on their classification as for-profit or nonprofit organizations. Sources of income can include fees and charges, rentals, donations, investors, investments, sponsorship, and tax support.

Fees and Charges

Many ways of collecting income through fees and charges relate to the purpose of the recreation facility and the desire for users to access a product. Fees and charges can come from the following sources:

User fees and charges are a major source of income for recreation facilities.

- Ticket sales
- User fees
- Membership fees
- Retail outlets

The amount of the fee is based on direct expenses resulting from the delivery of the product in the recreation facility. These expenses may include construction, mortgage, personnel, supplies, maintenance, utilities, and overhead costs.

Market factors also influence fees and charges. The simple business principle of supply and demand affects the ability of recreation facilities to charge more for certain products. If the existence, appearance, and service quality of a recreation facility are in demand, the facility can charge higher fees and thus generate greater income. The condition of a recreation facility in relation to its ability to generate income should never be underestimated. The amount of income deemed adequate is based on the mission of the agency in addition to its classification as a for-profit or nonprofit facility.

Programming Revenue

For many facilities, a significant portion of revenue is obtained through the programs and events that occur within the facility. The amount of revenue generated from a facility's programs and events is often linked to the number of programs and events offered as well as the cost recovery framework adopted by the facility or agency. Many agencies develop cost recovery categories that include varying cost recovery levels for each category. For instance, an agency may develop a cost recovery framework that includes a category of programs with targeted cost recovery levels of 0 percent (i.e., 100% subsidized). On the other end of the cost recovery framework might be an enterprise category with targeted cost recovery levels of +100% (i.e., 0% subsidized with surplus revenue generated). The facility's programs and events would then be assigned a cost recovery category based on their type, purpose, and target market, and a fee structure would be established based on the targeted cost recovery level.

Rentals

Some recreation facilities may rent space or equipment to generate income. Renting is an option when interest exists to use space or equipment and customers are willing to pay a rental fee. Recreation facilities that often provide rental opportunities include park pavilions, public pools, community-center meeting rooms, banquet halls, and athletic facilities. The rental cost to the customer varies according to what is being rented, the going rate for such a rental, and whether an agency is public, private, or nonprofit.

Donations

Many recreation agencies create an interest in and image of their facility that results in an opportunity for donations. If a recreation agency appeals to a community, particularly if it provides services for young people, financial support through donations may be an option. It is especially the case in public or nonprofit settings such as local schools, park and recreation departments, and other organizations where public interest (rather than making a profit) is central to the mission of the agency. Donations can also offer tax advantages to the donor, which presents an even better opportunity for those who can afford it to extend their financial support.

Donations can also be given in the form of in-kind gifts (also discussed in chapter 7) for recreation facility projects. When an interested party places a monetary value on a donated asset, intangible item, labor, or service supplied for a recreation facility project and receives a tax advantage in exchange, it is considered an in-kind gift. Some facility programs and equipment needs can depend partially or entirely on donations for support.

Investors

An individual or group of individuals with adequate financial resources, or investors, can provide funds for a recreation facility project in the hope of eventually receiving a dividend on their investment. Investors have a percentage interest in a for-profit recreation facility. For example, private golf courses (particularly high-end courses) may have one or more investors who provide financial resources for the construction and continuing management of the facility. A return on the investment greatly depends on the profitability of the facility.

Investments

Recreation administrators can invest excess cash in marketable securities to generate income. Certain recreation facilities may generate excess income beyond expenses during a fiscal year. In these cases, it may be possible to invest the excess cash rather than let it sit idle in a checking or savings account. Investments can be short term or long term, and they can be in the form of interest on bonds and notes or dividends on shares of stock. Investment strategies should be investigated thoroughly before implementation. Financial consultants can be a valuable resource; administrators should consider meeting with them before choosing to invest funds to produce additional income.

Sponsorships

Since 2000, recreation agencies have received a steady increase in support of their financial responsibilities through **sponsorships**. This form of fiscal support usually results from cooperative interests between two agencies who are both looking to gain something from the sponsorship. Usually, a sponsor offers financial resources to help with expenses in exchange for access to advertising space or promotional exposure. Income from sponsorships can be used to defray operational expenses, complete facility projects, satisfy equipment needs, or pay for employee expenses. Sponsorship income is not usually part of the annual budget unless it is a long-term arrangement that can be counted on year after year. Many professional sport facilities generate significant income from sponsorship arrangements. In these cases, a facility may give naming rights to the sponsor in exchange for a long-term (often 10+ years) commitment. Recreational facilities have also been successful on a smaller scale, recruiting sponsors for items such as score-

Usually a sponsor offers financial resources to help with facility expenses in exchange for advertising space at the sponsored facility.

© Human Kinetics

boards or wall space in ice arenas or indoor soccer facilities.

Tax Support

Most public recreation agencies depend on some type of income from local, state, or federal taxes. The general funding philosophy of tax-supported facilities is that they serve the extensive needs of the community. These facilities include public schools, correctional settings, military bases, colleges and universities, and other municipal settings. Although most local public recreation agencies would be unable to operate without tax support, currently even professional sport venues rely more and more on tax support to finance construction. Tax support is not only important in construction; for public recreation agencies, it is essential for programming and daily operations. Tax support is highly political, and it evolves from political leadership that can persuade government entities to fund a public need. In most instances, residents of a taxing jurisdiction decide on increasing income through taxes by voting on a **referendum** in an election.

Fiscal Practices

Managing facility finances involves many more details and responsibilities than what has been presented in this material. In addition to having an understanding of expenses and sources of income in delivering the product, recreation facility managers must also organize and present systems for managing finances. The most common fiscal practices for managing finances include budgeting, accounting, and cost analysis. These complex tools should be understood in great detail before starting a career in leisure services. This section offers a brief overview of what is taught in classes for managing recreation finances.

Budgeting

Budgeting can be described as a systematic effort to project all income and expenses for a given length of time. Most recreation agencies budget in yearly cycles, submitting budget projections to the administration 3 to 6 months before a new fiscal year. The fiscal year is a 12-month cycle, which does not necessarily correspond with a calendar year, during which a recreation agency determines and monitors its financial condition. A financial forecast (budget) is critical because it allows for financial planning and anticipation of income and expenses for a fiscal year. Reviewing historical expense and income information when preparing budget requests, calculating inflation or other cost increases, and projecting anticipated revenue for the coming fiscal year is a common budgeting practice. Each facility has its own way of administering its budget. Recreation professionals must understand their role in the budgeting process. Two of the more common budgets utilized in recreation facilities include program budgets and performance-based budgeting.

Program Budgets

Program budgets are generally developed at the program level. These budgets are developed for each program area within the recreation facility. Typically, the facility's programming staff initiate the program budgets before combining and sharing them with the facility administrator(s). Program budgets require these three steps for recreation professionals:

1. Have a clear understanding of fees and charges associated with the program. These fees and charges should also be aligned with the facility's cost recovery framework (see Programming Revenue).

2. Guided by the information collected in step 1, develop a program budget for each program. A detailed list of the projected expenditures and revenues should be provided. In some instances, a description of the program area(s) may also be needed.

3. Develop a clear justification of the program's expenditures. Information pertaining to the need and intended use of the specific expenditure should be prepared.

Performance-Based Budgeting

Performance-based budgeting is based on the notion of using previous performance, or evidence, in the allocation of future funds. Performance-based budgeting is also called outcome-based budgeting, results-based budgeting, or priority-based budgeting. Performance-based budgeting focuses on areas or services within a recreation facility that are demonstrating success toward measurable goals. Those areas making measurable progress receive heavier investments or budgetary allocations. For instance, a recreation facility may notice an increase in rentals and participation in their adventure recreation services (e.g., climbing wall, excursions, trips). Responding to this increase, the facility may invest additional funds within their adventure recreation services area in the following year's operating budget.

At its core, performance-based budgeting is used to do the following:

- Promote accountability across various departments, divisions, or areas within the facility.
- Guide resource allocation that is grounded in results.
- Improve budget transparency (allocation decisions are based on previously established measurable goals).
- Promote a goal-oriented funding model.

Accounting

Recreation professionals must be aware of their accountability for funds generated at their facilities. Part of the budget process requires ongoing record keeping of income and expenditures, or *accounting*. Accounting practices are usually done by an accountant or fiscal officer in the organization, and they involve generating reports on a monthly, quarterly, and annual basis. These reports reflect specific income and expense categories. They are often compared with data from the previous year, other time frames within the year, or a predetermined budget that outlines management expectations. Administrators should regularly review these records from the accounting system or accountant. They should strive to keep facility expenditures within the budget to maintain income levels.

Cost Analysis

Cost analysis is the process of comparing and analyzing costs associated with delivering a recreation product in an effort to determine the true costs of delivering the product and applying ways to save money. Expenses have a direct correlation to the profitability of a recreation operation. Facility managers use the accounting systems and budget to see what costs are, but cost analysis goes beyond this step. It involves comparing data from previous years, finding trends, benchmarking income and expenses against similar recreation operations, reviewing internal and external influences, comparing vendors, and analyzing dramatic changes to thoroughly evaluate the costs of an operation. Ultimately, the cost analysis results in recommendations to reduce operational costs and provide savings.

Summary

Recreation facility managers must be aware of a wide variety of details in relation to managing finances. These responsibilities are integral to the viability of a recreation facility and can ultimately determine its success or failure. Competent recreation professionals acquaint themselves with their fiscal responsibilities and attend to these responsibilities on a daily basis.

REVIEW QUESTIONS

1. Define structural and support expenses. Provide two examples of each expense.
2. List three types of income for recreation facilities.
3. Why is it important for a recreation facility to have an equipment replacement plan?
4. Define investment income and sponsorship income.

CASE STUDY

To Golf or Not to Golf; That Is the Question

The Dyersville Recreation Department is a public agency that owns and operates three golf courses:

- *Walnut Point Golf Course* is a 9-hole, par 3 course catering primarily to recreational players. No tournaments are held at this course. It is located on the south side of the community. While this course is the most popular, it is the oldest and in need of the most repairs. No tournaments are held at this course, and the pro shop does not have any space for rentals or dining area. In addition to the maintenance staff that maintains all three courses, the course has a full-time golf pro and a part-time manager who works in the pro shop.

- *Fox Run Golf Course* is the newest course; it was constructed 10 years ago. It is an 18-hole course that can host tournaments and large outings, and it supports competitive play. The high school state golf championships were held at this site 2 years ago. Because of its competitive layout, the course does not receive as many golfers as Walnut Point or Cardinal Golf Course. The pro shop contains a spacious area for retail, a bar and grill area, and space for small meetings and gatherings. The course is located on the north side of town, and it employs two full-time golf pros and five part-time managers and other staff.

- *Cardinal Golf Course* is an 18-hole course located in the middle of town. Arguably the most scenic course, Cardinal has mature trees and beautiful landscaping, and golfers rate it as the best maintained course among the three courses. Golfers play more rounds of golf here than at Fox Run, but they play fewer here than at Walnut Point. The course exists primarily for recreational golfers, but it does host a few tournaments, leagues, and other fundraising outings. The clubhouse is larger than the one at Walnut Point; it supports a pro shop and a bar and grill, but it does not have a meeting area. Cardinal is also in need of a new roof for the clubhouse, new flooring surfaces in the clubhouse and bar and grill area, as well as a few other repairs are expected in the next 5 years. The course employs one full-time golf pro and five part-time managers or staff members.

According to director Bill Slagle, the grim realities of Dyersville's golf climate could lead Dyersville leaders to contemplate closing one of these courses. The discussion came as part of the city's annual golf focus group meeting at Fox Run Golf Course Banquet Facility. Golfers filled the room to hear a presentation of the status of the golf program and provide their input about its future.

"What's golf going to look like in the future? Are we going to be able to sustain golf the way it looks today?" Slagle said after the meeting. "If you looked at the national trends and the trends in Dyersville, you would think probably not." City Council President Jack Kenny said no decision had been made, despite ongoing rumors about a potential closure. "I think we're going to talk about financing in the future," he said. "Whether that entails closing a course or not, I don't know. I think we've got budget questions coming up, and we'll see." Overall, financial data presented a bleak picture. Despite cuts to staff and other expenses and continued efforts to diversify offerings, the courses continue to lose money. Golf's decline in the city is a reflection of national trends; according to Slagle, course closings have outpaced openings for the ninth consecutive year. In addition, the game generally isn't drawing young people.

During the focus group meeting, one golfer asked directly about the possibility of closing Fox Run Golf Course and what could be done with the banquet facility in that scenario. "I don't think any decisions have been made, but it will be a topic of discussion going forward: how we're going to create a sustainable future," Slagle answered. "The reality of it is that we're going to have to talk about that. We have to talk about sustaining an entire park system." Speaking after the meeting, Slagle said that on paper, Fox Run Golf Course would appear to be the most logical option if city leaders did decide to close a course. However, it is also the newest and arguably has the most potential. "Given the participation numbers, given all the indicators that you would use in making a decision, I think we need to be extremely careful before making a hasty decision based on numbers alone," he said. "I think we'll have to talk all the way through that and determine what the future would be."

The three golf courses together will see an expected 68,266 rounds this fiscal year, according to the city's presentation. That represents a dramatic decrease from 190,000 rounds 20 years ago. Golf is just one of the city's offerings, some of which attract more people. Pantherville Zoo drew 108,000 visitors last year, and the Dyersville Indoor Sports Center has had 110,000 visits. Overlook Adventure Miniature Golf course had more than 36,000 rounds. Officials report that the city's youth baseball and soccer offerings are also very popular. Slow income growth, population decline, and competition from more than 100 courses within a two hour drive have all taken their toll on the city.

Several golfers suggested some type of discount, such as cheaper rates in the afternoons or lower cart fees to encourage more play. This year, in an effort to draw more players, district officials did reduce fees at Fox Run Golf Course to US$29 for 18 holes with a cart. Officials said that while rounds at Cardinal increased, play at the other two courses decreased. The numbers also were not high enough at Fox Run Golf Course to make up the discount. "You have to understand that when you reduce prices, you have to increase volume," Slagle said. "Right now, in our environment, we're really not increasing volume. You also have to figure out how to finance the repairs, renovations, and updates needed at two of these courses. We have to decide if it is worth the investment and how to fund it."

John Davis, a former candidate for the city council, suggested that the city pursue more competitive tournaments and add video gambling. The latter comment drew some chuckles from the crowd. "OK, we laugh, but gambling machines are very popular, and they bring in a lot of revenue," Davis said. Wes Hillen, assistant men's golf coach for Iona University and one of the event's younger attendees, said he didn't think gambling or small price adjustments were the answer. Instead, he said the city must find ways to attract young adults, who could eventually raise their children with the sport. "When it comes down to it, it really is the younger kids," he said. Steve Myrvold, 72, has been playing golf in Dyersville since he was 12. He typically plays at Walnut Point, and he said most golfers choose that course or Cardinal.

Case Study Questions

1. As the director, would you eliminate one of the courses? If so, which one?

2. Two of the three courses are in need of significant repairs. What are at least two ways to possibly fund these renovations?

3. What are some alternative revenue sources that could be pursued at these courses?

CHAPTER 11

Managing Employees

LEARNING OBJECTIVES

At the completion of this chapter, you should be able to do the following:

1. Define the concept of staffing.
2. Explain job classification and its role in staffing.
3. Recognize the difference between the job description and the job announcement.
4. Examine the steps involved in the hiring process.
5. Recognize what a recreation administrator can do to create a good work environment.

The most important aspect of recreation facility management is selecting and assigning the appropriate people to perform the functions associated with delivering a product to users. The work environment often leads to relationships between the employee and employer that can last for many years. Recreation facilities require a diverse array of employees to fulfill their various responsibilities. The nature of recreation facility work includes a wide range of jobs, such as supervising facilities, training users on new activities, and marketing programs and services as well as performing simple maintenance tasks, coordinating space and equipment, and managing finances. Finding people to fulfill all of these tasks makes the process of recruiting, hiring, and training recreation facility employees extremely important.

The process of recruiting and hiring employees to fulfill job obligations associated with the delivery of a product at a recreation agency is called *staffing*. It is vital to have employees with appropriate skills assigned to positions that maximize their expertise in performing the functions of the position. Recruiting and hiring employees is a detailed process that requires a considerable amount of planning. However, before recreation facility managers can actively recruit employees, they must determine precisely what type of position they need to hire for and where that position fits within the organization. This process is called *job classification.*

Job Classification

The process of **job classification** places a value on each job that is required to fulfill the mission and goals of a recreation agency. This value determines the compensation and responsibilities associated with each position. Collectively, this process results in a hierarchical compilation of the job title and responsibilities of each job that is necessary to deliver the products of a specific recreation organization.

Recreation organizations vary in complexity and diversity. Some may not require a great deal of attention to managing the various jobs required for operations. However, all jobs in the facility need to be thoroughly analyzed, and that content needs to be organized into a meaningful structure. Some jobs require many technical skills; other positions require few, if any, such skills. As noted earlier, the first step in managing employees is to understand all the job responsibilities needed for operating the recreation agency and to classify all jobs. Job classification results in a clear identification of the responsibilities, duties, complexity, and scope of each position to determine an appropriate job title. An organizational chart is a common way to classify and organize positions (see figure 11.1).

Job classification also should reflect compensation for performing the job. All employees should be compensated fairly according to their responsibilities. Benefits such as health insurance, vacation and sick leave, and retirement

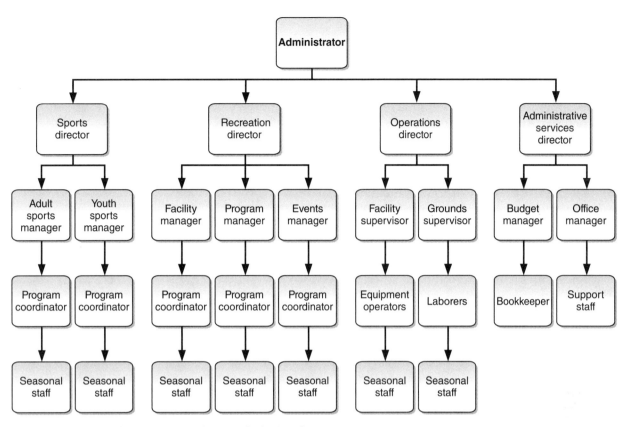

FIGURE 11.1 Sample organizational chart of job classifications.

plans are usually part of the compensation package, and they are critical to recruiting and retaining qualified staff. Usually, human resources management professionals establish compensation packages. However, recreation administrators bring expertise regarding the unique personnel requirements of the agency that can influence the compensation offered to potential employees.

Job Analysis

Once the job classification has been determined, the next step is to complete a job analysis. The job analysis is a process of gathering data about what individuals do in their jobs. The job analysis typically involves the following steps:

1. Identify the specific job to be reviewed. Understanding the specific position and hierarchy within the organization is the first step in this process.

2. Create a list of participants or staff to be involved in the job analysis process: A recommended approach is to involve all levels of staff in the process.

3. Review existing records and documentation to help with the job analysis process. Possible documents to review include organizational charts, similar job descriptions from other agencies, and other planning-related resources.

4. Determine the specific data collection method. Typical data collection methods include interviews of incumbents and supervisors, questionnaires, completion of task analyses, observations, or a combination of methods.

5. Implement the data collection method: Complete the process of collecting data as determined in the previous step.

6. Review and organize the data collected: The review of the job analysis data will lead to the development of a formalized job description for each position.

Job Description

Derived from the job analysis, the **job description** is a detailed document that includes all the responsibilities of the position. This information must be present to get the attention of prospective employees and also to eliminate unqualified applicants. A job description (see figure 11.2) includes the specific job area, its placement in the organization, and its responsibilities. This formal way of communicating job responsibilities to potential employees should be given detailed attention. Job descriptions also should be reviewed and updated regularly to reflect the addition or subtraction of responsibilities. Ultimately, the job description can serve as a contract between management and the employee. The job description could include the following information:

- Job title
- Job identification information (agency-related information, department, who job title reports to, job classification, etc.)
- Summary of the position
- Job domains and tasks
- Job specifications (required qualifications, working conditions, physical demands, etc.)
- Disclaimers

In addition, the job description is used during the performance evaluation (described later in this chapter).

Vacation leave may be one part of a benefit package that recreation facility managers offer their employees.
Jose Luis Pelaez Inc/DigitalVision/Getty Images

FUSION WELLNESS CENTER

Job Description

Title: Maintenance Supervisor—Facilities
Classification: Exempt
Reports To: Division Manager—Facilities
Job Summary: To plan and supervise building and facility management. Coordinate inventory control and inspection programs.

Domain: Personnel Management

Task Statements:

- Assist in recruiting, hiring and training staff
- Assist in managing and evaluating staff
- Provide ongoing direction, foresight and motivation to staff
- Provide technical resources and coaching to staff
- Document and address disciplinary issues with staff
- Prepare for and conduct staff meetings/trainings as needed
- Develop and monitor staff schedule
- Submit payroll information accurately and in a timely manner
- Adhere to and enforce staff compliance with organizational policies and procedures, and the strategic plan
- Ensure that employees are provided necessary training in usage of tools, equipment, machinery and personal protective equipment

Domain: Financial Management

Task Statements:

- Assist in preparing and monitoring budget
- Recommend purchase supplies, materials and equipment
- Accurately prepare purchase orders, check requests, requisitions and other financial paperwork

Domain: Administration/Organizational Planning

Task Statements:

- Establish and monitor goals and objectives
- Serve appointed committee assignments
- Attend staff meetings
- Attend workshops and seminars to develop professional growth and knowledge
- Be available for flexible work schedule, including evenings and weekends
- Assist in crew work schedule development in absence of Division Managers
- Direct annual cooperative purchase program
- Maintain current employee information in regards to the Parks
- Maintenance Management System (PMMS) records

FIGURE 11.2   Example job description.

Who to Include in the Job Analysis

Who should be involved in completing the job analyses for an organization? A recommended strategy is to include the incumbent (person currently in the job) and their supervisor in the job analysis for that particular job title. Including both the incumbent and the supervisor in this process allows both parties the opportunity to share their thoughts on the primary responsibilities associated with the position. In addition, this process encourages discussions on any discrepancies in their perspectives, facilitating a more open and transparent understanding of the position.

Recruitment and Selection Procedures

Once the job has been classified and analyzed and the job description has been written, the recruitment and selection processes can take place. At this point, recreation administrators and recreation facility managers should be aware of the regulations that affect the selection of prospective employees. Human resources departments and legal counsel for agencies can provide information regarding hiring practices. In addition, a number of handbooks and other resources are available online, such as the website Free Advice. Recreation administrators must base hiring decisions on the competency of the person applying for the position while also taking into consideration laws, ethics, and practicalities. For example, it is illegal to discriminate against an applicant based on race, sex, or age. Human resources professionals can advise managers on the various laws and regulations that apply to the hiring procedures of the organization.

The responsibilities of many positions require recreation facility managers to make difficult choices in hiring applicants. Applicants will have to display a variety of talents, skills, and abilities. The basic steps of the hiring process should remain the same for every position in the organization. However, the challenge of selecting the best candidate for the position becomes more demanding as the responsibilities of the position increase. The steps in the recruitment and selection processes include the following:

1. Job announcement
2. Application screening
3. Interview
4. Assessment exercises
5. Job offer

Job Announcement

The first step in recruiting potential candidates for recreation facility positions is to make a formal **job announcement** (see figure 11.3), also called a *job posting*, that can be used to create candidate awareness of the opportunity. This announcement could be advertised in local newspapers, in professional journals, on job search websites, and on facility bulletin boards where potential candidates might look for job opportunities. Another resource for promoting employment opportunities is referrals from existing employees. Some organizations even provide referral bonuses to employees, especially for high-level positions that are more difficult to fill. Often, current employees have friends or other professional contacts who may be interested in a job opportunity. If a position is at a higher level in an organization, it is common to make the job announcement available to a larger pool of candidates. Lower- and entry-level positions tend to be advertised on a regional or local scale, but they can also be posted to a national audience.

Every job announcement should include the deadline for submitting applications as well as the contact information (person and address) for sending the completed application. The job announcement should also specify what documents to include in the application. Some agencies require that a résumé be sent with a formal application letter. It is also common for agencies to require letters of reference or an application form, which can be obtained from the hiring agency.

SPLASH COVE HARBOR & RECREATION INDOOR PARK

Program Manager - Aquatics, Teens and Special Events

Job Title: Program Manager - Aquatics, Teens and Special Events
Agency: Splash Cove Harbor & Recreation Indoor Park
Salary/Pay Information: $70,000 - $85,000
Essential Duties: The Program Manager – Aquatics, Teens and Special Events position will work in conjunction with the Splash Store Supervisor, Recreation Supervisor, and Childcare Supervisor to ensure that all customers of Splash Cove Harbor and Recreation Indoor Park obtain a complete and well-rounded health and wellness experience. In particular, the Program Manager – Aquatics, Teens and Special Events will:

- Manage all personnel within the aquatics division. Expected tasks include: recruitment, hiring, training, evaluation, and general management.
- Responsible for financial management of aquatics division including the purchasing of supplies, materials, and equipment as well as supervision of the department's budget.
- Engage in organizational planning that is representative of the aquatics department's needs.
- Provide effective communications and customer service through cooperative relationships and oral/written communication.
- Ensure safe work habits and proper (accident/incident) reporting procedures within the aquatics division.
- Provide aquatics programming and guidance to program instructors.
- Market the aquatics division and its programming/services.

Educational & Experience Requirements: Candidates must meet the following educational and experience requirements:

- Bachelor's degree in Leisure Studies from a National Recreation & Park Association (NRPA) accredited university or related field with 2-3 years progressively responsible experience in programming
- Valid Illinois driver's license
- Current CPR and AED certification
- Current Certified Aquatic Facility Operator or Pool Operator with 1-year aquatic facility operations experience
- Proficient in computer word-processing and spreadsheet software applications
- Good problem-solving, presentation, communication and organizational skills

Physical Requirements: Candidates must be able to perform the following:

- Visual and hearing acuity to perform job-related functions
- Ability to lift up to 50 pounds
- Ability to talk, kneel, stoop, bend, grasp and reach
- Ability to spend up to 50% of work time standing and/or walking
- Ability to spend up to 40% of work time reading and/or working at computer terminal
- Ability to spend up to 10% of work time performing physical labor

Closing Date to Apply: Open until December 15th
How to Apply: Interested applicants can apply online at www.splashcoveharborrecreationpark.com/applications. Applicants will be required to submit a resume, cover letter, and three professional references.
Contact: Contact Ron Warren at rwarren@schrpark.com or via phone at (123) 234-5678 with any questions.
Benefits: Full-time employees of the Splash Cove Harbor & Recreation Indoor Park receive medical, vision, dental insurance and a healthy retirement program. Discounted use of Splash Cove Harbor & Recreation Indoor Park services are also provided to all employees.
Splash Cove Harbor & Recreation Indoor Park is an Equal Opportunity, Affirmative Action employer. Minorities, women, veterans and individuals with disabilities are encouraged to apply.

FIGURE 11.3   Example job announcement.

Application Screening

Once the application deadline has passed, recreation facility managers must review the submitted application materials to determine which candidates to interview. Assessment of application materials should be as objective as possible, and it should be based on the selection criteria and specific screening requirements listed in the job description. Some applicants can be eliminated from the pool by simply not meeting the minimum requirements of the job. For example, an applicant may not have the educational background or the years of experience required for a higher-level position. These applicants should be removed from further consideration.

It's not uncommon to receive a large number of applications for some recreation positions. Depending on the position, a multistep process may be necessary to narrow the field of applicants to a manageable number to interview in person. Recreation facility administrators and managers may choose to conduct phone interviews to narrow the field. This process also eliminates travel expenses for candidates or the agency. Ideally, the initial screening process should lead to a ranking of the top three to five candidates for the position. These candidates should be advanced to the next step in the hiring process, the interview.

Interview

A common practice for interviewing the top three to five candidates is a face-to-face interview with the supervising staff member.

Occasionally, a team of staff members including the supervisor, potential coworkers, a lower-ranking worker, and possibly a member of the board or administration may participate in a group interview. Another potential member of the interview team is a representative of facility users. Whatever process is chosen for the interview, it is critical that the interview questions be carefully prepared in advance. The questions should be crafted to determine if the candidates possess the most important competencies required of the position. In determining questions to ask, it is necessary to avoid questions that are illegal. It is not legal to ask personal questions that are not related to the position, such as questions about religion, marital status, and family status. If there is uncertainty about the legality of a question, the interviewer or interview team should refer to legal council within the organization or the U.S. Equal Employment Opportunity Commission (EEOC).

Each candidate should be asked the same questions; the responses to each question should be noted and later compared when selecting the most qualified candidate. This consistent process ensures that each candidate is given a fair and equal opportunity to earn the position.

Assessment Exercises

Depending on the complexity of the position, assessment exercises may also be included in the interview process. For example, if the position requires the applicant to be compe-

---

CHECK IT OUT

Providing Candidates With the Good, the Bad, and Even the Ugly?

A goal of the recruitment process should be to provide candidates with an overview of all aspects of the job. In fact, agencies should share both the desirable and less-than-desirable aspects. Known as providing a realistic job preview (RJP), agencies should inform candidates about the positive and potentially negative aspects of the job experience. Open and transparent conversations can go a long way in creating an environment of honesty, and they reduce quick voluntary turnover from staff who are hired only to be shocked by the unexpected aspects of the job. Agencies can provide an RJP through a tour of the workplace and working areas, and a frank discussion of all aspects of the job.

tent in writing, it is appropriate to include a writing exercise. Positions that require certain maintenance skills, such as operating heavy equipment, may include a field exercise to have the applicants display that particular maintenance skill. Positions that require extensive use of certain computer software may include an exercise that tests the use of that software. These exercises complement the face-to-face interview in an effort to fully assess the competencies of each candidate.

Following the conclusion of the interview and assessment exercises, candidates should be ranked in sequential order based on how they meet the competencies of the position. In a situation where two or more candidates are ranked closely, the recreation facility manager may wish to conduct another round of interviews. At the conclusion of the interview process, the appropriate agency representative should make a job offer to the candidate and negotiate the details of the offer. The job offer should provide the potential employee with an offer of a starting salary and benefit package. The benefit package could include medical and dental benefits, vacation days, personal days, and any other work-related benefits such as the use of a vehicle, compensation time, or an expense account. The prospective employee may wish to negotiate the salary and benefit package. Once it has been agreed upon, the agency may require that the prospective employee sign a contract verifying the agreed amount.

On-the-Job Training

The final stage of the staffing process involves conveying the job responsibilities directly to the new employee. The employee may have a certain level of experience and education that influences the orientation required. The orientation process may include giving the new employee a tour of the facility, meeting a variety of agency staff members, training on the use of computers and other equipment, and reviewing personnel manuals to acquaint the employee with the benefits and policies of the agency. Even if an employee has been hired from within the organization, it is still important to provide a complete orientation for the new position.

Every recreation agency has unique training circumstances and conditions that need to be brought to the employee's attention; therefore, the new employee usually meets with various agency staff, including the administration, supervisors, and coworkers. In addition, workshops and retreats may be offered to review both general and specific job responsibilities. It is important for recreation administrators to convey the specific responsibilities of a job and ensure that the employee understands them. Training is especially important in technical areas of recreation facilities, including the operation of recreation equipment, such as weight machines or machinery; maintenance; and facility scheduling practices, including software programs.

For a training program to be successful, a genuine commitment from the trainers and all levels of management is essential. This commitment requires the active participation of recreation facility managers throughout the entire training program. It is important for managers to motivate the trainees, to understand the trainees' knowledge and experience, and to set goals so that they have something to reach for. Managers and supervisors need to be involved in training in case any misinformation is provided or the new employee does not interpret information or responsibilities correctly. Managers closely involved in the training of a new employee can make corrections immediately before further problems arise. The goal of any training program should be to provide new employees with every opportunity possible to succeed in their new position.

Performance Appraisal

Recreation facility managers must monitor, assess, motivate, and offer constructive input to employees. Essentially, they have to assess employee performance and correct the areas where expectations are not being met. One of the ways to correct or compliment employee performance is through a performance appraisal. A **performance appraisal** (see figure 11.4) is a formal process resulting from the observation and evaluation of an employee in an effort to assess how the employee is meeting expectations.

Recreation facility managers should reinforce positive job performance when an employee is performing job responsibilities as expected or is exceeding expectations. When expectations are not being met, managers should provide direction and help to keep employees focused on their responsibilities. When employee performance consistently fails to meet expectations, termination may be necessary. Certain procedures should be followed when considering termination of an employee. Procedures may include the following:

- Written or verbal evaluations
- Counseling
- Written assessment
- Written warnings

These procedures should be followed until the situation leaves no alternative but to terminate the employee. The termination of an employee

Professional Performance Appraisal

Employee Name _____ Title _____
Supervisor Name _____ Title _____
Department _____ Review Period _____

Ratings

Consistently outstanding: Consistently exceeds expectations and demonstrates high performance on this responsibility.
Excellent: Exceeds expectations; work is typically above required performance on this responsibility.
Good: Meets expectations; satisfactory performance on this responsibility with some room for improvement.
Improvement required: Below expectations; needs significant improvement on this responsibility.
Not applicable: Too new in position to demonstrate competence or category not applicable to this position *(rarely relevant)*.

BEHAVIOR RATINGS

Behavior	Rating	Examples of observed behaviors
Teamwork		
Customer service		
Judgment and decisiveness		
Planning and prioritizing		
Initiative		
Open-mindedness and adaptability		
Communicating effectively		

Supporting comments _____
_____
_____
_____
_____
_____

JOB-SPECIFIC RATINGS

Responsibility or goal	Rating	Examples of observed behaviors

Supporting comments _____
_____
_____
_____
_____
_____
_____

SUMMARY

Areas of strength	Areas for development
•	•
•	•
•	•
•	•

Overall rating _____
Supporting comments _____
_____
_____
Employee comments _____
_____
_____
_____
_____

Employee signature _____ Date _____
(to acknowledge receipt)
Supervisor signature _____ Date _____
Second level signature _____ Date _____

FIGURE 11.4 Sample professional performance appraisal.

is a difficult process for both the supervisor and the employee, which reinforces the importance of a thorough and thoughtful hiring process that results in selecting the best candidate for a particular position. The termination of an employee often indicates that the hiring process was flawed.

An employee grievance procedure should be in place to allow employees to express their concerns. This process provides for external review of the employee's performance and also a review of the employee's supervisor. To address these types of concerns, managers can be provided specific personnel and human resource management training.

Types of Employees

Often, recreation facility managers underestimate how much is involved in keeping a facility at its optimal level of operation. Recreation facility managers have to supervise a wide variety of employees in order to keep a facility operating efficiently. Broadly, recreation facility employees are described as either internal or external.

Internal Employees

Certain roles and responsibilities can be fulfilled as part of the in-house (internal) staffing operation. In these cases, the job function is directly influenced by administrative operations. Internal employees can be identified in four general categories: administrative, supervisory, specialized, and maintenance or operations.

Administrative Employees

Administrative employees represent the executive level of an organization. The highest-level person may be the chief executive officer (CEO) in the private sector or the administrator or director in the public and nonprofit sectors. This person's role is to make all decisions that affect the mission and vision of the organization. Depending on the complexity and size of the recreational facility, this person may or may not be involved in its day-to-day operational decisions. All other employees ultimately report to this person.

Usually, a representative of the owner or administration is in charge of daily facility operations; this person is the recreation facility manager. Recreation facility managers may need years of experience and specific certifications or degrees in order to perform their responsibilities. They are in charge of employees, budgeting, office management, and all other responsibilities that support the administration of the facility. These professionals should be trained, experienced, and capable of overseeing all facets of recreation facility management. In more complex facilities, additional managers may be in charge of certain areas. For example, a resort hotel may have a front-desk operations manager, a food-service manager, a housekeeping manager, a retail manager, and a concierge manager.

Supervisory Employees

The person responsible for reviewing the work of one or more subordinate employees is called a **supervisor**. In some organizations, this person may also be called a *coordinator* or *foreman*. Supervisors have full responsibility for the employees in their area and accept the responsibility for accomplishing the tasks that recreation administrators assign them. Supervisors are representatives of the administration, and they are often held responsible for their employees' performance. They have an important influence on control, motivation, and quality of the job performed.

Specialized Employees

A variety of job functions in recreation facilities require specialized employees (specialists) who have received training to assist in delivery of the recreation product. In terms of recreation and leisure activities, specialists may be skilled in aquatics, therapeutic recreation, and fitness, among others. Specialized recreation certifications include the following:

A therapeutic recreation specialist will require extensive training in their field before they can become certified to do their job.

FG Trade/E+/Getty Images

- Certified Park and Recreation Professional (CPRP)
- Certified Park and Recreation Executive (CPRE)
- Certified Therapeutic Recreation Specialist (CTRS)
- Aquatics Facility Operator (AFO)
- Certified Playground Safety Inspector (CPSI)
- American College of Sports Medicine (ACSM) Exercise Specialist
- American Council on Exercise (ACE) Group Exercise Instructor

Certifications usually have specific requirements that a person must meet before they can even take a certification exam. For example, a person may be able to sit for the CPRP if they meet the following requirements (found at NRPA.org):

- They have just received, or they are about to receive a bachelor's degree from a program accredited by the NRPA Council on Accreditation.
- They have a bachelor's degree from any institution in recreation, park resources, or leisure services, and they also have no less than 1 year of full-time experience in the field.
- They have a bachelor's degree in a major other than recreation, park resources, or leisure services, and they also have no fewer than 3 years of full-time experience in the field.
- They have a high school diploma or equivalent, and they have 5 years of full-time experience in the field.

Certified Park and Recreation Professional (CPRP)

Did you know that there are nearly 7,000 Certified Park and Recreation Professionals (CPRPs) in the United States?

A specialist can also be an employee with training who assists in keeping the facility operational. Areas of responsibility that require this type of specialist include plumbing, electrical systems, mechanical systems, horticulture, motorized equipment maintenance, graphic design, and event planning. These positions may be full-time commitments and have a designated physical location within the agency that houses their particular function. Separate physical areas for these functions are especially prevalent for hotels, resorts, convention centers, and other large recreational facilities.

Maintenance or Operations Employees

Maintenance or operations employees consist of skilled, semiskilled, and nonskilled employees. The maintenance process may only include regular cleaning, upkeep, and minor repairs that can be done by nonskilled or semiskilled employees. Specialized tasks, such as plumbing or welding, require the expertise of a skilled employee. The size and classification system of the agency dictate the number of maintenance employees needed. As the agency increases in size, maintenance responsibilities become greater and more specialized.

In addition, the more a facility is used, the greater the maintenance responsibility becomes. Imagine an indoor sport facility where a basketball game is played one day, followed by a concert the next night, followed by a convention or ice hockey game the next day. This type of multiuse recreation facility may require leadership for coordinating maintenance-related functions in a timely fashion to facilitate the numerous uses of the facility. Janitorial services, minor repairs, event setup and takedown, and leaf and snow removal can be so extensive that maintenance efforts at some recreation facilities can be very demanding for just one person to handle. Maintenance responsibilities can require several types of employees, including janitors as well the types of maintenance employees mentioned earlier.

Today's recreation facility users place a high value on pleasant, comfortable, and properly functioning environments. Facility maintenance employees have a significant impact on creating this environment. The work of these employees helps create the image of a recreation facility.

External Employees

Many functions in the recreation environment are accomplished by outside (external) companies or people. The use of external resources to accomplish a task is called **outsourcing**. This option is often exercised when a recreation organization is relatively small. Outsourcing can be a viable option when the agency cannot afford to have a full-time staff person for a particular facility need. It provides an effective, cost-efficient means of addressing a specific and sometimes infrequent organization responsibility. External employees can include management professionals, field experts, vendors, and volunteers.

When recreation facility managers decide to outsource a job, they often use a formal written agreement, or contract. A contract can protect both parties and ensure that the recreation administrator's expectations are met. These contractual relationships may be specific to each job assigned to an outside source. For example, an ice arena may have a contractual arrangement with a vendor who specializes in cooling repairs. This agreement should stipulate how to contact the vendor's maintenance representative during operational hours or after hours, how soon the vendor will respond to a call from the recreation facility manager, how much the vendor charges per hour, and when the contract expires.

Management Professionals

Other types of management professionals may be required to be part of the administration and delivery of a product. Many revenue-producing facilities have large budgets and generate significant revenue. Examples of these recreation facilities include water parks, professional sport stadiums, and hotels and resorts with recreation amenities. Even smaller organizations may generate enough revenue to warrant considering assistance from outside accountants and other financial consultants.

The inherent risk for accidents, injuries, or other legal concerns in recreation facilities creates the possibility of lawsuits. In addition, contracts with employees or vendors often need to be professionally and legally prepared. These situations necessitate professional assistance from a lawyer.

Some recreation production efforts may require the availability of a member of the medical profession. A large special event, such as a fireworks show, national track and field meet, softball tournament, or aquatic event may warrant on-site medical staff. These outside resources could include trainers, nurses, emergency medical technicians (EMTs), and physicians.

Some outdoor recreation facilities require the assistance of horticulturists or landscape architects. Horticulturists or landscape architects are often important resources for park and recreation agencies, colleges and universities, and hotels and resorts, where the outside appearance and natural landscape of the facility need to be presented in an appealing fashion.

Finally, in almost every recreation facility development project, consultants are necessary to conduct feasibility studies. In addition, as discussed in chapter 6, the design of a recreation facility almost always requires a professional architect. In some cases, these professionals could be placed on a retainer and paid an annual fee so that they are available as needed.

Field Experts

Much like the specialists who are hired and trained within an agency, the facility may need to hire external field experts to respond to certain problems. Field experts may have a trade that is necessary to keep the facility operational. For example, plumbers, electricians, tree surgeons, general contractors, or laborers can provide expert assistance for specific tasks.

Recreation facility managers should research the expertise or certification of outside specialists to make sure they are qualified to complete the necessary task. In some instances, their fees may be higher if they have attained a certain level of education or certification. Outside experts who are insured to protect themselves and the work they do may also charge a higher fee. Recreation administrators should make sure that any work done by an outside expert is clearly specified and documented.

Vendors

Outside companies usually provide a product (e.g., fertilizer, concessions, or sport supplies) or a service (e.g., mowing, snow removal, or uniform laundering). These outside companies, or **vendors**, endeavor to create an ongoing relationship with recreation facility managers. A vendor may or may not have a warranty responsibility for the product or service they provide. However, it is in the best interest of the vendor to provide a quality product or service in order to maintain a positive relationship and generate continued business with the recreation agency. This ongoing relationship can result in the vendor providing assistance to the organization in the form of advertising or sponsorships or offering accelerated delivery or discounts on products in an effort to maintain a good working relationship with the recreation facility manager. Vendors can be a valuable resource. The relationship between management and vendors should be nurtured to benefit agency operations.

Volunteers

Although not technically an agency employee, volunteers represent another external workforce that is beneficial to the delivery of services at a recreation agency. Many municipal or nonprofit recreation organizations use volunteers to meet a variety of needs. The role of volunteers can be sophisticated or basic. In either case, volunteers help fulfill production responsibilities as well as facility needs. Volunteers typically fill these types of roles:

- Planting trees
- Mowing grass
- Painting rooms
- Controlling crowds
- Serving food
- Coaching youth sport teams
- Ushering art events
- Serving as docents in a museum
- Supervising youth sport leagues
- Working backstage for theatrical productions

Using volunteers can offset the cost and supplement the work of employees while also creating a positive impression of the organization. If volunteers are an important component of an organization, their recruitment, training, and retention is a critical management task. Recreation facility managers can recruit volunteers from a broad cross section of any community. University and college communities can attract student volunteers to encourage service learning and to fulfill class requirements. Schools may encourage students to volunteer for the benefit of the community and to teach long-term volunteerism. Recreation facility users are also a good volunteer resource. In addition, retired workers are often interested in volunteering for a variety of recreation-related needs, and they may have the time and experience to manage numerous responsibilities.

Recognition should also be an important part of working with volunteers. Recognizing volunteers for their contributions to the facility and agency is an important way to communicate appreciation and promote retention. The recognition can be informal or formal.

Recreation facility managers have many opportunities to use volunteers to supplement the work of their paid employees.

Jose Luis Pelaez Inc/DigitalVision/Getty Images

Common volunteer recognition activities include the following:

- Inclusion and recognition in reports
- Dinners or banquets to recognize the volunteers for their efforts
- Awards
- Publicity or recognition in meetings
- Gifts
- Other tangible expressions of appreciation

Work Environment

Employees perform best when they are in a comfortable and safe work environment. Recreation administrators are responsible for creating a safe and appropriate environment for employees to meet their obligations without stress resulting from the workplace condition.

Work assignments should be planned, organized, and presented to employees with full understanding of the conditions of the environment to which they are assigned. Employees in an unpleasant work environment are not as productive as those who are comfortable. However, some work environments cannot always be comfortable and safe because of the nature of the work. Employers can help to minimize discomfort even when they cannot completely eliminate it, such as in these cases:

- Many outdoor maintenance tasks expose employees to extreme weather. Providing appropriate clothing and other safety items such as goggles, gloves, steel-toed shoes, and high-visibility uniforms can decrease employee injuries and increase productivity.
- Employees who lead fitness or dance classes are at risk for injury because

Outfitting outdoor recreation employees with the proper safety equipment to perform their job is crucial for providing them with a safe work environment.

of the physical nature of the position. Providing surfacing materials that minimize slips and falls as well as installing efficiency systems that adequately cool classroom space can reduce health risks. Providing continuing education opportunities for these employees to improve their technique can also create a safer environment.

- Employees who work in outdoor recreation spaces leading outdoor excursions are in positions where safety is vital. Providing the proper gear in terms of footwear, ropes, and helmets as well as spending the time to make sure the outdoor space has as few risks as possible can help create a working environment where the employees feel safe.

Even office employees should be provided with conditions conducive to increased productivity and decreased risk of injury. Appropriate lighting, comfortable and ergonomically engineered office chairs and computer accessories, and hands-free phone accessories can minimize eye strain, neck strain, carpel tunnel syndrome, and other common office-related injuries. Recreation facility managers must do everything they can to protect employees and provide them with a comfortable environment as they fulfill their responsibilities.

Professional Development

Professional development begins once the employee has been hired. Ensuring employees have the knowledge, skills, and abilities to be successful in their job not only is important for the organization but can also motivate employees and support employee retention. At a minimum, professional development should include two elements: onboarding, and ongoing training and development programming.

Onboarding

Sometimes called orientation, employee onboarding is an experience or series of experiences focused on acclimating the new employee to the agency. Onboarding serves as an opportunity for the agency to showcase its workplace culture, and it is typically customized based on the employee's position and desired objectives. Despite the varied nature of onboarding programs, each experience should strive to achieve at least the following short- and long-term goals:

- Socialize the employee to the workplace and job expectations.
- Save time by helping the employee acclimate to the job and workplace more rapidly.
- Provide a clear, realistic overview of the job.
- Reduce the new employee's anxiety about the new job and workplace.
- Help improve employee retention, reducing employee turnover.

Ongoing Training and Development Programming

The scope and responsibilities of recreation facility professionals frequently change due to internal and external shifts or trends. Ongoing training and development opportunities are critical to ensuring that employees keep pace with these changes. These opportunities can be in the form of in-service training opportunities, or professional conferences or workshops. Agencies may also consider job rotation, mentoring, or expanded job assignments to support employee growth and development of new skills. When appropriate, agencies can also encourage employees to pursue professional certifications. Many of these professional certifications require individuals to successfully pass a test to earn the certification, then complete ongoing training programs to maintain the certification.

Employee Relations

Employee relations can be one of the most important and challenging considerations in the recreation work environment. Fair and consistent treatment is critical in relating to employees. Policies, procedures, rules, and regulations should be clearly communicated in employee handbooks that all employees receive during job training. In addition, the ability to interact and negotiate with employees can be instrumental in maintaining employee morale and support. Recreation agencies can incorporate various activities into the work environment to create a positive atmosphere. They can organize social functions, staff retreats, and other activities that encourage a team environment. Recognizing employees for outstanding achievement or for years of service are other ways to enhance employee relations. Maintaining a professional and enjoyable work environment contributes to increased productivity and job satisfaction.

As discussed earlier in the chapter, a well-thought-out and thorough job description establishes a framework of responsibility that can help greatly with employee relations. Nevertheless, problems may arise that can lead to disagreements (grievances). When a grievance occurs, it must be formally addressed in a process that ensures a fair and objective review of the situation. Having a peaceful resolution to a grievance can help maintain a productive and efficient work environment.

Summary

Considered the most important aspect of a recreation facility manager's responsibilities, hiring and retaining staff begins with proper classification of jobs within the agency and detailing specific requirements in accurate job descriptions. These initial steps help ensure that agencies hire qualified employees. Once an employee has been hired, job training and performance appraisals must be conducted. In addition, the agency is responsible for providing a work environment that allows employees to be safe and productive, helping to deliver the core product to facility users efficiently and effectively.

REVIEW QUESTIONS

1. What is a job analysis, and how is it different from a job description?
2. What information should be included in a job description?
3. List the elements to include in a job announcement.
4. What are some strategies to use when an employee repeatedly fails to meet the expectations for the job?
5. Provide an example of an internal employee and an external employee.
6. What is onboarding, and why is it an important part of employee management?

CASE STUDY

Phone Etiquette Training

You are the facility manager of the South John Indoor Sports Center (SJISC). One of your employees is Susan Murray, the assistant facility manager of the SJISC. One of Susan's responsibilities is to supervise the membership sales staff. Overall, Susan likes supervising the membership sales staff at the SJISC. The membership sales staff at the SJISC are responsible for communicating with facility users, updating membership accounts and files, and providing information to facility users and other staff.

Typically, the membership sales staff Susan supervises answer questions about the SJISC's services, provide information about membership accounts, and modify files so that they are up to date and correct. The membership sales staff were hired only recently to handle the increasing volume of direct SJISC membership calls more efficiently by using the newly installed online customer information system.

Unfortunately, the planning for the new membership sales team was not done well. The online computer system was purchased and installed before the actual operations consultants were brought in to fully orient everyone on the new system. As a result, Susan was given the responsibility for getting the membership sales team up and running within 1 week. Susan had to make some quick personnel selections and take care of a lot of administrative details within a short period.

Now, three weeks after receiving the assignment, Susan feels quite a sense of accomplishment. She has been lucky that things have worked out as well as they have. In fact, the only thing Susan is concerned with now is the way in which the membership sales staff handle phone calls from customers who are interested in a membership at the SJISC.

Susan knows that good telephone etiquette is essential to the successful accomplishment of the membership sales team's mission, but staff use many different styles in answering the phone and do not follow basic rules. For example, the membership sales staff commonly neglect to put customers on hold while they search for information. When asking questions, they do not explain the reason for the inquiry; they do not verify information; and, at times, they may react defensively when they do not know the answers. These are the major—but not the only—things they do wrong.

Susan completed an informal training needs analysis, and she now knows that she must train the entire membership sales staff in techniques of proper phone etiquette. While the staff members do appear interested in participating in the training, no external training program is available to which Susan can send staff. Therefore, Susan must provide the training (and ongoing coaching) to the staff while they are on the job.

Susan has reached out to you for insight into how to best manage this situation.

Case Study Questions

1. Identify two or three strategies that you and Susan could use to help the membership sales staff improve their phone etiquette.

2. As Susan's supervisor, how would you appraise her performance in handling this situation?

3. Create or describe how you could evaluate the training.

PART IV

UTILIZATION OF RECREATION FACILITIES

Recreation facility managers should coordinate all of the activities that take place in a facility. Facility procedures and policies allow for effective and efficient use of the core product, ancillary spaces, and core product extensions in a facility in order to ensure a positive experience for users. By maintaining equipment, being aware of risks, preparing for disruptions, and responding appropriately to emergency situations, the recreation facility manager ensures that the facility is properly maintained and secure for users.

CHAPTER 12

Circulation, Safety, Control, and Security

LEARNING OBJECTIVES

At the completion of this chapter, you should be able to do the following:

1. Recognize the role of signage in circulation and control.
2. Explain how environmental conditions in a facility are related to safety.
3. Examine the concept of risk management.
4. Recognize the various internal and external forms of control in a facility.

Recreation facility managers must be aware of issues associated with user and employee behavior. From a management perspective, it is much easier to influence employees than users. Users create the greatest challenge for management because they can exhibit such a wide variety of behaviors while using a facility. In an effort to control user behavior, recreation facility managers must have systems in place to direct and monitor users in the facility. These systems include facility circulation, safety, control, and security.

User Circulation

In the early stages of any facility development project, especially the design phase, a great deal of attention is focused on the **circulation** of users throughout the facility. Whether it is an indoor or outdoor recreation facility, the ability for users to get from one place to another easily and safely is critical to the efficient utilization of a facility. In creating good facility circulation, the following concepts must be considered:

Located in West Lafayette, Indiana, the West Lafayette Wellness Center declared a Promise of Inclusion, which is evident in its amenities as well as its overall facility design. The amenities include the following:

- Gender-neutral, single-stall bathrooms, showers, and changing areas
- Multicultural toys in child play areas
- An elevator
- Innovative cardio equipment used in physical therapy
- Three ADA compliant entries into the pool as well as a water wheelchair

Planning for the West Lafayette Wellness Center began in 2016. The organization sought input from the public with a concentrated effort on obtaining feedback from accessibility advocates and groups that are typically underrepresented in the community. Guided by this input and the city's core values, a financial and community needs feasibility study was completed in 2017. One year later, the design phase of the West Lafayette Wellness Center began. It focused on universal design principles (see chapter 8) with a facility layout and amenities that would support safe and secure access for all.

Special attention was given to the potential barriers associated with specific design features as well as their effect on the circulation of user traffic. The design of gender-neutral spaces was a key element in the facility's design. For instance, an innovative restroom and locker room design concept featured more individualized, private areas for users, which contrasted with the traditional multiple-fixture restroom and locker room spaces that can present barriers for many individuals. The design team also recognized the need to orient and educate facility users on these unique spaces that challenged traditional design features.

In addition to signage, the design team used visual cues, or sight lines, to help users better recognize the *public* and *private* zones within the locker and restroom spaces. According to Ross and Fischer (2022), visual connections in spaces can support users' ease of movement, and they are central to safety and security in inclusive locker rooms and restrooms. These design principles resulted in the development of locker rooms and restroom spaces that were some of the first of their kind in the state of Indiana. In particular, the handwashing and locker area zones are considered *public* (as opposed to *private*); they include visible glass partitions with open views of the gym and aquatic center. The visible access to these areas also helps with security efforts in this area. In contrast, individual, full-length doors (replacing the traditional stall doors) are used in the *private* zones of these spaces, and they include access to showers and toilets.

Other principles of universal design have been applied throughout the facility. Many of these measures support a more secure and safe space for users, including an indoor space for child supervision, wider doors for sport wheelchairs, and a clear wayfinding navigation design within the facility. The careful and inclusive design of the West Lafayette Wellness Center is a welcoming space that strives to protect the privacy of its users while providing a safe and secure environment for all.

- Circulation areas
- Signage
- Comfort for efficiency and aesthetics

Circulation Areas

Recreation facility managers must coordinate the comprehensive space of a facility in terms of how users access various areas of it. In addition, each area of a facility relates to others in design and function, which affects facility management practices. Within every indoor or outdoor recreation facility, certain areas have the specific purpose of circulating users throughout the facility. These spaces usually include hallways, stairways, landings,

Some facilities are so large in size that more than one level of hallways, landings, sidewalks, and stairways may be necessary to accommodate user circulation.

Ezra Shaw/Getty Images

corridors, and pathways. Entrances, including atriums or lobbies, are additional areas that facilitate user access to a facility. Exterior circulation areas could include roads, sidewalks, trails, and paths that provide access to parking or other auxiliary components of a facility.

Some facilities have commodity and food-service outlets whose success can depend greatly on patterns of user circulation. Probably the most important area of any facility is its production space, where the core product and core product extensions are delivered. All of the previously mentioned areas should facilitate access to the primary product area in a smooth and functional fashion.

Signage

Fundamental to efficient circulation patterns in a recreation facility is a signage system to communicate information that allows ease of movement throughout the facility. Facility signs (discussed in chapters 8 and 9) create visibility of various destinations. Signage should have consistent colors, fonts, and sizes throughout the facility while also using those and other features (e.g., shape) to indicate contrast in spaces and encourage efficient circulation patterns. The location of signs in the facility is also important. A larger facility should have large signs and maps to assist users in moving through the facility.

Technology plays a significant role in supporting interactive and individualized experiences between the facility user and signage. Common features of technology-based signage include the following:

- Digital monitors with touch-screen features
- QR codes on signage to provide additional information about the site or experience

- Availability of free Wi-Fi within the facility that can share facility-related information to users when they access the service
- GIS data layering and mapping

Other circulation enhancements include color-coded lines on floors or walls that assist users in locating specific areas. Reception areas should also be appropriately located to provide information to users on how to find desired areas. In addition, facility employees facilitate circulation by assisting users as they travel from place to place. Sometimes, barriers and fences are strategically placed to influence direction and control access to areas.

Comfort for Efficiency and Aesthetics

A large part of circulation is creating a sense of comfort or satisfaction for people as they move around a recreation facility. Certain applications can maximize this effort, such as configurations or systems that incorporate designated lines to make waiting time more pleasant for users. Entertainment, including videos or television, murals, paintings, music, and landscaping, can be provided for users' enjoyment or distraction while they are moving or waiting. Where appropriate, seats should be available, especially if extensive waiting or delays are likely. These provisions are particularly important for older adult users. Some facilities may require coverings or awnings in order to shelter people from inclement weather or intense sun. Entrances and exits for a single area may need to be located in completely different areas to avoid congestion.

The best use of these elements can be seen in major theme parks and the techniques they use to enhance customer comfort. Lines for attractions are often intentionally configured to limit views of the line length. Television monitors are placed in many waiting areas or lines to entertain customers while they wait. Background music is also used to enhance the experience as users wait in lines. Additional comfort features include water misters, air-conditioning or heating, and structures intended to shelter users from inclement weather.

Safety

Recreation facility managers must ensure a safe environment for employees and users. This care involves sensitivity toward the well-being of facility users and employees. Managers must consider many factors in providing a safe environment, including the product, equipment, weather, design, and user attitudes and behavior. As they set out to provide a safe environment, managers should consider the following points:

- User age
- Activity participation
- Experience level
- User behavior
- Environmental conditions in specific areas

User Age

The age of facility users requires specific safety management practices. Ages may vary widely depending on the core product, and facility managers will have different degrees of responsibility depending on the age of the users. If the average facility user is between 18 and 65 years old, users are expected to be responsible for their actions. However, management practices require a heightened alertness when users are below age 18 or when parental supervision is not expected. Young people have limited life experience and cannot be expected to be fully responsible for their actions. They could behave inappropriately, be distracted, or simply do something that a mature person would not. On the other end of the spectrum, older-adult users, although more mature, may have reduced physical capacity and require assistance. Recreation facility managers must be aware of the ages of the people using the facility and take appropriate action.

Corner Captains and Safe Passage

Initiated in 2008, the Safe Passage program in San Francisco's Tenderloin neighborhood utilizes volunteer Corner Captains who stand along a designated route to provide assistance and a safe presence for children during their after-school commutes. At the height of the COVID-19 pandemic, Corner Captains also worked with the Tenderloin food pantry and assisted with grocery delivery. Safe Passage focuses its efforts on three pillars of safety: education, visibility, and engagement.

Activity Participation

Participation in any recreation activity comes with some inherent risk; therefore, observing activity participation is an important part of operating a facility. Depending on the core product, activity levels can vary greatly from nonstrenuous and casual to highly physical and competitive. Extreme levels of activity can create a dangerous environment by leading to significant fatigue, altercations between par-

ticipants, and other actions that could result in potential injury to facility users and employees. Recreation facility managers have the responsibility to care for users and employees and to be aware of their activity. Managers may require that employees be certified to administer first aid and cardiopulmonary resuscitation (CPR). They may also need to take action to modify any activity that may result in potential injury or jeopardize users' safety and well-being.

For extremely difficult activities that require a high level of experience, such as scuba diving, an elevated level of supervision is required.
dstephens/E+/Getty Images

Experience Level

All users and employees come to a facility with unique skills and abilities. Similar to age, experience can also influence management practices. The use of certain equipment or the delivery of certain products may require instruction before use. For example, it is common for fitness facilities to provide equipment orientation to new users. For more difficult activities, recreation facility managers could provide screening, testing, or certification for people to attain the appropriate license or experience before using a product. For example, it is common for people who are interested in scuba diving to complete a basic level of training before attempting a dive in uncontrolled conditions.

On the other hand, user knowledge of the specific recreation activity could be expected for less-difficult activities, with managers only required to observe users or employees in a supervisory role. This difference in experience levels will influence employee assignments for product delivery.

User Behavior

Facility users come with a variety of interests, attitudes, and capacity to control their behavior. Although most users are responsible, sometimes events occur that result in altered behavior, creating a negative situation. For example, participants competing against each other in an adult softball program may get into a verbal or physical confrontation after a hard slide to break up a double play. Although this type of behavior cannot be completely anticipated, management should be prepared to address these kinds of situations and any potential conflict that may result from user interactions.

Users' interests vary, and each user expects a different experience from a facility. For example, some users view trails in a park system as an escape to nature and a tranquil and peaceful experience. However, others use the trails for intense experiences such as mountain biking. If these users access the same areas at the same time, conflicts may arise. It is important to address these differences in behavior through rules and policies that are communicated through signage.

Although conflicts may be rare, recreation facility managers must constantly remain sensitive to unexpected behavior and have a system in place to respond to it, including an incident report (see figure 12.1). It can be a significant concern if unexpected behavior involves a large group. Such situations should be handled carefully, avoiding unnecessary escalation.

Environmental Conditions in Specific Areas

Environmental conditions can affect the state of mind and possibly the physical condition of users and employees. It is especially the case with outdoor recreation facilities where extreme temperatures or unexpected changes in weather can occur. In such situations, it becomes the recreation facility manager's responsibility to make appropriate decisions to protect users and employees who face environmental conditions that could affect their well-being. An example of a common safety concern for outdoor recreation facility managers is inclement weather (particularly lightning strikes) that can cause the temporary closure of an outdoor recreation facility such as an aquatic, baseball, softball, football, or soccer facility (see table 12.1). Rules and procedures need to be in place for closing the facilities quickly for the safety of users and employees. It is common for these recreation facilities to have access to weather information through television or other weather-alert devices. New technology has presented options such as lightning-detection devices to assist facility managers in protecting the well-being of users and employees.

The comfort and satisfaction of users of an indoor facility depend on the climatic conditions created by the HVAC system in the facility. Environmental conditions rarely create an unhealthy situation in indoor facilities, but the potential exists. Recreation facility managers must be aware of the fact that their environment has the potential to create problems.

FIGURE 12.1 Incident report.

TABLE 12.1 COMMON ENVIRONMENTAL THREATS

Type of threat	Examples	Proactive strategies
Weather related	Lightning, severe rain or storm, tornado, earthquake, fire	• Provide warning devices (e.g., signaling flags, sirens, flashing lights, app alerts) in areas with history of extreme weather. • Provide on-site signage. • Develop relationship with local media to broadcast information and warnings.
Wildlife related	Plant and animal dangers	• Provide guidelines for safety in areas of potential danger (e.g., food storage while camping). • Post signage with information on insects and poisonous plants.
Society related	Shootings, vandalism, terrorist, riots	• Use electronic surveillance and effective lighting. • Coordinate with local, state, and federal law enforcement during large-scale events. • Use security gates and search procedures.

Areas for concern in indoor environments include monitoring chlorine levels at indoor pools and monitoring ammonia or exhaust levels at indoor ice rinks. Detection devices serve as alarms when certain chemicals reach an unsafe level; for example, carbon monoxide detectors are programmed to beep when they sense a high level of the toxic gas.

Recreation facility managers must be able to recognize an unsafe situation and have the authority to take action to remedy it even if it means shutting down the facility or equipment. This action could include removing equipment from an area where it does not function as designed. For example, if a weight machine is improperly functioning or loses a bolt, users should not have access to it. On-site facility personnel must immediately address this situation by using signs or taking the equipment to a maintenance or storage area. Consistently monitoring a facility and having maintenance schedules in place for equipment can minimize such situations.

Risk Management

Risk management is a key safety function of recreation facility management. It involves analyzing the existing facility, evaluating the goals and objectives of the agency in terms of the product, and examining product utilization from user and employee perspectives in order to identify and minimize potentially hazardous situations. Risk management attempts to eliminate injuries, accidents, and the potential for costly damages or lawsuits. Precautionary measures also raise awareness of potential risk among employees and users. When developing a risk management program for a facility, managers should understand and consider the following:

- Leadership
- Safe amenities and facility spaces
- Safe delivery of facility programs and services
- Ongoing safety audits
- Hazardous materials identification and protocols
- Reporting

Leadership

Recreation facility managers should establish a risk management program that includes a primary person (called an officer) as well as an advisory group (called a committee) to ensure successful delivery of the core product. These two sources serve as a leadership team

that accepts responsibility for administration of a facility risk management program. The risk management team develops a program of action by reviewing the facility, its core products, and its core product extensions and identifying any risks to users and employees. This team is responsible for implementing the precautionary system, and it also has the authority to take appropriate steps to avoid dangerous situations. Recreation facility managers often serve as the officer for risk management activities.

Safe Amenities and Facility Spaces

Throughout the facility planning, design, construction, and operation phases, the facility manager and risk management team should ensure compliance with relevant local, state, and federal standards. Many of these standards and regulations will be associated with various aspects of the facility including various physical dimensions, overall layout, fire, emergency, health, and local building codes. During this phase of the risk management program, facility staff should also be concerned with identifying and addressing any potential hazards.

Safe Delivery of Facility Programs and Services

Safety is the foundation of any facility program and service. Facility managers must ensure that facility programs and services are organized and facilitated by competent professionals who follow acceptable delivery standards. Established performance expectations and standards of care should be established for the delivery of programs and services within the facility. When staff lack the appropriate skills, facility managers must provide training to ensure the facility's programs and services are delivered in a safe and efficient manner.

Ongoing Safety Audits

It is important to have a system of ongoing inspections where all facets of product delivery are assessed from a risk perspective. The inspection process can include instruments such as checklists that cover every aspect of a facility, including

- employees,
- equipment,
- maintenance schedule,
- policies and procedures,
- job descriptions, and
- operational items.

Inspections should be performed regularly. The frequency of inspections can be daily, weekly, monthly, or annually depending on the facility and the product. The level and intensity of facility usage influences the need for more frequent or less frequent inspections.

Recreation facility managers should routinely observe employees in the performance of their duties in an effort to minimize risk of injury. Employee education, certification, and relevant work experience all influence employee safety. Inspections should be conducted regularly to make sure employees are doing their jobs in a safe way that minimizes risk of injury.

Equipment should also be inspected on a regular basis to ensure it will not wear out or break down. An equipment inspection checklist is helpful for documenting equipment conditions. A checklist should be designed for each piece of equipment based on the characteristics of the equipment. For example, vehicles have a specified maintenance schedule. A vehicle may need its oil changed every 3 months or 3,000 miles (4,828 km). Tires may need to be rotated every 10,000 miles (16,093 km). A golf course mower may need its oil changed every 500 hours of use or its blades sharpened once every 2 weeks. Equipment manufacturers provide maintenance and operational information in the manuals they provide with the equipment. Managers should keep this information in a file in the event of a malfunction. They should consider the amount and type of use when evaluating equipment and when replacing it, based on manufacturer recommendations.

Inspection of facility areas and equipment should be done regularly. Recreation facility managers never know when an unsafe condition may develop. All indoor and outdoor surfaces should be checked for hazards before a facility opens for use. Safety devices such as lighting, fire extinguishers, signage, storage, and exits should be inspected annually.

Finally, systems that contribute to an emergency process, such as exit doors, public-address systems, hallways, and stairways, should be inspected annually. Early warning systems and internal communication systems are essential elements of an effective precautionary system; they should be inspected monthly. Following all inspections, all monitors or committee members should hold a meeting to report their findings as described in the next section. In addition to regular safety inspections, facility personnel should practice emergency procedures and drills (see chapter 15).

Hazardous Materials Identification Protocols

Many facilities rely on chemicals and other potentially hazardous materials to support their daily operations. Facility management should develop specific policies and procedures for safe storage, handling, and application of these materials. In the United States, the Occupational Safety and Health Administration (OSHA) requires that organizations maintain a Safety Data Sheet (SDS), a recognized information source that outlines the handling and storage of these materials. Manufacturers of hazardous chemicals are required to provide SDSs for each chemical they produce. SDSs include a description of the hazardous material, the first aid procedures associated with exposure to the material, and how to flush the material off of one's skin or from one's eyes. The SDS also provides detailed instructions for managing a spill of the material.

Reporting

The final component of a risk management program is making sure that any inspections, situations, conditions, and incidents are documented, reported, and stored for future use. These reports need to summarize what conditions exist or what potential problems could occur. When documenting incidents, the following information should be included on an incident report form:

- People affected
- Witnesses
- Nature of incident
- Severity
- Medical attention required
- Comments by the injured and witnesses

Recreation facilities should have accident report forms readily available so that when a user or staff member experiences an accident, an employee can promptly fill it out (see figures 12.2 and 12.3). The accident report form can be used for medical, legal, and insurance purposes. Therefore, it should be completed in great detail, including the previously listed information. When a facility user is injured, the form should also provide the opportunity for an employee to indicate specifically where on the body the individual was injured, the type of injury, the status of the injured person, how the injury occurred, and contact information for the injured person and all witnesses to the incident.

All of the risk management information should be brought together in a formal plan for implementation. The plan should be conceived with the understanding that it should be flexible and sensitive to changing users, employees, facilities, and equipment. It should identify all risks, express potential effects, and provide ways to minimize, control, or avoid them. The entire risk management plan should be available to all levels of management. Management is responsible for minimizing these dangers to provide a safe, meaningful experience in all areas of the facility. Other reports that are often part of a precautionary system could include facility and equipment maintenance logs and checklists (see figure 12.4) and reports for user concerns that reflect a pattern or a potential problem (see figures 12.5 and 12.6).

Control

Control involves the practices that recreation facility managers implement because they are

FIGURE 12.2   Sample accident report form for the facility user.

Employee's Accident Report

Date of report _____

Personal Information

Employee's name _____

Department and division _____

Social security # _____

Home phone _____

Address (city, state, zip) _____

Date of birth _____

Gender ☐ Male ☐ Female

Marital status ☐ Single ☐ Married ☐ Separated ☐ Divorced

Job Information

Hours worked per day: _____ Days worked per week: _____ Shift: _____

Date of hire: _____ Wage basis: ☐ Hourly ☐ Salaried wage: _____

Work status: ☐ Regular full time ☐ Regular part time ☐ Temporary full time ☐ Temporary part time
☐ Seasonal ☐ Other: _____

Accident Information

Date of accident: _____

Time of accident: _____ ☐ a.m. ☐ p.m.

Date accident reported to supervisor: _____ Was report delayed?: ☐ Yes ☐ No

If yes, why?: _____

Exact location (address) of accident: _____

City property?: ☐ Yes ☐ No

City vehicles involved?: ☐ Yes ☐ No If yes, vehicle #: _____

From B. Beggs, R. Mull, M. Renneisen, and M. Mulvaney, 2024, Recreation Facility Management, 2nd ed. (Champaign, IL: Human Kinetics).

Detailed description of accident (what was employee you were doing and what tools, equipment, structures, or fixtures were involved?

_____

_____

Nature of injury (e.g., bruise, cut, strain, etc.): _____

Part of body (e.g., wrist, forearm, toes, etc.): _____

Was medical treatment sought?: ☐ Yes ☐ No If yes, where?: ☐ Promptcare ☐ Hospital emergency room

Will you miss at least one day of work?: ☐ Yes ☐ No

If yes, what is your expected return- to- work date? _____

Was the accident due to unsafe conduct on part of the employee or on the part of another employee?:

☐ Yes ☐ No

If yes, explain.: _____

_____

What should be done or has been done to prevent a recurrence of this type of accident? _____

_____

Give name of witnesses to the accident: _____

Authorization and Release for Disclosure of Medical Records and Information

I, (employee name)_____ , by the following signature, authorize any and all medical providers, including but not limited to physicians, therapists, hospitals, and laboratories, to disclose all medical records and information concerning my physical and mental conditions relevant to worker's compensation benefits and coverage to the legal department and the risk management division. This authorization includes both past and present medical information and written and oral communications.

I hereby release any medical provider disclosing information pursuant to this authorization from any liability that may result from such disclosure.

Employee's printed name _____

Employee's signature _____ Date _____

Return this form to risk management within 24 hours of accident.

From B. Beggs, R. Mull, M. Renneisen, and M. Mulvaney, 2024, Recreation Facility Management, 2nd ed. (Champaign, IL: Human Kinetics).

FIGURE 12.3 Sample employee accident report form.

2023	Pool (Preseason)	Status
Facility maintenance staff	Remove plywood from bathhouse vents (upper and lower). Store in safe and secure area.	
	Hang clock in activity pool.	
	Clean out filter rooms, main pool, and activity pool.	Probably already in pretty good shape.
	Move ice machine to pool concessions.	
	Replace ceiling panel with new one by electrical box in front basket room.	
	Hook up floatables with new locking devices; we will need these moved out of the bathhouse for pool cleanup.	
	Reattach shower fixture that has broken away from wall on men's side.	New parts being installed by facility maintenance staff.
	Hang large bulletin board in front entryway.	Operations staff has the board.
	Install stainless-steel grab bars on both sides of flume bottom of blue waterslide.	Can be done after opening.
	Power wash black algae from north and south side of bathhouse.	
	Test all fixtures in bathhouse (i.e., lights, outlets, plumbing).	
	Hang sunblock station.	Get with operations staff for location.
Sports maintenance staff	Remove plastic tie wraps from skeletons and put canopies up.	
	Remove lounge chairs from inside of bathhouses.	
	Move stuff out from under roofed area of concessions.	
Park maintenance staff	Repair bad areas of concrete deck.	Discuss locations with operations staff.
	Clean out drain in front entryway sidewalk and drain behind the office.	
	Fill in turf area on south side of filter room.	
Landscaping staff	Make landscaping touch-ups to exterior and interior of facility.	
	Add mulch to landscaping areas in and out of fenced areas.	Done.

		Status
Operations division staff	Call street dept. to have parking lot swept and relined.	Done.
	Design and construct sunblock station.	In progress.
	Get signs for new sign and sunblock station.	
	Call for sign corrections.	Done.
	Contract out for guttering on new filter building.	Done—being installed in May.
	Call for installation of new awnings at top of slides.	
	Hang large bulletin board for front entryway.	Call outside contractor.
	Treat soda fountain drain in concessions.	
	Call hardware store for office replacement door.	
	Fix trim piece on lifeguard cubbies.	
	Call for flowers.	
	Hang AED unit.	
	Call health dept. for inspection.	
Sports administrator	Install window well barriers on south side of bathhouse.	
	Call about slide drainage problem.	
	Plant grasses at east end of facility outside perimeter fence.	

From B. Beggs, R. Mull, M. Renneisen, and M. Mulvaney, 2024, Recreation Facility Management, 2nd ed. (Champaign, IL: Human Kinetics).

FIGURE 12.4 Sample pool facility opening checklist.

Citizen Report

Reporting Party

Name _____

Address _____

City _____ Zip code _____

Home phone _____ Business phone _____

Report taken by_____

Time _____ a.m./p.m. (circle one)   Date _____

Complaint

Suggestion

Info request

Commendation

Nature of Call

Building	Irrigation	Street furniture
Playground Park	Path/trail	Programs
Other Restroom	BBQ area	Floor

Details

Location of occurence _____

Time _____ Date _____

Action Taken

By _____

Position _____

Time _____

Date_____

Action taken_____

_____

_____

_____

From B. Beggs, R. Mull, M. Renneisen, and M. Mulvaney, 2024, Recreation Facility Management, 2nd ed. (Champaign, IL: Human Kinetics).

_____

_____

_____

Reporting party notified by _____

Time _____ Date _____

Phone _____ a.m./p.m. (circle one)

Date _____ Letter _____

Was the citizen satisfied with your response?   1-Very   2-Satisfied   3-No response   4-Not satisfied

Review

Division director _____

Comments _____

_____

Date_____

Administrator_____

Comments _____

_____

Date _____

From B. Beggs, R. Mull, M. Renneisen, and M. Mulvaney, 2024, Recreation Facility Management, 2nd ed. (Champaign, IL: Human Kinetics).

FIGURE 12.5   Citizen report.

Vandalism and Trouble Report

Site _____ Date _____ Time _____

Persons Involved

Name	Age	Address	Phone

Witnesses

_____

_____

_____

Nature of Offense

_____

_____

_____

_____

Action Taken at Scene

_____

_____

_____

_____

Were police called? ☐ Yes ☐ No

Investigating officer _____
                        Supervisor in charge

Damages

_____

_____

_____

From B. Beggs, R. Mull, M. Renneisen, and M. Mulvaney, 2024, Recreation Facility Management, 2nd ed. (Champaign, IL: Human Kinetics).

FIGURE 12.6   Vandalism and trouble report.

responsible for every person at their recreation facility. Whatever happens within a facility is ultimately the responsibility of management. Managers can demonstrate a caring attitude and take precautionary measures to avoid risks, but the bottom line is that they must exert reasonable control of the activities at their facility at all times. Control of a facility takes into consideration internal influences and external influences.

Internal Influences

Internal influences involve ensuring proper use of the facility and its equipment. To aid in this effort, certain guidelines, directives, and policies are created.

Policies and Procedures

Facility administrators must develop informational statements about limitations on what people are allowed to do while using the recreation facility. These administrative statements, known as **policies**, inform users and employees of what they may or may not do as they experience the product. Policies generally answer questions such as *who*, *when*, and *what*. In addition to limiting certain types of use, they can establish fees and charges, supervisory statements, access requirements, capacity limitations, and scheduling requirements, among other things.

At the same time, administrators need to share certain statements that help people know how to use a facility and its equipment; these statements are called **procedures**. Procedures create user and employee awareness of *how* and *where* they may be able to use the facility as designed. Examples of procedures include directional information, times and places of activities, announcements, and user application requirements.

Rules and Regulations

Rules are controls that place limits on specific actions of users and employees. Policies and procedures can manage passive use of the facility, but active use requires additional limitations. For example, this common sport

participation rule limits the age of users who may participate in a certain program: Participants in a 12-and-under baseball league may not turn 13 years of age by December 31 and still be eligible to participate.

External Influences

Local, state, and federal agencies, as well as professional associations, have established principles to protect people (both employees and users) in recreation facilities. These forms of guidance are considered external influences. Recreation facility managers must be sensitive to how these external influences affect their responsibilities. External influences include liabilities, codes, and standards.

Liabilities

A liability occurs when management had an obligation to protect the user or employee and failed to do so. This failure to exercise some degree of care by a reasonable person can be observed as negligence on the part of manage-

Signage can help inform users of rules and regulations of recreation facilities.
© Human Kinetics

ment. If negligence occurs, a user may make a claim, which could result in a lawsuit that provides damages equivalent to what the user may have experienced. These situations are known as a tort or a civil wrong, a private wrong, or an injury independent of a contract resulting in a breach of legal duty and responsibility to the user. These types of developments need to be avoided if at all possible. Potential lawsuits can place extensive demands on management and cause significant financial loss for the agency.

Generally, recreation facility managers take for granted that the users have the knowledge, experience, and willingness to accept responsibility for their actions, and they accept the idea that all users are responsible for how they use a facility. Although this **assumption of risk** can be a good legal defense in many situations, management should take precautions; they should let this defense be the exception and not the rule. In addition, assumption of risk is less of an option when providing a product to children and adolescents as well as older adults. Assumption of risk is intended to protect management; however, it also implies significant responsibility for recreation facility managers.

A recreation agency can make a viable defense claim when an incident results from an *act of God* (certain facility and environmental developments outside the control of management). Again, this defense should be an exception and not the rule when determining appropriate risk management at a recreation facility. Forces of nature often create situations that facility managers could have avoided. Extenuating circumstances, including floods, earthquakes, tornadoes, lightning strikes, and unforeseen sudden illnesses or death, could be perceived by the court either as situations where management should have taken necessary precautions or as acts of God that were beyond anyone's control.

An **attractive nuisance** is a condition that exists when a product that is not currently available is considered inviting or attractive to potential users. If the potential user could be a child or anyone else not realizing the hazard involved, management could be held responsible because the situation attracted the user. This responsibility applies even when the potential user should not have had access to the product. A common example of a recreation facility that is perceived as an attractive nuisance is a swimming pool. Recreation facility managers who are responsible for pools should always be sure that access is restricted by fences, lighting, and other reasonable control measures when the facility is closed.

A **standard of care** is usually established as a result of previous legal action or precedence. In this case, recreation facility managers who have the responsibility for supervising, instructing, or managing the facility must be familiar with information that is relevant to being responsible for use of the facility. Usually, professional associations and organizations communicate these standards through meetings or publications. Often, standards of care are minimal. For example, a recommendation to drag (groom) and line softball fields after every third game is a standard of care often used by the Amateur Softball Association (ASA) for national tournaments.

Many recreation facilities host special events such as athletic tournaments, fairs, and expositions. These events involve elements of risk that must be managed to keep participants as safe as possible while also minimizing the potential for incidents of liability for the facility or its agency. Many of these events involve multiple agencies, large crowds, emergency medical response units, public health officials, fire safety personnel, police, and unique parking demands. All of these moving parts require a great deal of collaboration and coordination to limit liability issues. While each special event is unique, common liability issues associated with these events include the following:

- Parking and traffic flow
- Vendors and contract service agreements
- Crowd control, and safety and security
- Injuries and challenges to participants
- Agreements, waivers, and releases of liability
- Background checks for employees and volunteers

Enclosing an entire aquatic area of a facility with a fence is a good way to limit access.
Nicholas Lamontanaro/iStock/Getty Images

Codes

Codes are legal guidelines or systems that set limitations or control mechanisms for recreation facility usage. They place restrictions and requirements not only on facility development but also on daily operations. Codes change, and facility managers should stay abreast of these changes. For example, construction codes are enforced during facility construction; they can affect facility location, structural makeup, sizes of areas, entries and exits, and space requirements. Other common codes that apply to recreation facilities include fire codes and facility capacity codes designed to assist in the safe operation of a facility.

Standards

Standards are another external influence on recreation facility managers. National associations create standards to provide guidance for the delivery and use of a particular product. Standards could also influence facility use, especially where a successful product is being delivered. Sometimes products can be so specialized that only the national association has the ability to oversee their proper application and use. Standards can apply to designing of spaces and areas, operation of a facility and equipment, ratio of employees to users, temperatures required for certain environment conditions, weather postponement, types of equipment for a job, level of attention and care to users and employees, and timing in getting specialized work completed.

Security

Security is one of the most important concerns in recreation facility management. Managers need to know that their facility and related equipment are safe from burglary, vandalism, and prohibited entry and use. Security is having a system in place to protect users as well as facilities and equipment from harm. Users and employees desire an environment free from the fear that they could be harmed or lose their belongings. When discussing security, the two most important aspects to consider are surveillance and access control.

Surveillance

A surveillance system allows management to keep close watch over space, equipment, and people. A variety of monitoring options are available. Although access control can play a large role in facility security, surveillance is a means of protecting a recreation facility—such as identification checks, gates, or security guards—without necessarily creating the discomfort that can occur with access control.

Lighting

Lighting can be a less intrusive option for securing a facility. It can include providing adequate lighting in and around a facility. Regular lighting automatically contributes to facility security because it gives the appearance that people are present, making it unattractive to unwanted intruders during nonbusiness hours. Security lighting enables employees to view areas at a distance to see what is happening and have time to respond.

Surveillance Cameras

Another form of surveillance involves video cameras and monitoring systems. Cameras act both as a deterrent and as a means for staff to view areas from monitors located at a control center. Two types of cameras are typically used in a security system. The first captures pictures in a still-frame format much like the way a typical photo camera captures pictures. The second type records action continuously. It can be fixed and only capture pictures from a limited area, or it can be mobile so that it can survey a wider area.

Surveillance cameras can be on continuously or triggered when motion, such as people

Surveillance cameras may be necessary to provide a secure, safe environment for facility users and employees.
MICHAEL KAPPELER/DDP/AFP via Getty Images

walking through a door or crossing a trigger device, occurs. Strategic hiding positions of cameras are based on the nature of the facility and what is to be recorded. Cameras can be hidden in overhead lights, in clocks, behind mirrors, or even within smoke detectors and ceiling speakers. Outside surveillance cameras can be placed on high poles and can have the capacity to zoom in on movement. As mentioned, cameras can also serve as a deterrent if they are positioned in areas where they can be seen. Multiple cameras can feed into one monitor and depict images from several locations. One disadvantage of this type of surveillance equipment is the cost. Some cameras are designed for night vision, which is even more expensive to purchase and maintain.

Surveillance Staff

Surveillance can also take place by staff designated to watch areas in and around a facility. This responsibility is part of the job for most employees, but it is not their primary focus. In some instances, a recreation facility may include employees whose sole purpose is observing and guarding the facility. These security guards are valuable because the visibility that results from their uniform and sometimes a marked security vehicle can deter unwelcome behaviors. Security guards usually have to meet predetermined qualifications, which can incorporate not only guarding but also emergency or disaster training. It is common practice for security guards to be fully evaluated before hiring, making sure they are properly trained for a particular recreation facility and product.

Watchdogs

An effective but inexpensive form of security guarding is the use of watchdogs or guard dogs. This type of security is generally used at facilities during the evening hours. When using watchdogs, facilities should post appropriate signs and warnings, and the dogs should be behind barriers. Dogs can be much cheaper than electronic surveillance devices, and they can be as effective as police officers. Advantages of watchdogs are that they can intimidate intruders; they have a keener sense of sight, smell, and hearing than humans; and their bark can serve as both a deterrent and an alarm. A disadvantage of watchdogs is the considerable amount of time and expense involved in caring for them.

Access Control

Access control is a security concept in which appropriate steps to influence who and what can enter an area or a facility are enacted. It keeps people out of a facility unless they are deemed appropriate for entry.

Generally, a facility has two areas: internal areas, where access control can be established, and a perimeter, which surrounds these areas. The perimeter may be enclosed by fences or other barriers, creating a boundary. Most facilities have a main entrance where perimeter control is maintained. Internal areas are enclosed by the walls, doors, counters, gates, or other barriers inside a facility. They include areas that are involved with the delivery of the core product and core product extensions. Different indoor areas may require different access control devices to limit access to the appropriate people.

Barriers or fences around the perimeter can be either natural or manufactured. Natural barriers include mounds, trees, bushes, and shrubs, whereas manufactured barriers usually involve some type of fencing or gate. These barriers can prevent intruders from entering a parking area or from driving into areas that need to be protected.

Barriers and fences can control entry to a facility, but access usually requires a system that identifies users and employees. Identification systems should be able to recognize people who have access to the facility or area. The most common system is to require a form of identification that has been authorized by

CHECK IT OUT
History of Access Control Technologies

Access control has a long history in facilities. Here is an overview of the evolution of access control technologies:

- Physical access control: Use of physical barriers (i.e., fence, walls, etc.)
- Mechanical era: Use of mechanical locks and keys
- Modern (digital) era: Use of hardware components powered by backend software platforms (web-based access control, Bluetooth access, authentication technologies, etc.)

management. Common forms of acceptable identification include the following:

- Driver's license
- Credit card
- School identification card
- Work identification cards
- Birth certificate
- Passports

Often these types of identification are required in order to create a specific facility identification card or membership card. More advanced identification techniques include voice identification, fingerprint identification, and retinal identification.

At some point, security needs to address door control, which involves a system of keying to create access to the facility. Key access includes padlocks, mechanical or combination locks, card swipe systems, or magnetically keyed locks. Each lock system provides a different degree of security; in other words, some locks are easier for an intruder to remove than others.

Advancements in communication technologies have led to substantial growth in the variety of access control technologies (Gips, 2020; see table 12.2). These advancements have allowed many facilities to limit or fully replace the mechanical lock-and-key system because standard keys and locks no longer fulfill demands for maintaining access control. Keys can be a weak link in any security system because they can be lost, stolen, and duplicated. In addition, the process of changing locks and reissuing keys is costly and time consuming.

TABLE 12.2   COMMON ACCESS CONTROL TECHNOLOGIES

Access control technology	Description	Example
Near field communication (NFC)	Devices communicate over the air interface (MHz frequency), developing an electromagnetic field between the devices when they are near one another.	Smartphone (waving phone next to door lock)
Radio-frequency identification (RFID)	Credential information is stored on a digital tag that is associated with the carrier. When the tag is in close proximity to the reader device, electromagnetic waves are used to read the tag and grant or deny access.	Key card, RFID chip, key fob
Physical access control system (PACS)	Uses personal information from a card and a card reader.	Encrypted badges, personal identification number (PIN) codes and passwords, key cards
Mobile access control	Converts a mobile device into an electronic key fob through an installed app on the device.	Smartphone
Wired access control	Is similar to other technologies, except the system relies on hardwired cables to transmit data.	Smartphone, PIN codes and passwords, key cards, cameras

Summary

Monitoring and guiding user and employee circulation, safety, control, and security is an important component of planning and operating a facility. By having effective systems in place, recreational facility managers can create a safe and comfortable environment that not only protects users and the organization but also enhances the recreation experience.

REVIEW QUESTIONS

1. Describe one or two purposes of signage in a facility.

2. What role does a facility user's experience level have in the creation of a safe environment within the facility?

3. Provide an example of an environmental threat that could affect a recreation facility.

4. Why are inspections an important component of a recreation facility's risk management program?

CASE STUDY

A Tragedy at the Y

The local community has a beautiful 120,000-square-foot (11,148 m²) YMCA facility, which includes five multipurpose courts, an indoor soccer complex, two golf simulators with driving and chipping areas, a 25-foot by 24-foot (7.6 m × 7.3 m) free-form climbing wall, a quarter-mile (400 m) mondo surfaced running track, cardio and strength-training equipment, and a 27-yard (25 m) swimming pool. Two lifeguards staff the swimming area during open swim, swimming lessons, classes, and special events.

The YMCA is very popular among the 155,000 residents of the community. Nearby communities also enjoy its services. Of all the facility's amenities, the pool area is the most popular. For instance, over 75 percent of the community participated in some type of swim program offered by the YMCA during the past year.

On one particular day, a large family reunion and birthday party took place at the YMCA. The family had rented the entire facility. When groups rent the facility, they can choose various facility amenities to rent by the hour. Because of the staffing and overhead expenses associated with the pool, the family opted to rent the pool from 5 p.m. to 7 p.m. that evening while they rented the rest of the facility from 12 p.m. to 9 p.m.

One hundred family members gathered to celebrate the special day. At around 4 p.m., one of the younger boys (5 years old) expressed a desire to go swimming but was told the pool was closed until 5 p.m. His parents also insisted he had to wait an hour until his food digested. He asked if he could walk around the swimming area and go to the rock climbing wall to watch his friends climb for an hour. He was given permission (by his parents) to do so; however, he never made it to the climbing wall. Instead, he went to the pool and in the water. Moments later an adult saw three boys screaming hysterically. The facility staff (two of which were lifeguards) were notified, and they immediately rescued the boy.

Unfortunately, the boy did not survive. Both lifeguards had correctly administered first aid and CPR until rescue workers arrived at the scene. The boy was later pronounced dead at the hospital.

Case Study Questions

1. If you were the supervisor of the facility and of the lifeguards, how would you handle their emotional well-being?

2. Based on the situation, what action, if any, would you take with your staff?

3. Your lifeguards are hurting emotionally from this tragedy. How could you develop a crisis management policy that you could implement in a situation like this one?

4. Your lawyer does not think a lawsuit will be filed, and they state that no lifeguard was at fault. Do you agree? Why or why not?

CHAPTER 13

Coordinating and Scheduling

LEARNING OBJECTIVES

At the completion of this chapter, you should be able to do the following:

1. Recognize the various approaches to maximizing facility usage.
2. Examine practices for facility supervision and user agreements.
3. Describe the purpose of a master schedule.

Recreation facility management requires extensive insight into two key subjects: coordination and scheduling. Each facility has unique policies, procedures, and systems to meet administrative expectations. Recreation facility managers are responsible for coordinating and scheduling space, people, and equipment efficiently. Because a variety of individuals and groups use a facility, coordination requires the careful integration of activities in the overall plan for use.

Coordinating

The goal in coordinating a recreation facility is to create an effective system that provides for the efficient use of all areas, personnel, and equipment in a harmonious and timely fashion. Managing individual and group use of a facility takes time and effort. Inefficient coordination can reflect poorly on management and product delivery.

Competently coordinated facilities can enhance facility usage. In addition to providing a positive and satisfying experience for users, competent coordination also allows for maximum use of the facility. Conversely, if not coordinated properly, maximizing facility use can create conflict. Recreation facility managers should be sensitive to potential coordination problems and be prepared to respond to coordination challenges when they occur. Most facilities have different levels of usage interest from internal and external users and, in some cases, employees. Multiple interests in facility use often create conflicts of interest, and recreation agencies must create policies to establish priorities for use. Even when policies are in place, ill will between competing user groups can occur, potentially having a negative effect on facility operations.

Another concern related to maximizing facility use is allowing for adequate preparation of the facility. The details for this preparation can be extensive. Typical arrangements to coordinate include the following:

- Dates and time commitments
- Setup and takedown
- Equipment needs
- Electrical needs
- Area load and layout
- Supervision
- Security requirements
- Access control
- Charges
- Food service
- Final written agreement

In the beginning, most recreation facilities have the available space to fulfill user needs. Over time, however, production areas can become crowded. Although this problem can be the result of demand for a product, it makes coordination challenging. Obstacles arise in meeting user needs when the facility has too many users or employees for the space available. Recreation facility managers should be alert to space limitations, anticipate solutions, and have appropriate responses that will help in the effort to coordinate facilities. An example of a space limitation is a golf course that has a waiting list for tee times. Managers can respond by limiting the number of tee-time reservations a person can have, altering the fee structure to encourage play at low-usage times, or adding facilities to meet the demand for additional golfers.

Recreation facility managers should consider the following five factors in their approach to coordinating maximal facility usage:

1. Leadership
2. Stakeholders
3. Seasonality
4. Time
5. Place

This task is an important part of the manager's job. Each factor is described next.

Leadership

Leadership refers to how recreation agency leaders influence facility usage so that it fulfills the mission of the agency. Is the mission to serve people, to make a profit, or both? Recreation facility coordination evolves from administrative priorities and the style of the agency executives. People- or service-oriented leaders may be so sensitive to users, schedulers, and employees that technical responsibilities may be compromised. On the other hand, they could be so driven by goals and profit that they lose sight of users' and employees' experiences. Understanding how leadership influences facility availability and coordination is fundamental for recreation facility managers.

Administrators have a philosophy about their product and how it should be produced and delivered; this philosophy is imparted in the form of a mission or vision statement. Employees should be familiar with this philosophy, and it should influence decisions regarding facility utilization. For example, a recreation agency may determine that a particular facility should be made available to tax-paying residents before other user groups. This philosophy would clearly affect the scheduling practices of the facility.

Stakeholders

Who are the users and employees (stakeholders) who will use a recreation facility, and what are their interests and needs? An appreciation for personalities, gender, race, social status, attitude, and motivation can make a significant difference in facility coordination. Understanding the various people who may use a recreation facility and enhancing their usage can lead to harmonious use of a facility while helping managers anticipate and avoid coordination problems.

Seasonality

Understanding *seasonality* is being aware of changes in recreation facility use as it relates

While space limitation might not be an issue when a facility is first built, demand for a core product can cause overcrowding in the facility's main area. Making changes in scheduling practices of a facility can help to solve this problem.
Scott Varley/Digital First Media/Torrance Daily Breeze via Getty Images

to certain times of the year. Busy times are the peak season, and slow times are the off-season. For example, baseball or softball facilities are likely to be busy in the summer and not so busy at other times of year. Seasons could also be affected by changes in weather conditions, which greatly influence what users do, such as using an aquatic facility. Facility coordination efforts can change dramatically as seasons dictate product interest and support.

Time

Facility usage also varies based on certain times of the day. Coordinating a recreation facility comes down to customer demand for a particular time. This particular time is often called *prime time*, and the opposite is *nonprime time*. Usage time could be divided into morning, afternoon, and evening time slots. Hours could be blocked into segments that are regularly scheduled for certain activities. For example,

an ice arena may reserve weeknights from 7 p.m. to 9 p.m. for public skating. This time may be blocked regularly based on user demand. Recognizing customer demand for facility time results in maximal use and revenue.

Place

Recreation facility managers must be mindful of the type of facility they are managing and how it dictates certain use and coordination limitations. Each facility has its own policies, procedures, rules, and regulations that influence coordination. For instance, a community center caters to users of all ages. However, it may include some spaces that children are not allowed to access for safety reasons. Conflicting group usage could also arise in a facility that has multiple spaces that can be used at the same time, such as a convention center or park with pavilions.

Happy users are the main goal of any recreation facility.
iStockphoto/Kennneth C. Zirkel

Scheduling

Scheduling is the act of assigning a time, place, and date based on a request for a particular use. In many facilities, the agency schedules its own activities related to delivering the core product. In other instances, facilities may be reserved by users. Recreation facility managers are responsible for facility scheduling, which can be a tedious and difficult responsibility. Scheduling responsibilities vary depending on the recreation agency and the facility. Additional influences on scheduling include the product, procedures, responsibilities, and policies. The following sections focus on these factors.

Product

Each facility has scheduling needs based on the core product. A schedule may be required for employees to accomplish operational tasks, responsibilities, and functions related to the product. A different schedule may be necessary to coordinate participants' use of the core product. Scheduling practices for products are based on one or a combination of the following: users, staff, space, and special events.

Users

Recreation facilities can have a number of users whose access to the core product may need to be scheduled. Depending on the use of the facility, varying degrees of user supervision may be required. Understanding users, the product they want to use, and how the facility can best serve them is an essential job function of recreation facility managers. Managers' knowledge of users can play a big part in how a facility is scheduled. Several factors can determine user nature and status, including product popularity, socioeconomic status, gender, age, special needs and interests, skill level, and willingness to pay. Achieving customer satisfaction through a needs assessment and appropriate allocation of space for their needs is an important goal in recreation facility management.

Staff

Scheduling of staff requires assigning the right individual to the right job at the right time.

The first step in this process is to identify the tasks and responsibilities to be performed in the facility and the staff who are capable of successfully performing these tasks. The next step in the scheduling process is the development of a schedule that includes the number of hours each staff member works per week and what days they are available. The number of hours for a job may also be dictated by budget constraints and by laws such as the Patient Protection and Affordable Care Act (ACA) in the United States. Furthermore, required breaks and limits on hours worked are factors to consider when scheduling staff.

Managers should also recognize the peak times within recreation facilities and their effect on staff scheduling. In particular, recreation facilities are often at their busiest when people have leisure time to spend. Staff must therefore work during evening hours, on weekends, and holidays as well as during weekdays throughout the year. Facility managers should strive to balance the amount of work assigned during holidays and weekends by assigning staff to a rotating schedule and by placing a limit on the amount of work any staff is required to perform.

Another way to approach balancing work assigned is to schedule staff not only for optimal job results but also for maximum personal satisfaction of the employee. When doing staff schedules, the facility manager must have the flexibility to consider alternative schedules of employees in the event of severe weather, outside obligations, or other disruptions in previously planned programs or activities.

Space

Another facility scheduling practice based on the core product is controlling facility use based on the area to be used. Recreation facilities may have any number of areas that need to be scheduled in a way that maximizes their use, whether they be hotel rooms, sport courts, theaters, classrooms, or outdoor areas. Some facility spaces require a completely different scheduling technique than others. Some spaces have laws that limit how many users can be accommodated at a given time. Each area of a recreation facility—or even the facility itself—

can be viewed as unique space with its own requirements for accomplishing utilization expectations.

Special Events

Auditoriums, stadiums, convention centers, arenas, hotels, and other facilities have venues with the potential for holding events that can attract large groups of people, also known as *special events*. Coordinating special events is one of the most complicated facility scheduling practices. Special events can originate in-house by recreation facility personnel, or they can be delivered by an outside agency requesting sole use of the facility. Event scheduling can be time consuming, and it sometimes requires legal consultation regarding responsibilities of facility personnel and limitations placed on them from an outside organization. Special events that may take place in a recreation facility include weddings at a country club or church, concerts in an arena or stadium, tournaments at sport complexes, or lectures in an auditorium. Event scheduling requires a great deal of preparation and attention to detail.

Procedures

Recreation facility scheduling is challenging, so applying a system of sound procedures can be invaluable. These procedures may be applied informally or formally. In most cases where effective and efficient management scheduling is observed, the following scheduling procedures are applied:

A large amount of planning and facility preparation is required before a special event; it usually lasts for the majority of the day.

Elenathewise/fotolia.com

How Common Are Special Events?

Special events are diverse; they range from single-day themed events to weeklong celebrations. Regardless of the type of event, these experiences represent an important component in recreation agencies' programming and services portfolio. According to the National Recreation and Park Association's *Agency Performance Review Report* (NRPA, 2022), 90 percent of agencies offer at least one special event on an annual basis. Clearly, special events are common!

1. Request
2. Log
3. Review
4. Response
5. Agreement

Request

The initial request for use of a facility may require a letter, phone call, or email formally requesting the facility. Often, some type of form must be completed (see figure 13.1). The request demonstrates a sincere interest from a potential user that should result in a response from facility personnel. Oftentimes, a web-based submission form allows the individual to complete and submit the request online. Many facilities publish a current availability calendar for each of the reservable facility spaces. This information can provide the potential user with up-to-date information on the availability for the facility space of interest.

A reservation request form often includes the name of the group or person requesting use; a contact person, address, phone number, and email address; the date, time, and space desired; and a statement indicating the nature of the event. This document represents the beginning of an arrangement where both parties are attempting to come to an agreement on all the details for use of the facility. Agreements are commonly called *permits, contracts,* or *facility use agreements.* Depending on the facility and the use requested, these agreements can be simple or detailed.

Log

When a request is received, it should be logged on a calendar, indicating the date and time of receipt. Recording the time of receipt can be important when multiple usage requests are submitted for the same time. If no predetermined policies are in place for establishing priority of use, a philosophy of first come, first served is often observed. As noted earlier, the use of a web-based submission process can provide a digital time stamp and provide immediate feedback to the potential user on the receipt of their request and the availability of the desired space.

Review

Each facility request should receive a complete review by appropriate facility personnel. More than one employee may review a request based on their area of expertise and level of authority. Depending on the nature of the facility and how often it is reserved for use by an outside party, some requests may not require an in-depth

FIGURE 13.1 Sample golf outing or tournament information form.

review and simply be scheduled into a date and time slot. Other requests may require that all variables and details be carefully considered before a determination of use is made. All final decisions regarding a request should be applied in a fair and equitable fashion.

Response

However a request is submitted, it should be responded to in a timely fashion. Each agency may have a policy stating the time that applicants can expect before receiving a response. Even if a request is denied, applicants deserve the courtesy of a prompt answer so that they can seek other arrangements. Acceptable response methods include a letter, an email, or a phone call to the person who made the request.

Agreement

Some recreation facility uses require a final, written agreement or contract. The agreement binds all details of the arrangement into a formal understanding between the potential user and the recreation agency. Some agreements or contracts may require the assistance of an attorney. The agreement should include details such as requirements for use of the space, equipment needs, food service, setup and takedown responsibilities, personnel requirements, safety and security concerns, length of use, and charges for use, misuse, or overuse. An agreement should clarify any details that are negotiated as the scheduling process evolves so that there no misunderstanding exists between the parties. Figure 13.2 shows a sample agreement.

Pool Rental Agreement

Name of group ____________________

Address ____________________

Phone ____________________

Representative of group ____________________

Reservation for *(circle one)*: Pool and waterslide Pool Wading pool only

Rental date_____/_____/_____, from _____:_____a.m./p.m. to _____:_____a.m./p.m.

General description of group *(circle one)*: Youths 17 and under Adults Families School group

Will your group need use of the wading pool for children aged 5 and under *(circle one)*? Yes No

Approximate # in group ________

Rental fee/hour $________

Total fee $________

I, as representative of the previously named group, hereby reserve the pool facility for the date and time indicated. As the responsible party for this group, I understand it is my duty to see that all pool policies and rules are followed by the group while using the facilities.

Please read carefully. We understand the following:

- Final decisions regarding closings and cancellations are at the discretion of the department staff only.
- Alcohol is not permitted.
- The premises are to be left in the same condition as when we arrived.
- All public rules and policies apply to private parties
- Food and drinks may be brought into the facility but eaten *only* inside the concession area.
- Our party will be allowed to enter the facility no earlier than the confirmed rental time.
- The entire fee will be due at the time of reservation.
- Reservations will not be taken earlier than 3 business days in advance of the rental date.
- The entire fee will be forfeited if the aquatic director is not notified of a cancellation 3 business days in advance of the reserved date.

Signature ____________________ Date ____________________

White copy—Office
Yellow copy—Pool
Pink copy—Patron

Payment	
Cash	
Check/money order	
Credit card	
School group subsidy	

From B. Beggs, R. Mull, M. Renneisen, and M. Mulvaney, 2024, *Recreation Facility Management*, 2nd ed. (Champaign, IL: Human Kinetics).

FIGURE 13.2 Sample pool rental agreement form.

Scheduling Techniques

Scheduling can be accomplished using various concepts and practices. Computers play a significant role in the facility scheduling process. Certain techniques can be applied to efficiently manage facility requests, which can involve diverse interests and a large number of requests. Ultimately, whatever system is in place should be tied into a facility master schedule.

A **master schedule** is appropriate when the facility receives many requests for its use. It records all users by date, time, space, and user contact information. Facility personnel should maintain the master schedule so that a current version is available at any time. It helps keep scheduling organized and avoids conflicts caused by overlapping bookings. One way to maintain a master schedule is to use a reservation book or computer software that allows for review of any time and place that has or can be scheduled. Using a single system ensures that all of the reservations are available in one central location and that all entries are as accurate and current as possible.

Facility software and web-based application systems assist in organizing facility scheduling processes. Facilities can use many of these programs to support the reservation process, including recurring schedules, and create master schedules while safeguarding against double-booking and other issues related to human error. In addition, these systems can be set up to create automatic reservation confirmation emails as well as provide facilities with customizable master schedules organized by facility area. Most of these programs also include features that support other facility operations, such as billing, invoicing, facility check-ins, rentals, and program or league management.

Responsibilities

Before making arrangements for use of the facility, a recreation facility manager needs to understand scheduling responsibilities. These responsibilities vary according to each facility and its function. Before finalizing the arrangements, it is essential to decide on and clarify certain expectations for recreation facility managers and users. These expectations are often communicated in writing, where both parties recognize their responsibilities. Users may need the agency to provide equipment, lighting, security, or other services. On the other hand, these needs may be the responsibility of the user. Other responsibilities may include setup and takedown, security, supervision, equipment, and safety.

Setup and Takedown

Most arrangements to use a recreation facility or an area require recreation facility managers or users to perform some type of setup. It is important to define in advance who is responsible for which setup and takedown tasks. For instance, if a group is reserving a room in a convention center for a meeting, they will need tables and chairs. Both parties should establish in advance whether the group or the convention center is responsible for setting up the tables and chairs. If the convention center is responsible for the setup, the users should explain how they want the room set up. This

In the final agreement, recreation facility managers must ensure it is clear who—the users or the facility staff—will be responsible for setting up the facility area and for returning it to its original condition.

© Human Kinetics

communication usually occurs when the agreement is signed.

Equally important is the need for a clear understanding regarding takedown responsibilities, especially if the users are responsible for this task. Users often do not have the same standards when it comes to returning a facility area to its original state. Recreation facility managers should clearly communicate (in writing) to what condition the facility should be returned when the use is completed. Clearly communicating cleanup expectations can save a lot of trouble and inconvenience for recreation facility managers.

Security

Some facility uses require special security measures. A user's request should be reviewed and any security requirements established in advance. Some recreation facility uses can create concerns based on the size of anticipated crowds, the possibility of unusual or unexpected behavior, or other reasons. For example, a recreation agency may require security for a use that involves the consumption of alcohol at the facility. Security arrangements regarding protection of people, facilities, and equipment may be necessary based on a thorough review of the user's request. These needs and whose responsibility it will be to establish security should be discussed and agreed upon in writing before final scheduling takes place.

Supervision

Most recreation facility use will require some level of supervision, which can be provided by facility personnel or by the user. Details on facility supervision must be clearly communicated when the user is responsible for providing supervision. Supervisory arrangements depend on the inherent risk associated with the type of use. Recreation facility managers need to make sure that users are fully aware of their supervisory responsibility; in turn, users must demonstrate the capacity to meet this need. The most common arrangement is when the recreation facility provides supervision with facility staff. In this arrangement, the user typically is responsible for reimbursing the recreation agency for this service.

Equipment

With most facility requests, users will need equipment for the activity they have planned. Recreation facility managers should communicate what equipment will be made available for use in addition to making sure the users know how to properly operate it. Users could also bring their own equipment to a facility, so a clear understanding of what equipment can be brought into a facility is important. In both cases, equipment damage could result. An understanding of each party's responsibility for equipment should be communicated in writing in the event that damage to the equipment or facility occurs. Equipment arrangements may warrant a separate written document expressing all obligations and financial responsibilities.

Safety

User safety is paramount in any recreation facility, especially when managers are scheduling a facility or delegating its use to an outside group. In addition to ensuring proper supervision, recreation facility managers should provide a safe environment, including safe equipment. If users are providing equipment, recreation facility managers need assurance that the equipment is in proper condition and is appropriate for the activity. Users must be aware of their responsibility for safety when providing their own equipment. In scheduling a facility for use, managers have to accept

CHECK IT OUT

Don't Forget to Inspect

Facilities should create an equipment inspection form to be completed before and after each equipment rental transaction. These inspections can help to ensure that no safety issues or defects to the equipment exist before and after operation.

responsibility for safety of both the area and the equipment involved. They must make sure all the details regarding safety are reviewed and documented in writing, creating a clear understanding of the responsibilities of each party.

Policies

Facility scheduling practices require the establishment of policies to protect everyone's interest and involvement. Policies also provide the basis for consistent and fair review of facility requests. Scheduling policies include charges or fees, prioritization, cancellation, damage, food-service policies, and insurance policies.

Charges or Fees

An established and well-planned policy statement for fees and charges is a critical component of recreation facility management. Depending on the type of use and scheduling arrangements, the agency can incur costs that necessitate the assessment of fees for reserved use. Fees come in many forms. Each facility has its own fee system for assessing charges to users based on the type and duration of facility use. Other factors that can influence fees include special arrangements, equipment, supervision, time of day, and time of the year. These charges need to be established in advance in a written policy, basing the amount on a fair assessment of all variables involved. Charges are usually intended to offset part of the construction costs, direct expenses related to the specific use, overhead, and a percentage for profit. Often, market conditions influence fees more than any other factor. Ultimately, fees and charges have a significant effect on the success of a recreation facility.

Prioritization

A typical user submitting a request for use of a recreation facility may not understand all the steps involved in the scheduling process. Further complicating this situation is when multiple requests are received for the same time and space. A policy stating how requests are received and prioritized should be in place to assist staff in determining which users' requests are to be granted and in what order.

This policy should outline how far in advance a request must be received, and that information should be shared with users. This approach allows time for making arrangements without excessive time pressure that can create misunderstandings and conflict.

Typical factors for determining priority of use include when the request is received, the nature of the group that is making the request, and the number of people being served by the use. The nature of the agency may also influence the priority policy. For example, a public recreation facility may prioritize local residents over nonlocal residents, whereas a private recreation facility may prioritize the group that will generate the most income for the facility.

Cancellation

Sometimes cancellations occur. A written cancellation policy ensures that recreation facilities are consistent in applying penalties or other consequences to users. A cancellation policy should specify any acceptable reasons for a cancellation so that users are aware of their obligations in advance. The cancellation policy should include a clause that stipulates a time frame when financial penalties will be invoked.

Sometimes users make arrangements to use a facility, but they don't show up or they don't use the facility as intended. Interested parties may make a preliminary request to reserve a facility, taking a lot of time to discuss arrangements with facility staff, and then never follow through with a formal request. To deter facility users from wasting facility resources, sometimes advance deposits are required in order to reserve the facility. Agency policies should clearly define deposit requirements and stipulations. Typically, a deposit is returned at the end of the use, providing the facility and equipment are not damaged. Reserving parties who fail to show up for the intended use may forfeit their deposit or a portion of it based on a reasonable percentage of the full charges. This practice makes users think twice about not showing up. Advance deposits demonstrate good faith on the part of the potential user, and they protect administrative time and effort.

A refund policy should also be in place; it indicates under what circumstances users may receive a partial or entire return of any fees paid. A policy statement should protect facilities from unwarranted requests while also returning to users all or part of a fee under certain conditions. A refund may be issued when user expectations are not met, an unforeseen change in the user's situation occurs, or the agency has a change in facility availability. Whatever the situation, the policy should include refund request details and be approved by the administrative authority of the agency. The agency could also use a refund request form, as seen in figure 13.3.

Damage

Use of a recreation facility can result in damage to the facility and equipment. These developments are often unexpected and are seldom addressed during scheduling discussions. Unfortunately, damages do occur as a result of unruly participants, vandalism, weather, or accidents. If no damage policy exists, the facility may have a difficult time recovering financial resources from the user group who caused the damage. A damage policy should be discussed in advance during reservation nego-

tiations with users so that they have full insight into their responsibility to protect facilities and equipment. Usually, some type of facility inspection occurs with facility personnel and potential users before usage, citing all areas and equipment conditions so that neither party is caught off guard by preexisting damage. Facility personnel should also conduct an inspection after use and document any damages caused by the user. A deposit fee is often incorporated into the facility use agreement; it states the conditions for the deposit to be returned to the user or retained by the facility after a final inspection occurs.

Food-Service Policies

Some facility users may want food and beverage products available during their use. Requests may include the sale, purchase, or distribution of food and beverages, including alcohol. Any food-service arrangement should clearly stipulate the facility user's responsibilities. If a third party provides food service, facility management must be informed of the caterer's credentials and licenses and review the contract between the potential user and food provider. If the facility provides food service, all menu items and pricing should be reviewed in advance so that no surprises or misunderstandings occur between the facility and user.

Whether the facility, the user, or a catering service provides the food service, facility personnel should inform users of licenses, codes, and requirements dictated by state and local government. The sale or distribution of alcoholic beverages presents additional issues for both users and facility operators. Certain restrictions will be imposed by state and local agencies, and a higher degree of supervision may be required. Additional liability to the user and facility operator because of the sale or distribution of alcoholic beverages may have financial or other implications. Food-service policies should clearly state limitations, restrictions, and expectations of the facility and the user.

Refund Request Form

Household name _____ Date _____

Address _____

City _____ State _____ Zip _____

Amount of refund _____ Participant name _____

Program _____ Class code # _____

Reason for refund _____

Requested by _____

Comments _____

_____

For Office Use Only

Approved by _____ Amount of refund _____

Account # _____ Project code # _____

Transaction fee amount _____ Return this form to refund clerk by _____

Check # _____ Date mailed _____ Receipt # _____

This form may be used only for refunds.

From B. Beggs, R. Mull, M. Renneisen, and M. Mulvaney, 2024, *Recreation Facility Management*, 2nd ed. (Champaign, IL: Human Kinetics).

FIGURE 13.3 Sample refund request form.

The facility user may supply food and beverages at a special event, or the recreation facility or a third-party caterer may supply them for a fee.

© Human Kinetics

Insurance Policies

Recreation facility managers may expect users to obtain insurance to cover their use of the facility. When insurance is necessary, the agency should have a policy statement that stipulates the type and amount of insurance coverage expected. The agency may also expect proof of insurance by requesting a certificate of insurance to ensure that the coverage is appropriate. The user's policy should cover all aspects of the use, including the areas and space used, interior and exterior equipment, people who are involved, and complete time span from setup through cleanup. The certificate of insurance should state the limits of liability and type of coverage provided, and the user should present it before making final arrangements.

Summary

Recreation facilities often serve the needs of many activities and programs. It is critical that activities be coordinated in a manner that maximizes facility use in an efficient and effective manner. Carefully coordinating activities can avoid conflict and result in positive experiences for both facilities and users. In addition to scheduling activities related to the core product and core product extensions, agencies often must work with their users in reserving and scheduling space for outside activities. By having procedures and policies in place for employees and users to follow, this process can run smoothly for all involved.

REVIEW QUESTIONS

1. Why is it important to consider stakeholder needs when coordinating maximum facility usage?
2. List the procedures associated with the facility scheduling process and provide a brief description of each.
3. What is a master schedule? What is its role in facility scheduling?
4. Create a sample policy that could be used to support the facility scheduling process.

CASE STUDY

Staff Scheduling

You are the assistant manager for the Hill Valley Recreation Center, a 150,000-square-foot (139,354 m^2) recreation facility. The facility includes office space, multipurpose courts, a one-eighth-mile (1/5 km) running and walking track (six lanes), a fitness area with resistance and cardio equipment, three studios for aerobic fitness and dance classes, a child care room, an indoor climbing wall, a lap pool, and an aquatic zone (including a lazy river, slides, and splash pad).

One of your primary responsibilities is the supervision of the recreation center's part-time staff. When developing the staff work schedule, the following parameters must be followed:

- Agency policy does not allow part-time employees to work more than 40 hours per week or more than 12 hours per day.
- Agency policy requires that all staff wear appropriate uniforms.
- The Hill Valley Recreation Center is open to the public during the following hours:
  - Monday through Friday: 5:00 a.m. to 10:00 p.m.
  - Saturday and Sunday: 6:00 a.m. to 10:00 p.m.
- An average breakdown of visitors or users at the Hill Valley Recreation Center is as follows:
  - Monday through Friday: 5:00 a.m. to 7:00 a.m. (average of 100 visitors per hour)
  - Monday through Friday: 7:00 a.m. to 4:00 p.m. (average of 40 visitors per hour)
  - Monday through Friday: 4:00 p.m. to 8:00 p.m. (average of 400 visitors per hour)
  - Monday through Friday: 8:00 p.m. to 10:00 p.m. (average of 30 visitors per hour)
  - Saturday and Sunday: 6:00 a.m. to 8:00 a.m. (average of 100 visitors per hour)
  - Saturday and Sunday: 8:00 a.m. to 10:00 a.m. (average of 70 visitors per hour)
  - Saturday and Sunday: 10:00 a.m. to 5:00 p.m. (average of 300 visitors per hour)
  - Saturday and Sunday: 5:00 p.m. to 8:00 p.m. (average of 70 visitors per hour)
  - Saturday and Sunday: 8:00 p.m. to 10:00 p.m. (average of 30 visitors per hour)
- Agency policy requires at least one staff member (can be more depending on the number of visitors) at each of the following areas within the Hill Valley Recreation Center:
  - *Front desk and check-in area*: All visitors must check in (swipe their membership card) or purchase a daily pass at the front desk before entering the facility. Two

members of front desk staff are needed during peak usage, and one is needed during non-peak hours.

- *Evening and weekend manager*: An evening manager must be in the facility from 4 p.m. to close on Monday through Friday and from open to close on Saturday and Sunday. The evening manager serves as the supervisor for all staff in the building and is your immediate subordinate.

- *General facility staff*: Staff that work under the supervision of the evening or weekend manager and are assigned to various facility areas (multipurpose courts, event setup, track supervision, open gym monitors, etc.). Two general facility staff members are needed during peak usage, and one is needed during nonpeak hours.

- *Lap pool and aquatic pool*: Two lifeguards are needed during peak usage, and one is needed during nonpeak hours.

- *Fitness area*: Two members of service staff (to answer questions, service equipment, clean, etc.) are needed during peak usage, and one is needed during nonpeak hours.

The available staff and their specific requests or preferences are listed here:

Front Desk Staff

- Mary—Can only work 2 weekends per month
- Jon—Can't work before 4 p.m.
- Natasha—Can't work on Saturdays or Thursdays
- Susan—Can work any hours
- Natalie—Can work any hours
- Torre—Has another job and prefers to work fewer than 20 hours per week
- Juan—Has another job and prefers to only work after 5:30 p.m. and fewer than 20 hours per week
- Anita—Can work any hours, but prefers mornings (if possible)

Evening or Weekend Manager

- Zeb—Can work any hours during the weekends but only Mondays or Wednesdays during the workweek
- Stephanie—Can work any hours
- Christopher—Can work any day except Saturday
- Nick—Can work any hours, but must have third weekend of month off for military obligation
- Mandy—Can only work Friday, Saturday, or Sunday
- Julie—Can work any hours

General Facility Staff

- Randy—Can only work after 4 p.m. and can only work two weekends this month
- Courtney—Can only work after 5 p.m.
- Carrie—Can work any day after 4 p.m.
- Jesse—Can work any hours
- Jasmine—Can work any hours

- Mike—Can only work Friday, Saturday, or Sunday
- Marcus—Can only work before 5 p.m.
- Megan—Can work any hours
- Michelle—Can work any day except Tuesday and Thursday

Lap Pool and Aquatic Zone
- Harold—Can work after 5 p.m. on Monday through Friday and all day on Saturday (can't work Sundays)
- Henri—Can work any time after 4 p.m.
- Katie—Can only work on Saturday or Sunday
- Karen—Can only work on Saturday or Sunday
- Katlyn—Can work any hours
- Karson—Can work any hours
- Margret—Can only work before 5 p.m. on Monday through Friday and is unavailable on weekends
- Missy—Can work any hours
- Mason—Can work any hours
- Nellie—Can work any hours
- Nancy—Can work any hours
- Zelda—Can work any hours

Fitness Area
- Pat—Can work any time before 6 p.m. any day of the week
- Norris—Can only work after 3 p.m. on Monday through Friday and prefers to only work two weekends per month
- Corey—Can work weekends only
- Carrie—Can work any hours
- Angela—Can work any hours
- Amy—Can work any hours, but only a total of 5 days per week (needs at least 2 days off per week)
- Lynne—Can work any hours after 4 p.m.
- Lynda—Can only work after 4 p.m. on Monday, Tuesday, Wednesday, and Thursday
- Katana—Can work Saturday and Sunday only and must have at least one weekend off per month

Case Study Questions
1. As part of this supervision, you must develop staffing work schedules for the 150,000-square-foot (139,354 m²) facility. Using the information outlined in the case study, prepare a 1-week staffing work schedule for the front desk staff

   Note: It is expected that the staffing schedule will attempt to minimize employee dissatisfaction.

CHAPTER 14

Maintenance

LEARNING OBJECTIVES

At the completion of this chapter, you should be able to do the following:

1. Explain how maintenance affects facility usage and operations.
2. Identify the categories of facility maintenance.
3. Recognize the processes involved in maintenance requests.

Maintenance as a management function can be a critical contributor to facility utilization. If not performed properly and in a timely fashion, it can have a negative effect on the core product and core product extensions. **Maintenance** includes any function associated with keeping facilities and equipment in proper, safe, and functional condition. It is a support service that is often performed behind the scenes. Terms associated with maintenance activities include the following:

- Clean
- Replace
- Repair
- Prevent

- Protect
- Preserve
- Fix
- Change over
- Set up

The goal of the maintenance function is to keep everything as close to its original condition as possible so that facility usage can take place as intended without safety concerns, distractions, delays, or disruptions.

In some agencies, maintenance functions are mistakenly regarded as a secondary responsibility; thus, maintenance is taken for granted and not given proper attention from management. However, poor maintenance practices

Environmental stewardship and sustainable practices have been the guiding principles of the Techny Prairie Activity Center since its beginnings. A groundbreaking ceremony was held on July 10, 2019, and the facility officially opened in January 2021. Managed by the Northbrook Park District in Northbrook, Illinois, the 44,200-square-foot (4,106 m²) facility is a future-forward building that uses net zero energy.

The Techny Prairie Activity Center is situated on a 6-acre (2.4 ha) property that was once the home of a large (over 300 workers) industrial kitchen products factory. The Northbrook Park District acquired the property in 2011, and the agency launched an extensive pollutant removal program to clean up the site. These efforts led to the repurposing of this industrial site to the Techny Prairie Park and Fields.

Situated in the middle of these scenic views of the prairie, the Techny Prairie Park Activity Center is a multipurpose facility that includes a fitness area, cardio and strength-training equipment, a gymnasium, a multipurpose room, an indoor track, fitness studios, and office space. Efforts to develop an eco-friendly facility were prioritized throughout the design, construction, and operations and maintenance phases of the project. For example, more than 800 rooftop photovoltaic solar panels generate enough (and sometimes more) energy to support the building during an entire 12-month period (Scovic, 2022). In addition, a 200-foot (61 m) bioswale in the parking lot utilizes native plantings that collect and filter storm water, which is eventually introduced into the Chicago River.

A landscape operations and maintenance plan was also developed to support sustainable practices at the center. No-mow spaces are utilized to decrease the use of chemicals and fossil fuel consumption. Plantings in naturalized areas were designed to support pollinators, and nearly 70 trees were planted in strategic locations. These features are just a few examples of the Techny Prairie Activity Center's future-forward focus that contributed to the facility being included on the Illinois Net Zero Honor Roll and Watch List by the Illinois Green Alliance (Scovic, 2022).

can have a negative effect on user satisfaction and product delivery. In some cases, lack of appropriate maintenance practices leads to compromising user safety. Maintenance should always be a priority function. Recreation facility managers must be committed to and involved in the maintenance process so that intended utilization can occur, leading to positive user experiences with the product.

Maintenance can be an indirect or a direct function of product delivery. In most instances, maintenance is an indirect function because maintenance workers seldom are in contact with users. Recreation facility managers often intentionally schedule maintenance functions for times when the facility is not being used. Scheduling maintenance functions during these times is critical for the efficient and effective completion of maintenance tasks so as not to interfere with administrative and delivery operations. Scheduling maintenance functions

can be challenging, particularly for recreation facilities that are in high demand. Maintenance tasks have to take place when the facility is not in use, which is often late at night or early in the morning. Recreation facilities that are extensive or have more complex products have unique maintenance scheduling challenges.

As mentioned, maintenance can have a direct effect on the delivery of the product. Therefore, it is important for maintenance leadership to understand facility usage, including what activities it involves, volume of users expected, preparation efforts, and consequences, so that they can realize how their role and decisions will affect utilization. If maintenance is required while a facility is in use, then management and maintenance leadership should devote time and effort to keeping user inconveniences to a minimum and ensuring that maintenance tasks do not negatively affect usage.

Maintenance functions require unique scheduling practices to avoid interfering with utilization of a facility.
© Human Kinetics

Safety

A top priority for every facility manager, safety is an important end result of good maintenance. Sometimes product usage results in the degeneration of the area or equipment, which can lead to hazardous conditions. For instance, playgrounds often have loose-fill surfaces such as wood chips or shredded rubber. If the playground has swings, usually children drag their feet under the swings, moving the loose-fill surface and creating an area directly under the swing with less surfacing for fall protection. Requiring the simple maintenance task of sweeping and leveling the loose-fill surface greatly improves safety in the swing area, diminishing the risk of serious injury. Other examples of unsafe conditions include a nail sticking out of a floor, security equipment that is not working, a hole in a playing field, a crack in a sidewalk, water on a floor, an emergency exit that is blocked, or ice or snow in parking areas. The maintenance staff is usually in the best position to see hazardous situations and correct them. Maintenance staff should also conduct regular checks of smoke alarms, security alarms, emergency lighting, and other safety mechanisms in a facility. Their role in protecting users and employees is invaluable in keeping a facility free from unsafe conditions and serious emergencies.

Annual inspections of all life safety systems for emergency disruptions, including fire alarm checks, should be documented to ensure that the systems will function as planned. Documentation would include a description of any maintenance practices that factor into the prevention process. In addition, any maintenance practice that is part of an evacuation plan should be included in the plan. For example, if an ice arena has an ammonia leak and the evacuation plan calls for a maintenance employee to shut down a series of equipment to limit further contamination, it should be documented in the evacuation plan.

Maintaining playground equipment and surfacing is critical to user safety and diminishing risk of injury.
Nannapat Pagtong/iStock/Getty Images

Facility Image

The end result of the maintenance function will influence users' perceptions of the facility. Their impression of a facility may include a sense of comfort and belonging or a sense of uncertainty or discomfort. Recreation facilities that are not clean, are unsanitary, have broken equipment, or have other poor maintenance practices can drive users away. For example, a person staying at a resort is much more likely to return to that location if the facility and rooms are clean and in good condition. The same holds true for users' experiences at a park or playground. If the area is clean and well maintained with no broken equipment, users are more likely to be satisfied with the experience than they would be if equipment didn't work or the area were dirty. Facility maintenance can make either a positive or a negative statement about the facility, the product, and management. Facility management should put forth every effort to maintain a positive image through good maintenance practices.

CHECK IT OUT
The Importance of a Good Front-of-the-House Impression

Commonly called the *front of the house*, the parking lot, landscaping, reception areas, and other areas of initial contact provide facility users with a first impression. Studies have shown that a facility has only about 7 seconds to make a first impression (Gibbons, 2018). In other words, potential facility users are not likely to get very far into the physical facility space before forming their impression. Facility managers should be asking this question: What can be done in these front-of-the-house areas to create a positive first impression?

Maintenance and Environmental Stewardship

In addition to safety and the facility's image, it is also important to recognize the relationship between a facility's maintenance activities and environmental stewardship efforts. A facility's focus on environmentally friendly and sustainable practices should be intertwined with the maintenance program. A quality maintenance program can help safeguard against overuse, help preserve the facility and its resources, and extend the life of operational equipment and tools. Recycling programs, facility or land use restrictions, integrated pest management policies, chemical use and disposal methods, and similar environmental considerations are just a few examples of the symbiotic relationship between a facility's maintenance and environmental stewardship activities.

Maintenance Types

The two general types of maintenance are routine and nonroutine. These two categories help to describe how tasks may be organized.

Routine Maintenance

Routine maintenance is ongoing maintenance that represents management efforts to keep facilities and equipment in proper condition from day to day or even hour to hour. Facilities depend on routine daily maintenance tasks to keep the production environment and equipment in its proper functioning state. Routine maintenance requires supervision, coordination, and attention to detail. These tasks are often performed around the delivery of the product, so they may be organized on a daily or weekly checklist and recorded on an inventory form (see figure 14.1). Routine maintenance tasks should not be interrupted; delays can result in problems. However, when routine maintenance tasks such as cleaning, trash removal, and maintaining an aesthetically pleasing environment are apparent to users, it indicates a well-organized and coordinated maintenance system.

Nonroutine Maintenance

Not all maintenance is routine. Many circumstances exist where nonroutine activities

Facility Maintenance Inventory Form

Facility items		Condition	Location of problem	Comments
General	Sport activity areas	Pool #1			
		Pool #2			
		Basketball court #1			
		Basketball court #2			
		Racquetball court #1			
		Racquetball court #2			
		Exercise or weight room			
	Office areas	Office #1			
		Office #2			
		Office #3			
		Break or meeting room			
		Reception or lobby area			
	Locker and storage areas	Women's locker room			
		Men's locker room			
		Storage area #1			
		Storage area #2			
	Safety	Fire alarm system			
		Security system			
		Sprinkler system			
		Back-up generators			
Structural	Interior	Ceiling			
		Floor			
		Walls			
		Windows			
		Doors			
	Exterior	Roof			
		Gutter and downspouts			
		Wall treatment			
		Windows			
		Doors			

From B. Beggs, R. Mull, M. Renneisen, and M. Mulvaney, 2024, Recreation Facility Management, 2nd ed. (Champaign, IL: Human Kinetics).

Facility items		Condition	Location of problem	Comments
Utilities	Water and sewer	Water lines			
		Sewer lines			
		Water heaters			
		Water treatment systems			
		Sink and shower fixtures			
		Toilets			
		Drinking fountains			
	Electric and gas	Electric lines			
		Gas lines			
		HVAC systems			
		Electrical fixtures			
Grounds	Vegetation	Trees and shrubs			
		Grass			
	Parking and Walkways	Parking lot #1 (asphalt)			
		Parking lot #2 (gravel)			
		Sidewalk #1			
		Sidewalk #2			
		Mulch path			

Conditions: S = Satisfactory condition
H = Hazardous condition
R = Routine maintenance needed
M = Large-scale maintenance needed (more than $500)
m = Small-scale maintenance needed (less than $500)

From B. Beggs, R. Mull, M. Renneisen, and M. Mulvaney, 2024, Recreation Facility Management, 2nd ed. (Champaign, IL: Human Kinetics).

FIGURE 14.1   Sample daily maintenance inventory form.

require maintenance attention, including projects and unforeseen, preventive, and cyclical maintenance. Nonroutine maintenance usually requires extra attention, especially as it relates to the coordination and scheduling of work that is needed. When these situations develop, a system is initiated that recognizes a need and then issues a response to take care of it.

Projects

From time to time, facilities and equipment require work resulting from damage, breakdown, or failure. This work is considered a project, which may require planning and design. Nonroutine maintenance projects may include repair, renovation, or refurbishing of flooring, walls, turf, or equipment. These projects may or may not be preplanned, and their accomplishment could require a short or long time. As projects are scheduled, the work area must be blocked off from the public for their safety. It is a good idea to post a notice in advance about any projects that are being completed so that users and employees are aware of the time frame during which an area or piece of equipment will be unavailable.

Unforeseen Maintenance

Often, nonroutine maintenance tasks fall under the category of unforeseen maintenance. Frequently they are the direct result of wear and tear from facility and equipment usage. A maintenance system should be in place to repair areas or equipment when they simply reach a point where they do not function as intended. These cases can be an emergency (the problem is addressed as soon as possible), or they can be scheduled to be addressed when resources and time allow. Examples of unforeseen emergencies include the following:

- Trees falling over power lines
- Water leaks that affect delivery operations
- Toilet overflow
- Electricity or light failure

Other unforeseen maintenance tasks that may not require immediate action include the following:

- Locks not functioning
- Vehicles not starting
- Broken windows
- Water damage
- Any area or equipment that can be scheduled for repair without disrupting facility usage

Preventive Maintenance

Recreation facility managers try to avoid unforeseen maintenance through preventive maintenance. **Preventive maintenance** is applied in anticipation of what needs to be done to protect areas and equipment from wearing out, failing to operate, or breaking down. This nonroutine practice is usually planned, but it most often results from a judgment based on the level of use and wear of areas or equipment. This preventive system recognizes potential problems and then attends to them, increasing the longevity of areas and equipment and ensuring their protection. When managed properly, preventive maintenance can decrease or even prevent area and equipment problems and possible hazards. Examples of preventive maintenance include the following:

- Changing oil and rotating tires on vehicles or maintenance equipment
- Pruning trees around electrical wires and buildings
- Controlling insects and pests
- Refurbishing floors
- Painting surfaces
- Repairing cracks in concrete and asphalt surfaces

Cyclical Maintenance

Another type of nonroutine maintenance is cyclical maintenance. Although cyclical maintenance is performed on a schedule, it occurs infrequently and is not considered routine maintenance. **Cyclical maintenance** is a nonroutine application that is initiated as needed and performed with a complete set of tasks designed to restore an area or piece of equipment to its desired state. Cyclical maintenance incorporates several steps in order to complete

Preventive maintenance can decrease or prevent facility problems. Pruning trees around the facility could prevent damage to the facility at a later date.
CasarsaGuru/E+/Getty Images

a full process or cycle. An example of a cyclical practice is maintaining turf areas, which requires soil preparation, seeding, fertilizer, watering, mowing, and aerating. These practices are repeated in a cycle (usually seasonally) and can be planned in advance.

Areas of Maintenance

Whether routine or nonroutine, maintenance tasks can be broadly categorized into the following areas:

- Building maintenance
- Grounds maintenance
- Equipment maintenance

Building maintenance involves indoor facilities or structures, including rooms, corridors, stairwells, lobbies, lounges, and offices that need to be kept clean, functional, and safe.

Specific building maintenance tasks include the following:

- Sweeping
- Mopping
- Picking up trash
- Window washing
- Watering plants
- Dusting
- Vacuuming
- Deep cleaning carpets
- Changing lights
- Repairing windows and doors
- Plumbing
- Performing electrical or mechanical repairs

Grounds maintenance can have several meanings depending on the recreation

Infield grooming is a form of grounds maintenance.
© Human Kinetics

facility. An outdoor facility such as a park or playground primarily requires grounds maintenance. In addition, exterior and landscaping care of a recreation building falls under grounds maintenance. Grounds maintenance is often the first thing users see and thus it affects their first impression of a facility and its curb appeal. This maintenance category incorporates all the necessary activities associated with keeping the outdoor areas attractive, functional, and safe. It includes tasks such as the following:

- Snow removal
- Leaf removal
- Tree pruning
- Watering
- Fertilizing
- Weed control
- Grass mowing
- Pest control
- Disease control
- Trash removal
- Shrub trimming
- Grooming of infield surfaces

Equipment maintenance refers to maintaining items and mechanical systems that support a facility or help to make the product efficient and functional. It can include maintenance equipment and any equipment that fulfills product delivery. It can also include technical equipment for the efficiency support systems that provide comfort to users and employees as well as assistance with product delivery. Certain equipment can be susceptible to damage and wear, resulting in demanding maintenance work. Examples of maintenance in this category include the following:

- Repairing machines
- Replacing parts
- Cleaning
- Rotating and replacing tires
- Sharpening tools
- Servicing HVAC equipment

Maintenance Systems

The production and delivery process should not be subject to negative developments because of facility maintenance practices. A recreation facility is designed to create and deliver a product without disruptions. Recreation facility managers should ensure that a maintenance system is in place that attends to all nonroutine developments before they negatively influence operations. Maintenance systems should be created in the most effective way possible, and they should include planning, work orders, and work assignments.

Planning

Fundamental to a sound maintenance system is having a plan in place for addressing all potential facility and equipment maintenance concerns. A maintenance plan should incorporate both short-range and long-range planning. Planning is critical because so many details are involved with the maintenance responsibilities of a recreation facility. The key to planning is to anticipate deterioration, repairs, and replacements rather than react to them. This responsibility can be demanding. Not everything can be foreseen, and unexpected developments require a planning system that addresses whatever *may* occur. Planning must be evaluated regularly and modified as necessary. In order to keep facilities and equipment functioning properly, inventory, assessment, and task identification are often built into the maintenance planning process.

Inventory

A basic task of a maintenance system is creating and maintaining a complete inventory of everything that exists in the agency. This process creates precise records for reference whenever necessary so that accurate information exists, leading to proper planning. Detailed information about every aspect of a facility and its equipment is usually gathered to reflect quality, quantity, condition, number, type, size, cost, age, and location. Facility managers and maintenance leaders can use this information to help with planning various areas of maintenance, including budget, development projects, emergency assistance, preventive steps, production concerns, and the need for extra help.

Assessment

The facility assessment process allows maintenance employees to contribute to a systemized maintenance plan. This type of assessment does not address user needs; instead, it focuses on the maintenance needs of a facility as identified by maintenance personnel. Maintenance employees can be scheduled to perform a visual check of a particular area or piece of equipment. This inspection can be scheduled regularly as the maintenance employees perform routine tasks associated with their position. Maintenance employees are in the best position to recognize limitations that need to be identified for both short-range and long-range maintenance planning. These assessments can lead to discovery of structural problems, unsafe situations, efficiency system failures, potential emergency situations, and other routine and nonroutine maintenance concerns. This information should be incorporated in a plan to address the facility or equipment problem. Assessment results can also be interfaced with formal feasibility studies or risk management plans and needs assessments that may be underway. Assessing facilities and equipment is a proactive effort

CHECK IT OUT

A Multibillion-Dollar Backlog of Deferred Maintenance

When confronted with budgetary reductions, a common strategy of many recreation facilities and agencies is to defer previously scheduled, bigger (and more expensive) maintenance projects. Called *deferred maintenance*, these projects could include a roof replacement, new windows, flooring upgrades, and other tasks. According to the NRPA's Park Metrics (NRPA, 2022), local park and recreation agencies in the United States have more than an estimated US$60 billion worth of deferred maintenance.

that helps identify and solve problems before they can affect product success.

Task Identification

Before initiating nonroutine maintenance work, someone needs to submit information regarding the maintenance concern. This information can come from observations or assessments by maintenance employees, production staff, or product users. It can be presented through verbal complaints, user complaint forms, or staff requests for assistance. Each option should cite some type of problem that needs attention. Management should be prepared to receive this information, which may be relayed in a negative fashion, with sensitivity. This feedback is important because it offers information that could have a negative effect on delivery operations and customer satisfaction. Once maintenance situations are identified, they should be placed into a work-order system that addresses maintenance concerns in a timely fashion.

FIGURE 14.2   Sample maintenance request form.

Work Orders

When a nonroutine maintenance issue is identified, the organization needs to have an action system that evaluates the problem, makes a judgment, prioritizes it with all other needs, and then assigns an employee to attend to it. This responsibility can be demanding, especially in a large agency. The response to a maintenance issue should be organized through a formal maintenance work-order system that includes a control center as well as a job form and number.

In the work-order system, a formal documenting process should begin when someone identifies a maintenance issue and makes a request. This request is a written or electronic form that identifies the category of work, its location, its nature, and whether it is an emergency (see figure 14.2). Some emergency situations may be handled by telephone, postponing the completion of this form until a later date. The request form usually requires a signature from the person completing it, along with additional information such as the department, telephone number, email address, and detailed description of the nonroutine request

for service. This request initiates a process that takes administrative time and effort and has a financial impact on the agency.

Control Center

After a request form is completed, it is often routed to a central place for review and assignment; this location for maintenance operations is the control center (some facilities may use a different name for it). This stage of the process is administrative in nature; it represents the authority in receiving, reviewing, assigning, and supervising work. During this stage, an administrator or manager prioritizes all work, assesses costs involved, coordinates and assigns workers, and oversees work from beginning to end. This stage also includes keeping pertinent records and documenting all work performed.

Job Form and Number

A job form represents the official assignment of the work that needs to be done. As part of the form, a description of the work is included along with a job number, which serves as an identification code for the work. This number is usually logged in a sequence that can be applied to a written or computer-generated form. The job form and number assist in keeping accurate records, provide easy access for review, and track all work as it is being completed. It authorizes and assigns the work to a specific maintenance employee or team that usually stays with the job through completion. Copies of the form are made available to the requesting person or unit, the maintenance employees completing the job, the control center, and the administration so that all parties can be updated on the status of the job.

Work Assignments

After the control center has processed the request, an administrative manager assigns the job. Work assignments can be influenced by the extent and degree of the work required,

Trash removal is one of many tasks that a maintenance unit may be responsible for in a park.
MediaNews Group/Contra Costa Times via Getty Images

availability and ability of workers, financial resources available, and level of demand. A work assignment requires management to supervise the work in progress and make sure that it will get done correctly and on time. Work assignment options depend on the structure of the agency and the type of work to be completed; these options include units, specialized crews, and outside contractors.

Units

One approach to getting nonroutine work accomplished is to have it performed within a particular unit. A unit is a component of the maintenance division that responds to agency-generated work requests. It has the benefit of being familiar with agency facilities, grounds, and equipment and their respective maintenance needs. A unit could be a complete area or a building with a crew that is responsible for all maintenance operations within that area. For example, a park maintenance unit may be responsible for mowing, trash removal, equipment repair, irrigation system repair, horticulture maintenance, and so on.

Advantages to a unit approach to work assignments include employees becoming familiar with maintenance of particular facility areas and ease of determining responsibilities. This type of system also breeds a high level of loyalty and pride within the unit. On the downside, employees need to learn a variety of jobs, supervisors must have diverse capacities to oversee work and equipment, and a unit approach may not make the most efficient use of expensive equipment.

Specialized Crews

Specialized crews consist of people who are trained to have specific skills. Examples of specialized crews include tree surgeons, mechanics, carpenters, locksmiths, plumbers, and electricians. Because of their experience or certifications, they are considered experts and their work is expected to be of the highest quality. These specialists could be the only ones who can competently complete a particular task. Large recreation agencies may have enough specialty work to keep these types of employees busy.

Specialized crews could be scheduled to move from one area or facility to another to perform their work. Advantages of this system are that crews become extremely proficient at their work, expensive equipment is used efficiently, and the chance of accidents is lower because of workers' experience and knowledge. Some disadvantages are that repetition of work tends to create boredom and mediocre work, and the assignment of a specialized crew to a variety of locations results in time lost for travel.

Outside Contractors

Recreation agencies use outside contractors when a task cannot be accomplished internally, it requires specialized employees, or it is simply more efficient to contract out. Advantages of contracting out certain tasks include well-trained workers, no capital investment in equipment, no in-house personnel problems such as unqualified staff, appropriate insurance protection carried by the contractor, and decreased workload for in-house maintenance staff. On the other hand, disadvantages for contracting out maintenance include loss of control of when and how work is completed, higher costs, less vested interest in the facility and operations by external employees, and potential difficulty in coordinating a contractor's time with facility usage.

Arrangements with outside contractors should always be completed through a formal process. The contract requires careful attention; it must be written clearly with precise task descriptions to avoid mistakes or miscommunications. When work is contracted out, it is advisable to provide agency supervision of the task to ensure that the work is completed as expected.

Other Maintenance Considerations

Each maintenance consideration has a unique role that should be incorporated into a comprehensive maintenance system. In addition to the basic categories of maintenance, management must also account for supervising maintenance activities, keeping maintenance records, establishing maintenance manuals, housing maintenance shops and storage facilities, inspecting maintenance work, and maintaining efficiency systems.

Supervising Maintenance Activities

Supervision of all employees is paramount to effective recreation service delivery. Often nonroutine maintenance employees may work in a location where supervision is not present; however, to avoid a lack of effort, their work needs to be monitored regularly. The supervision of maintenance employees is not easy. Care and tact are high priorities, especially when supervising work that has demanding requirements. Supervisors need to be able to have difficult conversations and share sensitive information with employees and do so in such a manner to preserve professional relationships. Managers need to establish a system to monitor and control work performance, especially when working less-trained or noncertified staff.

Keeping Maintenance Records

Records regarding assigned work should document the time required to complete a maintenance task as well as track costs, including labor, materials, and overhead. Keeping records helps with budgeting, maintenance accountability, and showing proof of work. Maintenance records can be extremely beneficial if legal action is taken against a recreation agency because they prove that routine maintenance tasks are completed. Records can also help with scheduling subsequent projects and employees because requests may parallel those for past work.

Using maintenance management software and web-based application programs can support maintenance record-keeping activities. Many of these programs enable maintenance staff to record activities on equipment, create scheduled service appointments, and send automated reminders to optimize repair times and overall efficiency of the maintenance program.

Establishing Maintenance Manuals

Maintenance manuals are instructional documents that provide written descriptions, photos, and diagrams that explain exactly what is required in the proper care of facilities and equipment. These manuals are particularly valuable for equipment or facilities that are highly technical. They provide details on everything required to keep the equipment or facility functioning effectively, often including a step-by-step checklist or system that guides employees through the work process. These manuals play an important role in effective maintenance operations. Manuals assist with keeping detailed information available to present and future maintenance employees and with keeping maintenance tasks organized.

Housing Maintenance Shops and Storage Facilities

Large, multifaceted recreation agencies that have both indoor and outdoor facilities could have an extensive maintenance operation that incorporates a specialized maintenance shop or department. Large recreation agencies sometimes have specialty areas that house particular maintenance functions in order to minimize the expenses involved with renting equipment, hiring outside expert assistance, and contracting out work functions. These shops can be created and maintained as independent departments with specific functions and equipment needs. Typical independent shops or departments include the following:

- Paint shops
- Machine shops
- Carpenter shops
- Key shops
- Plumbing shops
- Landscaping shops

These areas could also be located in a maintenance control center or in a storage and warehouse facility, which is another important maintenance-related space.

Storage facilities or warehouses contain equipment, bulk supplies, spare parts, and other maintenance items. Often they are incorporated with the control center for appropriate supervision, control, and distribution of the items. These areas often store items that require protection, including chemicals, flammable materials, paint, gasoline, fertilizer, paper goods, and production supplies. Some of these items are purchased in bulk in order to save money, and a storage area or warehouse houses them until they are needed. Some of the bulk supply items commonly purchased and stored include grass seed, light bulbs, toilet paper, soap, and hand towels.

Sustainable Practices

Sustainable practices are not just a good component of a maintenance program; they are expected. Common activities that support sustainable practices within a facility's maintenance program include the following:

- *Sustainability analyses.* Facilities should perform regularly scheduled assessments of existing maintenance equipment practices to identify any potential inefficiencies. The utilization of technological resources (e.g., data tracking software) can aid the facility in better understanding its current practices and identify areas for potential improvement.

- *Energy efficiency.* As equipment ages, it likely becomes less efficient to operate. Guided by the sustainability analyses, equipment that is, or has become, less efficient to operate should undergo updates to improve its efficiency. In some instances, it may also be more efficient to recycle and replace the older equipment with an upgraded version.

- *Eco-friendly supplies.* Toxic chemicals (e.g., glyphosate herbicides, certain cleaning products) used to support the facility's operations should be scrutinized, and facilities should consider strategies to reduce or replace these supplies with eco-friendly alternatives.

- *Recycling.* Receptacles for recyclable materials should be available throughout the facility. Traffic flow analyses should be performed to determine areas of high use, and receptacles should be located accordingly. In addition to establishing recycling activities to support facility user groups, facilities should also implement a system for recycling maintenance and operational materials. Recycling of used office supplies (e.g., paper, printer toner, outdated equipment) as well as maintenance materials (e.g., used mechanical oil, chemicals, broken equipment) should be standard practice for the facility.

Inspecting Maintenance Work

An important component of maintenance is keeping a facility and its equipment safe for users and employees. Any number of conditions can have a negative effect on delivery operations. In addition, codes, rules, and regulations that are enforced by local, state, and federal building inspectors must be followed.

External inspectors from local, state, and federal governing bodies regularly conduct formal reviews and write reports that reflect problems with facilities and their production process. Inspectors could require that corrections be made, issue a citation and a fine, and even shut down the facility for not meeting requirements. Maintenance employees are often looked upon to understand these requirements and be responsible for proper preventive maintenance. Members of in-house maintenance staff often conduct regular checks to avoid negative consequences during inspections. Areas that are frequently inspected for proper maintenance include fire codes, electrical standards, plumbing, area capacity, ventilation, and sanitary conditions.

Maintaining Efficiency Systems

The need to make a recreation facility functional and comfortable relies greatly on elaborate efficiency systems, which require maintenance employees to keep them working properly. Indoor recreation efficiency systems include HVAC systems, security systems, restrooms, plumbing, and lighting. Outdoor systems include irrigation, lighting, security systems, restrooms, and public-address systems.

How well these systems work—especially at times of high use—is a significant factor for recreation facilities. Whether this work is to be performed internally or contracted out, it is a crucial responsibility. Maintenance staff should also be familiar with utility monitoring and repair. Interruption of water or electrical service, waste removal, or communication systems could result in negative consequences for users and hence the recreation agency. Maintenance employees who have the ability to repair efficiency systems are valuable resources for a recreation facility.

Summary

Although maintenance is not the main focus of recreation facilities, it is an integral part of efficient operations. When facilities establish maintenance procedures and have policies in place to govern maintenance, users can have a safe recreation experience. In addition, a well-maintained facility creates a positive image for the core product and the organization, and thus users are more likely to return.

REVIEW QUESTIONS

1. How are facility safety and maintenance related?

2. What is the *front of the house* when considering a facility's maintenance plan?

3. Provide an example of (a) a routine maintenance task and (b) a nonroutine maintenance task.

4. What are some ways a facility can integrate eco-friendly practices into their maintenance plan?

5. List and briefly describe the typical elements that should be included in a facility's maintenance system; provide one or two sentences for each element.

CASE STUDY

The Employment Interview and Job Hunt

You are on the job hunt! You have been in the field of recreation for 3 years, and you think that you have gotten about all you are going to get (professionally) out of your current role as an assistant facility manager of a community recreation complex. You are enjoying your current position, but you are eager to challenge yourself in different ways, acquire new skills, and grow as a professional.

While you are actively searching for that next opportunity, you are also being somewhat selective in where you apply as well as what you might accept should you receive an offer. Because you are happy in your current position, you feel you can be a bit more selective; you do not want to be overly aggressive with your search. Embracing this mindset, you have spent the past few months watching the job boards and networking with your contacts to learn about any new opportunities.

Two weeks ago, you learned of an opportunity that intrigued you; a position for director of facilities and operations position has become available. The agency would be slightly smaller than your current agency. In addition, the position would allow you to manage a more diverse set of facilities, namely, a combination of indoor and outdoor sites. You are hoping the smaller agency size and the variety of facilities will allow you to get involved in projects that you will likely not tackle in your current position. Overall, you are excited about the potential with this position and decide to apply.

Within 3 days of applying, you are contacted for an in-person interview. You are surprised by their quick response to your application. A tour and in-person interview has been scheduled. During the tour, the executive director of the agency drives you to the two park sites and indoor facility you would be responsible for if you were hired. While it is during the daytime hours of a weekday, you notice both parks are nearly empty with only a few visitors.

The parking lots for both parks have several potholes, and one large waste receptacle with no lid appears to be overflowing with trash. The landscaping around the entrance signage is overgrown with weeds. It also appears a few of the lights in the parking lot are broken. During the tour, you do get a chance to walk into the park as the executive director shows you the various amenities within each site. Once in the park, you are pleased to see all of the amenities are in safe, working condition. Most look relatively new and reasonably well maintained. The outdoor green areas appear to be mowed, signage in the park is clean and informative, and you can see a great deal of potential for these sites.

During your tour of the indoor facility, you notice a few pieces of fitness equipment that are not working, and they have signs on them indicating they are out of order. While the main areas appear to be clear of dust and debris, you do notice a few areas where cleaning could be improved. Finally, you also notice that the lights for each facility space are on even though no one is using about half of the spaces.

After completing the tour, you and the executive director sit down in the conference room for a conversation. The executive director asks for your opinion on the sites that were toured, and you also get a chance to ask a few questions. During this discussion, you learn that the agency uses outside contractors to clean the indoor facility. These crews work only in the evening because the agency does not want to have cleaning crews disturb the facility users during its open hours in the daytime. The cleaning crews are provided with a specific list of areas to service or clean. According to the executive director, the cleaning crew has done a solid job cleaning those areas on the list. However, a challenge occurs when other areas need to be serviced or during the daytime hours when a situation might arise (spills, overflowing garbage cans, etc.). In such instances, the agency's facility's maintenance supervisor, who works out of another building, is tasked with responding to the situation.

The agency utilizes a maintenance and cleaning crew for the two outdoor park sites as well. Similar to the indoor facility, these crews focus their efforts on addressing tasks the agency has provided to them.

In an effort to prepare you for the interview, the executive director warns you that several of the questions will likely center on how the agency, and the facility and operations director in particular, will work to improve usage at these sites. You thank the executive director for the insight, and you both head into the administration building for the interview.

Case Study Questions

1. During the interview, one of the interviewers asks, "We collect feedback from individuals that use the amenities in our outdoor park sites and, overall, they are pleased with what we offer. However, we feel the actual number of users in relation to our market is still low. Based on what you saw today, what are some ways we might be able to make our outdoor sites more appealing and increase traffic to these sites?"

2. Another interviewer asks, "What do you think about our use of outside contractors to clean the park sites and facility? If you were in this role, what would you see as advantages or disadvantages to using these outside contractors?"

3. During one of your responses to an interview question, you mention your observations that parts of the indoor facility might have benefited from some spot cleaning during the daytime hours. One of the interviewers asks how you might address that issue. How would you respond?

4. Overall, what do you think? From your perspective, what could be one or two positive aspects of accepting this job (if it were offered to you)? What might be one or two concerns associated with accepting this job (if it were offered to you)?

CHAPTER 15

Emergencies and Emergency Responses

LEARNING OBJECTIVES

At the completion of this chapter, you should be able to do the following:

1. Recognize the varying degrees of disruption in facility activities.
2. Recognize the various catalysts for disruptions in recreation facilities.
3. Understand the systems that should be in place for an emergency response.

In recreation facility management, the administration influences all operational functions to create a process that delivers a product as effectively and efficiently as possible. Whatever the product, recreation facility managers focus on influencing usage to lead to satisfaction and success. At some point, disruptions (either gradual or sudden) can throw the production process into disorder, interrupting the expected delivery of service. When a disruption occurs, the management response must provide appropriate attention to eliminate the disruption. Recreation facility managers play an important role in preparing a facility for disruptions and for executing emergency procedures.

Disruption in Facility Activities

Delivery of a recreation product can occur daily, weekly, or monthly. Accordingly, operational efforts can become routine simply based on repetition of usual responsibilities and tasks. Whatever the time frame, the product delivery has been planned, organized, and directed, and the users' perception is that all elements of the production process are under control.

One of the unfortunate aspects of facility management is that things do not always go as planned. In spite of the best precautionary

Built almost 75 years ago, the Dennis Malone Aquatic Center (DMAC) is an indoor aquatic facility in Bristol, Connecticut. The DMAC is owned and operated by the City of Bristol's Parks, Recreation, Youth and Community Services. Amenities in the DMAC include a 185,000-gallon (700 m³) indoor pool, six swim lanes, and a 1-yard (1 m) diving board. Open year round, the DMAC hosts a variety of aquatic exercise classes, swim lessons, open swimming, and competitive swim training sessions.

The emergency action plans utilized by the City of Bristol in general, and the DMAC in particular, are especially impressive. A 2022 class IV (population 30,001-75,000) finalist for the NRPA's Gold Medal Award, the City of Bristol and their DMAC facility adopt a training mindset in the fostering of a culture of safety and emergency preparedness. According to Jaimie Clout, aquatics supervisor, a constant message reinforced with their aquatics lifeguards is that "they are the 'first,' first responders and they must train like that" (Clout, 2022). The City of Bristol and the DMAC embrace this mindset, and they train staff for worst-case scenarios.

Regular risk assessments are routine at the DMAC and the city's other facilities. Inventories of these areas and the levels of risk within these spaces are completed and updated by staff to ensure the emergency response plans are current and appropriate. More recently, the City of Bristol has examined their spaces for opportunities related to physical and mental health and potential (elevated) risks or threats for these areas. Potential risks related to behavior, special populations, advanced medical emergencies, and age are all considered and integrated into their emergency action planning activities.

measures and control practices, disruptions can still occur. It is management's role to anticipate these potential disruptions, accept the responsibility for every situation, and be prepared to respond in an organized fashion.

Degrees of Disruption

Disruptions come in varying degrees and in a wide range of conditions. Minor disruptions could include concerns such as toilets overflowing, lights not working, negative user behavior, equipment malfunctioning, comfort systems (e.g., HVAC) breaking down, weather problems, crowd control, and more. Even these minor unexpected situations can often be time consuming and challenging to resolve. If they are not dealt with properly, they could escalate into more serious situations. It is usually the responsibility of management to address unexpected disruptions and implement appropriate action. Responses to unexpected disruptions could include a call to maintenance to fix an equipment-related problem, a call to security to deal with user behavior, or a verbal warning given face-to-face or over a public-address system to caution against unacceptable user behavior. Whatever response is required, recreation facility managers have to be in a position to address the disruption so that the production process can continue.

A fact of recreation facility management is that unexpected disruptions can also be severe. These unexpected situations extend beyond usual circumstances, and they could affect users' and employees' physical or emotional well-being. They may be perceived as minor at first, but they can quickly escalate to a dangerous level. Extreme disruptions can place both users and employees in a situation that requires emergency attention and assistance. Examples of major disruptions include severe weather, equipment breakdowns that stop product delivery, extremely negative user behavior, crowd panic, or severe health problems such as heart attacks, strokes, or accidents leading to bodily injury. Recreation facility managers should have an appropriate precautionary plan and response in place to address any development of an extreme nature. Disruptions that are not managed appropriately can evolve into serious injury, emotional trauma, defamed reputations, damaging lawsuits, or sanctions of irresponsibility. Ultimately, a disruption of this nature could lead to the demise of a recreation facility. Plans for emergency response are discussed later in this chapter.

Some extreme conditions can result in life-threatening situations. A worst-case scenario, such as a fire, tornado, hurricane, earthquake, flood, violence, or crowd panic, can end in the death of a person or group. In some cases, investigations reveal the lack of a planned emergency response system. Although the production process can be time consuming for recreation facility managers and not every extreme situation can be completely anticipated or controlled, it is vital to be prepared for extreme conditions that can cause life-threatening situations.

Catalysts for Disruption

Every user expects the usual delivery of a product. Employees also expect the routine of providing the same product day in and day out. However, situations develop that cause disruptions, and these disruptions have unique characteristics in different parts of the world. Certain regions may be susceptible to specific natural disasters, such as earthquakes, floods, mudslides, rockslides, avalanches, tornadoes, or others. Management should consider this factor when creating a plan to respond to disruptions. The nature of the product may also affect the planned response to a potential disruption. For example, the sheer physical size or geography of a ski resort may require a specific planned response to a participant's ski-related injury or to an avalanche. In contrast, the limited physical size of an indoor facility may require a much different response to a participant injury. Each facility, its location, and its type of product must be evaluated to plan for potential disruptions.

The evaluation process includes being aware of the catalysts that create disruptions, especially those that affect participant and employee safety and well-being. The disruption catalyst could be the product itself, maintenance,

Recreation facility managers need to be prepared to address out-of-control behavior from users. One way to prepare is to employ security staff to control the crowd.

weather, fire, threats, crowd behavior, or a combination of two or more catalysts. Initially these catalysts could be perceived as relatively harmless, but they could evolve into something more severe and challenging to management.

Product or Service

The nature of the product may create disruptions. These situations may not necessarily be part of the usual production process, but they can create delays that need to be addressed. Some examples include mechanical breakdowns such as lighting failure, spectator misbehavior, and equipment malfunction. Any of these occurrences can create delays and frustration. The most common disruptions are when users become ill or injured. These events may require medical or emergency treatment, which can disrupt product usage. Recreation facility managers should keep their focus on the production and delivery process and be aware of how the intended use may result in disruptions for those who are using the facility.

Maintenance

Maintenance functions not performed in a timely and efficient manner can disrupt facility operations. Examples of disruptions include unfinished facility repairs, nonfunctioning equipment that needs to be fixed or replaced, setup that has not been completed in a timely fashion, and sidewalks not cleared of snow. Maintenance disruptions are unfortunate because they are usually preventable if they

Recreation facility managers must be prepared for any type of injury that may occur while a user is participating in a core product's delivery. It may even include contacting medical staff outside of the facility for help.

© Human Kinetics

are identified in a timely manner and appropriate action is taken. Maintenance disruptions can be minimized through proper planning, good communication, and the presence of a sound maintenance system. Management needs to communicate with maintenance and production personnel to coordinate and anticipate maintenance-related disruptions. Applying preventive measures, conducting inspections, and initiating a well-thought-out and documented preventive maintenance plan (described in chapter 14) should minimize these concerns.

Sometimes the use of chemicals may be necessary in the production and maintenance process of recreation facilities. Recreation facility managers must be aware of the potential danger to users and employees that could result from the use or storage of chemicals. Incidents involving chemicals occur when inappropriate use or an unexpected release of chemical agents occurs. This type of disruption negatively affects the production process, creating potential harm for users as well as employees; it should be avoided at all costs. Chemical spills may require an evacuation or the activation of an emergency plan. The following are general guidelines for responding to chemical spills:

- Notify the facility manager on duty.
- Evacuate the area of the spill or evacuate the facility (depending on the size of the spill and the chemical).
- Contact the fire department, or call the emergency number (911 in the United States).
- Attend to people who may have come into contact with the chemical. Remove clothing, and flush skin with water.
- Follow chemical guidelines for cleanup.

A more detailed plan for dealing with chemical situations should be in place for all recreation facilities. In the United States, the Centers for Disease Control and Prevention (CDC) provides guidelines for chemical storage, which should be incorporated into this plan. Facility management should be aware of the responsibilities associated with the use and storage of chemicals.

Weather

One of the most common outdoor recreation facility disruptions is inclement weather. Even when inclement weather is anticipated, it can have far-reaching negative implications for the facility. Recreation facility managers could even be held responsible for not providing appropriate warnings as dangerous weather situations develop.

Each facility has its own potential weather situations that require a plan of action to protect participants and employees. Depending on the region, these extreme conditions may include tornadoes, hurricanes, earthquakes, landslides, floods, and avalanches. In some parts of the world, extreme heat and humidity or cold can affect participants' and employees' physical and emotional well-being.

Seemingly typical weather conditions can quickly become extreme. Light snow can turn into a blizzard with excessive snow that can limit access to and from a facility. Excessive rain can create flooding that can have severe ramifications. Heat or humidity can reach such high temperatures that people's health becomes compromised through heat exhaustion or heatstroke. When weather conditions deteriorate while an indoor or outdoor recreation facility is in use, managers must remember that they are responsible for the people at the facility.

Fire

Another common yet unexpected disruption in facilities is fire. Lightning, electrical problems, human carelessness, spontaneous combustion, and intentional arson can cause fires. Fires in recreation facilities are extremely dangerous; the danger is not only from the fire but also from the resulting smoke and crowd panic. Facility managers and staff should take precaution to prevent fires and to extinguish them if they occur. Fires have resulted in innumerable deaths throughout history. Evidence has shown that many of these deaths could have been avoided with proper management or preventive measures. Typically, city, state, or federal laws require indoor facilities to have fire response mechanisms, including fire alarms, fire extinguishers, sprinkler systems, and other devices to protect facility participants and employees. Management must be aware of potential fire hazards, and they must take every precaution to prevent them and respond accordingly. Standard procedures in the event of a fire include the following:

- Activate the fire alarm system.
- Call the fire department or emergency number (911 in the United States).
- Notify the facility manager on duty.
- Evacuate the building.

Facilities are usually required to post these procedures. Once the building has been evacuated, the manager should meet the fire department as they arrive at the facility to provide information about the fire and the facility. If the fire is small, facility staff may use a fire extinguisher to put out the fire. However, if they have any doubt about whether they can put the fire out, they should not attempt to extinguish the fire and should evacuate the facility.

Threats

Unfortunately, the term *terrorist threat* has increasingly become common. This type of disruption can occur with or without warning. In some cases, a disturbed person or group informs a facility of a bomb or other dangerous device in a facility. This action could create a disruption that leads to the evacuation of the facility. In other cases, the threat comes without warning. In this situation, management is forced to respond to the threat after the action has occurred.

Unfortunately, little can be done to deter such actions. The greatest challenge to recreation facility managers in this case is making the judgment to accept the terrorist threat as reality and not a hoax. In situations of this nature, it is best to be proactive, evacuating the facility and calling emergency personnel to assess and contain the potential threat. Virtually all communities have an emergency management response system in place. The

A fire is an extreme emergency that may have life-threatening consequences. Recreation facility managers should minimize fire risks and have a response system in place in the event of a fire.
Stevecoleimages/E+/Getty Images

U.S. Department of Homeland Security (DHS) regularly updates the status of threat and guidelines for dealing with threats. Information can also be obtained by contacting the local emergency response agency.

Active Shooter

According to the DHS, an *active shooter* is someone who is actively engaged in killing or attempting to kill people in a confined or populated area (2008). In most cases, active shooters use firearms, and their method and pattern is highly unpredictable. In the United States, many active shooter situations are over in 10 to 15 minutes and before law enforcement is able to arrive on the scene (Federal Bureau of Investigation, 2022). Because of the quick nature of these situations, facility managers and users must be prepared to deal with an active shooter situation. Several federal agencies have developed a set of response strategies for facilities to follow in the unfortunate event of an active shooter. These strategies are outlined in the sidebar "Run. Hide. Fight."

Facility managers should establish an emergency action plan (EAP) for active shooter situations. The EAP should include the following elements:

- Emergency reporting procedures and contact information
- Evacuation plans, including escape plans and route assignments as well as evacuation policies and procedures
- Local hospital information
- Emergency notification system to alert all facility spaces or areas, law enforcement, and hospitals

Training exercises should be scheduled regularly to prepare staff in how to effectively respond to these unfortunate situations. At a minimum, training programs should educate staff on facility floor plans, evacuation routes, security plans, and crisis kit organization. Working with local law enforcement and other local emergency response units can be an effective strategy in the development of thorough training programs.

Crowd Behavior

Anytime the core product draws a large number of people in one place, the potential for a crowd-related incident becomes a concern for recreation facility managers. In typical circumstances, crowds can be a positive part of a facility, generating energy and enthusiasm for a product. However, recreation facility managers should be prepared to make efficient and effective decisions to ensure safety when crowds begin to get out of control or participate in disruptive activities. Crowds can be dangerous because disruptions can trigger panic or irrational actions. Crowd behavior can range from supportive and participatory to rebellious and hostile.

In the past, deaths have occurred as a result of crowds that are out of control. People have been trampled and killed at concerts with large crowds. In some instances, people have been unable to evacuate crowded nightclubs in a fire, resulting in death. This type of situation can be one of the most demanding facility responsibilities to plan for and control. Management should take every precaution to assess crowd behavior to avoid the development of inappropriate behavior and, when necessary, take appropriate action to prevent crowd behavior from getting out of control.

Emergency Responses

Recreation facility managers should have a system in place to appropriately respond to whatever disruptions occur. Emergency

---

CHECK IT OUT

Characteristics of an Active Shooter

According to the U.S. Department of Homeland Security (DHS), active shooters typically select victims at random, making prior detection difficult.

Run. Hide. Fight.
Recommended Strategies With an Active Shooter Situation

When Visiting a Facility for the First Time

- *Assess.* Orient yourself to the environment and potential dangers.
- *Exits.* When visiting a facility, take a moment to identify the two nearest exits.

In the Event of an Active Shooter Situation

- *Run.* If it is safe to do so, run to the nearest accessible escape path and evacuate the premises.
- *Secure and hide.* If evacuating the facility is not an option, get into a room and secure the door. Hide behind heavy or large items. Remain quiet.
- *Last resort. Fight.* If a shooter is in close range and you cannot flee, your chance of survival is much greater if you try to incapacitate the shooter. Be aggressive and commit to your actions. Throw items, yell, and improvise weapons against the shooter.
- *Call 911.* When and if it is safe to do so, call 911.

When Law Enforcement Arrives

- *Remain calm.* Follow the officers' orders and instructions. Avoid quick movements toward the officers.
- *Hands.* Remove any items from your hands. Show or raise your hands. Keep your hands visible to law enforcement.
- *Let them do their job.* Don't stop to speak with the officers or ask them for help. Allow the officers to do their job.

From United States Department of Homeland Security, *Active Shooter: How to Respond*, (Washington, DC: Department of Homeland Security, 2008).

responses vary; they are determined by the type of facility, the catalyst, and the product that is being delivered. It is vital that management be fully aware of not only the potential disruption but also the coordination of an appropriate emergency response.

Each recreation facility should have a system in place that can respond to disruptions when necessary. This action must be effective and efficient in order to minimize the damage to facilities and equipment and, most important, to attend to situations that could affect participants and employees. Facility managers must provide leadership and take action by handling disruptions, requesting support from law enforcement and medical personnel as judged appropriate, and facilitating steps to evacuation if needed.

CHECK IT OUT
Brainstorming Helps!

How can a facility prepare for all of the possible emergencies? It can be a difficult task. One strategy is to brainstorm the worst-case scenarios, answering the question *What should be done if the worst happened?* Attempting to tackle these situations by imagining them in advance can allow facility staff to more clearly and logically flush out an EAP that best addresses the worst-case scenario.

Leadership

Management must demonstrate leadership in making appropriate judgments for action when a disruption occurs. As discussed earlier in this chapter, all facilities and equipment can experience varying degrees of disruption. Recreation facility managers must make the appropriate decision, anticipate potential disruptions, and have proper procedures in place for dealing with these situations.

Some recreation facilities will respond to these situations with a few special arrangements, whereas others will need to provide the highest level of security and medical care. The cost to provide appropriate responses could be prohibitive for some recreation facilities. However, proper precautions can

Pool lifeguards, supervisors, and managers are delegated by the recreation facility manager to represent their facility and respond to disruptions. These employees are trained for their responsibilities, and they are certified in standard first aid (SFA) and CPR.

VanHart/fotolia.com

result in cost avoidance. Failing to take any precautionary steps can result in more serious and costly problems. Management should be aware of potential disruptions. Supervision and warnings are two key actions that help fortify recreation facility managers' leadership role in responding to disruptions.

Supervision

Recreation facility managers cannot be in all places at all times. Often, responsibilities for reacting to emergencies are delegated to qualified employees. The delegation process authorizes the appropriate person to represent and take appropriate action on behalf of management as necessary. Possible employees who might be delegated this responsibility include supervisors, ushers, guards, attendants, and officers. Generally, these employees or volunteers should be in a position to manage disruptions or emergencies at the facility. Depending on the product and potential situations, various levels of training and certification could be required of employees in these supervisory roles. Facility supervisors are typically certified in CPR, standard first aid (SFA), and the use of portable defibrillators. Other certifications may be necessary for certain facility personnel, including lifeguard training, water safety instructor training, or certified pool operator training. Supervisory employees usually function as observers, requesting assistance, taking appropriate action, reporting disruptions and emergencies, and responding to any incident that arises.

Warnings

Every facility, equipment included, should be designed to minimize accidents or injuries. Occasionally, the design, construction, or renovation of a facility can result in unintended disruptions to the delivery of a product. Often, these unintended consequences are not discovered until the facility is in use. It is incumbent on recreation facility managers to notify users or employees when they discover a part of the production process that can lead to injury. In these cases, managers should provide advance warning. Warnings should be displayed and accurately worded so that all users and employees are fully aware of the potential for injury.

Taking Action

Some disruptions can escalate to the point that immediate action is required. The degree to which this action is required depends on the disruption and its severity. The response of recreation facility managers should be neither excessive nor incomplete. The three basic steps for taking action are as follows:

1. Assess
2. Attend
3. Refer

Assess

Supervisory staff, along with other employees involved with the production process, should have the ability to observe and evaluate what is going on in the delivery of a product. If a disruption happens to occur, staff should remain calm and assess the situation. Previous employee training will provide proper knowledge and techniques to accurately assess and address the disruption. The ability to accurately assess and respond appropriately is important. An inappropriate assessment can sometimes lead to a response that is worse than no response at all.

Attend

An emergency response plan should exist that attends properly to any disruption. Appropriate action could be as formal as SFA, CPR, preventive disease transmission (PDT), or announcing warnings. Other responses to less threatening situations include resolving conflict, repairing equipment, or diverting attention from disruptions. When proper attention is not given, the consequences could be extensive for all involved. The importance of this aspect of facility management cannot be overstated.

Refer

In most cases, supervisory staff can handle disruptions by providing appropriate attention. However, sometimes these developments need

Sometimes facility use requires the assistance of law enforcement personnel to control the area and help avoid any emergencies.
KAMIL KRZACZYNSKI/AFP via Getty Images

to be referred to outside parties after the initial action is taken. A referral may entail bringing investigators to the site, an ambulance for medical assistance, or police to assist with people who may need to be removed. Occasionally, a referral is necessary when a disruption exceeds the ability of management to respond.

Law Enforcement   Some disruptions can be anticipated because of large crowds, social tension, high intensity, or skill level of participants. Even with qualified staff, recreation facility managers can anticipate disruptions that exceed their capacity. In these instances, proactive managers may have security guards or police at the facility to assist with potential disruptions and to serve as a deterrent. However, the use of law enforcement should not be excessive; too much police presence can have the opposite outcome of what is desired.

Medical Assistance   The delivery of some recreation products can create situations that require responses beyond SFA, CPR, and PDT. Although these activities may have inherent dangers, their popularity and participant involvement is not diminished by the potential danger. When necessary, management may have medical personnel on site to assist with any injuries. Some examples of medical personnel used in the recreation environment include trainers, paramedics, nurses, EMTs, and doctors. These medical personnel have varying degrees of training that would allow them to attend to a more severe situation. Depending on the type of activity, some or all of these personnel may be warranted at a recreation facility. It is management's responsibility to anticipate these developments and make sure the appropriate assistance is available.

Evacuation

Catalysts such as chemical spills, bomb threats, threats of violence or death, fire, hurricanes, floods, and earthquakes can be so serious that management must have a system established for evacuating the facility. Catastrophic developments require immediate action to remove people from a facility or place them in a position that protects them from harm.

Disruptions of catastrophic proportion are infrequent, and most recreation facility managers have never had to initiate an evacuation plan. Even though such occurrences may be rare, they can still occur. Recreation facility managers should have an established and practiced evacuation plan in the event an evacuation is necessary. This evacuation plan should describe employee responsibilities, include basic facility information such as location of emergency exits and safe locations, and list other actions that should be taken in the event of an emergency. Facility managers should conduct drills every six months to practice these evacuation plans.

When developing an evacuation plan, it is important to keep it as simple and concise as possible. Disruptions can vary so greatly that the plan could require unique and immediate interpretation by staff in tenuous circumstances, which means keeping the plan simple and concise is a must. An evacuation plan should include these three components:

1. Assessment or inquiry
2. General information
3. Action steps

Assessment or Inquiry

One of the first things that recreation facility managers should do when creating an evacuation plan is to check with fire, law enforcement, and emergency personnel for any local requirements regarding an evacuation plan. Fire, police, or other municipal agencies often have requirements for building evacuation. Local codes or ordinances can also stipulate what kind of plan should be in place.

Recreation facility managers should also ascertain if an emergency planning group is available. Many U.S. communities have a designated emergency planning group that has developed an emergency response and evacuation plan. This group is a resource whose guidance should be followed with any facility evacuation plan.

For an additional resource, recreation facility managers can also use evacuation plans obtained from similar facilities. Although these

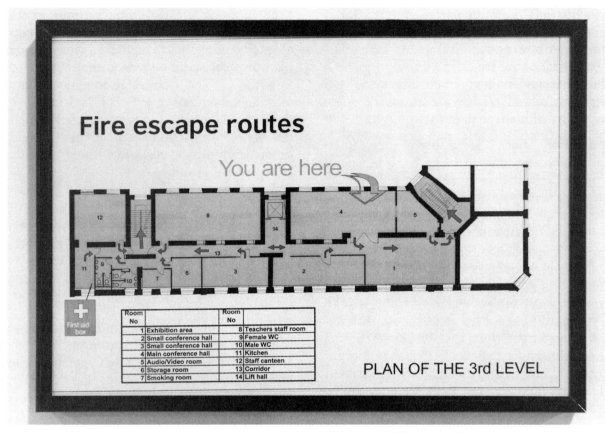

It is important to post an emergency plan where it is easily accessible by all facility staff and users.
Bzzz/iStock/Getty Images

plans do not always match the facility plan, they could help with format, resources, and general information.

General Information

Any evacuation plan should be in writing, and it should be put in a highly visible and accessible place where facility personnel can locate it in an emergency situation. The evacuation plan should state general information identifying the users, core product, core product extensions, mission, and goals and objectives. These statements help emphasize the activity level, involvement of staff, and interaction that takes place in the facility during an emergency situation.

An emergency and evacuation plan should include a specific policy statement that ensures the safety of users during an emergency. In addition, it should show the relationship and coordination with all local emergency service agencies (fire, police, medical, emergency). The information should reflect a full description of the facility, making references to architectural drawings, space capacities, physical layout, entrances and exits, primary and secondary communication systems, and the location of any emergency command center. The architect or a fire marshal can help with understanding this information and assisting in preparing the emergency and evacuation plan. It is also prudent to provide local fire and police agencies with copies of the facility blueprints for use in emergency situations.

Action Steps

When an evacuation is required, certain action steps must be initiated. Responsibilities should be identified, delegated, and explained to facility personnel before emergencies occur. In addition, these specific situations should be addressed:

- What happens if main entrances are blocked?
- How do users and employees with disabilities exit safely?
- Should certain instructions be disregarded if conditions change rapidly?
- What happens if electrical power is lost?
- If a child care facility is on-site, how will children be evacuated, especially if they are too young to move independently?

The procedures for executing the evacuation need to be clearly documented for full understanding. All employees need to know what the procedures are and how their role relates to other steps in the process. Ongoing training and rehearsals should be conducted to reinforce employee knowledge and practical application of the evacuation plan.

An evacuation plan should include any forms or reports necessary to assist with revisions or improvements to the plan. Documentation should include details of simulation exercises, all staff training, and inspections in case a critique is necessary either before or after an evacuation.

Finally, potential serious disruptions should be defined based on the location of the facility, its structure, and the product usage. Recreation facility managers should remember that each disruption may have different factors to consider when determining the appropriate action steps to implement.

Summary

Emergencies and disruptions in providing the core product and core product extensions are not common; however, they do occur. It is the role of recreation facility managers to provide leadership for employees and users in responding to these situations. A prepared response and an evacuation plan for catastrophic disruptions can lead to a safer response for all involved.

REVIEW QUESTIONS

1. Provide two examples of a minor disruption and two examples of a life-threatening disruption that can occur in a recreation facility.
2. Describe the typical steps involved in managing a fire-related disruption in a recreation facility.
3. Outline the recommended strategies in responding to an active shooter situation in a facility.
4. Why is it important for a facility's evacuation plan to be simple and concise?

CASE STUDY

Adventure Center Coming to the Lynne Lake Retreat and Conference Center

You are the property manager for the Lynne Lake Retreat and Conference Center (LLRCC). The LLRCC is located in a rural setting with the nearest town, Waverly (population 7,800) approximately 5 miles (8 km) west of the property. Despite its rural location, the LLRCC is sandwiched between two larger cities (with populations over 1 million) that are both approximately 1.5-hour drives from the site.

The LLRCC is a private organization that has been in operation for over 50 years. The 200-acre (81 ha) property includes the following:

- An 80-acre (32 ha) lake
- Motel-style lodging for up to 1,000 guests
- 200 RV full-service hookups

- Lynne Lake Center, which includes a dining hall and four meeting rooms
- Recreation complex with a gym and indoor pool
- Outdoor athletic fields, beachfront area with a climbing wall, and hiking and walking trails

The LLRCC can accommodate groups as small as 50 to as large as 1,200 as overnight guests. Groups can book all-inclusive packages that bundle lodging, meeting spaces, buffet dining, and general recreation activities and experiences. Groups can also customize their experience by reserving specific spaces and amenities on the property.

During the last 5 years, reservations have steadily increased about 4 percent year-over-year. The facilities continue to be popular with many groups who book return trips to the LLRCC. Word-of-mouth advertising has also helped the business; many guests and groups cite the LLRCC's exceptional customer service, general maintenance, and the overall quality of the accommodations as the primary reasons for their enjoyable experience. In addition, data collected from guests after their stay has identified an adventure-based recreation space as the LLRCC's top missing amenity and service.

Responding to the steady growth, financial stability, and the post-visit survey data, the CEO of the LLRCC decided to invest in the development of a new adventure-recreation facility on the LLRCC's property. Named the Lynne Adventure Center, the new facility includes a high ropes course, zip line areas, low ropes team initiatives, a climbing and traversing area, and escape rooms. The zip line platform, located on the top level of the Adventure Center, opens to the outside; the actual zip line cable runs outdoors. Each space was developed with the goal of fostering team-building opportunities for groups and their guests.

As the property manager, you supervised the planning, design, and construction of the Lynne Adventure Center. A groundbreaking ceremony for the center was held 18 months ago, and the facility was completed less than a month ago. You will also be responsible for the overall operations of the new Adventure Center once it is officially open to guests later next month. Before the Lynne Adventure Center is made available to guests, your CEO has asked you to develop the appropriate policies, operational procedures, staff training needs, and emergency response plans.

Case Study Questions

1. Brainstorm a list of possible disruptions that could require the Lynne Adventure Center to temporarily close.

2. Consider the list developed in question 1. Identify the specific emergency response plans that would need to be developed for the Lynne Adventure Center.

3. As a property manager, you will need to develop the appropriate emergency response plans for the Lynne Adventure Center. What are some resources or strategies you could use to help in developing these plans?

4. Should any outside entities be included in the Lynne Adventure Center's emergency response plans? If so, who?

PART V

TYPES OF RECREATION FACILITIES

There are many types of recreation facilities. The most common types include parks, playgrounds, aquatic parks, and recreational sport facilities. Whether they are designed to provide a service or to produce a profit, each type of facility has the potential to generate revenue for an organization, an agency, or a surrounding community. To operate a facility effectively, recreation facility managers must understand the unique characteristics of that facility type.

CHAPTER 16

Parks and Playground Facilities

LEARNING OBJECTIVES

At the completion of this chapter, you should be able to do the following:

1. Identify the various types of parks and their characteristics.
2. Recognize the design factors that make each park unique.
3. Examine maintenance and safety practices used in parks.
4. Recognize the various types of playgrounds and their purposes.
5. Explain the concept of use zones and fall protection in playgrounds.
6. Recognize the characteristics of various types of playground surfaces.

Parks and playgrounds are outdoor amenities that are part of every community. These facilities can be core products or core product extensions of another facility. Parks are outdoor spaces that provide an opportunity to connect with nature, whereas playgrounds are facilities with equipment and structures that provide physical challenges and are primarily geared toward children. It is common to see playgrounds built within a park, but it is important to distinguish between them because they have unique characteristics.

Parks

Parks are prominent in the fabric of communities all over the world. A **park** can be defined as an outdoor space made available to the public, often provided by a public agency, for the benefit of the citizens of a community, state, or country. Public parks are owned and operated by tax-supported government agencies, including local municipality, state, or national systems. Private parks are typically owned and operated by either corporations or private organizations

Industry Profile

Officially opened in January 2022, the Louis A. DePasquale Universal Design Playground is a 30,000-square-foot (2,787 m²) play area in Cambridge, Massachusetts. Located in the City of Cambridge's Danehy Park, it is the city's first playground to fully incorporate the seven principles of universal design (see chapter 8):

1. Equitable design and use
2. Flexibility in use
3. Simple and intuitive use
4. Perceptible information
5. Tolerance for error
6. Low physical effort
7. Size and space for approach and use

Each of these principles was considered in nearly every facet of the playground and its equipment. The park was designed for all ages; the playground's key amenities include the following:

1. Junior and senior play areas to support various age levels and experiences.
2. Slides with horizontal tubing to allow users to hear and feel when sliding.
3. Swing and spin zone and climbing slope to promote both independent and interactive play experiences.
4. Music area where users can play chimes or simulate rain sounds. The space also has plantings to foster sensory (smell, sight, touch) stimulation.
5. Sensory walk zone, which includes a pathway with various accessible surfaces that support users with or without mobility devices and provide changes in tactile and auditory responses as users navigate through it.
6. Sensory hilltop that is reached after completing an accessible labyrinth pathway.
7. Art-play sculpture with curving wooden planks, window features, and handholds for climbing.
8. Poured-in-place rubber surfacing use zones around the play equipment that provide non-slip, cushioned, fall-protection surfaces for users.
9. Splash pad for use in the summer months that includes junior and senior play features and seating for caregivers.

Over 50 trees were planted throughout the playground, and the wood used in most of the playground was sourced from harvested black locust trees (which are resistant to decay and rot) from an earlier city project.

Further integration of the community into the park is evident in the paintings along playground walls, which were completed by a local artist with autism. The playground is named in honor of Cambridge's city manager, Louis A. DePasquale, who was instrumental in the playground's universal design focus.

that provide opportunities for employees or members. Parks have many benefits:

- Parks offer a respite from urban areas, congestion, pavement, and other manufactured features.

- Parks provide natural habitats for wildlife and plants.
- Users may appreciate the ability to connect with nature in park settings.

- Users may also be able to use park areas to improve physical fitness through running, walking, hiking, biking, and other outdoor activities.
- Parks can have economic benefits; they may be designed to generate revenue if they have fees associated with them.
- The value of property in the vicinity of parks is higher than property not located near parks.

Parks can exist in a variety of settings, including woodlands, mountains, deserts, rain forests, beach areas, and underwater reefs. They can also simply be a neighborhood area that has a playground or ball field available for residents.

Types of Parks

Parks range in size, shape, function, and amenities. Most parks are owned and operated by some form of government system that is supported with tax dollars, fees and charges, donations, or all these sources. The most common public parks can be classified as neighborhood, urban, community or regional, linear, state, and national parks. Specialty parks can be public or private, depending on who owns them. They include theme parks, aquatic parks, and sport parks, and they are usually operated with the primary objective of generating revenue.

Neighborhood Parks

Neighborhood parks serve relatively small areas of a community; by definition, they are located in a neighborhood, often in a densely populated area. Generally, users or neighbors can access neighborhood parks by walking. These types of parks are generally 15 acres (6 ha) or smaller, and they offer amenities such as a playground, park benches, a picnic shelter, and an open area for multipurpose use.

Neighborhood parks are located in a specific neighborhood, which is often densely populated.
Russell Monk/The Image Bank RF/Getty Images

Urban Parks

Urban parks serve the most densely developed areas of a community. Urban parks tend to be fairly small, and they are usually bordered by a combination of residences and businesses. These types of parks often include hard surfaces such as concrete or pavement to accommodate the high traffic expected. Park benches, tables, and occasionally performance stages are common in urban parks. Depending on the location of the park, a playground may also be included.

Pop-Up Parks

A relatively new type of recreational space is the pop-up park. **Pop-up parks** can be permanent or temporary installations, are typically small in size (in the United States, referenced in square footage rather than acreage), relatively low in cost and maintenance, and provide cities with community-gathering spaces and opportunities to connect with nature (Collins, 2019). Most pop-up parks are located in urban areas and aim to provide more green space in these areas. Another trademark of these spaces is the ongoing amenity changes. For example, a 7,000-square-foot (650 m^2) pop-up park may include artwork, seating, planter beds, and food trucks; 6 months later, it might have an outdoor piano and host bands.

Community or Regional Parks

A **community park** (also called **regional park**) is larger than a neighborhood or urban park. Typical size can range from 15 acres (6 ha) to several hundred acres. This type of park consists of a broader range of amenities that attract users from a greater geographic area. Users are more likely to have to drive to a community or regional park. For this reason, large parking facilities are common. Typical features include all of the amenities commonly found in neighborhood parks, in addition to sport fields; hiking, biking, and skating paths; aquatic facilities; formal gardens; water features; zoos; museums; and other recreation attractions.

Linear Parks

The linear park is generally found along a stream, river, or wetland area or an abandoned railroad bed. By definition, **linear parks** are long or linear in nature, and they may connect to other similar parks. When two or more linear parks are connected, they are called **greenways**. Often, a trail system is incorporated in a linear park. In the United States, the Recreational Trails Program created a movement aimed to convert abandoned railroad corridors into trails for use as alternative transportation routes as well as for recreation. Funding from the federal government passed down to state and local governments assists in the development of these trail systems throughout the United States.

State Parks

A state park is usually larger than a community or regional park, but it may have similar amenities. **State parks** are owned and operated by a large government unit, and they serve those within the boundaries of the state and others who come to visit from outside the state. In the United States, state parks are operated by the Department of Natural Resources (DNR), a state department. In Canada, the system of parks similar to state parks are provincial parks. These types of parks are usually created to preserve natural areas such as water features, deserts, trees, and other unique attributes of the geographic area where the park is located.

CHECK IT OUT

Parks Are Everywhere!

According to NRPA's *2022 Agency Performance Review* (2022a), the typical park and recreation agency offers one park for every 2,323 residents with over 10 acres (4 ha) of parkland for every 1,000 residents.

State Park Sites

There are more than 6,600 state park sites in the United States that span more than 14 million acres (5.6 million ha). California has the most state parks (270), followed by New York (215) and Washington (212). Kansas has the fewest state parks, with the number being as low as 26 (National Park Trips, 2021).

National Parks

National parks share many similar characteristics with state parks. **National parks** are usually owned and operated by the national government, and they serve all those within that nation as well as other visitors from around the world. In Canada, these parks are administered by Parks Canada. In the United States, national parks are operated by the National Park Service (NPS), a division of the Department of the Interior. These types of parks are usually created to preserve natural areas that include unique features of the geographic area where the park is located. Users typically have to drive or fly a considerable distance to access a national park. Some well-known U.S. national parks include Glacier National Park in Montana, Carlsbad Caverns National Park in New Mexico, Yellowstone National Park in Wyoming, Hawaii Volcanoes National Park, Grand Canyon National Park in Arizona, Everglades National Park in Florida, and Rocky Mountain National Park in Colorado.

Specialty Parks

Some facilities include the word *park* in their name or description. Although not generally considered to be parks in the same way as the

The Grand Canyon is one of the United States' National Parks, which are operated by the National Park Service (NPS); people travel from hundreds or even thousands of miles away to visit each year.
Maridav/iStock/Getty Images

parks described earlier, they do have some similar characteristics. Unlike the parks previously discussed, specialty parks may be operated in the public or private sector, and many are constructed with the intent to generate revenue. In addition, specialty parks are designed with a specific purpose in mind; examples include theme parks, aquatic parks, and sport parks.

Theme parks offer an entertainment experience that is designed to attract visitors. Although the same description could apply to other parks, a theme park is a constructed facility that doesn't usually rely on natural features. Common examples of theme parks in the United States include Walt Disney World, Disneyland, Six Flags America, Holiday World, and Kings Island. A management system operates these types of parks, which are designed to produce a profit.

Aquatic parks may also be designed to produce a profit. They may be operated by a municipal government or a private company. At aquatic parks, water features or aquatic facilities are the main attraction. Aquatic parks may offer water slides, activity pools, wave pools, serpentine waterways for rafting, jet sprays, splash pads, lap pools, and other amenities that allow users to interact with water. (See chapter 17 for more details about aquatics and aquatic parks.)

Skate parks are designed for skate-related recreational activities, including skateboarding, scooters, BMX bikes, wheelchairs, and in-line skating. Several municipal government agencies operate skate parks in their communities; a few are managed by private organizations. Skate parks typically include prefabricated or concrete structures and obstacles to challenge the skater. While prefabricated structures are generally less expensive to build, the concrete structures tend to require fewer repairs or maintenance in the longer term.

Another type of specialty park is the **sport park**, which features a sport or a combination of sports as the core product. Sport parks may be operated by a municipal government or a private company. They may provide multiple sport areas for one particular sport or for various sports. These parks are often constructed to host community, state, or national sport events that may attract numerous participants, creating a significant economic impact on the community where the park is located. Sport parks also include professional sport venues that are owned and operated by professional sport organizations. They, too, have a significant economic impact on the community.

The main area at an aquatic park consists of a pool or other large water features.

kali9/iStockphoto/Getty Images

Park Design

The design of most park areas relies on the natural features of the area. Landscape designers and design architects (the expert consultants often hired to design parks) attempt to complement the natural features of the area in their design. Every park has a unique design based on its intended location and size, flow, amenities, and programs.

Location and Size

The location and size of a park influence its design. The topography of the area must be taken into consideration as well. Slope, valleys, soil types, and existing vegetation can be used as part of the design, or they may have to be altered to create the park. Natural features (e.g., mountains, lakes, streams, rivers, oceans, beaches, trees, rock) affect where park features can be located. Often these features are the attraction that creates customer interest. Competent landscape architects incorporate these features into the design of a park as part of an effort to minimize alteration of the natural conditions.

Parks can vary in size from less than an acre (0.4 ha) to thousands of acres. Generally, urban areas have smaller acreage for parks because of the density of the population and the value of land in densely populated areas. However, the exception is in some major cities where civic leaders and landscape architects had the vision to preserve significant acreage for the future use and enjoyment of their residents; examples include Central Park in New York and Forest Park in St. Louis.

Urban or neighborhood parks may have limited land mass, which affects the amenities that may be included in the design of the park. Because these types of parks often serve smaller geographic areas, they may have limited or no parking areas. In contrast, larger parks, including community, state, or national parks, may incorporate significant parking areas in their design to accommodate a large number of patrons who drive to the park.

A common practice in park design is to locate certain areas together. For example, playgrounds or other activity areas, such as sport fields or courts, typically have restroom and parking areas nearby. Parks where wooded areas, rock formations, trails, water features, or other natural elements of interest exist should be designed for appropriate access while limiting the possible negative effect of that access on the features that make the park unique. Railings, pathways, gates, and other barriers may be necessary in order to limit access to these features and to protect visitors from danger.

Parks that attract a high volume of users, particularly specialty parks, will need numerous parking areas and extensive restrooms to accommodate visitors. Pathways (hard or soft surfaced) should be placed in high-traffic areas to lead visitors to various features of the park. Exterior lighting may be necessary in parking areas, around restroom facilities, and along pathways to increase user safety in the later hours of the day. Regardless of size, parks must take into consideration how patrons will use the site. Landscape architects and other consultants often assist with the design of park facilities.

Flow

The design of the park entrance or reception area should consider the maximum flow of user traffic, including what the load will be at any single moment, and ensure that adequate space exists to handle user needs in entering and exiting a facility. A reception or entrance area naturally has the potential to cause lines to form. In certain park facilities, users may have to wait a long time to access the product. Adequate space to accommodate customer waiting should be incorporated into the design of any park facility. Special consideration should be given to park facilities that attract large numbers of users and long lines with considerable waiting time (discussed in chapter 12).

Amenities

Most park users have expectations for basic furnishings, including benches, tables, trash receptacles, signage, dog waste stations, water fountains, cooking grills, and other amenities. Because they enhance the core product, amenities are considered core product extensions. The vast size of certain parks often requires many amenities spread out over the entire park. Due to the extensive use of amenities, a replacement plan that factors in the life span of each amenity is an important management consideration.

Programs

Park areas are generally designed for unstructured leisure experiences; in other words, they are designed for people to use at their own pace and for individual reasons. However, park areas may also be used for programmed activities. Programs that take place in a park can include nature programs, sport programs, camp activities, special events, youth programs, and senior activities. A park can be an excellent resource for outdoor activities; programs that include these activities typically take place during warmer months.

Park Areas

Parks contain a variety of areas that enhance the core product and are important to users. These areas can include a welcome center, shelter buildings, food service, restrooms, equipment rental or checkout, retail outlets, trails, and playgrounds.

Welcome Center

Some park areas combine a reception area (welcome center) with administrative offices. Welcome centers serve several functions, including fee collection, information exchange, and emergency personnel access. These areas may be combined to maximize available space or simply because it is more efficient for the operation of the facility. Combining these areas into one location provides access for administrative personnel to assist customer service staff and respond quickly to customer questions or emergencies. In many respects, a reception area is an extension of administrative offices.

Shelter Buildings

It is fairly common for most parks to have some type of physical structure that provides shelter from the elements. Shelter buildings may be fully enclosed for the comfort of users, or they may be open to the elements, only providing cover from rain, snow, and sun. Occupancy of shelter facilities can be controlled with a reservation system or allowed on a first come, first served basis. Park agencies often charge a fee to reserve a shelter, basing the amount of the fee on the shelter size and amenities provided.

Conveniently locating a welcome center at the front area of a park will make it easy for users to pay fees, receive information, or locate emergency personnel.
Jamie Squire/Getty Images

Food Service

Depending on the location and type of park and the likelihood that patrons would benefit from vending or food service, parks may choose to incorporate vending or food-service areas. Park areas that draw a substantial number of visitors (e.g., state, national, or specialty parks) may choose to offer full-service restaurants to serve customer needs. Smaller parks (e.g., community, neighborhood, or specialty parks) may offer a limited-service concession or vending option. The agency that is responsible for the operation of a food-service area must consider the added responsibilities it requires, including waste prevention and removal from natural park areas, and balance those responsibilities with their goal of service or profit. (Food-service is discussed in more detail in chapter 18.)

The high visibility of a welcome center, park entrance, or major attraction makes for a good food-service location. This service should be located near the main thoroughfare of the park in order to capitalize on the traffic in this area. High visibility can be important to the success of food service.

Restrooms

Restroom facilities are often a fundamental need at parks. Restroom options can range from portable toilets or outhouse pits to the customary fully plumbed system. When selecting restroom facilities, park administrators should consider the typical length of stay of visitors in addition to the environment of the park. Natural areas may have attractions in locations that have limited plumbing access. In these areas, the more primitive restroom facility may be the only option. Parks in urban areas or theme parks that attract a large number of visitors with children are more likely to offer fully plumbed restroom facilities.

Food-service areas can be used as a way to increase revenue at an outdoor facility, but including a food-service area also requires waste prevention and removal from the park areas.

Equipment Rental

Park operating agencies should analyze the potential equipment needs of visitors. Where possible, equipment rental or checkout should be considered in order to provide a service and generate revenue. Managers of theme parks may provide stroller rentals to visitors with children. Aquatic parks often offer rental of cabana or lawn furniture in addition to snorkeling or diving equipment, boats, Jet Skis, canoes, paddleboats, kayaks, and necessary safety equipment such as life preservers. Parks with cross-country or downhill ski areas may offer ski equipment rentals. Each park area should analyze the rental opportunities available based on the core product.

Retail Outlets

Some park areas offer retail outlets, pro shops, or gift shops that serve as core product extensions. Depending on the type and size of the park, the retail outlet may be as simple as counter space within the welcome center or it may be a separate area located close to the welcome center or the core product area. Visitors to state, national, or theme parks may wish to remember their visit with a souvenir. Common souvenirs include T-shirts, sweatshirts, hats, coffee mugs, key chains, stuffed animals, calendars, and DVDs.

Incorporating these retail functions into a high-traffic area increases user awareness of the retail outlet. It is also a good business practice that enhances the functionality of the facility.

Trails

A common element in a park is a trail. Trails are paths or tracks in a natural outdoor area that are designed to be used for a variety of activities, such as walking, jogging, hiking, horseback riding, cross-country skiing, or biking. Some trails are also designed for motorized vehicles.

Retail outlets at recreation facilities allow users to purchase items of convenience, such as food, or they may allow users to purchase a souvenir to help them remember their visit.
Jeffrey Greenberg/UCG/Universal Images Group via Getty Images

An important consideration in trail design is to make sure the trail is properly sloped for water drainage. If water settles into places on a trail, the trail can erode and become unsafe for users. Trail designers need to create a gradient of 3 percent to 4 percent to allow water to run off the trail.

Playgrounds

A play area or playground can greatly enhance the park experience and serve as a major attraction, particularly in neighborhood and urban parks. Play areas can provide many physical challenges and opportunities for social interaction for children. Equipment in a play area can range from swings and slides to climbing walls and jungle gyms. The type of equipment in a play area will dictate the type and age of users. A number of considerations regarding play areas are presented later in this chapter.

Park Operations

Operating a park requires that a management system be in place to coordinate basic park functions. Park operations functions include access control, fee collection, maintenance, safety, and security. The implementation of these considerations varies depending on the type, location, and size of the park.

Access Control

The process of managing customer or visitor entry into a park area is called **access control**. Access control can vary according to the type of facility. For example, a state or national park may require users to enter the facility through a gated area staffed by park employees who limit access by charging a fee or restrict access to limit park usage or for safety purposes. Certain restrictions or policies may limit access to a particular park area. For example, local community or neighborhood parks may have policies that identify park hours while they have no physical access controls in place. Specialty parks are likely to incorporate park hours, an access-control system, and admission fees.

Various access-control systems may be used, including gates, turnstiles, counter areas, and ticket booths. Some of these areas may use card-reading equipment and metal detection or X-ray screening devices. Personnel involved in facility access control include attendants, receptionists, customer service representatives, security personnel, ushers, and ticket takers.

Fee Collection

As mentioned earlier, some park facilities collect a fee before permitting access and use of the area or product. Access-control or reception areas can incorporate this function by using a staff member and equipment, including a cash register, credit card machine, or computer, to assist with fee collection. Park facilities may collect fees each time a user accesses a facility (admission fees), or they may collect fees in one lump sum, such as through memberships or season passes.

Maintenance

When most people think of parks, they visualize open spaces with trees, grass, flowers, water features, and other amenities. However, as described earlier, a wide variety of park areas exist. Each area may incorporate manufactured structures that provide a core product or a core product extension to support the purpose of a user's visit. These park areas can be vast, and they can have a number of areas and facilities that require a great deal of maintenance. The following facilities may be located in a park setting:

- Restrooms
- Concession or food-service areas
- Shelter buildings
- Parking facilities
- Roads
- Paths
- Trails

Parks usually have vegetation to maintain. This vegetation can include trees, flowers, shrubs, aquatic plants, and grasses, in addition to other flora. Vegetation maintenance can vary greatly depending on the region; therefore, park employees need specific knowledge of vegetation management based on the location of the facility. For example, vegetation in arid areas may require different irrigation practices than vegetation located in climates where rainfall is more consistent. Qualified arborists and vegetation specialists should be employed when vegetation requires specialized maintenance.

Nearly all parks have the basic responsibility of maintaining some type of surface area. As discussed in chapter 6, a wide variety of surface types exist, and they need to be maintained. In areas where grass is prevalent, simply mowing grass areas on a regular basis may be a basic maintenance practice. In park areas where snow is prevalent or even necessary to deliver a product, such as downhill or cross-country skiing, the maintenance of this surface will require specific equipment and maintenance practices. The grooming of snow for skiing requires specialized practices and equipment to provide the desirable surface for park users. In most cases, snow removal is required in order to allow use of parking areas, roadways, or trails.

Trails also require considerable maintenance attention. As mentioned previously, one of the most important parts of trail maintenance is to make sure the trail is properly sloped for water drainage. Trail slope should be considered in the design phase of the trail construction, and trail maintenance crews should examine the trail on a regular basis, after periods of high usage or periods of inclement weather. By maintaining moving soil to divert drainage areas or to build up areas, maintenance crews can ensure that the trail will provide a safe experience for users.

Safety

Park users have a basic expectation that their visit to a park will be a safe one. It is incumbent on management to limit the risks associated with delivery of a service in a park area. Common safety practices include signage that warns users of potential risks, brochures, or other literature designed to educate users of risks, and barriers that limit access to areas that may pose risks.

Management can also institute regular inspections and maintenance of park areas to ensure that surfaces and amenities are safe to use. This variety creates a significant responsibility for recreation facility managers, who must assess risks and then implement maintenance and management practices to protect park users. A typical example of this practice is the routine inspection of park playground equipment for safety concerns. This practice is so common that park maintenance employees are often required to take courses offered by professional associations to become certified playground safety inspectors. (See Playground Maintenance, later in the chapter.)

Security

Park security is a significant concern for management. The sheer size of some park areas makes security a challenging aspect of recreation facility management. It is common for parks to have staff on-site to provide assistance to users or to enforce park rules and regulations. These employees may be patrol personnel, park police, or other security personnel. Other personnel, including gate attendants and maintenance employees, may also have some basic security responsibilities.

Some larger parks face tremendous challenges in limiting access to their areas. At best, parks may have perimeter fencing or other barriers that limit access and keep park assets secure from those who would poach resources within the park. Signage indicating park boundaries may also warn those who would enter that they are trespassing on park property.

Playgrounds

Playgrounds are an integral part of a community, and they can be an auxiliary to many types of facilities. Playgrounds are typically located in parks, schools, child care facilities, housing complexes, and community centers. Playgrounds can be included in the design of restaurants, resorts, and other commercial establishments that attract families.

On the surface, playgrounds appear to be a fun attraction for children to play on. However, a well-designed playground is more than just an area to play. All playgrounds should be designed to foster the physical and social development of children. Physical development

Playgrounds allow children to develop social skills as they learn to play with other children; for example, they take turns using the equipment found on the playground.
Cavan Images/Getty Images

takes place as children climb up, down, and through play equipment. Social development takes place as children learn to play together and get along with each other. A well-designed playground provides spaces and amenities that allow for these and other opportunities.

Playground Equipment

Playground equipment varies in the type of physical challenge provided. The equipment selected for a playground should reflect the age of the users. Typically, playground equipment is designed to meet the needs of two groups: preschool and school-age children. In the United States, guidelines established by the Consumer Product Safety Commission (CPSC) are typically adopted by state departments and dictate safety recommendations for playground equipment for these age groups.

In many playgrounds, children of both age groups may be using the equipment. In this case, the age-specific equipment should be kept in different areas of the playground. Because most playgrounds are not supervised, it is the responsibility of adults to make sure that children are using age-appropriate equipment. If a preschool child climbs up a larger slide or uses an overhead climber, a greater chance of injury exists. It can also be problematic if older children use preschool equipment because they can damage the equipment that is not designed for larger users.

Equipment for Preschool Children

A playground designed for preschool children (aged 5 and younger) should include equipment that is less than 5 feet (1.5 m) high, which is typically no higher than the average preschool child can reach. Any elevations in the equipment should be accessible by ramps or small stairway areas. In addition to being low to the ground, equipment should be selected that provides opportunities for children to play together.

Equipment for School-Age Children

For children age 6 and older, playground equipment should provide a greater physical challenge than preschool equipment, such as more opportunities for climbing. Equipment should also include chances for children to develop arm strength by providing overhead ladders and arm swings. School-age equipment should be no higher than 8 feet (2.4 m) above the ground.

Playground Safety

When designing a playground and selecting playground equipment, safety should be the top priority of recreation facility managers. In the United States, the CPSC tests and evaluates

playground equipment, and agencies should strongly consider choosing equipment that has been certified by the CPSC. The CPSC tests equipment to ensure that it doesn't have entrapment areas where children could get their limbs or heads stuck. The CPSC also tests the material that equipment is made from to make sure it is durable and can support the stress that children impose during play.

Certified Playground Safety Inspector (CPSI) Guidelines

One of the most recognizable and leading certifications in playground safety in the United States is the Certified Playground Safety Inspector (CPSI) program. Offered through the NRPA, the CPSI is a professional certification. More specifically, CPSI professionals acquire competence across these five core playground safety domains:

School-age playground equipment should not be more than 8 feet (2.4 m) high, and it should provide children age 6 and older the opportunity for greater physical challenges.
© Human Kinetics

- Playground equipment hazard identification
- Recognition of the necessary surface requirements for the safe use of playground equipment
- Determination of appropriate playground environment, including age-appropriateness, use zones, accessibility, design and layout, and overall equipment (e.g., products, trends, recalls)
- Completion of audits, inspections, and maintenance of playground equipment
- Development and supervision of an overall playground equipment risk management plan

Professionals earn the CPSI certification through the successful completion of an exam. The CPSI certification is valid for 3 years, and professionals can renew their certification by successfully retaking the CPSI exam.

Playground Use Zones

The CPSC also provides guidelines for equipment use zones. A **use zone** is the space below and around a piece of equipment that should have some type of fall-absorbent surface and be free of other equipment. The use zone, which is also called the *safety zone*, provides adequate space to prevent injury should a child fall from the equipment.

Use-Zone Size

The size of the use zone is typically dictated by the height of the equipment, the ground, the type of play or movement taking place on the equipment, and whether the equipment is stationary (see table 16.1). For equipment that

TABLE 16.1 PLAYGROUND USE-ZONE GUIDELINES

Playground equipment	Use zone	Example
Stationary equipment	Use zones should extend a minimum of 6' in all directions from the perimeter of the equipment.	A spring rocker that is 2' wide × 4' long Sides/width: 2' (rocker width) + 6' (use zone) + 6' (use zone) = 14' Front + Back: 4' (rocker length) + 6' (use zone) + 6' (use zone) = 16' Use-zone dimensions: 14' × 16'
Swings	Sides: Standard use zones of 6' Front: Twice the height of the structure/beam of the swing Back: Twice the height of the structure/beam of the swing	A swing that is 10' wide and has a height of 8' Sides: 10' (swing width) + 6' (use zone) + 6' (use zone) = 22' Front: 8' height × 2' = 16' Back: 8' height × 2' = 16' Front + Back: 16' + 16' = 32' Use-zone dimensions: 22' × 32'
Slides	Sides: Standard use zones of 6' Front (ladder side of the slide): Standard use zones of 6' End of slide chute: Slides 6' and under should have a 6' use zone. Slides taller than 6' should have a use zone equal to the height of the slide up to 8'.	A slide with a standard 3' wide slide chute and is 8' high and 12' long (back of ladder to end of slide chute) Sides: 3' (slide width) + 6' (use zone) + 6' (use zone) = 15' Front: 12' (length of slide) + 6' (standard use zone) = 18' End of slide chute to back: 8' height = 8' use zone at the end of slide chute Front + Back: 18' + 8' = 26' Use-zone dimensions: 15' × 26'

Adapted from U.S. Consumer Product Safety Commission, *Public Playground Safety Handbook*, (Washington, DC: U.S. Consumer Product Safety Commission, 2015).

is stationary, the standard use zone is 6 feet (1.8 m) beyond the perimeter of the structure. Equipment that is not stationary will require a larger use zone; in most instances, the use zone is specific to the equipment.

A swing is one piece of standard nonstationary playground equipment with specific use-zone guidelines. The use-zone guidelines for swings require the use zone to extend twice the height of the swing structure in front and back of the swing. For example, a swing structure that is 8 feet (2.4 m) high should have 16 feet (4.9 m) of use zone on the back side of the swing and 16 feet of use zone on the front side of the swing. On the sides of the swing, where no movement is taking place, the standard 6 feet (1.8 m) of use zone applies.

Use-Zone Surfaces

As mentioned, use zones also include surfacing. Although cost plays a role in selecting a surface, the most important factor for selecting a safe surface is fall protection (see table 16.2). *Fall protection* refers to how absorbent a surface is, or how much give a surface has. Each surface provides a different degree of fall protection. A playground can use two basic categories of surfaces: loose-fill surfaces and unitary surfaces.

- *Loose-fill surfaces* are the most common. They include materials such as sand, pea gravel, wood chips, shredded rubber, and synthetic wood fibers. These surfaces require containment and maintenance on a regular basis to prevent displacement. As a loose-fill surface is moved around, it becomes displaced and its fall-protection qualities are altered. Each loose-fill surface varies in fall-protection qualities and the depth of material that should be maintained. Typically, shredded rubber and synthetic wood fibers are more absorbent than other loose-fill surfaces, and they do not need to be maintained at a depth as great as sand, pea gravel, and wood chips.

- *Unitary surfaces* provide a surface that cannot be displaced. They typically take the form of rubbery tiles that are interconnected. Unitary surfaces are much more expensive to purchase and install than loose-fill surfaces, but they keep their fall-protection qualities and are much easier to maintain.

Accessibility: ADA Guidelines and Universal Design

The type of surface selected also affects the **accessibility** of the play area. Titles II and III of the Americans with Disabilities Act (ADA) require, among other things, that newly con-

Acceptable and Unacceptable Playground Use-Zone Surfaces

Acceptable
- Engineered wood fiber
- Wood chips
- Sand
- Pea gravel
- Synthetic or rubber tiles
- Shredded rubber
- Mats
- Poured-in-place rubber
- Impact attenuating synthetic turf

Unacceptable
- Concrete
- Blacktop
- Packed earth
- Grass

Adapted from National Recreation and Park Association, *The Daily Dozen: A 12-Point Playground Safety Checklist* (Ashburn, VA: National Recreation and Park Association, 2022).

TABLE 16.2   PLAYGROUND USE-ZONE SURFACING: TYPES, MINIMUM DEPTH, AND MAXIMUM FALL HEIGHT

Playground use-zone surface	Minimum depth (in.)	Maximum fall height (ft)
Sand	9*	4
Pea gravel	9*	5
Wood mulch	9*	7
Wood chips	9*	10
Shredded or recycled rubber	6	10

*Loose-fill materials will compress at least 25 percent over time due to use and weathering. For example, if a depth of 9 inches is required, the initial fill level should be 12 inches.

Adapted from U.S. Consumer Product Safety Commission, *Public Playground Safety Handbook*, (Washington, DC: U.S. Consumer Product Safety Commission, 2015).

structed or altered playgrounds be readily accessible to and usable by individuals with disabilities (U.S. CPSC, 2015). Unitary surfaces and loose-fill surfaces of shredded rubber and synthetic wood fiber are considered accessible. The surfaces of sand, pea gravel, and wood chips are not considered accessible and therefore do not meet ADA guidelines. In playgrounds, ADA guidelines can be applied to the accessibility of playground equipment. An entire playground area is not required to be accessible, but people in wheelchairs must be able to access play equipment.

Universal design principles for playground equipment should aim to create an environment that can be used by everyone without

Playground use zones help to prevent serious injuries to children if they should fall while playing on the equipment.
© Human Kinetics

Weather Matters!

According to the NRPA (2022b), temperature, UV rays, and overall weather conditions can affect the shock-absorbing properties of playground surfacing materials.

any adaptations or retrofitting. Universal design for playgrounds extends beyond physical accessibility; it not only creates spaces for everyone to use regardless of physical ability but also takes into account users' cognitive, sensory, and emotional conditions. Integrating the seven principles of universal design, use-zone surfaces within the playground should subscribe to the ADA guidelines noted earlier while also considering a mixture of these ADA compliant surfaces. The varied ADA compliant surfaces can support individuals with or without mobility devices while also providing tactile and auditory responses from the changing surfaces (e.g., changing surface as user enters a new play space). Plantings near the use zones could also be incorporated to elicit senses of smell, sight, or touch.

Playground Supervision

Playgrounds are primarily supervised by adults visiting the area with children. Most playgrounds are not equipped with staff to supervise use; however, recreation facility managers must design the play area in such a way that adults can easily supervise it, by following the tenets of the Playground Safety Checklist (see figure 16.1). Considering the following factors in the planning phase can lead to making supervision easier:

1. In selecting a playground site, management should consider locations that minimize potential hazards, such as busy roads or areas near water that could be attractive nuisances to children.

2. Sight lines are an important element in being able to supervise a playground. Spaces where sight lines are restricted by vegetation or manufactured structures should be avoided. When equipment is placed in a playground, it should be

located in such a way that the equipment doesn't limit the sight lines.

3. Signage is another way that management can assist in supervision of a playground. By providing signs that communicate age appropriateness of equipment and rules for a play area, adults may better understand how to supervise play on the playground.

4. Management can facilitate playground supervision by providing support amenities in the playground area for adults. Permanent benches in predetermined areas informally direct adults to those areas where they will be better able to supervise. In addition, adults will be more likely to sit in the playground area instead of on benches in areas outside the playground.

5. Providing other amenities such as trash receptacles, water fountains, or restrooms makes adults and children more likely to stay in the playground area and leads to fewer instances of inadequate supervision.

Playground Maintenance

Playgrounds must be maintained in order to ensure a safe user experience. As mentioned in the discussion of playground surfaces, it is important that the depth of loose-fill surfaces be maintained in order to maintain fall-protection qualities. An example is the area directly below a playground swing. It is common for users to drag their feet and displace a loose-fill surface below the swing. By raking the area and adding loose-fill surface material, the depth can be reestablished. Maintenance crews should examine surfaces in fall-protection areas on a regular basis. Maintenance crews should also be aware that rain can erode loose-fill surfaces.

PLAYGROUND SAFETY CHECKLIST

The NRPA offers the following 12-point checklist for individuals to consider prior to allowing children access to the playground:

1. *Proper surfacing*: Is the surface soft enough to cushion a fall? Unacceptable surfaces would include: concrete, grass, blacktop, or packed earth.
2. *Accessibility*: The American with Disabilities Act (ADA) requires newly constructed playgrounds to comply with the appropriate ADA guidelines. Some of these guidelines include accessible routes to the playground, appropriate surfacing, and a variety and number of play opportunities.
3. *Adequate supervision*: Are the play areas easy for the caregiver to observe the child(ren) playing? As the caregiver, it is important to understand the basics of playground safety.
4. *Age-appropriate equipment*: Is the equipment and setting appropriate for the age of the child(ren) at play? Signage that indicates the appropriate ages should be provided. In general, free-standing climbers, chain and cable walks, seesaws, or vertical sliding poles would not be age appropriate for preschoolers.
5. *Proper equipment*: Does the playground have safe and appropriate equipment for the space and supervision? Typical equipment that should not be available on a public playground includes free-swinging ropes, swinging exercise rings, trampolines, heavy metal swings, and trapeze bars.
6. *Adequate use zones*: Does all of the playground equipment have adequate space beyond the equipment areas to support its safe use? In general, a minimum of 6 feet (1.8 m) is required around all playground equipment.
7. *Protrusions and entanglement hazards*: Are any protrusions present that could cut or impale a child? Are any choking or entanglement hazards present?
8. *Head and neck entrapment*: Are any parts of the playground equipment places where a child's head or neck could become entrapped? The equipment should have no openings that measure between 3.5 and 9 inches (8.9-22.9 cm).
9. *Trip hazards*: Are any areas potential trip hazards for the child(ren)? Common trip hazards include tree stumps or roots, rocks, and changes in surface elevations.
10. *Sharp edges*: Do any areas on the playground contain sharp edges? Visual inspections of the playground equipment can help in identifying any concerning areas.
11. *Proper maintenance*: Does the playground appear to be well-maintained? Safe playground equipment should undergo regular inspections and preventive maintenance.
12. *Inspected by a CPSI*: Are these regular inspections conducted by a CPSI? A CPSI certified professional should complete regular inspections of the playground equipment to ensure everything is in safe working condition.

Adapted from National Recreation and Park Association, *The Daily Dozen: A 12-Point Playground Safety Checklist* (Ashburn, VA: National Recreation and Park Association, 2022).

FIGURE 16.1 NRPA 12-point playground safety checklist.

After inclement weather, crews should examine these surfaces.

Maintenance for playgrounds also applies to playground equipment. Most pieces of playground equipment have bolts or screws that should be tightened on a regular basis. Playground equipment manufacturers usually provide maintenance guidelines when selling their products. It is good policy for maintenance crews to establish a schedule for checking equipment and surfaces to ensure the safe experience of playground users.

To ease supervision by caregivers at public playgrounds, the team can take several actions during the planning stage, such as not building the playground near a busy traffic area, not limiting the sight lines in the playground, posting signs that include rules for play, providing benches for parents in the play areas, and providing amenities nearby.
© Human Kinetics

Summary

Parks and playgrounds provide opportunities to participate in a variety of recreation activities in an outdoor setting. Parks can take a number of forms, and they can be an effective source of revenue generation. Playgrounds are prevalent in many settings, and they play an important role in the physical and social development of children. Attention should be given to the planning of parks and playgrounds to ensure that users have a safe and satisfying leisure experience.

REVIEW QUESTIONS

1. Describe the difference between a neighborhood park and a community park.
2. Provide an example of a specialty park.
3. Why is flow an important element to consider when designing park spaces?
4. Describe the general differences between the characteristics of playground equipment for preschool children compared to school-age children.
5. What is a CPSI?
6. What are the standard use zones for stationary playground equipment?
7. Identify two surfaces that are acceptable for playground use zones and two surfaces that are unacceptable.

CASE STUDY

Plans for a New Playground

You are a park superintendent for Whispering Pines State Park. Whispering Pines State Park is a midsize park for your state, and you have served as the park superintendent for the past 2 years. The park includes an 88-acre (35 ha) lake, multiple picnic areas and shelters, 50 primitive camping sites, and 122 camping sites with electrical hookups. A restaurant is located in the park. It is operated by a private vendor on a 3-year contract.

Whispering Pines State Park also has a large (over 25,000 ft², or 2,322 m²) playground near the restaurant that receives a great deal of use during the peak summer months. A smaller playground is situated near the east boat ramp recreation area. While not as large as the main playground, it includes swings, slides, a climbing structure, and spring riders. Seating for observers and caregivers is present outside the playground's use zone.

You recently applied for and received a grant to support the development of a third playground. Plans are for this playground to be located between primitive and non-primitive campsites. Space is available next to the shower facility, and feedback from campers has suggested a playground near this area would be widely supported. You envision the playground to be slightly smaller than the park's largest playground, with equipment to support a variety of ages.

Case Study Questions

1. What are some possible use-zone surfaces to use for this new playground, which would support both ADA and universal design guidelines?

2. Consider the seven principles of universal design and identify at least four ways in which the playground could support these principles.

3. You plan to have a slide on this playground. The slide will include a standard chute size of 3 feet and it will be 10 feet long and 7 feet high. Calculate the minimum use-zone dimensions to accommodate this slide.

4. To save money, your regional director encourages you to consider using pea gravel as the use-zone surfacing around the slide. From a safety standpoint, is pea gravel an appropriate use-zone surface material for the slide? If not, what are some possible alternatives?

5. You would also like to include a swing set on the new playground. The planned dimensions for the swing set would be 10 feet high by 20 feet wide. Calculate the minimum use-zone dimensions to accommodate this swing set.

CHAPTER 17

Aquatic Facilities

LEARNING OBJECTIVES

At the completion of this chapter, you should be able to do the following:

1. Recognize the various types of aquatic facilities and the experience that each is designed to provide.
2. Identify the type of staff required for operating an aquatic facility.
3. Examine the practices used at an aquatic facility to ensure a safe experience for users.
4. Explain terminology associated with aquatic maintenance.
5. Recognize the various types of delivery areas in an aquatic facility and the types of programs that might be offered.

Aquatic facilities provide opportunities for users to engage in activities in spaces where water is a part of the experience. Similar to parks and playgrounds, aquatic facilities can be core products or core product extensions of another facility. Aquatic facilities have become immensely popular; they are a common amenity in many recreation facilities. They can vary from a small eight-lane lap pool to a large, multi-attraction aquatic center with slides, wave pools, child swim areas, and other unique attractions. Aquatic facilities generate revenue, offer diverse aquatic opportunities, and provide participants with a unique leisure experience.

Types of Aquatic Facilities

Aquatic facilities can be found in indoor and outdoor settings that may be natural or manufactured. Typically, aquatic facilities fall into one of four categories: waterfronts, pools, splash pads, and water parks.

Established in 1955, the Tualatin Hills Park and Recreation District (THPRD) is the largest special district in the state of Oregon, encompassing nearly 50 square miles (129 km²). The THPRD provides a variety of parks, facilities, and programs to approximately 250,000 residents in the Beaverton, Oregon, area. More specifically, the THPRD manages 117 park sites, 1,500 acres (607 ha) of natural areas, 405 community garden plots, three skate parks, five off-leash pet areas, 27 miles (43 km) of streams, three lakes, over 100 tennis courts, nearly 150 multipurpose athletic fields, 60 basketball courts, 104 baseball and softball fields, four community murals, six recreation centers, and 70 miles (113 km) of trails.

In addition to all these parks and facilities, the THPRD also operates eight aquatic centers throughout the Beaverton community. The eight aquatic centers provide a variety of classes, amenities, and opportunities for the community. For example, the Conestoga Recreation and Aquatic Center is a full-service aquatic complex that offers after-school camps, aquatic fitness programming, aquatic dance, and sport-related services, while the Tualatin Hills Aquatic Center hosts competitive swim clubs and community swim lessons through its 50-meter pool and Oregon's only 10-meter diving platform.

The THPRD's commitment to aquatics is evident not only in the variety of their aquatic facilities but in their programming as well. The THPRD has been a regular partner with the USA Swimming Foundation, which has allowed the district to provide free swimming lessons for hundreds of kids each year. Water safety is also important to the THPRD, as is evident by their aquatic life skills and safety programming that reaches over 30,000 swimmers annually, including 2,000 who experience disabilities (Tualatin Hills Park & Recreation District, 2017).

The THPRD has been innovative and resourceful in their efforts to maintain these aquatic centers. For example, the THPRD developed and implemented an innovative cost-recovery methodology to support the agency's backlog of park and facility maintenance needs. These efforts led to their deferred maintenance funding growing from about US$1 million in 2007 to US$3.5 million in 2017 (Tualatin Hills Park & Recreation District, 2017). This additional funding supported improvements to several of the aquatic centers, including HVAC efficiency upgrades, ADA-related improvements and barrier removals, and roof repairs.

A testament to the THPRD's facilities, parks, and services, the district has been a finalist for the National Recreation and Park Association's Gold Medal Award multiple times.

Waterfronts

A **waterfront** is an outdoor aquatic facility located at a lake, beach, river, or quarry. The aquatic space includes all open water; that is, the facility is not contained in a closed environment. Weather plays an important part at all waterfront facilities. It determines what activities are offered, when the activities are offered, whether the facility opens, and where participants can swim. Waterfront facilities are commonly used for swimming, boating, and fishing. Beach facilities and marinas must be aware of changing tides and varying aquatic animals, and they must have staff members who are trained to deal with swift currents and safety concerns.

Pools

Pools are the most common and basic aquatic facility. Pools may include a diving board or slide, but for the most part, they offer few amenities. The traditional pool may include lap swimming areas and a diving well (an area of deep water suitable for diving). Detached diving wells have become more common; because they are a separate pool, they tend to be much deeper. A current trend in aquatics is **leisure pools**. This type of pool moves from the traditional square or rectangle shape to a variety of formats, and it does not include areas for competitive swimming. Pools can be located indoors or outdoors. They are frequently found in recreation centers, health clubs, country clubs, and hotels.

Splash Pads

Splash pads are interactive playgrounds; they are equipped with a variety of motion sensor nozzles that spray water upward from the splash pad deck or from decorative, playful, shower-style features (Gardner, 2018). Splash pads have little to no standing water. The water supply for the splash pad can be recycled water that is treated, or it can be fresh water. Splash pads are typically accessible to all, with textured-based surfaces that include nonslip materials to minimize slipping and injuries. Furthermore, users of splash pads do not need any swimming skills, and most splash pads are unsupervised. Construction and maintenance of splash pads are considerably less demanding than for a pool, making them attractive options for many agencies and communities.

Water Parks

Every year, **water parks** become more widespread across the United States. These facilities incorporate different water features designed for maximum entertainment. Features at these facilities include water slides, wave attractions, spray features, slow-moving water attractions (e.g., a lazy river), toddler play areas, and shallow entries. Similar to traditional pools, water parks can be indoor or outdoor facilities.

Aquatic Facility Construction and Accessibility

Water parks and pools are manufactured aquatic facilities. Basic construction is usually a concrete basin with a few options for liners. Sometimes tile is installed on the pool basin and deck. Both concrete and tile can become a

Water parks are popular recreation areas, and they can be indoor or outdoor facilities.
iStockphoto/Edwin Verin

Construction of most aquatic facilities starts with a concrete basin.
Jeff Clow - Fotolia

slippery surface hazard. To combat this hazard, tiles should be one square inch (2.5 cm²), and all decks should be slightly sloped toward a drain to prevent standing water.

Facility accessibility is also important. Accessibility enables all participants to use facilities regardless of disabilities. The Americans with Disabilities Act (ADA) outlines accessibility requirements that should be followed for aquatic areas. These three innovations help make a pool more accessible:

1. Movable ramps and stairs allow access to the facility through an easier entry point for those with limited mobility.

2. A chairlift runs on electricity or hydraulics to move participants from the deck to the water with ease.

3. Movable floors allow the floor of the pool to be moved to any depth to allow various groups of participants the opportunity to be in the water. These floors are becoming popular in new facilities.

Aquatic Facility Operations

Aquatic facilities require a number of key management functions in order to efficiently operate. The facility must be adequately staffed,

The average cost of a 50-meter by 25-meter pool with a ceramic tile floor is US$350,000, and regrouting costs are US$15,000 every 15 years (Hughes, 2019).

The Americans with Disabilities Act (ADA) sets forth requirements to make aquatic areas accessible for people of all abilities.
© Human Kinetics

safe, and well maintained. In addition, it must have proper mechanical systems and quality aquatic equipment.

Aquatic Facility Operator Guidelines

One of the most recognizable and leading certifications in aquatic safety and operation is the Aquatic Facility Operator (AFO) certification program. Offered through the NRPA, the AFO is a professional certification for people who work on swimming pool operations. More specifically, AFO professionals acquire competence across four core swimming pool domains:

- Water chemistry and disinfection
- Mechanical systems and operations
- Health and safety
- Aquatic operations

Professionals earn the AFO certification through two options: the successful completion of a 2-day training program and exam or the successful completion of a proctored exam. The AFO certification is valid for 5 years. Professionals have two ways to renew the certification: successfully retake the AFO exam, or complete 20 hours of approved continuing education and training in the aquatic operations and management field (NRPA, 2018).

Staffing

Staffing is one of the most important concerns that facility managers will encounter when managing an aquatic center. The most important consideration when hiring staff is finding properly trained and certified employees. Certification must be obtained before employment occurs. Aquatic staff may include lifeguards, instructors, and additional staff.

Lifeguards

Lifeguards are the lifeblood of an aquatic facility. Most facilities have lifeguards and head lifeguards. Lifeguards are first and foremost responsible for the safety of participants in the aquatic area. This responsibility can include enforcing facility policies, administering emergency care, surveying the water, and performing other duties as assigned. Head lifeguards perform basic personnel management responsibilities, and they are also responsible for standard lifeguard duties. It is important to ensure that lifeguards are properly certified. Certification should include lifeguard training, cardiopulmonary resuscitation (CPR), stress first aid (SFA), preventing disease transmission (PDT), automatic external defibrillation (AED) training, and lifeguard supervisor certification. These certifications ensure that lifeguards are properly trained in handling emergency aquatic situations.

Instructors

Aquatic facilities rely on many types of instructors for their programming needs, such as swim instructors, water exercise instructors, and aquatic therapists. In addition, aquatic classes may warrant instructors for self-contained underwater breathing apparatus (scuba), sailing, canoeing, and kayaking. When dealing with a large number of instructors, recreation facility managers may find it beneficial to hire an instructor supervisor or coordinator. This position is closely related to that of head lifeguard; the person in this position is in charge of supervising the instructor staff and scheduling aquatic space for each class.

Swim Instructors   The most common type of aquatic instructor is a swim instructor. These instructors are responsible for teaching participants the skills needed to be a swimmer. All swim instructors should be certified as water safety instructors as well as in SFA, CPR, and AED use.

Water Exercise Instructors   Fitness instruction is another key aspect of aquatic operations. Water exercise is a low-impact fitness option that offers an alternative to traditional land-based aerobic and weight training. To properly

teach these classes, water exercise instructors are needed. They should be certified as water exercise or exercise instructors and hold the same safety certifications as the swim instructors, including SFA, CPR, and AED.

Aquatic Therapists   Closely related to water exercise is aquatic therapy. These instructors are specialists in rehabilitation or therapy with older populations or people with disabilities. Aquatic therapists' certifications should be based on industry standards for therapists, and they should include certification for safety standards such as CPR, AED, and SFA.

Other Instructors   Although the swim and fitness aquatic programs are the most popular, many new courses are becoming successful that require many types of instructors. Some facilities offer scuba classes, which require not only SFA, CPR, and AED certifications but instructors who are knowledgeable in local diving locations. Club sports—including swim

Swim instructors are the most common type of instructors at an aquatic facility.
FatCamera/E+/Getty Images

teams and dive teams—may have instructors or coaches depending on the facility and the availability of funds for the club. Sailing, canoeing, and kayaking instructors should be knowledgeable about their type of water craft. All of these instructors should also be trained in CPR, AED, and SFA.

Additional Staff

Aquatic facilities may have additional staffing needs. Maintenance personnel are essential to any facility, but they are especially crucial for aquatic facilities. These professionals are tasked with making sure the mechanical, chemical, and sanitation systems of the facility are functioning properly, efficiently, and in accordance with health and safety codes. In addition, janitorial staff are vital to the upkeep of the aquatic venue. Custodians take care of all cleaning, supplying, and beautification projects. If an aquatic facility operates concessions or pro shops, it may become necessary to hire staff to manage and operate these amenities as well.

Fee Collection

Aquatic facilities are revenue-generating facilities. Revenue is typically generated through fee collection, where users pay a fee before permitting access to the aquatic area. Access control by staff members and equipment (e.g., cash register, credit card machine, or computer) is utilized to assist with fee collection. Aquatic facilities may collect fees each time a user enters a facility, or they may collect fees in one lump sum in the form of memberships or season passes.

Aquatic Facility Safety

Safety is a primary concern in aquatic facility management. When working around a water environment, each decision regarding safety is one of life and death. Safety has many components, including standards, codes, and safety training for all staff. These workplace practices are designed not only to protect the aquatic users but also to keep staff members healthy and safe as they perform their duties.

An important aspect of aquatic safety is **access control**, the process of managing entry into an aquatic area. Because aquatic facilities offer an inherent risk of drowning, it is important to limit access to the aquatic area. In most settings, fencing the area and establishing a staffed entrance are strategies for limiting access. The entrance area is also where admission fees are collected and passes are checked.

Standards and Codes

Standards and codes affect many businesses, agencies, and organizations that people come into contact with daily, including aquatic facilities. Standards are the broad guidelines that facilities strive to follow in their everyday operations. Codes are rules and regulations that are mandated by federal, state, and local governments. They state minimum standards that must be met in order for a facility to remain open. They are usually enforced by random inspections that help to determine state or local licensure.

State and local bathing codes vary, so it is important that facility managers check with local and state government offices to ensure that they have the most current copies of all codes and regulations pertaining to aquatic facilities. State codes cannot be less stringent than federal codes, and local codes cannot be less stringent than state codes. The codes can become more regulatory as they move down the governmental chain. Typically, bathing

---

CHECK IT OUT

Model Aquatic Health Code

The Centers for Disease Control and Prevention (CDC) publishes the Model Aquatic Health Code (MAHC), which is based on the latest science and best health and safety practices in pools, spas, hot tubs, and splash pads. The MAHC guidelines aim to be comprehensive, providing insight into cutting-edge design, construction, operation, and management needs of today's public aquatic facilities (CDC, 2022).

codes contain information regarding safety, sanitation, equipment, and bather loads.

In the United States, the Occupational Safety and Health Administration (OSHA) protects employees in a variety of work settings. It plays a major role in regulating jobs that have primary responsibilities involving chemicals, drugs, bodily fluids, and other potential health hazards. Employees at an aquatic facility have the potential to come into contact with bodily fluids and chemicals on a regular basis.

Safety Training

Paramount to safety is certifying staff to respond to and effectively manage accidents. Many agencies provide basic certifications in SFA, CPR, PDT, AED, lifeguard training, and the like. One agency that provides many of these certification necessities is the American Red Cross. Two other agencies that provide many aquatic certifications are the Young Men's Christian Association (YMCA) and Jeff Ellis and Associates. All CPR guidelines are passed down by the American Heart Association (AHA; www.americanheart.org), and they also offer their own certification in this skill. Obtaining these certifications is crucial for all staff, not just aquatic personnel, because it enables anyone who works for the aquatic facility to help participants in need of assistance.

The key to effective emergency management is a solid emergency action plan. This plan allows staff to assist participants in emergencies in the best possible way. In aquatic facilities, an emergency action plan can encompass near-drowning experiences, spinal injuries, and non-life-threatening emergencies. Proper supervision should be part of any plan. Lifeguards practice supervision every time they sit down in their chair. By taking steps to ensure that participants are following the rules, they practice preventive supervision. Children need to be given special consideration in the aquatic environment. They often do not understand the serious threats an aquatic facility can pose. Because of their curiosity and willingness to try anything, they need to be given the utmost attention during supervision of a facility.

Maintenance and Hygiene

Maintenance and hygiene are essential to operating a safe aquatic facility. These two factors encompass a wide range of facets. Minor repairs come up almost daily; examples include replacing a broken handle on a bathroom stall or restringing a lane line. When dealing with minor repairs, addressing them as quickly as possible is critical because they can turn into major (and costly) problems later. Locker room sanitation must be done every day. This task can include scrubbing toilets, cleaning sinks, scrubbing floors, and hosing showers and other surfaces. Similar to locker room sanitation is deck sanitation. Every day, both before the facility opens and after it closes, the deck should be sanitized with a mixture of water and bleach. This practice will keep bacteria and other parasites from contaminating the pool water and ensure that the pool deck is user friendly.

To keep a facility looking professional for many years, preventive facility upkeep is essential. A fresh coat of paint each year on the walls and pool (manufacturers' guidelines for pools should be accounted for first) will lengthen the life of the facility. Appliances such as air conditioners, toilets, sinks, and hand dryers should have routine maintenance performed on them according to manufacturers' guidelines to ensure a long life span. At times, it may be necessary to make updates to an aquatic facility. These modernizations will keep users satisfied with the facility and wanting to come back. Before undergoing any major renovations, check with local government agencies for the proper building codes and permits. It is also imperative to make sure updates meet ADA standards.

Mechanical Systems

The heart of any aquatic facility is the mechanical system that filters and sanitizes the water. The first consideration in an aquatic mechanical system is the pump. This piece of machinery circulates the water throughout the aquatic venue. Pumps can be placed before or after the filter, which is the next key component of

An aquatic area must be sanitized periodically with a mixture of water and bleach to kill bacteria and other parasites and keep them from contaminating the pool water.
© Human Kinetics

a mechanical system. Various types of filters exist, but the two main types that recreation facility managers may encounter are sand filters and diatomaceous earth (DE) filters. Both of these systems trap loose materials in the water and put the filtered water back into circulation. The last main part of a mechanical system is the sanitation system. The two most recognized chemicals used in aquatic sanitation are chlorine and bromine. Chlorine is the most widely used sanitation chemical; it comes in gas, liquid, and tablet forms. Tablets are the most common form used in systems today. Gas chlorine is not commonly used because of the dangerous properties it possesses when under pressure in a cylinder. All three aspects of the aquatic mechanical system—the pump, the filter, and the sanitation system—must work together to provide a safe and clean environment for participants.

To ensure that the aquatic mechanical systems are running efficiently, routine maintenance should be performed on them. **Backwashing** the pump and filtration system should be a weekly process. This process involves putting the pump on in reverse to stir up the sand in the filter and remove the buildup of materials from the system. Sanitation systems also require basic maintenance. They must be cleaned and refilled regularly according to manufacturers' maintenance guidelines. Failure to clean a system can lead to buildup of the sanitizer and hinder the performance of a system. Seasonal pools have the added burden of winterizing, or closing the facility for the off-season. This task can include draining the pool, cleaning and dismantling the sanitation system, cleaning the pump, putting away all movable pool equipment, and locking down the facility.

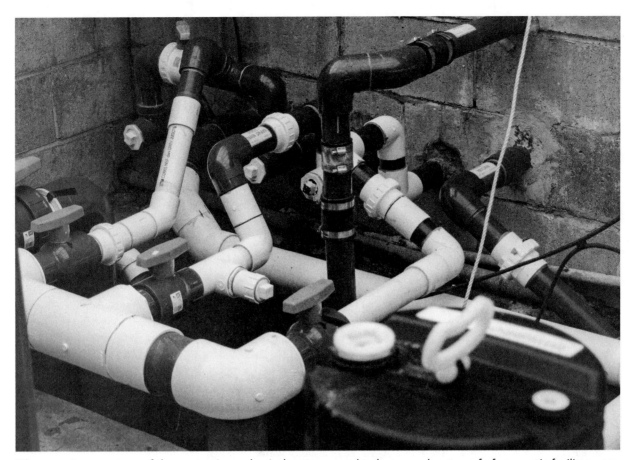

Filters are just one type of three aquatic mechanical systems used to keep pool water safe for aquatic facility users.
© Human Kinetics

Certain safety concerns arise when dealing with pumps and chemicals. For instance, all personnel should know the location of the emergency pump shutoff and how to operate it. This switch will shut off all mechanical systems in the event of an emergency. In addition, some pool chemicals can cause burns and other health problems. These chemicals should be handled with extreme care. Recreation facility managers should provide proper safety equipment and information to all employees who may come into contact with these chemicals. When storing chemicals, it is necessary to read the labels and fact sheets to make sure that the chemicals can be stored together and know where they should be stored. All chemicals should be stored in a cool, dark area. Improper storage can lead to a wide range of problems, including corrosion of the storeroom and health hazards.

Aquatic Deck Surfaces

The surfaces of aquatic decks should allow users to safely navigate the pool while also supporting qualified lifeguard movement, viewing, and quick access to all parts of the pool. While state codes specify the acceptable and unacceptable aquatic decking surface options, the most common surfaces include the following:

- Poured concrete
- Brick or precast cement pavers
- Stone tiles
- Manufactured acrylic surfaces
- Epoxy-type coatings

Regardless of type, the deck surface material should be uniformly constructed with easily cleaned and slip-resistant materials. All materials must be nontoxic, suitable for a pool environment, and generally impervious to water. In addition, any sharp edges should be smoothed, rounded, or beveled. Any cracks or gaps in the deck surfacing must be less than 3/16 inch (0.4 cm) wide with maximum vertical elevation differences of 1/4 inch (0.6 cm) (CDC, 2022).

Aquatic decks must also have a minimum of 4 feet (1.2 m) of clearance from the pool's edge to the fencing or other obstruction. While 15 feet (4.5 m) of clearance is recommended to support the safe flow of user and staff traffic, the 4-foot minimum is required along all sides of the pool.

Aquatic Facility Equipment

Without the equipment that goes inside of it, an aquatic facility is just another body of water. Many types of equipment are available to allow recreation facility managers to provide almost unlimited types of programming; they include rescue and safety equipment, instructional and fitness equipment, swimming and diving equipment, and general aquatic equipment.

Rescue and Safety Equipment

The most important equipment in an aquatic facility is rescue and safety equipment. This equipment can include items such as rescue tubes, ring buoys, reaching poles, backboards, rescue boards, and various other pieces that a lifeguard may need when performing a rescue. Part of the rescue equipment (called personal protective equipment, or PPE) is extremely important because it keeps employees safe from disease transmission. Such equipment can include rescue masks, gloves, aprons, and other items that put a barrier between the rescuer and the victim. Rescue and safety equipment also includes first aid supplies, such as adhesive bandages, blood spill kits, gauze pads and bandages, slings, antibacterial cream, ice packs, glucose, and general safety supplies.

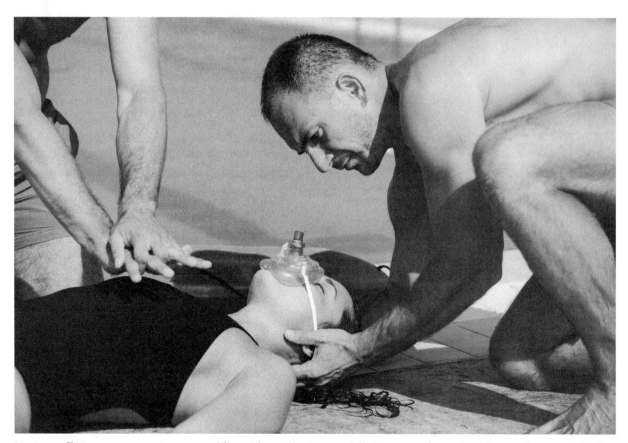

Having sufficient rescue equipment and first aid supplies is especially important for maintaining a safe aquatic facility.
Microgen/iStock/Getty Images

Instructional and Fitness Equipment

Instructional and fitness equipment form the core of aquatic programming equipment. Instructional items may include water noodles, water toys, and the like. Instructors use various products while teaching, so it is best to find out what they need and order equipment accordingly. An aquatic facility can include a wide range of fitness equipment, such as kickboards, pull buoys, aqua jog belts, and wrist weights. Many people mistake aquatic fitness for swimming laps. This misconception leaves out the many aspects of water that make it a perfect medium for fitness. Fitness in aquatics can include programs such as aqua aerobics, classes for participants with fibromyalgia,

and aqua step aerobics. These aerobic fitness classes can provide a low- or high-intensity workout, and they tend to be less stressful on bones and joints. Facility managers should take these benefits into consideration and provide equipment accordingly.

Swimming and Diving Equipment

Swimming and diving clubs and teams also have a great deal of equipment at an aquatic facility. Swim groups have the usual kickboards and pull buoys, but they also have specialized equipment, such as fins, resistance trainers, weight sets, and hand paddles, among others. Dive groups may have dry-land boards, crash mats, trampolines, and other equipment to help them practice a dive before trying it on

Having the essential equipment for swim instruction and fitness instruction will help managers provide successful aquatic programs.
© Human Kinetics.

the real board, where serious injury can occur if it is not done correctly. Recreation facility managers may not be responsible for the team or club equipment, but they should be aware of the equipment used because it may be stored or brought into the facility.

General Aquatic Equipment

Aside from the specialized aquatic equipment, every facility has general equipment that should be taken into consideration. Tables, chairs, and lounge chairs are the most widely used nonprogramming equipment at aquatic facilities. They are useful for people participating in aquatic activities and for those who would like to bring participants or watch them. Such pieces of equipment should be checked daily to make sure they are in working order because they are the most likely to wear out. Other equipment that recreation facility managers may find at an aquatic venue includes benches, umbrellas, cleaning equipment, lane-line spools, computer timing systems, bleachers, trash cans, and office supplies.

Aquatic Facility Product Delivery Areas

As mentioned in the Staffing section, an aquatic facility includes a number of production delivery areas. Restrooms are ancillary production delivery areas that support the core product, and they are often included in locker rooms. Another type of production delivery area is the retail outlet. Retail outlets are core product extensions where users may purchase merchandise or equipment as a part of their aquatic leisure experience. Production delivery areas that focus on the core product include areas for informal swim, instructional swim, fitness programming, special events, intramurals, clubs, and athletic teams.

Informal Swim Area

Informal swim is the easiest area to schedule and the most crucial to any aquatic facility. Most people think of informal swim as lap swimming. Although lap swimming does occur during informal time, the concept encompasses all types of activities that participants might choose to do. Whether the activities involve swimming laps, jumping off the diving board, aqua jogging, or simply chatting with friends, informal swim should be the primary focus of recreation facility managers because it is where a facility will see the most participation.

Instructional Swim Area

Instructional swim is the second most popular activity at aquatic facilities, and it is the one that will garner the largest profits if promoted, offered, and run properly. Swim lessons make up the bulk of instructional swim time, and scheduling them is of great importance to the success of instructional swim. These programs are typically offered during peak times, which include the late afternoon, early evening, and weekends, so as not to conflict with school schedules. During the summer, it is more common to see instructional swim offered throughout the day. Swim lessons for preschool children can be offered on weekday mornings and early afternoons, but they should also be offered during peak times to account for working parents.

Swim lessons can be offered to children as young as 6 months to adults who are 100 or more years old. It is imperative to keep the instructor-to-student ratio low but cost effective. In addition to group swim lessons, private and semiprivate lessons are another great service to provide. They give participants either one-on-one instruction or lower instructor-to-student rations. They also bring in extra revenue because their fees can be relatively high.

Swimming and diving lessons represent the traditional instructional programming offered at aquatic facilities. However, newer forms of instructional programming are being offered. Scuba instruction is growing rapidly. Sailing, canoeing, and kayaking are popular at facilities with outdoor capabilities, and innovative classes such as surfing or water skiing can add to the variety of programming. When deciding what programs to offer, it is important for recreation facility managers to think about what they can actually do within their facility. Although participants may desire a surfing class, if there are no facilities available where the class can be conducted, offering the class is impossible.

Fitness Programming Area

Water fitness (called water exercise) has become a more popular dimension in aquatic facilities. Water exercise can incorporate many facets of aquatic activities. Lap swimming can be considered water exercise, but most think of it as a traditional class with an instructor. Water exercise includes swim conditioning, aqua jogging, water aerobics, and aquatic yoga. An interesting spin-off concept from traditional fitness programming is personal aquatic training. Similar to personal training, personal aquatic training is one-on-one exercise with a certified trainer in the aquatic environment. It is a more recent trend in the field of aquatics, but recreation facility managers should be aware of it because it is gaining popularity.

Closely related to fitness programming is aquatic therapy. As mentioned earlier in this chapter, water has many properties that make it the ideal environment for people who may need less impact on their joints. Seniors are finding benefits from classes aimed at strengthening the body to help alleviate the symptoms of arthritis. Athletes are using the water to help recover from injuries and surgeries. In addition, people with disabilities are able to use the water to gain range of motion that makes everyday life easier.

Special Events Area

Special events are a prime time to showcase a facility and what it has to offer. These programs can range from a daylong event to a once-a-month community offering. During special events, participants who would not usually be using the facility have the opportunity to do so. Family swim time is the easiest special event to program, but it needs the most attention from a risk management standpoint because

Water exercise is popular among users at aquatic facilities.
Luis Alvarez/Digital Vision/Getty Images

small children will be using the facility. It can be scheduled daily, weekly, monthly, or at other designated times. Family swim is exactly what it sounds like; it's a time for families to have fun exploring aquatic activities together. Facility rentals are another type of special event that can bring in large revenue. Many groups may want to use the facility, and it is the job of recreational facility managers to prioritize these groups and schedule space accordingly. (See chapter 13 for more details on special events and facility rentals.)

Intramural, Club, and Athletic Programming Area

The next tier of aquatic activities delves more into competitive swimming and diving. Intramurals is the most informal type of swimming competition. All levels of swimmers partake in competition based on cooperation and fun. Events can range from traditional competitions to more inclusive events such as a dog-paddle or cannonball competition. This type of event is usually a daylong tournament with men's, women's, and coed teams.

Club programs are a more formalized system of aquatic competition. In addition to competitive swimming and diving, groups form clubs for water polo and synchronized swimming. They typically have weekly (or even daily) practices and a set meet schedule. A club schedule can also include invitational meets, championship tournaments, and other national competitions.

Athletic teams are the traditional varsity swimming, diving, water polo, and synchronized swimming teams. These teams practice daily; sometimes, they practice two or three times a day. Meet schedules can vary based on the season of the sport, so recreation facility managers should be aware of the season of each sport that they supervise. At times, a facility may be called upon to host a championship

Many details go into planning a swim or diving meet, including coordinating schedules, timelines, facilities, and staff preparation. The recreation facility manager should request help from people who have knowledge of this type of event to make sure all details for the event are covered.

Jupiterimages/Getty Images

meet or competition. These meets can range from a local all-city meet to an international championship. Each event has different needs and concerns, so facility managers should surround themselves with people who are knowledgeable of the event. The meets require attention from facility managers in coordinating schedules and timelines, as well as facility and staff preparation, which can take weeks or even months to develop and implement. These types of events can raise revenue not only for the facility but also for the surrounding community as an economic stimulus.

External Support

Certain services are vital to an aquatic facility, but facility employees may not be able to pro-

vide them. This is where external personnel such as emergency medical personnel; police, security, and fire personnel; food-service personnel; computer and information technology personnel; and maintenance service personnel help to fill in where needed.

Emergency Medical Personnel

Critical in the emergency action plan, emergency medical personnel are the next link in the chain of survival for an accident victim if on-site staff are unable to handle an emergency on their own. Emergency medical technicians (EMTs) and paramedics can provide a standard of care above that of the lay rescuer. They can also transport victims to a medical facility where they can receive advanced care faster.

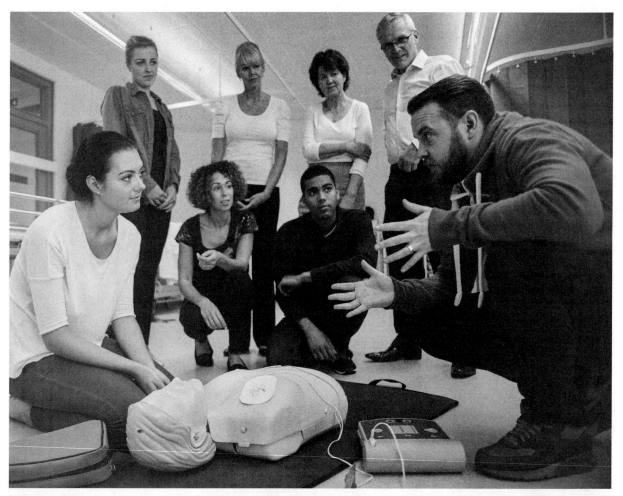

Aquatic facility managers should establish contact with local emergency personnel and review the facility's emergency action plan.

sturti/E+/Getty Images

Aquatic facility managers should have contact with local emergency personnel to review the facility emergency action plans and determine the logistics of possible emergency scenarios.

Police, Security, and Fire Personnel

Police and fire rescue services are integral to emergency service systems. Facility managers should have contact with these services because they are important to all emergency action plans. Fire rescue services can help address where participants should go in the event of a fire or other emergency. Police have their obvious job of upholding the law, but they can also be brought into a facility to provide security. Security services can also be performed by a third-party organization that specializes in them.

Food-Service Personnel

Some aquatic facilities offer a food-service area. Recreation facility managers must decide whether the service will be done in-house or contracted to a third party. In either case, food-service health and safety codes are an important consideration. This section does not delve deeply into the components of food service, but facility managers should be aware that such services do exist at aquatic facilities. For more detailed information on food service, see chapter 5.

Computer and Information Technology (IT) Personnel

As technology grows, a growing number of aquatic facilities are using computers and the Internet in their everyday business. Although

some aquatic and recreation facilities may have their own information technology (IT) services, a third party may provide this service. Computers and IT services are useful for facility managers in programming, personnel management, marketing, and many other areas. Recreation facility managers must become aware of such technologies through continued professional development and training, and they must surround themselves with experts in the field.

Maintenance Service Personnel

As mentioned earlier, the mechanical systems of aquatic facilities can be extremely intricate and sometimes frustrating for recreation facility managers. If a properly trained aquatic specialist is not on staff, managers can hire a third-party contractor who specializes in aquatic maintenance. Contracting this type of service can be more expensive, but it ensures that a trained professional is working on the systems. Third-party vendors can also perform general maintenance. Facility managers should make themselves aware of the costs associated with these services. If the laborers are in a union, facility managers should also stay informed on union policies.

Summary

Aquatic facilities have many unique properties that can overwhelm recreation facility managers who do not understand the intricacies of successfully running a facility of this type. With the increased revenues being generated by pools and water parks today, it is of great importance that recreation facility managers understand how to adequately staff these facilities and create a safe aquatic environment.

REVIEW QUESTIONS

1. Identify three advantages of a splash pad.
2. What is an AFO, and why are they important in the operations of a swimming pool?
3. What are some ways to improve a pool's or water park's accessibility?

4. What is backwashing?

5. Identify the most commonly used surfaces for pool decks.

6. Identify at least two external agencies that support the safety training of employees of an aquatic complex.

CASE STUDY

Recruitment Falling Short at Black Hills Community Parks and Recreation Department

You are the aquatics coordinator for the Black Hills Community Parks and Recreation Department (BHCPRD). You were just hired last month, and you are quickly gearing up for the busy summer season that is 5 months away. While you have been with the BHCPRD for only a month, you really enjoy the community, your coworkers, and your supervisor. Everyone has been extremely supportive as you settle into your first full-time job in this exciting career.

One of your first tasks is to begin assessing your summer staffing needs. During this assessment, you learn that approximately 100 lifeguards and 25 support staff (concessions, admissions, general supervision, etc.) will be needed to maintain the same service quality as last summer. You also discover that nearly 50 percent of the staff from last year are no longer available because they secured other jobs, moved out of the area, or graduated, or for other reasons. Based on these projections, you will need to hire at least 45 new lifeguards and 15 new support staff.

Overall, the anticipated turnover rate of last summer's staff is not surprising. Summer turnover rates for these seasonal positions have typically been high because over 98 percent of last summer's staff are high school or college students with schedules and plans that change from year to year. You initiate several staff recruiting initiatives to attract applicants to the available positions.

After a month of running various staff recruitment campaigns, you are disappointed that your applicant pool is limited to only 20 applicants. You had spoken to several of your coworkers and your supervisor for guidance on recruitment activities that had been successfully used in the past. Each of these recruitment strategies (visiting local universities, attending high school job fairs, and posting on social media) was implemented along with a few others that you added. Clearly, these efforts did not produce the same results as they had in past summers.

Of the 20 applicants, 15 of them meet the minimum qualifications for employment while the other 5 do not (and therefore must be removed from further consideration). You have spoken with several of your coworkers and supervisor to learn they are also experiencing below-average applicant pools for their summer positions. As a new employee, you are eager to have a great first summer season; however, you are growing increasingly concerned about a possible staff shortage and its effect on your aquatic operations.

Case Study Questions

1. What are some additional strategies you could employ that may attract a larger, more diverse pool of applicants?

2. If you are unable to hire the same number of lifeguard staff as last summer, what are some of your options from an operations perspective?

3. If you are unable to hire the same number of support staff as last summer, what are some of your options from an operations perspective?

CHAPTER 18

Recreational Sport Facilities

LEARNING OBJECTIVES

At the completion of this chapter, you should be able to do the following:

1. Identify the various types of recreational sport facilities.
2. Recognize the general design considerations for recreational sport facilities.
3. Examine the operational practices of recreational sport facilities.

Sport facilities can range from a community soccer field in a small, 5-acre (2 ha) neighborhood park to a multimillion-dollar complex that encompasses over 50 acres (20 ha) and includes several sport fields. Regardless of size, sport facilities represent a significant part of the scope of operations for many recreation facility managers. **Recreational sport facilities** include a large variety of outdoor sport fields and areas. Examples of sport facilities include baseball and softball fields, football fields, soccer fields, running tracks, lacrosse fields, and cricket fields. Recreational sport facilities provide opportunities for users to engage in sport-specific activities. These facility areas can be core products, or they can be core product extensions of another facility. With the

increased popularity in sports such as soccer and cricket, the number of recreational sport facilities has grown since the early 2000s. In addition, these recreational sport facilities are a common amenity for many agencies and can vary in size and scope. Many generate revenue while they provide participants with a unique leisure experience.

Types of Recreational Sport Facilities

Outdoor recreational sport facilities vary from amenities within a park or facility to large-scale venues. They can be classified into these four categories:

Located in York County, South Carolina, Field Day Park at Lake Wylie opened in 2020 following 2 years of construction. Field Day Park at Lake Wylie is a 50-acre (20 ha) complex that includes a community building, two pavilions, three baseball and softball fields, six pickleball courts, walking trails, a playground, and a score tower. In addition, the complex has three multipurpose turf fields that can be used for soccer, rugby, and flag football games.

Costing US$13.5 million, Field Day Park has become a local destination for sport events. The park has also attracted individual and group participants from outside the community through its hosting of regional football combines, travel baseball team workouts, and large-scale tournaments. While sport events represent the primary amenities at Field Day Park, the site also regularly hosts other recreational activities such as concerts, movies in the park, food truck Fridays, and other special events. Several of the sport fields and amenities are also available for daily or hourly rentals.

A first of its kind for York County, the three baseball and softball fields have natural grass outfields and synthetic turf infields, allowing for games to still be played in wet weather conditions. Another unique feature of Field Day Park at Lake Wylie is the partnership that was established with the local college, Belmont Abbey College. This partnership provides Belmont Abbey College with exclusive access to one of the turf fields for its athletic teams. More specifically, six of the college's teams practice at Field Day Park: rugby, field hockey, men's and women's soccer, and men's and women's lacrosse.

1. Open-play recreational sport fields
2. Encapsulated stadiums
3. Multifield recreational spectator safety and performance
4. Multipurpose recreational sport complexes

Open-Play Recreational Sport Fields

Open-play recreational sport fields are often located in parks or adjacent to other recreation facilities. These fields are primarily used for open-play, instructional, or general recreation programming. Often, open-play fields include a single sport field, are less than 5 acres (2 ha) in size (depending on the specific sport), and are used to meet the needs or interests of a local group of people (e.g., neighborhood, school, church).

Encapsulated Stadiums

Encapsulated stadiums are those recreational sport fields that are surrounded or housed within a protected space. Encapsulated stadiums are typically single-field constructions with mass seating, fencing, and natural landscaping that surrounds the field. The singular field may support multiple purposes such as football, lacrosse, soccer, track, and various special events. Encapsulated stadiums are commonly used for competitive sport events or other large events (e.g., concerts, convocations, exhibitions, rallies). These venues are typically located near the community's major highways and other transportation infrastructure to support the large crowds navigating to and from the stadium. In addition, they require large parking areas.

Multifield Recreational Spectator Safety and Performance

Multifield recreational sport facilities (complexes) include several sport fields of the same type in one location. While the actual size of each facility depends on the specific sport field dimensions, many of these complexes are more than 10 acres (4 ha) in size; some span more than 50 acres (20 ha). Multifield recreational sport complexes experienced significant growth in response to the growing youth

Encapsulated stadiums are common for sporting events with large crowds.
Galina Barskaya/fotolia.com

sport movement of the late 1980s. Designed to support multiple games at the same time, these complexes allow facility managers the ability to host larger-scale leagues, tournaments, and other events. Multifield sport complexes should be conveniently located near main highways, public transportation, pedestrian walkways, and bikeways to support the large number of participants and spectators.

Multipurpose Recreational Sport Complexes

Multipurpose recreational sport complexes include fields that support a variety of sports. In particular, the dimensions and markings on the field(s) can accommodate multiple uses, such as football, soccer, lacrosse, field hockey, and more. Multipurpose facilities are becoming increasingly popular because they represent a more cost-effective facility and they allow for

more flexibility in the types of activities that can be played on the fields. Similar to multifield complexes, multipurpose recreational sport complexes are often used to host organized programming and events such as concerts, celebrations, tournaments, and competitive sport events.

Despite the potential benefits of multipurpose recreational sport complexes, these facilities also present some challenges for facility managers. The visual appearance of multiple markings on the playing field can be distracting for athletes, officials, and even spectators. A recommended strategy for addressing this potential issue is to use different colors for each of the sport's field markings. Sometimes, multipurpose recreational sport complexes can create scheduling challenges for facility managers when multiple sports are competing for the use of the shared field space. For example, a multipurpose facility that supports both football and soccer may find times when teams and athletes from both sports wish to use the space at the same time. Managers need to plan carefully to create a schedule that supports the equitable use of the field.

Recreational Sport Facility Construction Considerations

Whether the facility manager is tasked with constructing a new sport facility or renovating an existing area, they should consider these five overarching factors:

1. *Budget.* In general, all types of construction projects are approved with the understanding that they will be constructed within a predetermined amount of financing; sport facilities are no different. The project team needs to plan carefully throughout the entire design and construction phase to ensure construction or renovations of the sport facility are completed within the previously established budget.

2. *Accessibility.* Whether it be a new site or an existing site in need of renovations, the recreational sport facility should be easily accessible by all.

3. *Water.* Nearly all of the outdoor sport facilities in North America must contend with water. Excessive water or areas of standing water on the playing field can make the space unsafe for use, resulting in temporary closures or postponed games and activities. To maximize safety and use, construction should include proper drainage and use grading techniques within the facility.

4. *Existing site conditions.* The physical location of the sport facility must also be considered. Questions to address during the planning phase of a sport facility construction or renovation project include the following: What is the site's topography? How well does the soil drain? Can the site also support traffic and spectator demands?

5. *Surface.* Consideration of the sport facility's playing surface is also required. The playing surface should be smooth and even to support safe play and use.

These factors should guide the planning, design, and construction of sport facilities. It is also important to note that the application of these factors can vary by the type and intended use of the sport facility. For instance, surface considerations might represent a more important area of focus for a youth baseball field, while the location of a multifield soccer complex in relation to major traffic arteries in the community might assume a greater significance in another community. Simply put, these overarching factors will likely vary in importance, and they should serve as practical guidelines to use in sport facility development.

General Design Criteria for Sport Facilities

Facility managers should consider some general design criteria that apply to recreational sport facilities. The criteria align with the five factors previously discussed (budget, accessibility, safety, location, and surface), and they support safe and playable sport fields. Each of these criteria are discussed in the following sections.

CHECK IT OUT
Sport Field Line Marking Colors on a Multipurpose Field

While no rules exist regarding the line colors for each sport, a commonly accepted practice is to use white lines for football marking, yellow for soccer, and blue or red for lacrosse (Novak & Maguire, 2012).

Player or Participant Safety and Performance

Safety of the sport facility is of utmost importance. The first safety consideration is the size of the site. The site should be an appropriate size to safely support the sports to be played. It's also important to consider that many sports require space that goes beyond the dimensions of the court or field. Sports such as tennis, volleyball, basketball, baseball, softball, and table tennis should have adequate space for players to go beyond the court markings while playing. For example, a tennis player serves from beyond the endline and may spend much of the match hitting shots outside the court markings. Other sports, such as baseball and volleyball, allow for players to leave the field or court area to make a play. In a sport setting, this additional space is called a use zone. Space for the sport activity itself, as well as the use zones

and any spectator needs, should be carefully considered in determining the appropriate size. Overall traffic safety is also an important factor to consider when assessing the size of the site. The play areas should be located at a safe distance from vehicular traffic, bicycles, and pedestrians. Fencing or landscaping (e.g., shrubs, trees) can be installed to separate the playing areas from traffic areas (see table 18.1). Accessible parking lots and walkways should also be available to support direct access to the sport facility.

For recreational sport facilities with multiple fields, playing fields should be organized by age or level of play. For instance, elementary and high school soccer fields should be located in different areas to avoid errantly kicked balls drifting into the other fields and potentially causing serious injury. Installing a divider or barrier can also aid in isolating the areas.

TABLE 18.1   TYPICAL PLAYING-FIELD SPACE REQUIREMENT

Sport	Recommended space needed for playing area
Baseball, youth	2-2.5 acres (per field)
Basketball, youth (with 10' use zone around perimeter)	5,040 ft² (per court)
Basketball, adult (with 10' use zone around perimeter)	7,280 ft² (per court)
Bocce ball	1,134 ft² (per court)
Disc golf	Varies (2-3 holes per acre)
Football, touch or flag	1 acre (per field)
Horseshoe (pitch)	1,400 ft² (per pitch)
Ice skating or hockey	22,000 ft² (per rink)
In-line skating or hockey	28,000 ft² (per rink)
Platform tennis (with 3' sideline and 8' endline use zones)	1,800 ft² (per court)
Rock climbing (climbing walls)	Varies (at least 2,000 ft²)
Shuffleboard	520 ft² (per court)
Skateboarding (skate park)	Varies (~7,000-12,000 ft²)
Softball, fast and slow pitch	1.7 acres (per field)
Soccer, youth	1.14 acres (per field)
Soccer, adult	1.9 acres (per field)
Tennis (with 12' sideline and 21' endline use zones)	7,200 ft² (per court)
Volleyball	5,000 ft² (per court)

Source: Outdoor Recreation Facilities Guide (IDNR, 2006).

At the design phase, the team should consider existing and future environmental conditions that potentially affect the sport facility. Distracting noises near the site, such as train horns or nearby industrial activity, can negatively affect participants and spectators. Prevailing winds and any nearby pollutants should also be assessed. Recreational sport facilities should never be located near utility wires or poles.

Recreational sport facilities should be oriented to protect both participants and spectators from the glare of the sun. While the ideal orientation of the sport fields may not be possible, keeping athletes from directly facing the sun (particularly during the early morning or late afternoon hours) is the goal. The long axis of rectangular shaped sport fields should generally be at right angles to the late afternoon sun rays. While the sun's positioning in the sky varies throughout the year, the sun's positioning during the midseason of the sport should serve as the guide for orienting the long axis at a right angle to the late afternoon sun. Orienting softball and baseball fields is more complicated because of the varied angles of play occurring on the field. However, priority should be given to the pitcher, batter, and catcher because they are typically the most vulnerable positions. Thus, the field should be oriented according to an axis line drawn from the catcher to the pitcher. For many geographical locations, this line would suggest the tip of home plate through the pitcher's mound and second base should point in an east–northeast direction.

Spectator Safety and Performance

Most recreational sport facilities attract crowds of spectators. A spectator can be a supportive family member, a friend, a team fan, or someone who is there for the simple pleasure of watching the sport. Spectators are an integral element of the recreational sport facility, and their safety is arguably as important as athlete safety. Spectator areas should be free of any potential trip hazards, be well lit, and include appropriate signage to inform spectators of facility policies, safety warnings, emergency procedures, and other necessary information that supports their safety.

The safety of the spectators also largely depends on the safety of the seating. Sport facilities containing bleachers or stadium seating should undergo regular inspections and preventive maintenance procedures to ensure these areas are safe to use. While the type and amount of seating within sport facilities varies, every facility must consider two factors: protection from balls and other equipment used during play and protection from those situations when an athlete's movement extends beyond the field of play. The most common method used to reduce the number of times balls exit the playing field is the use of a screen or fence. The screen or fence should be located between the playing field and spectator seating areas. This protection is particularly important for sports such as baseball and softball, where balls are regularly hit out of the area of play. A recognized strategy to protect spectators from players extending beyond the field of play is to restrict spectators to areas beyond the field's use zones. Athletes and coaches can be allowed to be within the field's use zones, with spectators positioned just beyond those areas. In cases where multifield layouts are present, allowing spectators between the adjacent playing fields is not advisable.

Grading

The playing areas and fields within recreational sport facilities should be relatively level. To support appropriate water drainage, many sport fields have a slight slope to direct water off the playing area. One of the first tasks during the construction or redevelopment phase of a sport facility is the completion of a survey. The survey should include dimensions and elevations at specific points on the playing area. Surveys are completed through the use of scopes with levels, transits, elevation rods, and marker stakes.

Scope Equipment

Scope equipment can vary from a simple builder scope and level to a more sophisticated system. Simple scope equipment is positioned on a stand and requires the surveyor to manually adjust the stand's legs to get the scope level. Once level, the scope is used to obtain elevation readings at various points on the field using the elevation rod. More advanced equipment includes automatic or laser grading levels that can more quickly obtain elevation readings with a higher level of precision.

Transits

Transits are also positioned on a stand with adjustable legs and are used in two ways. They either set a straight line and an angle to measure the playing field's boundaries, or they establish a percentage of slope on the playing field (typically done for drainage purposes). Most transits also include a level, which can be manual or digital devices.

Elevation Rod

The elevation rod is used to measure the elevation differences throughout the site. In the United States, elevation rods are typically calibrated in feet and inches. The elevation rod is a long, straight portable post that has foot and inch readings vertically labeled. The elevation rod is typically held by a surveyor, and it is located at various points within the site. The level or transit device is stationed at another location, and it is used to obtain elevation readings from the elevation rod. Readings are taken from these various points and plotted on a contour plan to determine specific grading needs for the site.

Elevation Marker Stakes

Wooden stakes, commonly called grading stakes, that are secured into the ground with markings on them are also used in surveying. The markings help inform the contractor or excavator whether the area needs cutting or filling to reach the appropriate elevation and grading for the sport field.

Surfaces

Recreational sport facilities need to be large enough to support the rules and regulations of the sport or activity for which they are intended. These facilities also need to have a surface that allows the users to participate safely and at a reasonable level of competition. In many instances, recreational sport facilities are designed to support multiple sport and even nonsport purposes (e.g., a football field used for concerts). Thus, these facilities must have surfaces that are not only safe but also resilient enough to support all of their intended purposes. To ensure both safety and resilience, the facility manager must consider the following surface characteristics:

1. *The levelness of the surface*: Overall levelness can have an influence on important elements of the ball used in the sport, such as its bounce trueness and predictability of ball response and movement.

2. *The surface's hardness*: Hardness can affect several factors of game play, including speed of play, athlete movement, and injury potential.

3. *The traction provided by the surface*: Traction influences speed of play, athletes' direction changes, and injury potential resulting from slips or collisions.

Selection of the appropriate surface depends on several factors, including local conditions, intended level of play (e.g., youth, adult, competitive, recreational), and the criteria outlined in previous sections of this chapter. What works for one facility may not be realistic or desired by another. The predominant surfaces used for the playing areas of recreational sport facilities are discussed next.

Natural Grass

In the United States, these five grasses are most commonly used as turfgrass for a recreational sport field:

1. Bermudagrass
2. Kentucky bluegrass
3. Tall fescue
4. Perennial ryegrass
5. Creeping bentgrass

Kentucky bluegrass, perennial ryegrass, and creeping bentgrass are used primarily in cooler regions of the United States. Kentucky bluegrass is generally slower to establish from seed, has strong surface resiliency, and has moderate wear resistance over times of heavy use. Perennial ryegrass has faster growth rates (from seed) and very strong wear resistance compared to Kentucky bluegrass, but its appearance is often considered less visually appealing. Because of these qualities, when seeding sport fields in cooler regions that support sports requiring heavy traffic and rapid movement (e.g., for football, lacrosse, rugby, soccer, baseball, and softball), facilities often use a mixture of Kentucky bluegrass and perennial ryegrass.

The third cool-region grass is creeping bentgrass. Creeping bentgrass has the slowest seedling growth rate, but it can tolerate regular mowing as low as 0.25 inch (0.6 cm) high. Creeping bentgrass is often used for grass tennis courts, lawn bowling, and croquet fields.

Tall fescue can be used in transition or warmer regions of the United States. Tall fescue has excellent surface resiliency and wear resistance with a moderate growth rate. Limited to warm-climate regions, bermudagrass also has strong surface resiliency and wear resistance. However, bermudagrass has a slower growth rate compared to tall fescue. Facilities in warmer regions often use a mixture of tall fescue and bermudagrass to support sports requiring rapid player movements and heavy traffic (e.g., football, lacrosse, rugby, soccer, baseball, and softball).

Synthetic Turf

Rising to prominence in the 1960s with the Houston Astrodome's AstroTurf, synthetic turf has vastly improved since its early days. Today's synthetic turf systems primarily include a fill-in system. While variations exist, most fill-in systems consist of 2.5-inch (6 cm) long vertical polyethylene, polypropylene, or nylon fibers attached to a porous polyethylene backing that is infilled with approximately 2 inches (5 cm) of crumb rubber that serves as dirtlike material between the blades of synthetic grass (Rogers, 2008). Some synthetic turfs use a combination of sand and rubber crumb infill, and they may include a polyurethane pad that is placed under the backing for additional cushioning.

In preparing the site and providing proper drainage for the field, a geotextile fabric-type liner is installed, followed by an 8- to 12-inch (20-30 cm) subbase of gravel or sand. Drain tiles are also integrated into the subbase to capture and carry water away from the field's playing surface. Once the subbase has been installed, the site will typically involve a surveyor to mark the field's layout followed by the installation of the synthetic turf. Synthetic turf often comes in 5-yard (4.6 m) panels that are rolled out and seamed together by sewing, gluing, or a combination of both (Rogers, 2008). Finally, a heavy roller goes over the seams, and field markings are installed.

Here are the benefits and drawbacks of synthetic turf (Jenner, 2019):

Benefits

- It has a longer playability season (for those in colder and wetter climate regions).
- It can be used more quickly after rain and wet weather.
- It does not require a rejuvenation period, which is common practice on natural grass fields.
- It has longevity; its typical life span is 10 to 15 years.
- These fields can be lined and used for a variety of activities.
- It requires lower maintenance costs.
- It can support more activities and events per year compared to natural grass fields.

Drawbacks

- Up-front costs are more expensive than for natural grass fields.
- After a predetermined life span, most manufacturers recommend replacement of the entire synthetic-turf carpet, which can be expensive. This is not an issue with natural grass fields.
- It likely requires the use of a consultant during various phases of the planning, design, and installation.
- Dozens of options exist for the top 3 inches (7.6 cm) of the synthetic pile, which can be overwhelming when trying to plan for a multi-use field.

Synthetic Turf's Growth

More than 8,000 synthetic turf sport fields exist in North American schools, colleges, parks, and professional sport stadiums (Ford, 2021).

Concrete

Poured surfaces such as concrete are used in some sport facilities. Concrete surfaces can typically be used year-round, and they provide a multifunctional space to use for a variety of sports and activities. While the installation costs are higher, concrete surfaces are durable with lower maintenance costs.

Asphalt

Typically less expensive than concrete, asphalt is also a durable, year-round playing surface for facilities. Maintenance costs are also lower compared to natural grass, and the surface can be used for multiple purposes. Asphalt can also be combined with other surfaces (e.g., rubber, synthetic materials) to enhance its cushioning for sports such as track and field.

Drainage

As noted earlier, most sport fields have a gradual slope on the playing area to support the efficient removal of excess surface water. Most sport fields have a gradual slope of about 1 percent. In addition to surface drainage, subsurface drainage should be considered. It is often necessary to consult with a soil engineer to ascertain the specific subsurface conditions.

Communications

Most recreational sport facilities require a communications system in place to support game-day operations. At a minimum, most communication systems include public-address or announcing equipment, a press box, telecommunications, and a scoreboard with

A scoreboard can be an essential tool in a communication system.

Galina Barskaya/fotolia.com

controls. The locations and controls for this equipment should be determined early in the site planning process; some may require the routing of wiring and other equipment to support its operations.

Lighting

Lighting needs must be considered for those recreational sport facilities with plans of night use. Outdoor lighting comes with unique challenges that are not present in indoor spaces. Furthermore, lighting for sport events has its own set of needs and considerations. Facility managers often work with lighting experts to provide the proper level and quality of light required for the particular sport. Information on the types and particular levels of lighting for specific sports is covered in chapter 6.

Parking

Nearly all recreational sport facilities need parking to support the numbers of athletes, spectators, and staff. Parking spaces should be clearly marked; they should ideally be constructed in locations that have the highest concentration of users while also not impeding playing environment or interfering with pedestrian traffic. For venues requiring large parking areas, careful planning is crucial. The facility design team should conduct an assessment of traffic patterns in the surrounding area to determine appropriate entry and exit points. Parking is covered in detail in chapter 5.

Storage and Service Areas

Sport facilities require equipment in order to effectively operate and maintain the playing areas and ancillary spaces. When feasible, storage and service facilities should be situated nearby and readily accessible. These facilities should include space for storing operation and maintenance equipment, restrooms, and, in many instances, locker rooms or shower facilities for athletes, coaches, and officials.

Operation of Sport Facilities

To operate efficiently, a recreational sport facility requires several important management activities. These activities include finding adequate staffing and ensuring proper maintenance.

Staffing

Staffing represents a critical element for the effective and efficient operation of a recreational sport facility. Specific staffing needs vary based on the scope and size of the recreational sport facility. However, typical staff include managers, officials, instructors, and maintenance and operations staff. Their roles and responsibilities are discussed next.

Managers

The recreational sport facility manager is responsible for mobilizing, organizing, and applying the facility's resources (human, physical, financial, and technological) toward quality services and experiences within the facility. Managers of recreational sport facilities also assume a leadership role to ensure the efficient and effective use of these resources. Depending on the size and scope of the facility, the manager may serve in a full-time or part-time capacity. In some cases, the manager may be responsible for the leadership and coordination of multiple facilities.

Officials

Most sport facilities host recreational or competitive events. Whether they host league events or large-scale tournaments, officials are needed to support safe and fair game play. The level of play determines the level of training required for the official. For instance, an official for a youth recreational soccer league match might require the completion of a half-day training course offered by the local park and recreation department. In contrast, officials for a competitive travel club soccer tournament

An "Official" Workout

Enjoy exercise? Interested in becoming an official? Why not do both at the same time? According to the National Association of Sports Officials (2022), basketball officials run between 1 and 4 miles (1.6-6.4 km) during a competitive basketball game.

may require more extensive training and demonstrations to trained observers, leading to the attainment of a national-level certification.

Instructors

Like most recreation facilities, instructors play a significant role in the on-site facilitation of programs, clinics, events, and camps for recreational sport facilities. Common programming opportunities within a recreational sport facility include sport-specific instructional programming, clinics, camps, and special events. The supervision of and training for instructors are often the responsibility of the facility manager or their staff. When dealing with a large number of instructors, facility managers may find it beneficial to hire an instructor supervisor or coordinator.

Maintenance and Operations Staff

Maintenance and operations staff are important to any facility, and recreational sport facilities are no different. Maintenance and operations personnel are charged with the oversight and coordination of most of the facility's physical resources, including turf management, landscaping, seating and structures, equipment, mechanical systems, chemical systems, and sanitation systems associated with the facility. These professionals must ensure the facility is functioning in a safe, efficient, and effective manner while also in accordance with health and safety codes.

Concessionaires

Depending on the facility, an on-site concession service may be provided. In those instances, concession staff are needed to support these services. Concession staff may be employ-

ees of the agency or facility, or they may be outsourced. Concessionaires are responsible for the planning, ordering, preparation, and delivery of food, snacks, and beverages to the facility's users. Concessionaires should be focused on meeting the needs and interests of the facility's users while also adhering to health and safety codes.

Gate and Security Staff

Some large-scale recreational sport facilities are revenue-generating facilities. Some of these venues require on-site fee collection prior to admission into the facility. In these instances, access-control areas typically include staff and equipment, including a cash register, credit card machine, or computer, that are utilized to assist with fee collection. Security personnel may also be a part of a recreational sport facility to support the safety of spectators and facility users.

Security and Emergency Medical Personnel

Large-scale recreational sport facilities typically have game-day operations staff who are responsible for enforcing facility policies and procedures and general facility supervision. At times, these facilities may also require additional support, such as emergency medical or security personnel. They are typically not employed by the recreational sport facility; rather, they represent a form of external support for the facility.

Emergency medical personnel represent a critical element of the recreational sport facility's emergency action plan. They provide support for people injured in accidents when on-site staff are unable to handle the emergency on their own. Emergency medical personnel can also transport injured people from the recreational sport facility to the appropriate care facility. Facility managers should be engaged in regular communication and work closely with emergency medical personnel to ensure response plans remain current and are as effective and efficient as possible. Communications should also extend to local fire and law enforcement agencies to keep all emergency service personnel apprised of the facility's emergency action plans. Facility staff should undergo regular scenario-based training exercises to ensure that all appropriate staff are able to execute the facility's emergency action plans.

In addition to supporting a recreational sport facility's emergency action plans, local law enforcement can also be brought into the facility to provide security during large-scale events. Managers can also hire third-party security companies to support the facility's security needs. Having on-site law enforcement who can provide quick response times during these large events can help keep some situations from escalating and becoming unmanageable or dangerous.

Maintenance

A recreational sport facility must have a well-developed maintenance program to ensure that the facility is functional, attractive, clean, sanitary, and safe. Despite the diverse nature of recreational sport facilities, some core elements should be integrated into the facility's maintenance program. These elements include legal requirements, inspections, maintenance standards, routine and preventive maintenance, and repairs and renovations.

Legal Requirements

Local, state, and federal regulations must be considered as part of the facility's maintenance program. Recreational sport facilities comply with these regulations to avoid fines or closures. Categories of regulations that generally affect recreational sport facilities include the following:

1. *Accessibility.* Multiple U.S. federal laws (Architectural Barriers Act of 1968, Rehabilitation Act of 1973, ADA of 1990) outline the need for facilities to be accessible to individuals with disabilities. In many instances, state and local laws exist that complement these federal laws by requiring public facilities to be accessible by all people.

2. *Building codes.* Generally determined at the local level, building codes outline construction processes as well as the configuration and layout of mechanical, electrical, and plumbing systems within the facility. Codes for a facility's emergency systems (e.g., fire, sprinkler systems) are also required. Regular on-site inspections by local authorities are completed to ensure the recreational sports facility's compliance with these codes.

3. *Environmental protection laws.* Depending on the facility, some environmental protection laws may affect the maintenance program. Common environmental issues affecting recreational sport facilities include surface water runoff; chemical storage, application, and disposal procedures; and assessment processes for hazardous waste or other toxic materials.

4. *Health codes.* Recreational sport facilities providing food and beverage services must adhere to local health codes and regulations. Health code officials often conduct inspections of the facility's concession and food preparation areas as well as food-service and food handling practices to ensure compliance.

5. *Safety mandates.* One of the most significant mandates concerning the safety of a recreational sport facility's maintenance program is outlined in the U.S. federal government's Occupational Safety and Health (OSH) Act of 1970. Expectations and responsibilities related to workplace safety for both employers and employees are specified within the Occupational Safety and Health Administration (OSHA).

Inspections

Inspections are an integral part of the recreational sport facility's maintenance program, and they should occur on a regular basis. Depending on the facility, inspections may occur at various times—daily, before opening or closing, or seasonally. User safety is the primary reason for these inspections. Inspections should focus on determining if the recreational sport facility has an acceptable level of maintenance present and the area is safe with no hazards present. The facility manager often develops guidelines and procedures for handling situations when unacceptable conditions are found within the facility. When defective conditions are found, typical responses to these situations may include the following:

- The completion of a work order or procedure to have the hazard repaired
- A partial opening of the facility with the hazardous area being closed until it is repaired
- Complete closure of the facility until repairs are completed

Each of these responses considers safety to be the top priority.

Maintenance Standards

All areas within a recreational sport facility should have well-developed maintenance standards. Standards should specify the maintenance that is required and the level of performance that is to be achieved. For instance, a maintenance standard for natural grass turf areas of a soccer field may be developed as follows:

> Soccer field turf will be mowed on a regular schedule at the following mowing heights: 1.5 inches in the spring season, 3 inches in the summer season, and 1.5 inches in the fall season. The mowing schedule will ensure that no more than one-third of the grass blade will be cut at a single mowing.

Routine and Preventive Maintenance

Routine and preventive maintenance tasks for a recreational sport facility vary slightly depending on the specific facility. However, most recreational sport facilities require the completion of routine maintenance tasks such as turf care, mowing, tree and shrub care, landscaping, and general building cleaning and maintenance. Some of these tasks may be informal, while others may require a work-order request. The work order will outline the specific maintenance services to be performed. Preventive maintenance procedures within the recreational sport facility seek to prolong the life (or prevent the failure) of the facility's equipment and structures. Regular inspections can aid the facility manager in developing preventive maintenance schedules for the facility. Routine and preventive maintenance are also discussed in chapter 14.

Repairs and Renovations

Repairs and renovations within a recreational sport facility are commonplace given the heavy usage that places stress on this type of facility. Repairs can be as basic as replacing the net on a soccer goal, or they can be more extensive projects such as the complete renovation of a football stadium's press box. Depending on the extent of the repair and the level of expertise required, outside contractors may be required. In those instances, a bid for the contractual work will typically be prepared. The bid should clearly detail the scope of work and operational considerations associated with the repair project. Once bids are received and reviewed by the facility manager, an external contractor can be selected and hired.

Summary

Recreational sport facilities have experienced significant growth since the early 2000s. The unique characteristics and uses of these facilities present a different set of challenges and opportunities for the facility manager. From the management of a single baseball field in a neighborhood park to a 50-acre (20 ha) soccer complex that serves an entire region, these facilities must be closely monitored to support their safe use and enjoyment.

REVIEW QUESTIONS

1. Identify at least two advantages of a multipurpose field compared to a multifield complex.
2. What are two benefits and two drawbacks of synthetic turf?
3. Describe the two primary safety factors to consider for spectator seating.
4. What are the most common types of natural grass used in North America's cooler regions?
5. Identify the typical equipment that should be included in a sport facility's communications system.

CASE STUDY

New Athletic Fields for Steeltown College

You are an associate athletic director for Steeltown College Athletics. Steeltown is a modest-sized college with approximately 7,000 undergraduate students. Located in the Midwest, Steeltown College was founded in 1877. It is affiliated with the NCAA Division II level. Steeltown College Athletics supports 10 women's and 10 men's teams, and it competes within the Bluestem Prairie Conference.

Historically, Steeltown College's athletic teams have regularly competed for conference championships and have enjoyed sustained success during the past 25 years. Building on this success, the college recently acquired land as part of an in-kind gift from an alum. The 30-acre (12 ha) property is located on the edge of town, and it is approximately 1.5 miles (2.4 km) from the Steeltown College campus. The property is square to rectangular in shape, measuring approximately 3,960 feet long by 3,300 feet wide (1,207 × 1,006 m).

The Steeltown College president has indicated the property will be used to support the college's athletic programs because several of the team's facilities are outdated and in need of significant upgrades and repairs. One of the more neglected athletic team facilities is the one used by men's baseball and women's softball teams. Both teams currently use the local community's fields for practice and games. The president of Steeltown College would like to use part of the 30-acre (12 ha) property to build a softball field and baseball field for the two athletic teams.

The president and athletic director have discussed these plans. As the associate athletic director, one of your responsibilities is the oversight of facilities and related activities (e.g., facility development, renovations, upgrades). The athletic director has invited you to join in these discussions and would like your input.

Case Study Questions

1. What are some questions you will need to consider as you reflect on the location of the 30-acre property as it relates to its location to campus and general traffic? Create a list of the questions that you would need to answer.
2. The president wants feedback on the advantages and drawbacks to using natural grass or synthetic turf for the two fields. Create a list of advantages and drawbacks for each option.
3. Based on the lists created for question 2, which surface option would you recommend?
4. In addition to the two fields, what other amenities for the 30-acre property should be considered to support the two sport facilities?

Professional Associations

Use this list of professional associations as a resource in managing recreation facilities.

American Academy for Park and Recreation Administration (AAPRA)

American Camp Association (ACA)

American Mountain Guides Association (AMGA)

American Therapeutic Recreation Association (ATRA)

Association for Experiential Education (AEE)

Association of Outdoor Recreation and Education (AORE)

Canadian Parks and Recreation Association (CPRA)

Canadian Therapeutic Recreation Association (CTRA)

Centers for Disease Control and Prevention (CDC)

Climbing Wall Association (CWA)

Club Management Association of America (CMAA)

Consumer Product Safety Commission (CPSC)

Environmental Protection Agency (EPA)

International Association of Amusement Parks and Attractions (IAAPA)

International Association of Convention and Visitor Bureaus (IACVB)

International Association of Venue Managers (IAVM)

International Council on Hotel, Restaurant, and Institutional Education (CHRIE)

International Festivals & Events Association (IFEA)

International Live Events Association (ILEA)

Leadership in Energy and Environmental Design (LEED)

National American Association for Environmental Education (NAAEE)

National Association for Interpretation (NAI)

National Association of State Park Directors (NASPD)

National Collegiate Athletic Association (NCAA)

National Council for Therapeutic Recreation Certification (NCTRC)

National Education Association (NEA)

National Intramural-Recreational Sports Association (NIRSA)

National Park Service (NPS)

National Recreation Association (NRA)

National Recreation and Park Association (NRPA)

National Sanitation Foundation (NSF)

National Society for Experiential Education (NSEE)

National Tour Association (NTA)

North American Society for Sport Management (NASSM)

Occupational Safety and Health Administration (OSHA)

Outdoor Industry Association (OIA)

Professional Convention Management Association (PCMA)

Resort and Commercial Recreation Association (RCRA)

Society for Accessible Travel & Hospitality (SATH)

Society of Health and Physical Educators (SHAPE America)

Society of Outdoor Recreation Professionals (SORP)

Student Conservation Association (SCA)

The Academy of Leisure Sciences (TALS)

Travel and Tourism Research Association (TTRA)

United States Green Building Council (USGBC)

USDA Employee Services & Recreation Associations (ESRA)

Wilderness Education Association (WEA)

World Leisure Organization (WLO)

World Tourism Organization (UNWTO)

World Travel & Tourism Council (WTTC)

World Waterpark Association (WWA)

Accredited Academic Programs

This appendix contains a list of universities with academic programs accredited by the Council on Accreditation for Parks, Recreation, Tourism, and Related Professions (COAPRT). Use it as a resource for recruiting and hiring students who are graduating from certified academic programs.

Appalachian State University	Ohio University
Arizona State University	Old Dominion University
Arkansas Tech University	Pittsburg State University
Brigham Young University	Radford University
California Polytechnic State University	San Francisco State University
California State University, Long Beach	San Jose State University
California State University, Chico	Shepherd University
California State University, Northridge	Southeast Missouri State University
California State University, Sacramento	Southern Connecticut State University
California State University, Fresno	Springfield College
California University of Pennsylvania	St. Joseph's University, New York
Central Michigan University	State University of New York, Brockport
Chicago State University	State University of New York, Cortland
Clemson University	Texas State University
Dalhousie University	University of North Carolina, Greensboro
East Carolina University	University of Idaho
Eastern Kentucky University	University of Mississippi
Eastern Washington University	University of Missouri, Columbia
Frostburg State University	University of New Hampshire
George Mason University	University of Northern Iowa
Georgia Southern University	University of St. Francis
Grambling State University	University of Tennessee, Knoxville
Illinois State University	University of Toledo
Ithaca College	University of Utah
Kent State University	University of Wisconsin-La Crosse
Longwood University	Virginia Wesleyan University
Middle Tennessee State University	Western Carolina University
Minnesota State University, Mankato	Western Illinois University
Missouri State University	Western Kentucky University
North Carolina Central University	Western Washington University
North Carolina State University	Winston-Salem State University
Northern Arizona University	York College
Northwest Missouri State University	

access control—A concept in security in which appropriate steps to influence who and what can enter an area or a facility are enacted.

accessibility—The ability of all participants to access and use facilities.

accounting—The documentation of incomes and expenditures associated with operating a facility.

administrative equipment—Equipment that supports the administrative and executive operation of the facility.

administrative functions—The ultimate executive system that influences the desired results or outcome of an organization; includes planning, organizing, directing, and controlling.

ancillary spaces—Areas in a facility that support the core product.

aquatic facilities—Facilities where the core product revolves around aquatics.

aquatic parks—Aquatic facilities with features such as water slides, wave attractions, spray features, slow-moving water attractions (e.g., a lazy river), toddler play areas, and shallow entries.

area function—The activities that will take place in a specified area.

area impact—The effect the area will have on a facility as well as the effect a facility will have on the area.

assessment—Used in determining the need for a facility, it is critical in influencing a facility's construction. Assessment can range from very informal to very formal.

assessment fee—Fee collected for a short duration by members, customers, or patrons for an improvement to a facility.

asset management—The concept of documenting the age and predicted life span of various facility components.

assignable square footage (ASF)—The total number of usable square feet that can be occupied or assigned for actual use or space that is required for delivering the core product and core product extensions.

assumption of risk—Assuming of any risk that may be involved in a facility or activity.

attractive nuisance—A condition that exists when a product or service that is not currently open or available is considered inviting or attractive to a potential user.

auxiliary space—Space in a facility where ancillary spaces and core product extensions are delivered.

backwashing—A process used in an aquatic facility that involves putting the pump on in reverse to stir up the sand in the filter and get the buildup out of the system.

bond—A method of raising funds for public facilities involving the selling of bonds to be paid back by the recreation agency at a later time.

bond issue—A method of raising funds for public facilities. It is often the primary source of funds for local or state capital construction projects. The process incorporates the issue of tax-exempt bonds for the general public to buy with a return of the principal amount, plus interest, after a certain time or investment period.

bottom line—A result that shows a net profit.

budgeting—A systematic effort to project all income and expenses for a given period.

building efficiency—A measure of percentage of a facility that is used to deliver the core product and core product extensions.

capital costs—Costs involved in constructing a facility.

change order—An actual or written design order that authorizes the contractor to make the proposed change in the work at the construction site.

circulation—The ability for a user to get from one place to another easily and safely.

codes—Control guidelines or systems that set limitations or control mechanisms pertaining to recreation facilities and equipment usage.

commodity outlet—A core product extension that can provide unique support and enhance revenue generation for a recreation facility.

community park—*See* **regional park**.

comprehensive plan—A document that provides a long-range agency-wide outlook with a generalized overview of operational activities and capital projects.

construction manager—Employee from the construction management firm who ensures that contractors are performing the work as described in the blueprints and specifications for a project.

contingency—An amount of money set aside in the overall project cost to take care of unexpected developments that can come up after design and during construction.

control—The practices that management implements for taking charge and ultimately being responsible for every person at their recreation facility.

controlling—The process of supervising, assessing, and correcting employee performance and resources to ensure successful delivery of the product.

core product—The organizational directive and primary service delivered by an agency.

core product extensions—Directives that exist to complement or supplement the core product and generate revenue.

cost analysis—The process of reviewing, comparing, and dissecting costs, associated with delivering a recreation product or service in an effort to determine the true costs of delivering the product and applying ways to save money.

cost containment—Assessing space in order to make it as efficient as possible from the perspective of revenue versus expense.

customer relations—The recreation professional's ability to relate, share, and interact with users; also called *user relations*.

cyclical maintenance—Nonroutine maintenance that incorporates various steps over time in order to complete a full process or cycle.

delivery operations—Presenting the product to the user or participant.

depreciation—The process whereby the value of recreation facilities and equipment decreases by a certain percentage each year.

design stage—Early stage of a facility development project that involves bringing together all relevant details of assessment and planning and integrating them into documents that diagram and describe the design of the construction.

design team—Consists of a team leader or architect, administrators from the recreation agency, and the construction manager. This group works together in a cooperative and professional fashion to bring the project to reality.

directing—The process of guiding or channeling people or groups within an overall management system.

economic impact—Refers to money that will be spent by users and employees at the facility directly or indirectly (at other businesses or agencies in the community).

efficiency—Relates to how well management uses a facility and other resources in maximizing revenue opportunities while minimizing expenses.

efficiency systems—The electrical and mechanical equipment that supports the overall use of the facility.

elasticity—The amount of give in a surface.

employee—A person hired to work for a recreation agency.

employee relations—The recreation professional's ability to relate, share, and interact with staff.

environmental impact—Considered to be negative and relates to the damage that the facility may have on the environment.

equipment—Any item, object, or thing, mechanical or otherwise, that enhances the production process of the product.

equipment diversity—The variety of purposes and functions that can be served by equipment that is specifically designed to meet the needs of delivering a specific product.

equipment maintenance—Maintaining items and mechanical systems that support a facility or help to make the product efficient and functional.

expendable equipment—Equipment related to the delivery process that is used with the expectation that it may get lost, broken, or worn out. Usually, it is replaced within 2 years.

extensiveness—Number of various products or services provided at a facility. It indicates the complexity of recreation facility management, which encompasses a wide range of responsibilities, such as risk management, maintenance, and unexpected disruption in product delivery.

external support systems—Responsibilities and tasks accomplished outside the organization by partnering or contracting with outside agencies.

facility—The leisure services environment where activities occur.

fall protection—Safety characteristics that refer to how absorbent a surface is or how much give a surface has when a fall occurs.

feasibility study—Formal assessment used to determine if a facility design project is financially viable for an agency.

final blueprints—The actual drawings or design documents with which contractors will communicate to subcontractors and craft workers the specifics on what is to be constructed.

finishing stage—Represents work done by the contractors that includes painting walls, installing light fixtures, hanging doors, and installing windows and floor coverings. It is one of the last stages of construction.

fixed equipment—Equipment that is firmly attached as part of the structure of a facility and is usually installed during construction.

fixed-price bid—A system where all designs and specifications for the project are awarded to one general contractor to complete all the work. A lump-sum option results in a single sum of money paid for all work to be accomplished. *See also* **lump-sum bid**.

flexibility—A recreation professional's awareness of the possibility of the need for adjustment in facility usage and management.

focus group—A group process for gathering information, usually consisting of people who represent various segments of users and stakeholders. A facilitator guides the group through questions regarding facility needs.

foot-candle—Unit of measure of the calculated supply of energy required to brighten an area with light.

gravity effect—Having multiple businesses in the same area where various types of people are drawn to and may end up spending additional money at nearby establishments.

greenways—When two or more linear parks are connected.

gross income—The total amount of money generated over a specified period.

gross square footage (GSF)—The total number of square feet of a facility established by measuring the outside (perimeter) of a facility and multiplying that measurement by the number of levels.

groundbreaking—Before the actual construction process begins, a ceremony is held to symbolize and recognize the official start of the project.

grounds maintenance—Keeping outdoor spaces clean, functional, and safe; it can include an outdoor facility and the exterior of an indoor facility.

illumination—The amount of light given off by a light source.

in-kind gifts—Labor or materials that a contractor or other interested party provides to a facility at no cost in exchange for a tax deduction or tax write-off for the amount of labor or materials donated.

influence—The act or power to affect an outcome.

internal support systems—Responsibilities and tasks accomplished within the organization.

job announcement—An official posting of a job used to solicit applicants.

job classification—Places a value on each job that is required to fulfill the mission and goals of a recreation agency. This process results in a hierarchical compilation of the type, number, and responsibilities of each job necessary to deliver the products of a specific recreation organization.

job description—A detailed document that includes all of the responsibilities and tasks of the position.

leisure pool—An aquatic area that can have any variety of shapes and does not include areas for competitive swimming.

linear park—A park that is generally found along a stream, river, or wetland area or along an abandoned railroad bed. It tends to be long or linear and may connect to other similar parks.

loose-fill surface—A surface that can be displaced.

lump-sum bid—A system where all designs and specifications for the project are awarded to one general contractor to complete all the work. A lump-sum option results in a single sum of money paid for all work to be accomplished. *See also* **fixed-priced bid**.

maintenance—The concept of keeping facilities and equipment in proper, safe, and functional condition; can be considered a support function.

management—The process of working with people and resources to achieve agency goals.

manufactured structures—Facilities that are conceived, planned, designed, constructed, and ultimately occupied by a management system to deliver a recreation product or service.

master plan—A formal comprehensive document that identifies the agency's facility needs and establishes the priority in which construction of new (or the renovation of existing) recreation facilities will occur.

master schedule—Records of the various uses of the facility by date, time, and space and contact information of the user group.

market segmentation—Targeting a particular segment of users by recognizing their particular needs and interests and then attempting to meet them.

marketing—Management's efforts to obtain and reach an audience in order to deliver a product to them.

multipurpose facility—A facility that incorporates two or more products that differ in their makeup and potential.

national park—A park that is usually owned and operated by a national government unit; it serves all those within that nation and others who visit from other areas of the world. It has many characteristics similar to a state park.

natural environment—Structure where little about the attraction or environment has been built or constructed by humans.

needs assessment—Formal assessment that helps an agency understand additional services and facilities that users would like to have provided.

neighborhood parks—Parks intended to serve relatively small areas of a community. They are often located in a densely populated area.

net income—The remaining funds after all expenses (including taxes) have been paid; also called *profit*.

nonassignable square footage (NASF)—The total number of square feet of space in a facility where activities do not take place, consisting primarily of nonactive ancillary spaces and circulation areas.

organizing—Involves recognition and assignment of specific tasks and responsibilities to employees and resources as well as designing areas and time assignments that relate to the product.

operational costs—Costs involved in running a facility.

outsourcing—Contracting services to outside vendors.

park—An outdoor space made available to the public and often provided by a public agency for the benefit and enjoyment of the citizens of a respective community, state, or country.

performance appraisal—A formal process resulting from the observation and evaluation of an employee in an effort to assess how the employee is meeting expectations and standards.

permanent equipment—Facility equipment that is not affixed to the facility but is necessary as part of the structure in order for the facility to operate or fulfill its intended purpose.

petition—A document stating that people agree on a certain issue or need. The petition usually has a formal statement that demonstrates a real or sincere interest or commitment by the petitioners in support of a project.

place—Where a product is distributed and allocated to target consumer markets.

planning—The act of anticipating through thought and, when appropriate, documentation, all facets that should take the organization to an expected level of success.

policies—Administrative guidelines that formally state limitations on what individuals are allowed to do while using a recreation facility.

pop-up park—Parks that can be permanent or temporary and are typically small with minimal cost. They are often located in urban areas, provide green-space and community gathering areas, and have ongoing amenity changes.

preventive maintenance—Maintenance practices that avoid unforeseen maintenance. This preventive system recognizes potential problems and then attends to them, adding longevity to areas and equipment and ensuring they are protected.

price—Cost to the consumer to acquire a product or service. This expense goes beyond the product's sticker price; it may also include time and opportunity costs, psychological costs, personal effort costs, and indirect financial costs.

primary space—Areas in a facility where the core product is delivered.

private sector—Designed to provide a product based on profit-oriented goals.

procedures—Administrative statements that help individuals know how to use a facility and its equipment.

product—The organizational directive and primary service delivered by an agency; it is the same as the core product (what the consumer receives from the business transaction or exchange). The product can be a tangible good or intangible service.

product delivery equipment—Equipment that relates specifically to the delivery of the product for which the facility was designed.

production—Creating the basis of how the product is delivered. It includes communicating basic information to recreation facility users and allocating the human and physical resources and other elements critical to the delivery of the product.

profit—Generating sufficient net income to exceed expenses.

programming—Designing and manipulating of leisure environments in an effort to promote the desired leisure experiences of participants.

progress meetings—Meetings scheduled on a regular basis by the construction management team with key people involved in the project to discuss the project schedule, provide updates on progress, and resolve issues or problems affecting construction.

project planning—A systematic anticipation of information through careful thought and documentation to develop a facility project.

project schedule—A conceptual plan that ideally reflects every phase of the project.

project statement—A formal planning document that assists in the architect's design of the facility. It serves as a transitional document between planning and design.

promotion—The advancement or appreciation of the status, position, or value of a product or idea. Promotion includes various strategies in delivering information, such as public relations, personal selling, sales promotions, publicity, and advertising.

prospectus—A formal summary of a business venture or facility project that may be used to justify funding or attract investors.

psychographics—Lifestyle information used in target marketing.

public sector—Designed to provide a product based on service-oriented goals.

punch list—Near the conclusion of a facility construction project, a system of assessing and recording everything that is to be finalized or corrected.

purchase order—A formal written request initiated for ordering equipment and arranging for delivery.

purchase requisition—A written request to administration to indicate a need for a particular piece of equipment.

recreation facility—A structure that exists and creates space for the core product and core product extensions.

recreation facility equipment—Items, objects, and things (mechanical and otherwise) provided by management to enhance, make functional, and complete a recreation product's administrative and delivery operations.

recreation facility management—Supervising staff, operating a facility, maintaining equipment, or running an event.

referendum—An issue on which the general public votes.

recreational sport facilities—A diverse number of outdoor sport fields and areas, including baseball or softball fields, football fields, soccer fields, running tracks, lacrosse fields, and rugby fields.

regional park—A park that is larger than either a neighborhood or an urban park. Typical acreage of this type of park can range from 15 acres (6 ha) to several hundred acres. This type of park consists of a broader range of amenities that will attract users or residents from a greater geographic area. Also called a **community park**.

renovation—The rehabilitation of an existing facility with steps taken to rearrange the space within an existing structure.

resources—Employees, money, equipment, and facilities.

retrofitting—The addition of new systems of technology to an existing facility.

security equipment—Equipment that is in place to protect the employees and users as well as the facility and its equipment.

self-parking—When a driver parks their own vehicle. It is the most common parking option.

separate-bid pricing—Quotes solicited from different general contractors for different elements of the construction process.

service area—The people within a certain distance of a facility who will be users of—and therefore served by—the facility. Depending on the type of facility, distance can be measured in actual geographic distance from a facility or it can be measured in the amount of time it takes to get to a facility.

service needs—The maintenance functions that a facility requires.

shop drawings—Interpretations of the blueprints by the contractor, or subcontractor, for approval by the architect. They support the blueprints and specification books in a project.

single-purpose facility—A facility that typically has only one product that is developed and delivered.

site analysis—Identifying a variety of factors related to the specific location being considered for a facility.

skate park—Spaces designed for skate-related recreational activities that typically include prefabricated or concrete structures and obstacles to challenge the skater.

slide characteristics—How much a surface allows people to slide when participating in activities.

social impact—How a facility will affect people nearby and other facility users.

space relationships—A component of a project statement describing how all the areas of a facility will relate to one another.

specification book—Important part of communicating the details of a project to the various contractors. It provides written detailed references to the blueprints; also called a *spec book*.

sponsorships—When an outside entity provides funds to a leisure service agency so that their business receives recognition of some type at the facility.

sport park—A park that features some type of sport or a combination of sport facilities as the core product.

staffing—The recruitment, hiring, and training of appropriate individuals who can facilitate the requirements for the product's success.

stakeholder—Someone who has a vested interest in an agency or facility.

standard of care—A legal concept that is usually established as a result of previous legal action or precedence.

state park—A park that is usually larger than a community or regional park but may have similar amenities. State parks are usually owned and operated by a large government unit.

strategic planning—A detailed, comprehensive process with several people involved in planning for an organization.

structural equipment—Items that are permanent or attached to the structure and are critical to the core product and core product extensions.

structural expenses—Expenses associated with maintaining or improving the physical structure of the facility.

structural material—The makeup of the materials that are used in constructing the facility.

structural square footage (SSF)—The square footage in a facility made up by the construction materials used for walls and permanent facility structures.

structures—Any recreation facility; all recreation facilities are considered structures.

supervisor—Job classification in which a person is responsible for reviewing the work of one or more subordinate employees.

supplies—Considered expendable items that are consumed or used up during the production process.

support—Activities that take place behind the scenes by personnel who are typically not out front or in contact with facility users.

surface parking—A parking area consisting of a single level surface.

surfaces—the outer area of a boundary such as a wall, floor, or ceiling.

surfacing—The type of material used to cover a surface.

survey—A common method for obtaining information; can be considered internal or external. An internal survey can be used in obtaining user or employee feedback regarding an agency's own facility or facilities. An external survey (also called *benchmark survey*) can be used in obtaining comparative information from other facilities with similar products.

sustainability—Operating a facility while minimizing the long-term effect on the environment.

synthesizing—Bringing the recreation product and space together as a useful experience for the user.

target market—A population with specific demographic or statistical descriptions or characteristics that are used in order to analyze and ensure the product's success. Characteristics may include age, sex, socioeconomic background, and geographic location.

tax levy—A portion of local taxes that is collected and earmarked for a specific recreation facility project.

theme park—A park with a specific attraction that is designed to appeal to customers or visitors from an entertainment or unique experience perspective.

topography—The natural condition of the land.

unitary surface—A surface that cannot be displaced.

uniqueness—The design, product being delivered, administrative styles, management philosophy, staff composition, and leadership qualities that make each facility different from others.

urban parks—Parks intended to serve the most urban and densely developed area of a community. An urban park is generally fairly small in size and is likely to be bordered by a combination of residences and businesses in a community.

use zone—The area required for participation in an activity and the areas beneath a structure that should have a surface that provides fall protection.

user relations—The recreation professional's ability to relate, share, and interact with users. Also called *customer relations*.

users—People who come to a facility to have a positive experience while using the product or service.

valet parking—Parking service where staff members greet customers at the facility entrance and take the vehicle to a different location or parking area to park it.

value engineering—When a recreation administrator and the contractor seek assistance from architects, engineers, and specialists to make sure bid prices accurately reflect details in the project specifications.

vendors—Outside entities that sell their product or services in a recreation facility.

water parks—Aquatic facilities that incorporate various water features designed for maximum entertainment of participants.

waterfront—An outdoor aquatic facility located at a lake, beach, river, or quarry.

BIBLIOGRAPHY

Bennis, W.G. (2009). *On becoming a leader: The leadership classic revised and updated.* Basic Books.

Boyd, J. (2019). Designing facilities for safety and security. *Athletic Business.* www.athleticbusiness.com/operations/safety-security/article/15157109/designing-facilities-for-safety-and-security

Centers for Disease Control and Prevention (CDC). (2022). *The Model Aquatic Health Code (MAHC): An all-inclusive model public swimming pool and spa code.* www.cdc.gov/mahc

Cipolla, K. (2013). Environmentally friendly locker rooms can lead to savings. *Club Industry.* www.clubindustry.com/commercial-clubs/environmentally-friendly-locker-rooms-can-lead-to-savings

Clout, J. (2022). Is your organization ready for an emergency? *Parks and Recreation Magazine.* www.nrpa.org/parks-recreation-magazine/2022/may/is-your-organization-ready-for-an-emergency

Cobb County Government. (2022). Braves stadium information. www.cobbcounty.org/communications/info-center/braves-stadium-information

Collins, L. (2019). Pop-up potential. *Parks and Recreation Magazine.* www.nrpa.org/parks-recreation-magazine/2019/september/pop-up-potential

Decatur Park District. (2011). *Nelson Park master plan: Decatur's lakefront—A community vision.* Decatur Park District.

DGI Communications. (2020). *What is digital signage? Here's how it can help your business.* www.dgicommunications.com/digital-signage

Energy Star. (2021). About Energy Star. www.energystar.gov/about

Farley, L.J. (2018). Construction 101: The basics of change orders. *American Bar Association.* www.americanbar.org/groups/construction_industry/publications/under_construction/2018/fall/construction-101

Federal Bureau of Investigation. (2022). Active shooter resources. www.fbi.gov/about/partnerships/office-of-partner-engagement/active-shooter-resources

Ford, T. (2021). Synthetic turf: Beyond the benefits for ball fields. *Parks & Recreation Business.* www.parksandrecbusiness.com/articles/synthetic-turf

GameTime. (2020). How much does commercial playground equipment cost? www.gametime.com/news/what-is-the-cost-of-commercial-playground-equipment-cost

Gardner, R. (2018). The splash pad revolution—Cool locales, hot commodities. *MSA.* www.msa-ps.com/the-splash-pad-revolution-cool-locales-hot-commodities

Gavin, M. (2019). Leadparkership vs. management: What's the difference? *Harvard Business School Online.* https://online.hbs.edu/blog/post/leadership-vs-management

Gibbons, S. (2018). You and your business have 7 seconds to make a first impression: Here's how to succeed. *Forbes.* www.forbes.com/sites/serenitygibbons/2018/06/19/you-have-7-seconds-to-make-a-first-impression-heres-how-to-succeed/?sh=5e8dcfbe56c2

Gips, M. (2020). Access control trends in 2022: The future of access control. *Swiftlane.* www.swiftlane.com/blog/the-future-of-access-control

Glen Ellyn Park District. (2022). About the park district. https://gepark.org/overview.

Hughes, W. (2019). Keeping a Campus Rec Center's Construction Budget Under Control. *Athletic Business.* www.athleticbusiness.com/budgeting/keeping-a-campus-rec-center-s-construction-budget-under-control.html

IDNR. (2006). *Outdoor recreation facilities guide.* Illinois Department of Natural Resources.

Jenner, C. (2019). Considering synthetic turf: What you need to know. *Parks & Recreation Business.* www.parksandrecbusiness.com/articles/2019/8/ln2xv2owppqx-17qdo858umq6uw0t2m

KMMO. (2022). Grand opening for the Heckart Community Center is scheduled for March 18. www.kmmo.com/2022/03/11/grand-opening-for-the-heckart-community-center-is-scheduled-for-march-18

Krysiak, M. (2022). 25 best tool inventory and equipment tracking software systems. www.camcode.com/blog/25-best-tool-inventory-and-equipment-tracking-software-systems

Lehdonvirta, V., Oksanen, A., Rasanen, P., & Blank, G. (2020). Social media, web, and panel surveys: Using non-probability samples in social and policy research. *Policy & Internet, 13*(1), 134-155.

Memmott, J. (2021). From pickleball to meditation, this $17M center in Chili offers a little of everything. *Democrat & Chronicle.* www.democratandchronicle.com/story/news/local/columnists/memmott/2021/11/18/chili-ny-community-center-activities-pickleball-meditation/8641073002

Myrick, S. (2019). LED lighting and IoT. *Parks and Recreation.* www.nrpa.org/parks-recreation-magazine/2019/april/led-lighting-and-iot

National Association of Sports Officials. (2022). Say yes to officiating: Recruit, retain & celebrate sports officials. www.sayyestoofficiating.com/become-a-sports-official/sports/basketball

National Park Trips. (2021). U.S. national parks by state. *Outside.* www.nationalparktrips.com/parks/us-national-parks-by-state-list

National Recreation and Park Association (NRPA). (2018). *Aquatic facility operator examination candidate handbook.* National Recreation and Park Association.

National Recreation and Park Association (NRPA). (2021). *Certified Playground Safety Inspector (CPSI) certification.* www.nrpa.org/certification/CPSI

National Recreation and Park Association (NRPA). (2022a). *2022 NRPA agency performance review report.* National Recreation and Park Association.

National Recreation and Park Association (NRPA). (2022b). *The daily dozen: A 12-point playground safety checklist.* National Recreation and Park Association.

Nielsen. (2015). 2015 Nielsen global sustainability report. https://engageforgood.com/2015-nielsen-global-sustainability-report

NCSA. (2021). List of colleges with varsity Esports programs. *Next College Student Athlete Report.* www.ncsasports.org/college-esports-scholarships/varsity-esports

Novak, M.J., & Maguire, P. (2012). The rise of the multi-purpose field: All the sports, all the time. *Sports Destination Management.* www.sportsdestinations.com/sports/sports-facilities/rise-multi-purpose-field-all-sports-all-time-5766

Peoria Sports Complex. (2022). *Facility history and facts.* Peoria Sports Complex.

Peterson, C. (2022). Recommended foot candle chart. www.ledlightingsupply.com/blog/recommended-foot-candle-chart

Pittsburgh Parks Conservancy. (2020). *Parks Are: beautiful. essential. safe. yours. 2020 annual report.* Pittsburgh Parks Conservancy.

Populous Events. (2018). College varsity eSports programs on the rise: How gaming is changing college for gamers. *Populous Magazine.* https://populous.com/populous-collaborates-north-americas-first-esports-stadium

Quan, S. (2018). OSHA regulations for restaurants. *Small Business.* https://smallbusiness.chron.com/osha-regulations-restaurants-58031.html

Rogers, J. (2008). To turf or not to turf. That is the question. *Illinois Parks and Recreation, 39*(4), 25-28.

Ross, B., & Fischer, D. (2022). Making wellness more inclusive. *Parks and Recreation.* www.nrpa.org/parks-recreation-magazine/2022/june/making-wellness-more-inclusive

Scalisi, T. (2022). 2022 Guide to U.S. building commercial construction cost per square foot. www.levelset.com/blog/commercial-construction-cost-per-square-foot

Scovic, J. (2022). Sustainable construction decisions: A natural solution for the Northbrook Park District. *Parks and Recreation.* www.nrpa.org/parks-recreation-magazine/2022/january/sustainable-construction-decisions

Sourby, C.A. (2022). Universal design. *inTERlink.* www.recreationtherapy.com/articles/sourbyuniversaldesign.htm

Srivastava, P. (2018). 6 ways facilities managers can support sustainable facilities. *Service Channel: Industry.* https://servicechannel.com/blog/6-ways-facilities-managers-support-sustainable-facilities

Tualatin Hills Park & Recreation District. (2017). *NRPA Gold Medal application.* Tualatin Hills Park and Recreation District.

Trotter, S. (2019). 8 steps to writing your equipment replacement plan. *Campus Rec Magazine.* https://campusrecmag.com/8-steps-to-writing-your-equipment-replacement-plan

U.S. Consumer Product Safety Commission (CPSC). (2015). *Public playground safety handbook.* U.S. Consumer Product Safety Commission.

United States Department of Homeland Security (DHS). (2008). *Active shooter: How to respond.* Department of Homeland Security.

United States Department of Justice. (2010). *2010 ADA Standards for Accessible Design.* Department of Justice.

United States Geological Survey (USGS). (2022). What is a geographic information system (GIS)? *USGS: Science for a Changing World.* www.usgs.gov

INDEX

Note: The italicized *f* and *t* following page numbers refer to figures and tables, respectively.

disabilities, people with. *See* accessibility; Americans with Disabilities Act
displays 85
disruptions in facility activities 263-269. *See also* emergencies
donations and contributions 138, 181
drainage
    of facilities 30-31, 327
    of parking areas 75, 76-77
    of trails 289
drawing area 118-119, 118*f*
drawing index 116, 117*f*
drawings, schematic 111, 112*f*
drawing title 118, 118*f*

E
eco-friendly supplies 13, 259
economic impact 65
education, in child care 93
efficiency 49-50
    assessments of 49-50
    building 128
    comfort for 214
    energy 13, 36, 259
    of operation 37
    of reception areas 77
efficiency systems 163, 163*t*, 260
elasticity 107
electrical blueprints 113-114, 120*f*
electrical systems 25, 26-27, 87
elevation marker stakes 325
elevation rods 325
emergencies 263-276
    active shooters 269-270
    brainstorming for 270
    crowd behavior 269
    degrees of disruption 264-265
    evaluation of catalysts 265-266
    fires 267-268, 274*f*
    maintenance disruptions 266-267
    terrorist threats 268-269
    weather 267
emergency action plans 316, 330
emergency response 269-275
    emergency medical personnel 316-317, 329-330
    evacuation 273-275, 274*f*
    inspections of equipment for 219
    leadership in 271
    medical assistance 273
    reception staff in 79
    taking action 272-273
employee management 189-207
    employee relations 38, 205-206
    job analysis 191-192, 194
    job classification 190-191, 191*f*
    job description 192-193
    on-the-job training 197

performance appraisal 197-199
professional development 205
providing applicants with all job aspects 196
recruitment and selection procedures 194-197
staffing process 11-12, 189-190
work environment 204-205
employees. *See also* employee management
    accident report form 221*f*
    in aquatic facilities 305-307, 317
    attitude of 78
    in child care operations 94
    in commodity outlets 85
    employment opportunities 39
    expenses from 177-178
    external employees 201-204
    internal employees 199-201
    interview and job hunt 261-262
    phone etiquette training 206-207
    professional development of 205
    scheduling 235, 244-246
    of sport facilities 328-330
    in surveillance 227
    training of 94, 205
    types of 199-204
encapsulated stadiums 320
energy efficiency 13, 36, 259
Energy Star label 36
engineering fees 129
environmental impact 65, 69. *See also* sustainable practices
environmental protection laws 330
environmental threats 216-218, 217*t*
equipment, facility 159-171
    in aquatic facilities 311-313, 311*f*, 312*f*
    budgeting funds for 178-179
    checkout and rental 98-101
    costs 125*f*, 129
    definition 12
    equipment complexity 160
    equipment diversity 160
    in facility requests 240
    inspections of 219, 240
    inventory and tracking software 169-170
    liability waivers 99-100
    maintenance of 254
    for management use 163
    in planning 69
    planning and delivering 153
    in playgrounds 291-292, 292*f*, 297
    purchasing 165-168, 167*f*
    receiving and distributing 168-170
    renting and leasing 170, 288
    replacement plans 178-179
    signage as 165

status of 161-162
structural 114, 163, 163*t*
types of 162-165, 162*t*, 163*t*
using 161, 170-171
equitable service delivery 4
esports 5, 40-41
evacuation plans 273-275, 274*f*
expendable equipment 162, 162*t*
expenses 174-180. *See also* costs
    structural 174-177
    support 177-180
extensiveness, in management 22
exteriors of facilities 27-29
external support systems 9-10

F
facilities. *See* recreation facilities
facility assessment 45-55
    for evacuation plans 273-275, 274*f*
    influencing factors in 46-50
    influencing techniques in 51-53
    initial proposal 53-54
    maintenance in 255-256
    process of 45-46
    in recreation facility development 21
    types of 45
facility design
    aesthetics 111
    blueprint reading 115-121, 116*f*, 117*f*
    blueprint types 111-114, 113*f*
    of child care centers 96-98
    of commodity outlets 86-87
    conceptualization 106
    design documents 112, 114
    design team 103-104
    equipment checkout and rental 100-101
    of facilities 22
    laws, codes, ordinances, and standards 114-115
    lighting 25, 104, 109-111
    of locker and shower areas 82-83
    materials 106-109
    mechanical systems 111
    parking 75-76
    of parks 284-286
    process overview 22
    of reception areas 80
    schematics 111, 112*f*
    signage in 153, 165
    site analysis 63-64, 106
    of sport facilities 322-326
    universal 148-149, 153, 295-296
    use zone dimensions 127*t*
facility image 250
facility management. *See also* administration

Brent A. Beggs, PhD, serves as director of the School of Kinesiology and Recreation at Illinois State University in Normal, where he previously served as a professor and director of the recreation and park administration program. Beggs has taught courses in facility planning and management for over 20 years and has a wealth of expertise in managing sport, fitness, and aquatic facilities in municipal and collegiate settings.

Beggs is a member of the National Recreation and Park Association (NRPA) and NIRSA (formerly National Intramural-Recreational Sports Association). In 2006 and 2008, he was awarded NIRSA's President's Award for Outstanding Writing in *Recreational Sports Journal*.

Richard F. Mull was an assistant professor in the School of Health, Physical Education, and Recreation (HPER) at Indiana University in Bloomington from 1972 to 2006. He also served as the director of the Center for Student Leadership Development, director of Indiana University's tennis center and outdoor pool, and special assistant to the dean for the auxiliary unit of the school of HPER. From 1972 to 1992, he served as the director of campus recreational sports at Indiana University (IU). In 2017, he was honored with the Founding Dean's Medallion by IU School of Public Health officials.

Mull brings the practical experience of over 40 years spent managing recreational sports to his work with students and to his writing of numerous publications and books. His professional contributions to the field led to his receipt of the 1989 Honor Award from the National Intramural-Recreational Sports Association (NIRSA). In 1994, he was inducted into the Professional Hall of Fame in the School of Physical Education at West Virginia University. For more than 35 years, Mull has served as a consultant and advisor in the field of recreational sports. He also served as chairperson of the NIRSA's Professional Development Committee, assistant chairperson of the NIRSA Standards Committee, and vice president of NIRSA. Throughout his career, Mull's special interests have included professional preparation, student development, management, and leadership.

Mick Renneisen served as the deputy mayor of Bloomington, Indiana, from 2016 to 2021 and as the director of the City of Bloomington Parks and Recreation Department from 1996 to 2015. He also served an adjunct instructor at Indiana University, teaching courses in recreation facility management for the School of Health, Physical Education, and Recreation for more than 10 years. Renneisen currently serves as a consultant in parks and recreation for local government and utility leaders.

Renneisen has more than 35 years of experience in managing and developing a variety of recreation facilities. In 2007, his department received the Gold Medal Award from the National Recreation and Park Association (NRPA). In 2008, he received the W.W. Patty Distinguished Alumni Award from Indiana University for his outstanding personal and professional achievement. He was responsible for the design and management of the award-winning Twin Lakes Sports Park, which received the Daniel Flaherty Award from Great Lakes Park Training Institute in 1993 and the Amateur Softball Association (ASA) Complex of the Year award in 1994.

Michael (Mike) A. Mulvaney, PhD, is a professor at the School of Kinesiology and Recreation at Illinois State University in Normal, Illinois. His research centers on management issues within public park and recreation agencies. Mulvaney has held the Certified Park and Recreation Professional (CPRP) credential since 2007.

Prior to obtaining his PhD, Mulvaney was employed with the Decatur Park District in Decatur, Illinois, in a variety of capacities, including facility management, fitness, programming, and special recreation. Mulvaney's teaching and research experiences have focused on management and organization of park and recreation agencies, human resource management functions in park and recreation agencies, and planning processes in park and recreation agencies. Mulvaney also has extensive experience in the development and testing of the effectiveness of various modes of instruction and their relationship to student learning of park and recreation concepts. Publications authored include textbooks, journal articles, and technical reports.